ABOUT THE AUTHOR

THEODORE H. WHITE was born in Boston in 1915. After graduating summa cum laude from Harvard University in 1938, he was recruited to cover East Asia for *Time* magazine, becoming chief of its China Bureau in 1945. This experience would inspire his first book, *Thunder Out of China* (written with Annalee Jacoby). After serving for a brief time as editor of *The New Republic*, he edited *The Stilwell Papers*. In 1948, he went to live in Europe, and his experience as a European correspondent led to *Fire in the Ashes*, published in 1953. That same year he returned to the United States to work as national correspondent for *The Reporter*, and then for *Collier's* magazine. After the collapse of *Collier's* in 1956, White turned to fiction, completing two novels, *The Mountain Road* and *The View from the Fortieth Floor*, in the next four years.

At the time *Collier's* closed down, White was planning a story on "The Making of the President 1956" for the magazine; he revived the idea in the next election year, resulting in his most famous book, *The Making of the President 1960*, which was awarded the Pulitzer Prize for General Nonfiction in 1962. White went on to produce three more Making of the President volumes, covering the 1964, 1968, and 1972 campaigns. Subsequently, he was author of *Breach of Faith: The Fall of Richard Nixon*, *In Search of History: A Personal Adventure*, and *America in Search of Itself: The Making of the President 1956–1980*. He was the recipient of numerous awards in addition to the Pulitzer Prize, and was recognized for his documentary work with Emmy Awards in both 1964 and 1967. White died in 1986 at the age of seventy-one.

D1019184

THE
MAKING OF
THE PRESIDENT
1972

THEODORE H. WHITE

THE
MAKING OF
THE PRESIDENT
1972

HARPER**PERENNIAL** ★ POLITICAL**CLASSICS**

NEW YORK • LONDON • TORONTO • SYDNEY • NEW DELHI • AUCKLAND

HARPER**PERENNIAL** ★ POLITICAL**CLASSICS**

A hardcover edition of this book was published in 1973 by Atheneum House, Inc.

THE MAKING OF THE PRESIDENT 1972. Copyright © 1973 by Theodore H. White. Foreword copyright © 2010 by Cokie Roberts. All rights reserved. Printed in the United States of America. No part of this book may be used or reproduced in any manner whatsoever without written permission except in the case of brief quotations embodied in critical articles and reviews. For information address HarperCollins Publishers, 10 East 53rd Street, New York, NY 10022.

HarperCollins books may be purchased for educational, business, or sales promotional use. For information please write: Special Markets Department, HarperCollins Publishers, 10 East 53rd Street, New York, NY 10022.

FIRST HARPER PERENNIAL POLITICAL CLASSICS EDITION PUBLISHED 2010.

Designed by Harry Ford

Library of Congress Cataloging-in-Publication Data is available upon request.

ISBN 978-0-06-190067-9

10 11 12 13 14   RRD   10 9 8 7 6 5 4 3 2 1

FOR

THEO BENNAHUM

—*whom I loved*—

1906–1972

CONTENTS

FOREWORD TO THE 2010 EDITION

It's odd to read the words of this volume—many of them admiring, if not approving, of Richard Nixon—knowing what happened next. Theodore White's author's note is dated June 8, 1973, a few weeks before White House Counsel John Dean's damning testimony before the Senate Watergate Committee. In another month we would watch Dean insist that it might be proven that the cover-up of crimes continued, and that it came from the president himself. In July 1973, Alexander Butterfield quietly told the committee that President Nixon had taped his conversations in the Oval Office. And the unraveling of the Nixon presidency became inevitable.

So it is odd, then, to read about the creation of the second term of that presidency, the tumultuous times that defined the 1972 campaign. And it is fascinating. For me, as I suspect for anyone "of a certain age," these pages evoke an amused nostalgia for when we were young and ready to take on the world. I remember the eighteen thousand screaming fans ushered to their seats by the likes of Warren Beatty, Jack Nicholson, and Julie Christie at the Fabulous Forum in Los Angeles when James Taylor, Carole King, Quincy Jones, and Barbra Streisand sang out their souls for George McGovern. But even then, as the crowds around us roared, those of us with any political sense knew that Richard Nixon was right on Election Day when he told Theodore White: "The election was decided the day McGovern was nominated." Once the Democrats made that choice, the president judged as he flew across the country to watch the returns at the White House, "the question after that was only how much. McGovern did to his party what Goldwater did."

But Nixon wasn't able to do for his party what Franklin Roosevelt did for his; he wasn't able to create the "new majority" he sought. Even as the president piled up one of the biggest landslides in history, White tells us "the President was bothered; the results nagged" because he couldn't bring the Congress, or ultimately the people, with him. While Nixon trounced his rival by the astounding margin of 61 percent to 38 percent, Republicans actually *lost* seats in the Senate and gained only twelve in the House of Representatives, leaving both houses well in the hands of a Democratic majority. The voters had sent a strong message to Washington—they were rejecting George McGovern more than they were electing Richard Nixon and the policies he stood for.

By Election Day the bare outlines of the Watergate scandal were known. The botched burglary of the Democratic National Committee in June had already been traced to the Committee to Re-Elect the President, gleefully dubbed CREEP by Nixon-haters. By October, more than three-quarters of the voters told pollsters that they had heard of the scandal, though most dismissed it as "just politics." Still, White muses, Watergate might have led to an unprecedented pattern of voter turnout: in several states more people cast their ballots for governor or senator than for president. And most of those ballots went to Democrats, but that didn't just happen by chance. Democratic Party leaders looked ahead at what they knew would be a debacle in November and took action. My father, Hale Boggs, was the majority leader of the House at that time. He and Hubert H. Humphrey, the former vice president and defeated 1968 Democratic nominee, mounted a frantic fall road trip in support of congressional candidates. In fact, the last time I ever saw my father was at a fund-raiser in Los Angeles, where he and Humphrey outdid each other in their purple pleas for the party. Shortly after that, while campaigning for Nick Begich, an endangered Democratic house member in Alaska, the plane carrying my father and Begich disappeared, never to be found. (In the 2008 election, with Republican Governor Sarah Palin on the national ticket, Begich's son Mark was elected as Alaska's first Democratic senator in eighteen years.)

The race for Congress was the one arena in the crazy campaign of 1972 where party leaders and organized labor could play a role. The AFL-CIO refused to endorse McGovern, ostensibly over his anti-Vietnam war stance. But White gives us one instance after another where labor and elected officials were excluded from the march that ended with the nomination of McGovern. And that offensive provides the heft of White's story; it's all here—starting with the commission formed by the Democratic convention of 1968 and chaired by McGovern that changed the rules for delegates, working through the primaries and caucuses and state conventions; and ending at the raucous Democratic convention in Miami, where the candidate cooled his heels until almost three o'clock in the morning waiting to make his acceptance speech while a parade of delegates insisted on having their say about minute details. I still laugh remembering my mother's wisecrack as we witnessed that convention from the prime real estate of my father's box. Scanning the scene, she fixed her gaze on one particular delegate and stammered, "Why would anyone wear shorts that short?" My husband, Steve, who was part of the team covering the convention for the *New York Times*, remembers his fiercely antiwar, pro-McGovern father looking at the chaos on television and concluding, "There's nobody there who looks like me."

A lot of America felt that way, despite the fact that 60 percent agreed with the basic thrust of the convention and the raison d'être of the McGovern candidacy—that the Vietnam war was a massive mistake. (Though White can't resist telling us that McGovern decided to run for president in 1962 long before the war was ever an issue. The reason? He had read *The Making of the President 1960*, and he thought he'd go for it.) But even as Nixon continued to wage war, mining the North Vietnamese ports and bombing Hanoi and Haiphong, he talked peace. And he walked it as well—dazzling White with his opening to China and his trip to Moscow, the first ever for an American president.

Theodore White had covered China for *Time* during and after World War II, and was a legitimate expert on that vast nation. Traveling with Nixon's press corps back to the country in 1972, White saw the China trip as the momentous occasion that it was, nothing less than "closing an epoch" of postwar foreign policy. The promise that Nixon offered in foreign policy, and his attempts at a pragmatic approach to domestic policy, understandably attracted not only the author but also the American people. That's why Watergate created such a "breach of faith"—a phrase that would become the title of White's next book, published in 1975.

But the full extent of Watergate was not yet known as the campaign of 1972 marched on toward Election Day. As Nixon's team ran ads highlighting the president's foreign visits, interspersed with staged rallies—and certainly no messy press conferences or interviews—the McGovern operation imploded in plain sight. In chronicling first the embarrassment over Thomas Eagleton's selection as running mate, and then the frantic search for a substitute after unceremoniously dumping Eagleton from the ticket, White provides some juicy stories I had long since forgotten. And putting together the predictable frustration of the losing candidate with the press with Nixon's longstanding hostility to the news media—allows the author an opportunity to do a riff (chapter 10) on the power of the press at the time. Reading his thoughts makes an old-fashioned reporter like me yearn for "the good old days," when newspapers were profitable and network news was watched by fifty million adults nightly (about half that number tune in today).

Many of the contemporaneous reviews of the book singled out White's section on the press, but with very different takes on his opinion. The book was applauded in the conservative journal *Commentary* by Harvard's James Q. Wilson, who called it "a brilliant analysis by a knowledgeable but detached insider." In the liberal *New York Review of Books*, however, Garry Wills scoffed: "White's indiscriminate celebration of the ruler shows up best in his long chapter on the press. There he tries to defend Nixon's nonexistent public sensitivity to the press, despite the fact that 93 percent of the papers endorsing a candidate last year came out for Nixon." To liberals, of course, any defense of Nixon at all was an offense.

Reading through the reviews, I feel as though I am witnessing a much more erudite and informed preview of the Fox News/MSNBC shouting matches of today. The changes in the media (a word White dismissed as an invention of advertisers) would certainly surprise the author. What else? The demise of the Soviet Union? Certainly. The rise of a capitalistic Communist China? Probably. The idea that energy issues still defeat us would surely depress him, given that Nixon named energy as his top agenda item for his second term. White was particularly obsessed with the problems facing America's cities in 1972, viewing them as something of a code for issues of race. He would be pleased, I suspect, to see some revival of our urban areas, and I think he would be flabbergasted to find an African American (a term that would have been unfamiliar to him) in the White House.

But that's because the country has changed greatly. In 1972, George McGovern thought he could mobilize women, the young—the 1972 election marked the first year that eighteen- to twenty-one-year-olds could vote—blacks, and the poor to go to the polls. He was wrong. As the Census Bureau dutifully reported the following year, "Females, Negroes, persons of Spanish ethnic origin, the youngest (18–34), [and] those in families of income less than $5000 . . . were less likely to register and vote." The electorate McGovern faced was almost 90 percent white, with "persons who are male . . . the middle age group (35–64), [and] those in families with incomes greater than $10,000," showing "higher levels of registration and voting."[1] By 2008, whites had dropped to 74 percent of voters, with blacks, Hispanics, and Asians adding up to more than a quarter of the electorate and women more than half, according to ABC News exit polls.

The election of 1972 was quickly overshadowed by the disgrace and resignation of President Nixon, which left a lasting mark on American politics. The "new majority" that Nixon sought to bring to the Republican Party—ethnic whites, Catholics, patriotic pro-defense workers—showed up in 1980, giving Ronald Reagan a Republican Senate for the first time in decades and a working majority in the House. And the Democrats spent the next several elections dealing with "McGovernization"—the image of a party "where nobody looks like me." Senator McGovern himself—one of the few key players in this book who is still alive and active today—understandably, rejects the term; however, it's now standard shorthand for both political parties when they veer toward the unelectable extremes.

---

1. www.census.gov/hhes/www/socdemo/voting/publications/p20/1972/p20-253pdf

Finally, as Teddy White predicted, George McGovern "introduced a new generation of young people to politics. Most would pass on, discouraged, to other things, the campaign of 1972 fading to a memory of their lives at springtime. But others, a handful, would remain to live and act within their party, wiser perhaps than before." Of that new generation, Bill Clinton would become the 42nd president of the United States, and his wife, Hillary Clinton, now the secretary of state, would run her own presidential campaign against a candidate she and her husband believed was McGovernizing the party. But in 2008—at last—American politics had moved beyond 1972.

—COKIE ROBERTS
October 2010

AUTHOR'S NOTE

This book would be incomplete without the author's thanks to those who helped.

Foremost among them is my friend Simon Michael Bessie, whose devotion has been extravagantly given to this work; he has hovered over every page and paragraph, trying to give the manuscript discipline and direction. Martin Plissner, political editor of CBS, has shared with me his unmatched lore of American politics; with his indispensable help, over his sometimes strenuous but rewarding protest, the themes of this book took shape. Hedva Glickenhaus has, for more than three years, been the chief conscience, stylist and researcher in this adventure; without her support and affection this book would never have been completed. Beatrice Hofstadter has contributed from her scholarship that perspective in American history which has helped me most in seeing 1972 against the background of our past. Two young reporters deserve special thanks: Mark Silk, whose range of research runs from supermarkets and census to Watergate; and David F. White, whose reportage runs from the New Hampshire primary to the Democratic convention in Miami. My thanks go also to George Backer, whose wisdom is a national resource.

A number of friends contributed substantial independent research. Among these, I wish to note most importantly Ms. Scottie Fitzgerald Smith. And then, Elaine Livingston, Marie Ridder, Eileen Hughes.

This book would never have appeared on time had it not been for two superlative professionals—Harry Ford, Vice-President of Atheneum, whose talents this year were pressed to the utmost by events which kept destroying deadlines; and to the unflustered Paul Hirschman, who, under all pressures, kept his cool to see us over the finish line.

I must thank all the campaign teams for the courtesies they extended. But, in particular, Ronald Ziegler of the White House, Richard Dougherty of the McGovern campaign, Daniel Hackel of the Humphrey campaign, Richard Stewart of the Muskie campaign, Tom Morgan of the Lindsay campaign, Mike Kelley of Senator Eagleton's staff.

I must thank Osborn Elliott, editor of *Newsweek*, for friendship, kindness, and concern which illuminated and warmed; Richard and Shirley Clurman, not only for hard thinking but for their persistent encouragement at the darkest time; Blair Clark and Heyden White for their insights.

And then follows the brotherhood of the press. All of us nurse from *The New York Times*, and I have found the dispatches of the *Times*'s campaign team, headed by R. W. Apple Jr., basic to all my own reporting. Martin Tolchin's series on the South Bronx, Tad Szulc's essay on E. Howard Hunt, and at least a dozen other specialized *Times* essays are high points in memory. The dispatches of Haynes Johnson and David Broder of the Washington *Post* enlightened all of us. So, too, did the reportage of the Knight newspapers, particularly that of Robert Boyd, Clark Hoyt and Loye Miller on the Eagleton affair. American political reporting, which roused the wrath of every candidate in the field except for George Wallace, reached new excellence in 1972. I would like to signal particularly the reporting of David Murray of the Chicago *Sun-Times*, Jules Witcover then of the Los Angeles *Times*, and Adam Clymer of the Baltimore *Sun*. Robert Healy of the Boston *Globe*, Edwin O. Guthman of the Los Angeles *Times*, Frank Morgan of *Newsweek* made specialized reporting available to me. Conversations with Meg Greenfield of the Washington *Post* and Marianne Means of King Features Syndicate brought fresh shared information and understanding. Columns by John Roche and Nick Thimmesch were extremely helpful; so too those of Hugh Sidey; and the cool civilized columns of Stewart Alsop in *Newsweek*, which held me, as so many others, on firm compass points. I would be remiss if I did not thank Richard Salant, President of CBS News, and William Leonard, Vice-President, for the resources and opportunities they offered me, and the pride of wearing their colors.

I know I have left out the names of countless reportorial companions of the road, from Collins Avenue in Miami to Commonwealth Avenue in Boston, from San Clemente, California, to Berlin, New Hampshire. With many of them I argued, with some I agreed, from all too many I have unconsciously plagiarized. To those to whose contribution and help I have inadvertently given no mention, I offer apologies; and hope to make amends the next time a volume of this series goes to press, God willing in a more tranquil country, in 1977.

JUNE 8th, 1973

THE END OF THE POSTWAR WORLD

I COULD see the fan of yellow water below shortly before the plane dipped into the overcast. We were coming in on China and the outpouring of silt was familiar. The Yangtze still flowed from the roof of Tibet, staining the Pacific with its mud fifty miles out to sea. That was the same. But so little else was. For several years the sense had been growing in me that nothing any longer was the same, no rules held, the world we knew was coming to an end.

But now in February, 1972, there was a recognizable time pivot: The President of the United States was on his way to China, and our press plane preceded his.

I had first landed at a Shanghai airfield twenty-seven years before, flying in from Tokyo the day after the Japanese had surrendered on board the U.S.S. *Missouri*. We landed that day long ago without permission, without warning, and a group of Japanese with drawn bayonets met us—we told them we were Americans, the Emperor had surrendered; we commandeered trucks and drove into Shanghai, through streets tossing with glee at the sight of American uniforms, then stayed at a hotel that night where all was free—room, food, liquor, girls—because we were Americans. The world then belonged to America—from the Golden Gate to Karachi no plane flew the sky, no ship sailed the seas without the let and knowledge of America.

Today, our plane had been given a ten-mile vector into Shanghai and we had been instructed not to stray from it.

We flew on from Shanghai to Peking that afternoon. Below: the unmistakable mark of the revolution—roads. Roads linking village to village, to town and to city; thirty years before, paved roads faded to dirt tracks twenty miles out of most major cities. Furrows: the peasants had worked their fields, years before, in garden patches, some as small as two or three acres—now the furrows of the collective farms stretched longer than the farms of Iowa. Water reservoirs: heart-shaped embankments cupping life-giving water, irrigating villages once permanently parched. And trees—trees in China!—lining roads. China had once been for us an expression of geography to do with as we wished. But revolution had visited here and stayed. China had now, at last, a government with power. We had come, at last, to deal with that power.

The next day in Peking, up early in the cold to journey to the airport to see Richard Nixon arrive.

I had visited the revolution in 1944 by flying to Yenan, the hill capital in the sere northwest, with the first American diplomatic mission to Communist China. Our pilot had sighted Yenan by the old yellow pagoda on the landmark bluff, swooped through gullies where dark ovals marked cave entrances, bounced down a rutted riverbed runway and lurched to a stop. Out from the plane had stepped Major General Patrick J. Hurley, his chest glistening with medals. He perceived a ragamuffin honor guard in padded quilting and, to their absolute bafflement, gave an Indian war whoop. Mao and Chou were a few minutes late. They jounced down from the hills in their most impressive conveyance, an old ambulance, tumbled out, then trotted unceremoniously across the runway to greet the American envoy. We climbed into the ambulance. Passing a flock of sheep, Hurley volunteered he'd once been a cowboy; Mao responded he had once been a shepherd; and, trading jokes, they began the first negotiations between Communist China and America in jovial goodwill. Two days later the negotiations stuck. Then stuck again in Chungking ten months later, and then hardened into hate.

The Chinese had persisted only briefly in the mood of Yenan. They had pleaded with Americans, in 1945, that they be allowed to send two delegates of their Politburo to talk to the President of the United States in Washington. They had been rebuffed. By 1952, in Korea, Chinese and Americans were killing each other. And the hate had persisted ever since, all dialogue between the two countries frozen into paranoia, [the whole world paralyzed for the entire postwar era by two systems of power which could not understand each other.]

For a generation the postwar Presidents of the United States, of both parties, saw the world as split between the clients of the Communist Revolution and the clients of the American Idea; and however correct the view of a world split between two monoliths may have been in the early postwar years, history itself wore the idea out. No man had believed more devoutly in the old view than Richard Nixon. Yet now, as President, he had come to realize that that world had come to an end. He feared the growing nuclear power of China, and wanted to talk about it. He had learned that the world of Communism was not a monolith, that a wedge of enmity was separating the Soviet Union and China. He knew his own people to be tormented by the war in Vietnam and sought now, not victory, but "peace with honor." He came to write an end to the history of the postwar world in China, where so much of it had been fashioned. With this act he would be not only closing an epoch, but beginning a Presidential campaign—for of all classic issues in American politics, peace-and-war is the most important. This is the ultimate responsibility the Constitution puts on a President.

For the Chinese, this morning of February 21st, 1972, was equally momentous. The airfield was almost barren, its far reaches color-flecked with white-on-scarlet slogans—"LONG LIVE THE CHINESE COMMUNIST PARTY" and "LONG LIVE THE GREAT SOLIDARITY OF ALL THE WORLD'S PEOPLE." The runway was immaculately swept, the terminal building glistened with a Swiss glossiness, the honor guard and ceremonial band stood stony-faced, husky, splendidly tailored in blue and olive green. In the chilly sunlight the faint shrill of Air Force One sounded at the distant end of the runway, and at 11:30 the silver-blue-and-white plane of the President touched down, to roll almost silently to the waiting greeters. Chou En-lai had materialized from nowhere and stood now at the bottom of the steps, still not old at seventy-three, his hair silvered, his long blue coat reaching down to the calves of his crisp gray pants; his right arm, wounded long ago in battle, stiff-cocked at the elbow.

The presence of Chou gave the greeting its meaning—the sparse gathering of Chinese newsmen and functionaries might otherwise have been an Oriental snub. Eighteen years before, at the Geneva conference on Vietnam, Chou En-lai had extended his hand in friendship to Secretary of State John Foster Dulles; Chou had remembered ever since how Dulles had spurned it, had turned his back and walked away. Nixon now extended his hand first; Chou took it in view of all the cameras, smiled, and in sight of millions of Americans watching back home, China was erased as the enemy. Richard Nixon, the peacemaker, had written his first message of the campaign of 1972.

Five hours later Nixon met Mao Tse-tung. That was a message for the Chinese people, not the Americans—the picture in the Chinese newspapers the next morning of Mao and Nixon sitting side by side, the shelves of Mao's private den overstuffed with books, both men smiling from easy chairs, flanked by Henry Kissinger on the one side, Chou En-lai on the other. The message that the picture bore to the Chinese people was clear: this visit was legitimate, the Chairman himself approved of peace; Chou En-lai's gamble on America in the intricate and perilous game of internal Chinese politics had the Chairman's sanction, too.

Yet the message Mao Tse-tung left with Richard Nixon was

equally important. Reminiscing, very guardedly and much later, the President reflected that most of his conversations with chiefs of state were absorbed with trivia, with "nitty-gritty," clogged with figures of Gross National Product, numbers of divisions, armies, navies, types of weapons, trade figures. With Mao, it was different. "You have to divide the politicians of the world," recalled the President, "into poets and pragmatists. Chou En-lai is part poet, part pragmatist; he has the surest grasp on the great issues of the world of any man I've met. But Mao is all poet. Maybe a revolutionary leader has to be a poet, he must be a dreamer. That's his strength. Mao thinks in conceptual terms. He probably couldn't tell you whether San Francisco or Los Angeles is larger, or the population figures of the United States. But he understands—what the United States means to the world, what Japan means, what the People's Republic of China means, what the U.S.S.R. means; he understands the changes in people, he talks in terms of a people's revolution, it's not an easy thing to describe . . . he doesn't talk in terms of next year, or even the next generation, but the next century. . . . He had no illusions that a handshake between us would change the deep differences in our philosophy, but he could see that at this time in history it was in the interests of his country and of ours, too, to cooperate. . . . He wanted to size me up. He'd read my statements and my background . . . he had to determine whether China and the United States could get along, whether I, from an ideological point of view, was an implacable enemy."

The two men and their aides were gathered, therefore, to discuss broad views, not details. In Nixon's words, as certainly in Mao's thoughts, the idea was "that leaders have got to talk about things in much broader terms, that day-to-day decisions down below will be influenced by how they size each other up, by their understanding of what brought them together." More than half the conversation was thus spent on what Mr. Nixon calls philosophical matters, the time cut by the time of translation between the two. Nixon began the talk very briefly by recalling his own record, his past hostility, his change of mind, his feeling that the two countries had been brought together by "a change in our interests." He had come "to seek peace." Mao responded without bitterness, without resentment, at one moment softly reaching over the tea table to hold Nixon's hand briefly in his. What Mao had to say is still secret, the minutes closed to all but two people in the White House. But Mao couched his response in hypothetical questions: why he thought as he did, why this, why that, explaining the Chinese point of view. They talked of Vietnam, but not for long; then of Japan; and of Russia. There was the problem of Formosa, which Kissinger described as a "murderously tough problem," and that problem perplexed the seven-day trip to its very end. But Mao's tone was gentle and soothing. They had come together to settle what could be settled now, and agreed, in Kissinger's words, "to leave to history what history had to settle."

What history had to settle remained all through the campaign of 1972 difficult to define, for the American people were seeking clear yes-and-no answers in an age of political transition. The postwar world was cracking up, and the settlements of the great war against Fascism which had left America master of the globe twenty-five years before were now as obsolete as the Treaty of Versailles or the Peace of Westphalia. A world power shift was going on, comparable to that of the 1840's and 1850's, when China had first been recognized by the Western powers as prey, when the 500-year war between England and France was fading to memory, when new entrants in the power world—Germany, Russia, America—were making their weight felt, when the old ideas of legitimacy and authority were dissolving under the acids of Marxist doctrine, American experience, industrial-technological innovation. So, too, now in 1972 a global power shift was going on.

Power relationships, when they change, crunch people who have no idea where the crunch and hurt come from, who cannot understand what has made them fat or now drives them from their homes. This was what was happening to Americans in 1972—the world was pressing on them, and pressing their politics at home, too, into strange new shapes. The changing world required a concentration of power in the President's hands greater than ever before to negotiate the perilous and delicate passage between two world eras. That concentration of power was changing the office of the Presidency at home as abroad.

I remember walking the beach of the Pacific at San Clemente in November on election weekend, as Kissinger tried to unwind from the negotiations going on between Hanoi, Saigon and the President's office. As we left his villa for a stroll Kissinger was indulging in a momentary burst of anger at the government of Thieu, which was then obstructing negotiations, and at George McGovern, who was denying the sincerity of the Nixon-Kissinger quest for peace.

Then, as we saw the children gathering kelp on the beach, and kicked the sand as we strolled, he relaxed and began to reminisce. As he recounted his story, events began to acquire a time frame. When Nixon first came into office and he, Kissinger, had joined the administration, various agencies of government had prepared study papers in foreign policy for their perusal—but the papers lacked any sense of the future; they were papers whose horizon was tomorrow, or next week. "It seemed as if American policy everywhere was simple—just get a pro-American government in power and keep it there." No real view of the world had come from the State Department.

Basically, thought Kissinger, the postwar foreign policy of the United States had once had a coherence—back in 1945 when it was first shaped. "It had a 'theory of power,' a 'theory of economics,' " said Kissinger, "and we saw the world as ours to defend against a monolithic Communism. Acheson and Dulles and Kennan all saw us as bringing our strength to a point where we could negotiate with the Communists— but negotiate about what? They never said. Their thought was that if we contained Communism long enough, Communism would change. But for them it was simple—the world was a confrontation between us and monolithic Communism."

Kissinger admired the policies of 1945—they had been based on a world view, a concept. But what we needed now was another, different concept. "How do you withdraw?" he asked. "How do you lessen the burdens and exposure and yet be the great international power? How do you get out of a situation where every single crisis around the globe gets dumped on us as America's problem? How do you limit this exposure and yet keep America a force for peace?"

Nixon had come into office, said Kissinger, with that necessary new concept, which he, Kissinger, shared: "What the world needed was a self-regulating mechanism." And if you were going to give the world a self-regulating mechanism of power, then the key was China. A week after his first inauguration, the President, who in those early days communicated with Kissinger usually by memoranda, instructed him to seek "unofficial contacts with China." This effort to unfreeze the world from the settlements of 1945 meant that you simply had to get to China as the first step—that, therefore, was the constant personal priority of the President. Then Kissinger went on to tell the story of how and where they had made contact with the Chinese state, how the first unsigned response from China had been delivered secretly, and said that Mao himself had noted and appreciated one of our gestures (on trade) that opened the way; but Kissinger himself will tell that story someday.

Not since I had talked with George Marshall long ago, and Dean Acheson during the dynamic days of American hegemony, had I heard the use of American power so carefully explained. Marshall and Acheson knew what they were doing and what power meant in the world abroad; so, too, did Nixon and Kissinger—they were building a frame: "There's room left in the frame for Europe, too," said Kissinger, "Europe must take its place. The trouble is that Europe has no world view of its own." Europe was turned inward, obsessed with details, uninterested in what lay beyond its peninsula. "Europe is all potential, but not there in fact yet," said Kissinger.

We came off the beach after a three-mile walk, climbing up the eroded duneland, and Kissinger began to notice that people were waving at him. They had been waving at him all along as we walked, but he had not seen them. A middle-aged man with gray fuzz on his chest asked if he could shake Kissinger's hand—he wanted to say simply he was grateful for peace. Kissinger became very boyish and shy, not his customary carriage; then said to me, "Where else—where else could it happen but in a country like this? To let a foreigner make peace for them, to accept a man like me—I even have a foreign accent."

Kissinger had put a time frame about what was happening to America. He had come to the United States a refugee from Nazi Germany as a boy of fifteen, in 1938, when the muscles of America were first flexing for combat, for the first testing of the use of power. America had treated him well. Under the GI Bill he had gone through Harvard, where he studied the structure of American power, then America's use of power; and then he had helped a President use that power as well as it had ever been used in the world at large.

But at home in America the use of this Presidential power was more complicated than it was abroad. If Nixon were to win his election by the expected margin on the Tuesday after I walked with Kissinger, it would be because of how he had used the power of the Presidency abroad; the diplomacy of the first four years could only be called majestic. But there would rise much later, in my mind as in the minds of so many others, the question of how large the margin would have been had the American people known of that family of obscenities which were to be jumbled together under the name "Watergate affair." And yet that family of obscenities flowed from the same management of power which had created the great diplomatic triumphs of the first Nixon administration. Of that story, and of the thinking and morality that begat Watergate, this book will have much more to say later. That corrosion of decency in power and fouling of the political process are as much a measure of the change in American life, and the end of the postwar world, as the open issues debated in the campaign itself.

I have had to write this book in a moment of passage which happens but rarely in American life—when the passing of a generation coincides with a crisis of conscience. As this is written, two former members of the Nixon Cabinet await trial, Federal grand juries in several cities are pursuing the trail of the greatest political scandal in American history, a Senate investigation is already exploring the entire political process and crimes of which the Nixon administration has been accused. And all this takes place against the background of another crisis, a change of ideas, at a time when the thinking of one generation has been worn out and the next system of ideas is not ready to replace it.

The change was easiest to see overseas, and there Richard Nixon led in understanding it. The world of 1945–1950 was a world of American design; except for Russia, which was to be contained, no balance or restraint limited either America's power or America's generosity to deal with that world as it wished.

By 1972, however, that postwar world was dead and awaited burial. The United States had in the 1950's encouraged the Common Market of Europe as a counterforce to Russia; now, not only was the Common Market a power force in its own right, but England, America's closest ally, had cast its lot in with Europe, not America. The trading system America had designed was totally obsolete—America could no longer both sustain and drain the free economies of the world, setting the rules by its own power. America had financed the recovery of Germany and Japan—but by 1972 recognized them as its chief trading rivals. America had pegged the world to gold in 1944—but now gold, man's oldest measure of value, had been erased as a measure of value by the United States itself. The postwar map had been sponged and its lines redrawn. Africa was almost entirely free. Pakistan, that artificial state, had broken apart. Despite continuing Arab hostility, the state of Israel was now sovereign and seemed both secure and permanent. Martial lines of settlement were elsewhere subsiding into uneasy but peaceful political acceptance—East and West Germany were negotiating their own way into the future, North and South Korea had begun to talk. Most of all, the Soviet Union and China were joining the world dialogue. The Russians had closed the missile gap; and, given parity in missiles, the Russians were finally talking to America about their most vital common interest: how to strike a balance of nuclear terror.

Anywhere one looked at the globe, it presented a fresh aspect for which no coherent doctrine existed. Not only was it a fresh globe—it was a thriving, prosperous globe. People lived better, ate better, slept better, survived longer over more of the world's surface than ever before. America had been more responsible for this global prosperity than any other country. It had created this new world out of self-interest—but the genuine goodwill and generosity that went along with its self-interest could not be denied. Yet both American self-interest and American goodwill were now checkmated by the world they had created.

Japanese and Russians, for example, were eating better than ever before in their history, but, like Americans, wanted more. Their ships and trawlers looted the oceans of the world for fish, ravaging the seabeds within twelve miles of American shores, Atlantic and Pacific. Japanese, who paid almost four dollars a pound for medium-grade beef, and Russians, who wanted millions of tons of grain to produce more meat, were competing with the American housewife at the supermarket for hamburger and steak. Hundreds of millions of previously illiterate people around the globe had been taught to read and write—and their appetite for the paper on which to print the words was shooting up the price of every American newspaper at home. What was happening in distant lands reached into every American family budget, pocketbook and holiday plan.

Energy, for example. Americans had multiplied by six their consumption of electric energy since the end of World War II, fouling their skies as they did so. They had also multiplied by four times their use of gasoline in automobiles. There was now no longer enough oil in the world as the civilization of wheels spread from America to Europe and Japan. The great world reserves of oil lay in the rickety principalities of the Middle East, whose accumulation of gold and dollars could now threaten the U.S. currency and the personal welfare of ordinary Americans. In every suburb of America or deep-center city, the energy crisis intruded itself. It intruded itself on those muggy days of August when the air-conditioning failed to work, on those sub-zero days in winter when the oil truck, short of supplies, failed to deliver fuel. The end of the postwar world abroad was at hand from coast to coast, whether Americans realized it or not.

The world abroad, as much as anything, had provoked the end of the era in American politics at home, too. The sharpest of these provocations was, of course, the Vietnam war, undertaken by a President without consent of Congress, without lust for territory or profit, in the name of a cause once honorable but ossified to dogma—and conducted with mindless stupidity. The war had provoked millions of Americans to ask why their sons should be sent to war without consent or apparent cause, and die in strange lands. What was politics all about? "Why am I in politics," a Wisconsin Democratic county chairman had asked me as early as 1967, "if they're going to take my boys and send them off to a war I don't believe in, and I can't do anything about it?"

But more than just the Vietnam war was pressing on American politics. Great ideas were changing. The idea of a free-enterprise economy, for example, was changing. That principal idea had fostered America's industrial power. It had been reconditioned in the Roosevelt revolution when the New Deal had insisted on supervising the investment process. It was now in the early 1970's changing again—the government was being asked to stand between the producer and the consumer as arbiter on wages and prices, on quality and value. The orthodoxies of the postwar world were trembling—the Keynesian theories of economics, the social workers' theorems of the Great Society were demonstrably inadequate. So, too, were engineering theories, planning theories, finance theories. The government had built highways which destroyed cities and ruined railways and public transportation; the government had financed suburbs with cheap credit and strangled the cities that lived inside their ring; it had pumped in education to create an elite without responsibilities; it had accepted, in noble, high conscience, the revolution of civil rights—but dumped its burdens on cities unable to sustain the burden; it had liberalized the immigration laws of the country—and overwhelmed, with a new absorption problem, cities already strained to the breaking point by the civil-rights revolution.

The politics of 1972 writhed under the strain of the thinking required, so coarsely translated on the stump or the airwaves. The rhetoric remained the same, but the country the rhetoric described was different. The climate of life had changed—from the irritable file at the airline gate where electronic eyes scanned your body for guns, to the supermarket where you studied the fine print on packages and tried to puzzle out which detergent or bug-killer you as a good citizen should buy. It was a period of passage in culture and response. The draft was over, thank God, after thirty-two years of conscription. The birth rate was down to its lowest point in American history—but was that good or bad? The privacy of grand juries, whose traditional secrecy was so essential to the protection of innocents under accusation, had been torn open by an enthusiastic press—whose own essential privacy of sources and reporting was, on the other hand, being challenged by the government. Labor unions, within government and outside it, were demanding the right to interrupt essential processes of service and survival with the same impunity with which they had won the right to interrupt the production of shoes, shirts and automobiles. Values were changing.

Even without the crunch on Americans from outside, there would have been a vast disarray of ideas in American civilization as the postwar world came to its end—what the New Deal had established thirty years before as the values of humanity, and what the Great Society had tried to put into institutional practice had run out of vitality, at home as abroad.

There was, thus, a turning point, which had not yet reached a clarity of options. No country moves forward more by ideas than America. And one of the problems of 1972 was that the idea system had become clogged by its own excessive outpourings. American intellectuals had written the Constitution, engineered the turn-of-the-century reform, provided Franklin Roosevelt with his blueprints of reorganization, armed America with marvels of technology during the Second World War. They had been rewarded with a gush of approval, with an outpouring of funds, private and public, that had all but choked off fresh ideas—like a garden over-seeded and over-fertilized. The American idea system poured out paper after paper, study after study, learned investigation after learned investigation on the race problem, the urban problem, the environment problem, the television problem, the violence problem, the identity problem, until clear thinking was suffocated by the mattress of scholarly investigation. ⌉

The problems came to their most acute edge for those who enjoyed, or aspired to, power. Richard Nixon was a President who repudiated most of the intellectually fashionable ideas of his time. Abroad, with the help of Kissinger, and with the authority Presidents traditionally enjoy in foreign affairs, he could work out his own ideas—with a clarity of vision and so tenacious a grip on reality that history must mark him among the great foreign-policy Presidents of the United States.

But at home, the use of power was more complicated.

Thus, irony: Richard Nixon campaigned in 1972, as he always had, against central power, against the idea of the omnipotent President doing his will from Washington. He was for returning home power to the people in their communities. But in practice he took to himself more personal power, delegated to more individuals of his staff the use or abuse of that power, than any other President of modern times. Faced by a hostile Congress, a hostile intellectual world, a hostile vanguard of the press/television system, a recalcitrant party of his own and a Democratic Party committed by definition to opposition, he abandoned all the old conventions of party politics.

His campaign was, therefore, a personal campaign and, above all, a campaign of issues. It was a campaign that never invited Americans to judge his use or manipulation of power, but only its apparent end results and its stated direction. He personally stood above detail, above the nitty-gritty of political mechanics. Mao Tse-tung would have approved of his long view. Americans overwhelmingly responded to Nixon's presentation of the issues—they chose his directions, freely and openly, as against the directions offered by George McGovern. And though McGovern tried, gallantly and eloquently, to turn national debate to a consideration of the style of power itself, he could not score the question through on the minds of people. That was left for the press to do later: to pose the question of internal power within the Nixon administration, and of how the President had let that power be used, and abused, to defile the laws of the country and the political process itself.

None of the changes that marked the end of the postwar world at home and abroad could fail to affect the vehicles of American power—the two great parties of tradition, the Republican and Democratic parties. By 1972 the parties had changed in character so fundamentally as to be almost unrecognizable, even to men who had made party politics their life study. The parties no longer controlled loyalties as they once had; the parties no longer delivered responses as they once had; the parties no longer related to government as they once had.

The process of degradation in American national politics had been going on, of course, for years before 1972. Election after election, from 1960 on, had seen the process increasingly polluted by money. A two-party total of $24,000,000 had been spent for the Presidential candidates of 1960. The sum had risen to $37,500,000 in 1964, to $100,-000,000 in 1968, and substantially more than $100,000,000 in 1972. Election trickery and deception had always been part of American politics—but beginning in 1964, in the Johnson campaign against Goldwater, trickery, espionage, counter-demonstration had first begun from the White House itself, condoned then by many because it was practiced against Goldwater, whom they despised. By 1972 the Nixon campaign had lifted trickery to the level of crime. The first mild and jocular adversary demonstrations planned against Goldwater by the White House in 1964 had by 1968 become a cult of politics controlled by no party, and of themselves escalated to riot in the street, maturing in the violence of conspirators seeking to hit and influence the national election process at its most vulnerable. The stage of politics was changing as television became its most important platform of action. Politics, in response, was planned increasingly for dramatic and visual effect. All the while, too, education, joining television, was freeing more and more millions of Americans from unquestioning obedience to past tradition, their union begetting what has been called the age of ticket-splitting.

America had not been born with a party system; the founding fathers had feared parties as the greatest possible danger to the republican system they envisioned. The party system had grown up in the first third of the nineteenth century as a way for people with common interests to band together to make power do what they wanted done. But the parties now, as the dying postwar world bequeathed the unbelievably complicated problems of this age of passage, were unable to perform the functions for which people had once intended them.

The transformation of the Democratic Party was a conscious one, as we shall see, although its consequences were completely unpredictable at the beginning of 1972.

The Republican situation was worse—the party was simply allowed to decay so completely that it played no role whatsoever as a national party in the national election of 1972. Both national parties as they presented themselves to the American people in 1972 had come, by no one's design, to reflect the wills and the personalities of two individual candidates. The candidates' personal staffs were responsible not to what their parties stood for, but to what they thought their candidates stood for. Neither campaign represented more than what its candidate said, or wanted, or permitted. Thus there came about, on the Democratic side, the buffoonery of the Eagleton affair. And, on the Republican side, something incomparably more disturbing—the felony of Watergate.

At the open level of dialogue, where issues were presented to the American people, Richard Nixon won by the greatest margin of votes in American history. No trickery was necessary to ensure that victory, and the political indecencies of his lieutenants clouded his victory in a way that could obscure both its meaning and the will of the people who voted for him.

Rarely had two candidates given Americans sharper choices. There was no doubt that the American people had grown suspicious about all governmental power—suspicious of what power could do, or undo, in their home cities; suspicious of its dictates to their communities in race relations; suspicious of its conscription of their sons to fight abroad; suspicious of its control over their purse and tax burdens. In this sense, Richard Nixon convinced the Americans, by more than three to two, that he could use power better than George McGovern—and how that came about is the story of this book.

The story of an election always belongs to the victor, as does this one. Nixon's triumph in the election of 1972 was won by a single man, adjusting America's role to the new world with an almost exquisite recognition of the passage of time, and a diplomatic finesse of conciliation and kill-power. He recognized best, and spoke most clearly for, the way Americans chose to live at home in their neighborhoods—or, at the very least, he persuaded an astounding majority of Americans that he understood their emotions and needs better than his rival. With his victory, he believed in all sincerity that he had been given a mandate to reorganize the American government to make it more responsive to what the voters had shown they wanted.

The after-fact that this genuine mandate might be denied him by Watergate, by the frightening way he had let his own appointees use his purposes to flout law—that is a story this book will inescapably, later, come to. But the book begins with how the people saw their leaders, and how the leaders saw their people, in America in 1972, when the postwar world was coming to an end—and how the people chose Richard Nixon.

THE
MAKING OF
THE PRESIDENT
1972

CHAPTER ONE

THE SOLITARY MAN

I T was to be Richard Nixon's last rally—and they wanted to make it splendid for him.

He had campaigned across the country the day before—in Chicago, Tulsa and Providence. This afternoon, Saturday, November 4th, 1972, he left the White House at 1:35 under clear blue skies, to prop-stop on his way home to vote in California. An hour's flight brought him in over the red earth and slash pine of the Piedmont to his first stop—a rally at Greensboro, North Carolina. He alighted to deliver the Presidential embrace to two obscure Republican candidates, for Senate and Governor, and was exhilarated when, returning to his plane, the crowd broke through the barriers—cheering and rushing him, snatching off one of his cufflinks in the crush. At dusk he paused again to speak at Albuquerque, the setting sun shafting shadows over the iron-gray mountains until, as he spoke, there he was alone in the darkness, silhouetted in floodlights. And then it was off again in the night for Ontario, California, twenty-five miles from his boyhood home, Whittier, for the last rally ever of Richard Nixon, candidate.

Everything his advance men could do had been done before he got there. But the rally was more than what they had prepared. Cowbells were clanking, hooters sounding, holiday horns blaring as his black limousine rolled down the roped-off lane from the plane toward the platform. There were perhaps 20,000 in the high stands and on the folding chairs, another 10,000 spilling over onto the field, and now they squeezed against the ropes—pounding on his car, clanging bells, squirting noise in his face. Somewhere in the distance a dozen bass drums were booming to the rhythm of clapping, but their thump-thud-thump was all but lost in the shrieks, the squeals, the roar of the crowd. It was a family crowd, and for the first time in a Republican rally in 1972 I noticed that blacks were present, too. The crowd surged, the car crawled, and he stood and waved while the roar rose higher and the crowd caught the thump of the bass drums and began to chant, "Four More Years, Four More Years, Four More Years." Little boys in colored football helmets were snatching drifting balloons from the air and cracking them pop-open, with the subdued crack of gunshots. A little Indian boy in a bright orange jacket sitting on his father's head almost tumbled into the President's car. The Secret Service ran ahead, pushing and shoving a way through the crowd that strained at the ropes of the lane. The car began to roll faster, and you could look up and see the panorama. Rallies in America are, by now, almost a thing of the past. There has been no tidal flooding of hundreds of thousands of people into the streets since Lyndon Johnson barnstormed New England in the fall of 1964, in the days before Americans learned how much easier it is to watch the candidates on evening television than in the street. But tonight was the old pageant, like a torchlight parade of Chicago Democrats, and was to be remembered as a moment of politics in passage: the arc lights criss-crossed the night sky with shafts of red, white and blue visible for thirty miles, the grandstand flags were repeated like tiny petals in the hands of thousands of youngsters. On the floodlit platform glistened what appeared to be an acre of bands—twenty-four of them, one learned later. The fan-bells of the tubas glistened like medallions in the distant rows—brass, gold, silver, blue and white. And the drum majorettes, a full corps of them in the uniforms of all the local high schools, were high-kicking with the music, pompoms in red and purple and green bouncing, shakos dancing. Then the music faded, and while the roar slowly died down, Richard and Pat Nixon were advancing to three tangerine-colored seats set alone on the forestage where Governor Ronald Reagan waited for them.

Richard Nixon had started here in Ontario, California, twenty-seven years ago—with some unremembered speech against Congressman Jerry Voorhis in the then 12th California Congressional. He had come a long way between that beginning and this return. One hoped now to catch a moment of poetry, or nostalgia, or even the sentimentality that could have been expected from Richard Nixon years ago. This crowd, if crowds have a personality, ached to cheer or cry. "No one loves Richard Nixon" had been one of the dominant clichés of American politics for years; but this crowd loved Richard Nixon, as did millions of others.

He came on easily, with no histrionics. He began by saying he had come that day from North Carolina, the home state of writer Thomas Wolfe. Wolfe had written that "you can't go home again"—but this crowd, he said, proved Wolfe was wrong. It was here, exactly twelve years ago, at one o'clock in the morning before the election in 1960, he recalled, that he had held his last rally of the campaign against Kennedy; California had been good to him that year. And he hoped he had kept the faith.

Then he settled into this, the last of his countless thousands of rally speeches, discarding his text, and this reporter watched the man he had followed for so many years in American politics. The Nixon of other years used to approach the rostrum on his toes, and, once there, his body-sway was an entertainment. His hips used to weave; sometimes one leg would curl up behind him; his hands would flail, weave, jab with an imaginary uppercut at his opponent. In emotional moments his eyes would close. His rhetoric would slash, pound, wander back through his boyhood and memories; he was, at one stage, the easiest public bleeder in American politics except for Hubert Humphrey; and at his peak he could arouse his partisans to frenzy.

Now there was neither frenzy nor sentiment in this Nixon, the President—and listening to him was a perplexity. So much in this man was persistent, consecutive, carrying through twenty-five years of national politics. The phrases floating over the sound system were part of what one had to recognize now, finally, as an unshakable philosophy. The key phrase, for example, tonight was, "I bring you Peace With Honor, not Peace With Surrender." He had first phrased it twelve years ago, against John F. Kennedy in 1960, as "How to Keep the Peace Without Surrender." And then his exhortation, the same as far back as one could remember, "Vote for What's Best for America"; and all the other phrases coming from the sound system: "Keep America Strong," "Strengthen the Peace Forces against the Crime Forces." They were old, all heard so often they had slipped from conscious retention.

Only in retrospect did one realize how much the substance of the man had changed. Not simply the newly grave, flat, unemotional tone of his voice, but the thinking. One could imagine him here, at his first rally, a freshman in politics, flogging the Democrats, as all Republicans did that postwar year, over the meat shortage and the meat prices and the meat rationing. One could imagine him, even better, inveighing, as he was to do for so many years, against the peril of Communism—above all, against the peril of Red China. But tonight, what his last rally heard was a statement of the essence of his case for re-election, as if he were a lawyer presenting a brief in court: He had brought peace. When he came to office, he said, 300 Americans a week were being killed in Vietnam; we had been on a collision course to greater war. Had he not acted, he told them, "we would have gone down the road to inevitable confrontation and nuclear confrontation and the end of civilization—I could not let this happen." And of China, yesterday's red menace, he was telling them, "Think of what it means fifteen years from now if they have a nuclear capability and there is no communication between us . . . nations of different philosophy must meet at the conference table."

The speech was simple, clear, forceful, but un-ringing. He was his own man, the President; he was not beseeching, or courting, or politicking; he was simply explaining.

But now he was coming to the end of his remarks. He gripped the lectern firmly with both hands and leaned forward, the wind ballooning his jacket out behind him. "Here in Ontario," he said, "in November, 1945, I held my first rally. Tonight as I speak to you in Ontario, it is the last time I will speak to you as candidate for any office—and this is the best rally. Thank you. Thank you." The old Nixon would have twanged every sentiment, would have tried to bring tears to the eyes, would have explored the limits of nostalgia. One waited for more. But he was through—like that, his last farewell to the stump.

It was a moment before the crowd realized that this last speech was over. And then, though wanting more, more, they cheered against the rising sound of the clanging, the singing, the beating of the drums. Nixon strolled across the platform shaking hands with old friends, occasionally reaching down to sign an autograph, his gravity gone and a wide, very boyish grin creasing his face. Then, abruptly, he vanished, leaving through a side gate to the helicopter that would lift him to San Clemente. There, that weekend, he would be studying the cables from Vietnam and, all by himself, putting the finishing touches on his personal plan for reorganizing the American government.

Of his re-election he had no doubt, nor did anyone else. He could spend the next few days at ease, carving a new outline for the next Presidency, imagining how he could make American government work if the power came to him in the measure he expected, and how America, by his design, could carve a new peace in the world.

Neither he nor anyone on his staff that weekend could conceive that the affirmative plebiscite on the Nixon record, so obviously swelling, would leave him so vulnerable and so isolated in the term to come. Very shortly, however, Richard Nixon was to become more powerful and more solitary than he had ever been before in his life—but that was not to happen until Tuesday, voting day.

On Tuesday, November 7th, the schedule called for him to board Air Force One at El Toro Marine Base in California, for the flight back to Washington, at 10:20 A.M.

Dawn had come four hours earlier through a low overhanging mist, the sun staining the undersides of the cloud bars pink. By voting time a cluster of fifty people—schoolteachers and schoolchildren, early-rising retirees and housewives—had already gathered at the Concordia Elementary School, a sand-colored stucco schoolhouse less than a mile from the President's Pacific seaside home in San Clemente. There, at exactly seven, a little boy shrilled, "Ooh—there's his big limousine now," and the black limousine was rolling along the oval drive lined by dwarf palms, cypresses and pines. At 7:01, as the President and Mrs. Nixon stepped out, Judge Mary Stamp stood before him, raised her hand in ceremony and said, "Hear ye, hear ye, the polls are now open."

Voter Number One of Precinct 48/146's 545 enrolled voters was thereupon handed his pink, newspaper-size ballot and the little blue electronic stamp which makes the balloting results machine-readable, and disappeared into Voting Booth Two. There were no less than twenty-four propositions and bond issues on the ballot in Congressional District 42 in California—two local, twenty-two statewide. Running the gamut from plebiscites on pot, pornography and the death penalty to the preservation of California's coastal beauties, the ballot reflected concerns which had scarcely been shadows on the mind when Richard Nixon had entered politics twenty-seven years earlier. Now he took his time—five minutes and twenty seconds—in examining and voting on each' proposition. Then he lingered to be photographed, handed out White House pens to the election clerks, autographed a picture thrust at him and, eleven minutes after his arrival, was en route back to his office in the summer White House.

By this time, in the East millions of voters had been balloting for hours; and as he was going through his mail with Rose Mary Woods, his secretary, she was interrupted by a telephone call. It was the first published tally on the wires: Dixville Notch in New Hampshire had voted 16 for the President, 3 for McGovern. Four years earlier Dixville Notch had voted 8 for Humphrey, 4 for Nixon. The President, as Miss Woods recalled, said nothing—only smiled, then went back to the mail. Miss Woods keeps ready a sampling of the more human mail gleaned from the torrent that floods the White House—letters from children, from bereaved parents of soldiers, from well-wishers, in the hand-scrawled style that yields the beat of emotion. When the President is not too busy, he enjoys reading such letters. And this was what he did that morning until his helicopter came to the pad outside his gate to take him to El Toro Marine Base, where Air Force One waited to carry him back to Washington.

Air Force One was airborne at 10:24, climbed over the tawny Santa Ana Mountains, rose over the huge Irvine ranch, nine times the size of Manhattan, cut quickly through low-hanging fog and in ten minutes was cruising at 33,000 feet over the desert, en route to Washington.

Except for Henry Kissinger, those admitted into the privileged forward compartments were all veterans of a similar flight made exactly four years before on Election Day, from Los Angeles to New York. In

1968 the mood had been both somber and comradely, the mood halfway between apprehension and anticipation, the plane festooned with balloons. The candidate that year had exerted himself to show the characteristic consideration that binds his personal followers to his career—sending for them and their wives, in groups of two and three, to thank and soothe them. Now he sat alone in the forward compartment of Air Force One; and the conversation in the compartments behind was laced with nostalgia and recall.

Air Force One, the President's plane, invites little conviviality. It had come into service in 1962 for John F. Kennedy, had been altered somewhat by Lyndon Johnson, then again been re-configured to suit Richard Nixon's personality. Johnson, a public man, had occasionally worked behind a plate-glass window so that anyone admitted forward to the working area could see the President of the United States doing his job. Now the plane reflected Richard Nixon's compulsive wish for privacy, and was severely hierarchical in configuration; he was invisible. The crew, the half-dozen rotating members of the press pool and Mrs. Nixon's hairdresser occupied the tail compartment, and none of them could go forward beyond it. Next forward came a staff-and-VIP guest compartment, decorated with two maps, one of America, the other of the world. Forward again came the working area, with its lounge, typewriters, desks and reproduction machines, served by the operational hard core—Haldeman, Ehrlichman and Ziegler. (It was in this area that Lyndon Johnson had stood and taken the oath of office on November 22nd, 1963, the blood-soaked Jacqueline Kennedy standing beside him.) Forward of the working area came the President's territory—a reception lounge for important visitors, usually occupied by Mrs. Nixon, the décor of the lounge all gold and blue, with bowls of fresh-cut flowers and hard candies adding color. Then a Presidential office; and finally the President's personal lair, no bigger than a Pullman compartment, where he could work alone at a tiny desk, from the one easy chair; or, when he chose, open out the folding bed and take a nap. Forward of that compartment were the Secret Service men, and yet farther forward, in the nose of the plane, a fifteen-foot panel of winking lights, buttons, switches, teletype and coding machines which reached to the signal consoles in Washington and the Pentagon and patched the President, if he chose, into every corner of his country and the globe, or, as Commander-in-Chief, to each of the nine Specified or Unified Commands of the Armed Forces. No one ventured forward from the rear of the plane to staff territory without permission; and no one on the staff, except Haldeman and Ziegler, ventured forth from staff territory to President's territory without being asked.

The mood was placid, "like coming home from an easy win at a football game," said someone contrasting it with the tension of the flight of 1968. There was Ziegler, constantly on the phone, relaying incoming press reports. Each Election Day, election officials in every state are asked by the press how the voting is going; and, invariably, every official reports that the voting is heavy and his state will set a record. So, today, too, officials were proclaiming that this election would set a record. All such predictions are true; given the growth of American population, each election turns out a larger total number than the election before. But over the past twelve years the percentage of those Americans eligible to vote who actually choose to vote has been dropping; and thus the record vote of 1972 was to turn out to be, in percentage terms, the lowest since 1948.

Champagne was served with a Mexican-American lunch and someone noted that it was the same which Nixon had taken with him for the Peking trip in February—a Napa Valley California champagne (Schwansberg 1970). Restlessly, Henry Kissinger paced the aisles, entertaining friends with his raconteur's flair, telling stories of a visit to Lyndon Johnson in Texas. Johnson had apparently mistaken him for a German dignitary (Kiesinger?) and lectured him on the Teutons of the Southwest. LBJ's home district was a German enclave; and had been the only district to side with the Union in Texas during the Civil War because, said LBJ, "Germans and Negroes have a natural friendship"; and, again, LBJ had told Kissinger how he had caused picnic tables, instead of hot-dog stands, to be installed around the LBJ ranch "because Germans are people who like picnics." Then Kissinger retired to the seclusion of the operations section to work out chess problems. In the working compartment forward they were playing a game, guessing how the nation's newspapers would handle tomorrow's story, inventing headlines. Ziegler brought the guests his favorite—the Washington *Post,* said Ziegler, would probably banner the elections as "MC GOVERN SWEEPS D.C.," with a subhead reading *"Nixon Carries Nation."*

Finch, the oldest veteran on Nixon's staff, was musing about the Cabinet changes to come, and the need for the President to address himself to the Watergate problem immediately after the election; but he did not see the President on the plane except in the presence of Haldeman and Ehrlichman, and the Watergate affair was not brought up.

The plane bore few problems. There was a complication created by a technicians' strike at CBS which might make it necessary for the President to decide whether to cross picket lines when he went to the Shoreham Hotel that night to address jubilant Republicans. But that was settled before the plane crossed the Mississippi. Haldeman, Ehrlichman, Ziegler, Finch discussed what should be their victory line, and the tone of the Republican spokesmen who would have to fill time on the air in what they felt would be a runaway election. They would be generous to the press this time—if asked, they would say they had had a fair shake; they would talk policy and issues, taking their text from the President's fourteen radio campaign speeches; and they hoped that when the night's returns were in they would be able to claim a "functional majority" in Congress. There seemed no doubt of this majority; shortly after eleven the UPI flash to the plane from the East had read, "At mid-afternoon, the first incomplete compilation of national returns gave Nixon 216 votes to 26 for McGovern—a majority of 89 percent." And down below, as the plane moved effortlessly across the Rocky Mountains, the face of the land was serene, snow-powder reaching down the slopes to the Plains states. There was nothing to be noted different from any other day in the land below when its people vote except, if one stretched the imagination, the highways seemed more bare than usual.

It was about half an hour before we touched down at Andrews Air Force Base that I was asked forward to the President's territory. He was sitting alone, the shades half drawn in his tiny cubicle, his hands neatly crossed over his knees, which were bent up so his feet could rest on the desk; beside him on the floor was a briefcase, with the familiar yellow legal pads on which he had just been scrawling.

He motioned me to the other chair in the cubicle, and I began by recalling the story he once told me of his flight back in 1968 when he had taken Mrs. Nixon and his two daughters aside, warned them privately of his fear, cautioned them against tears if he lost. The President nodded; it was different, yes. But he was in no mood for reminiscence—or jubilation, or euphoria. He had been working on his way back, and his tone was flat, matter-of-fact. Yes, people were saying this was going to be a landslide. "But what's a landslide?" he continued. "Down there" —waving with his hand to the window and the people below—"who remembers landslides, or electoral votes? Who remembers what Harding got? Or how Roosevelt did against Landon?"

What was important about this one, he explained, was that he thought he might have "shifted allegiances" this year. "Just think of the shift in the South," he said. People were going to say he got the South by racism; he knew what they were saying, but "You know what did it? Patriotism, not racism." Not only the South was shifting, but others— workingmen and Catholics, too. The Republican Party used to be a WASP party, he recalled, and he used to talk about it in the old days with Len Hall, who came from Nassau County. Len understood. You used to go to a Republican dinner in those days and there wouldn't be an Irishman or an Italian or a Jew there. If you could shift those allegiances permanently, then this landslide meant something. The trouble with McGovern was he took those people for granted—"You can't take people for granted any more," he said.

Vietnam was uppermost on his mind, it appeared, and he talked about that. "I never shoot blanks," said the President, "not when it comes to dealing with China or the Soviet Union." And he wasn't shooting blanks with the American people either, not when it came to Vietnam. He had the peace he promised; he would show it. The press disagreed with him so much, he knew, were so completely against his policy that they couldn't follow what he said. "I make my share of mistakes," said the President, "but one of their mistakes, because they disagree with me so much, they play right into my hands." He would have peace, he knew it.

I drew the conversation away from Vietnam and tried to bring it back to "Out There," where voting was still going on. Could he recognize the face of the country from the air? "I always recognize Chicago," he said. "I remember riding back from the West after the election in 1960, and coming over the mountains where we did so well, and seeing Chicago, and I thought of all the time I put in there and then how poorly we'd done." Then he brought the talk sharply back to today, to *this* election. Ten years ago, he said, who could have foreseen that we'd be doing better in New York than in California? This majority building up down there was a national majority, a real national majority. The West might be weaker than the rest of the country, but the South would be just as good as the rest of the country. Then a quick review: Oregon might be a surprise. So might Wisconsin. Michigan was always a tight state. He felt he would probably lose Massachusetts. But he would take South Dakota, McGovern's state, and West Virginia, Kennedy's state, and he relished the thought. His own guess was that he would probably get between 57 and 60 percent of the popular vote.

What were the key points in this year's campaign? I asked. "The election was decided the day McGovern was nominated," he said flatly; "the question after that was only how much. McGovern did to his party what Goldwater did." Then he ticked off the key dates and turning points of this victory: The day Wallace was out of the race, that came first. Then, the trip to Peking. Next, the decision of May 8th to blockade Haiphong and bomb Hanoi. Next, the trip to Moscow. Next, the economic decisions of the summer of 1971. And again he came back to the phrase that was holding him at the moment. He had tried to "shift allegiances."

The plane was now coming down under the overcast that had covered the country from the Mississippi to the Alleghenies, and lights of cities and towns were beginning to flicker, but he was paying no attention to the panorama below, he was off making his own points—that it wasn't going to be easy, even with a landslide.

"John Connally called up last night and he said to me, 'No two people have suffered more than you two. But there are as many things to bother you on the upside as on the downside. Too many people are going to say, now that he's won, he can do anything.' " The President reflected on Connally for a minute, and said he knew about Roosevelt's troubles after 1936's landslide. But he, Nixon, knew the names and the rules of the game. "I've always been fascinated by Disraeli and Gladstone," he continued. "Disraeli became Premier the second time when he was seventy years old, and he called Gladstone an exhausted volcano." He, Richard Nixon, was not an exhausted volcano. This second term was not going to be the fizzle of an exhausted volcano. He wanted me to know that he was going to be shaking the administration up; from Cabinet level all the way down, there would be new people, new blood, new ideas. But foreign policy seemed more important to him: "There are so many great things to do yet," he said, "if we can pull off the European Summit Conference!" Maybe his new relationship with Brezhnev would help. He was winding up now on the nuances of foreign policy, his favorite game, but as he began to detail his thoughts, the plane was coming down, and there, out the window, was the luminescence of Washington, all its floodlit shrines showing, glowing, disappearing, dissolving to runway lights. Then the plane's wheels were bumping ground and he was trying to sum it up, to compress all the great steps to come next, and the things he had already done. "It's just beginning," he said. "The first steps a baby takes are always the most exciting—maybe he grows up to run the mile in 3:50. We may make— we may break 3:50 in the second term, but . . ."

And now the staff was trying to ready him for departure, the camera lights outside flooding the fuselage of the plane, his helicopter waiting to take him to the White House, where the raw vote totals and key-precinct results would be pouring in to measure the allegiances he had hoped to shift.

It had taken only four hours and fifteen minutes to fly from Southern California to Washington. When he had first made that flight after his first election twenty-six years ago, it had taken thirteen hours. If the supersonic plane—which he privately hoped to set on the drawing boards in his second administration—came about, then the flight from coast to coast would take an hour and a half or two hours, less time than it had taken Dick Nixon in his boyhood to travel from Whittier to downtown Los Angeles and back.

So much had the world changed.

And he had helped change it.

But there would be much more known about the change later that evening than the simple fact of the Nixon landslide.

He dined alone with his family that night, and then, as the returns began coming in, he secluded himself, solitary again, in the Lincoln Bedroom on the third, or private, floor of the White House, with his briefcase and yellow pads, to receive occasional telephone reports from his two vote-analysis rooms, in the White House lobby and at the Shoreham Hotel. His family and his intimates sat in the long, gloomy hallway which Presidents use as their third-floor reception room; there they cheered the results that came in. They offered to send a portable television to the President where he sat by the fireplace, thinking his own thoughts, but he refused it.

There was still routine and ceremonial to go through to close what, in any man's life, had to be his greatest day. First was the ceremonial appearance on television for the nation, shortly after eleven o'clock and McGovern's concession, and he concluded: "I would only hope that in these next four years we can so conduct ourselves in this country, and so meet our responsibilities in the world in building peace in the world, that years from now people will look back to the generation of the 1970's at how we have conducted ourselves and they will say, 'God bless America.' " Then, after midnight, came a quick sortie to the jubilant Republican workers' gathering at the Shoreham Hotel, to thank them. Then, back to his hideaway office in the Executive Office Building, where he was joined by Bob Haldeman and Chuck Colson. They ordered a snack from the White House mess and idled the hours away until almost three in the morning as they sifted the late returns.

Their mood was relaxed, with the happy, spent energies of a great enterprise brought to conclusion, their planning now visible in solid votes that would go down in history. But the President had several annoyances beneath the warmth of victory. For one, his mouth bothered him—he had broken a crown at dinner; his dentist would have to fit him with an emergency temporary crown the next day when he was to be so busy; he feared that he had been stiff in his appearances on television because his mouth bothered him. He was also annoyed by the telegram he knew he had to send to McGovern; several drafts had been made and he had rejected them either as too curt or too effusive; he wished to be correct toward McGovern, but what rankled him beyond charity was McGovern's comparing him to Hitler: this he could not forgive. At length, speechwriter Pat Buchanan was located and summoned to the Executive Office Building to draft a message which would have the proper balance of magnanimity and coolness; but that message would not go out until the next morning. Then, finally, there were the returns themselves as they trickled into the hideaway office. These were more than an annoyance—they were a perplexity. The returns on the Presidential race itself could not be better, as large as his planning had ever hoped for. But the returns for his party, the Republicans—these were almost incomprehensible. Even under his personal joy and satisfaction, the President was bothered; the results nagged; he would talk about his unhappiness the next day at his Cabinet session; but it would take weeks before it sank in on him that, despite this personal triumph, despite all his talk of team and team spirit, he remained essentially alone.

The paradox of the returns had been building almost since he arrived back at the White House that evening at six o'clock. An hour before the national networks went on air to begin describing the riddle, the paradox had already been apparent to those who had access to the returns from the early states. Kentucky, for example, had gone overwhelmingly for Nixon, as expected, by 64 percent; but in the race for U.S. Senate, former Republican Governor Louie Nunn was running behind State Senator Walter ("Dee") Huddleston, Democrat. New Hampshire also was going for the President by 64 percent—yet Senator Thomas McIntyre, Democrat, was easily holding his seat against Nixon loyalist and former Governor Wesley Powell. In Vermont, the President was sweeping the state, but a young Democratic latecomer, Thomas Salmon, was apparently carrying off the Governorship. In Alabama, where the President was scoring a 72-percent majority, one of his favorite candidates for the Senate, Republican Winton ("Red") Blount, was being plowed under by long-term Democratic Senator John Sparkman.

It grew more contradictory as the evening wore on, for now added to the losses in the toss-up races were Republican losses where Democrats, in this year of Nixon's triumph, were ousting solid Republican Senatorial incumbents. As the President sat with Haldeman and Colson, his two closest political advisers, the news dribbled in—a sour undertaste to sweet victory. Margaret Chase Smith! An absolute fixture in the Republican firmament—being defeated by a newcomer Democrat in Maine. And J. Caleb Boggs of Delaware, of whom it was said he had shaken half the right hands in the state in his thirty years of public office, being defeated for the Senate by a young man, Joseph Biden, Jr., who would reach the Constitutional Senatorial age of thirty only a few weeks before he was due to take office. And Colorado—Nixon carrying Colorado by 63 percent while Gordon Allott, the party's third-ranking Republican Senator, was being put under by an ex-Republican turned Democrat only two years before.

Other results were to shape themselves in final figures later the next day, an almost crazy contrast between the Nixon/McGovern race for the Presidency and the Republican/Democratic contest for Congress. Nixon was swamping McGovern in Minnesota; but liberal Senator Walter Mondale was mounting a contrary landslide for re-election as Democrat. Iowa was giving Nixon a 210,000-vote margin, but dumping Senator Jack Miller, Republican. Ohio was giving Nixon an 883,000-vote margin!—but liberal-reform Democratic Governor John Gilligan had captured the Ohio lower house with a Democratic majority for the first time since the right-to-work hassle of 1958. The President was carrying the city of Atlanta—but that city's Congressional district, with a white majority, was electing its first black Congressman since Reconstruction, Democrat Andrew Young.

The old rule of thumb had it that for every percentile a President won over 55 percent, he could expect to drag in at least ten more Congressmen on the rising tide. But not in 1972. Nixon was picking up only thirteen Republican Congressmen nationwide, not nearly enough to shake the Democrats' grip on the lower House; and he was, in this year of landslide sweep, actually losing two seats in the Senate. Scholars had described well the growth of ticket-splitting among Americans in the sixties,[1] but the 1972 explosion of ticket-splitting was unprecedented. Nixon would have to face in his second term not only the same harassment, recalcitrance and adversary control of Congressional committees as he had in his first, but also that phenomenon which perplexed all serious students of politics—the break-up of the traditional party system of America.[2] Translated out of figures and historic analysis into personal problems, it meant, simply, that Richard Nixon, as he had been all his life, would be still a solitary.

Of all those who, in the weeks thereafter, reflected on the election of 1972, perhaps the solitary President understood it best. It meant that if he were to make his mark on history permanent, he would have to do it with greater individual boldness, with greater personal exercise of authority, than any victorious President before him. And that, in turn, meant that he would still be running, as really he always had been running, against the personality and work of Franklin Roosevelt.

Richard Nixon, when he muses about the great Presidents of the past, pays obeisance, as all do, to Lincoln and Washington, the mythic heroes of the line. When he comments publicly on the modern Presidents, his formal admiration goes either to Woodrow Wilson or to Theodore Roosevelt. But anyone who has talked to Richard Nixon, over a period of years and privately, knows that, without ever avowing it, he has been running against Franklin D. Roosevelt since he began campaigning for office. He speaks of Roosevelt not with bitterness or disrespect or anger—but in a way that makes clear in all conversation that his own measure of himself is a measure against Franklin Roosevelt. Both men have seen the problem in the same way: how to make the system work—at home as abroad.

In Richard Nixon's mind, in the way he has of keeping scores, as

[1] See, for example, *The Ticket Splitter: A New Force in American Politics* by Walter DeVries and V. Lance Tarrance (Grand Rapids, Michigan: William B. Eerdmans Publishing Co., 1972).
[2] See *The Party's Over: The Failure of Politics in America* by David S. Broder (New York: Harper & Row, 1972).

he does with baseball, football or voting results, only he and Franklin Roosevelt in all American history have run for national office—Presidency or Vice-Presidency—five times. The easy record reads that Roosevelt won four, lost one, and Richard Nixon won four, lost one. Roosevelt, of course, scored heavier, but between them, these two men go down as the most enduring American politicians of the twentieth century, and they span a period of fifty years of continuing American revolution.

Yet they are entirely different. Roosevelt had come of the patricians and rarely soiled himself with the nitty-gritty of mechanical politics. Roosevelt campaigned in another time, almost in another country. Large of vision, buoyant of spirit, steeped in history by family and blood, the lordly Roosevelt left it to his lieutenants to deal with the wards, the townships and regional power brokers, then pasted up his electoral votes, as he did the stamps his dealers brought him, in his album. It was quite clear always to Roosevelt what he was dealing with and what he had to do—and he did it easily.

Richard Nixon has always done it the hard way. The scar tissue had grown thick over him by the time of his re-election, a rigid self-discipline controlled the outbursts of emotion for which his enemies so long mocked him. But the hurt was there—for the remembered humiliations as well as the grudging later praise. By November of 1972, he had become far more his own man than Roosevelt ever was. Yet, paradoxically, this left him weaker—what he proposed to do, he would still have to do the hard way, alone.

Roosevelt brought with him to his exercise in political creations an entire party. Nixon came to the Presidency first as a marginal winner, and next, in November of 1972, as a spectacular personal victor, but stripped of control of both Houses of Congress, denied any tolerance by the "best thinkers" in American opinion. In his first term, with virtuoso personal diplomacy, he had perceived, then dismantled, the legacy of Franklin D. Roosevelt in world affairs; and then rearranged that world with a skill that the old grand master would have regarded with approval. In 1972, he had run, at home, against the coalition of forces Roosevelt had bequeathed his Democratic Party. At the personal executive level he had dismantled that coalition by what he called a "shift of allegiance." Yet, somehow, he had been unable to dismantle the Democratic Party itself.

Thus the great paradox. Obviously, in the politics of 1972, two entirely different stories are intertwined. There is the story of Richard Nixon, and how he, as President, read the nation's mood, to win the greatest margin of votes in American history. But then there is the rival story, of the various Democratic parties, whose inheritance from the Rooseveltian past had given them one of their greatest grass-roots victories at local and state level across the country—but whose choice of national leader to oppose Richard Nixon totally failed to catch the spirit of the times.

CHAPTER TWO

THE ROAD TO CEDAR POINT: FROM THE LIBERAL IDEA TO THE LIBERAL THEOLOGY

CHOOSING a Presidential candidate is the supreme exercise of an American political party.

But the nominating process is more than an exercise in power. In the symbolisms of the contest and candidates are reflected the entire culture of the nation as it changes, its surges of discontent, its stirrings of hope, its fantasies of fear and its yearnings for the new.

The contest among the Democrats in 1972 can be seen only in this light, a clash of ideas as much as a clash of power, for the contest, drawn out longer than any other in recent history, was met on classic issues: What is the purpose of a political party in a democracy? Can it respond to the people's will? From whom does it draw its authority?

One must go back all the way to 1968 to begin the story of the Democratic struggle in 1972—to be precise, to the hot and muggy night of August 27th, 1968, in Chicago, Illinois, when, in total confusion and a fit of absent-mindedness, the Democratic Party began what was to become a revolution in the structure of the oldest living political party in the world.

That Tuesday night it became clear to millions that neither the Democratic Party at its thirty-fifth national convention, nor the power it controlled, was responding to the will of the people. By accident of history, both had come into the hands of the wrong man; and that man even *in absentia* now held the convention of the party in his grip. At 2:43 in the morning of Tuesday, the Monday-night session of the convention had finally closed down in a barely subdued brawl over delegate credentials. Already, in the real city that night, affairs had come to blood as police and demonstrators charged and countercharged in Chicago's

Lincoln Park, clubbing and wounding each other in a street fight that left sixty injured. The delegates had dissolved that night to their hotel rooms and risen Tuesday morning, after what little sleep they could get, to the turbulence of caucuses, arm-twisting in hotel lobbies, reports of riots, and press conferences which bred more press conferences, all of them revolving around the central question of power at the moment: what to do about the war the Democratic Party had launched in Asia, which had cost 25,000 American lives at that point, and for which everyone vainly sought an end.

Technical control of the convention was secure. Hubert Humphrey, the favorite of the regular faction and the Southern faction, held the commanding votes. But the third faction, the insurgents, impotent as they might be on the floor, had a detachment of auxiliaries in the street which competed with the convention for the attention of the media and the country. On the wild fringe of the insurgency, irregulars of every political hue battled the police in public places. The Poor People's March, with its mules, its wagons, its blacks, paraded the avenues clamoring for the ear of the mighty as it marched from hotel to hotel. Tear gas eddied over Lincoln Park and Grant Park, and the police were barely able to drive back a mob of irregulars from the statue of General Grant over which they had planted the Viet Cong flag. Violence was the quality of the day—and on the floor, confusion.

The Tuesday session started at six that evening, with all the babbled issues of the day fused in a roar on the floor. Blacks and Southern whites were clashing. Newsmen were being beaten not only in the city, but also on the floor of the convention.[1] Grim guards patrolled the entries and aisles of the convention with an unprecedented brutality. The hall stank of stockyard offal, of sweat, of cigarette smoke; concessionaires refused to serve ice in drinks, lest delegates pelt each other with ice cubes.

Two overriding matters gripped the emotions of the delegates, as they gathered, to the exclusion of all formal transactions on the evening's agenda of deliberation. First was the debate over Vietnam—two conflicting resolutions, a "dove" resolution and a "hawk" resolution, were about to come down from the Platform Committee, scheduled to reach the floor about midnight. The second matter was the party's romance with Senator Edward M. Kennedy of Massachusetts. Would he, or would he not, consent to rescue the party from chaos by accepting nomination?

Distracted by such vivid claims on their attention, the delegates drifted in, took their seats slowly and passed, perfunctorily, by voice

[1] Of 300 newsmen covering the streets and parks of Chicago during the convention week, more than 20 percent were injured. Some 63 were physically attacked by police, and 13 had their equipment deliberately smashed.

vote without debate, a seemingly mild resolution offered by the Credentials Committee: to set up a committee to reform and improve the
delegate-selection process governing the convention of 1972, four years
hence.[2] The convention hall was still not full when, at 10:25, the chairman offered for consideration both a majority and a minority report
from the Rules Committee—but by now near-pandemonium was sweeping the floor. The New York and California delegations, largest in the
nation, had been seated at the very rear of the hall by Lyndon Johnson's
design and now, as the hours wore on, had begun to hoist banners
saying WE WANT KENNEDY. Delegates were listening by portable television or radio sets to stories of violence in the city outside; politicians
were darting through the aisles trying to stop or further the candidacy
of Teddy Kennedy; and all were girding for the battle over the resolutions on the Vietnam war. The words of the majority and minority reports of the Rules Committee floated almost unheard above the noise as
the sound system squawked incomprehensibly through the fog, the
smoke, the din. Had anyone cared to listen, he would have noted that
the minority report, which favored the abolition of the unit-rule system
of voting, did not simply urge or recommend a change; its language was
stark. It "required" that the next convention conform to the stipulations
laid down for reform. The minority report, if passed, would have binding effect on the convention of 1972. But few delegates were listening.[3]

Conventions are not deliberative bodies. They are power pits where
the chief transaction is measuring how much power has coagulated under what leadership to gain a floor majority. On the two contending
resolutions of the Rules Committee, there came now a power play authorized by Hubert Humphrey. Humphrey, a warm, moderate and humane man, had himself once been an insurgent and understood what
moved the insurgency. He, too, had once been locked out of power and
understood how bitter those locked out at Chicago now must feel. He
sympathized with most of the insurgent principles—that government,
party and power must be open to all groups, must be responsive to the
changing moods of the nation. Moreover, with the nomination assured
him, he would need the support of just these high-minded insurgents in
the campaign against Richard Nixon. Thus, Humphrey released his
delegates to vote their consciences. And what with the confusion, the
bloodshed, the weariness, the climate of violence in Chicago, it turned
out there were enough delegates to give the insurgency its only victory
of the convention. The minority report of the Rules Committee was
voted in over the majority report by a vote of 1,350 to 1,206—carrying
with it not only delegates of conscience, but the delegations of such
regular-controlled blocs as Missouri, Indiana, West Virginia and Mary-

[2] See Appendix B.
[3] See Appendix B for the text of the Rules Committee resolution.

land. With that vote, the delegates could proceed to discuss Vietnam—
and then ensued another near-brawl as House Speaker Carl Albert tried
to adjourn the meeting while hundreds of delegates yelled in protest. The
folklore of the convention ends that night with the television cameras
on Mayor Daley of Chicago, his finger making the unforgettable throat-
cutting gesture to signal for the thwack of the gavel that closed the session at 1:17 Wednesday morning, August 28th, 1968.

The rest of that convention belongs to the history of 1968—the
blood in the streets the following day, the vote on Vietnam, the simul-
taneous victory and humiliation of Hubert Humphrey.

But the transactions of Tuesday night, the votes on credentials and
rules reform, were the very beginning of the history of the Presidential
year to come. Few of the delegates who voted on either side had understood what they were doing. But in their innocence or inattention they
had voted for the most fundamental change in the party's long history.
The insurgency was now no longer an insurgency. The supreme body of
the Democratic Party, its convention, had issued title papers for reform
—legal, valid title papers on the party's future. The outsiders of 1968
would have full legal rights to debate and help set the terms on which
power in the party would be disposed of in 1972.

The semantic and legal confusion of these title papers should not
detain us here, although Constitutional lawyers may argue over them
for years. From the two resolutions passed by the convention, the National Committee was to paste together a directive, lifting words from
both resolutions, which ordained that all state Democratic parties must
give "all Democratic voters . . . a *full, meaningful, and timely* opportunity to participate in the selection of delegates" to the next convention
(italics added); and two commissions would be set up to carry out the
resolutions.

With this directive, the politics of the Democratic Party were to
disappear once more into the backrooms, from which they would emerge
in 1972 changed in structure—and totally split in philosophy.

The resolutions of the convention of 1968 said, in essence, to the
Democratic Party: Reform! And reform was long overdue, for its machinery had grown more arthritic and anachronistic even than that of
its counterpart, the Republican Party.

From the days of Thomas Jefferson and Aaron Burr, the Democratic Party, the people's party, had been also the professionals' party.
The professionals had nominated and elected a succession of men from
Andrew Jackson and Martin Van Buren down to Franklin Roosevelt
and Harry Truman who, by doing what the people wanted, increased
the professionals' power at their local base. Presidents so selected had
governed the country in years of glory; but the selection process itself

was closed. When the system went off the tracks, as it had under Lyndon Johnson, ordinary people were shut out. The new commissions ordained by the convention were designed to overhaul this system.

Choice of members of the new commissions would be up to the next National Chairman of the party. But the choice of that new chairman would be up to Hubert Humphrey, the defeated candidate and titular leader of the party—whose fancy had been caught, for months, by Senator Fred Harris of Oklahoma. Humphrey had briefly considered Harris for the Vice-Presidency at Chicago, then passed over him to choose Senator Edmund Muskie of Maine. Now it seemed to Humphrey that Harris was exactly the man who could pull the party from its past without shaking old loyalties. Harris was young (not yet forty), an eloquent liberal, blessed with a handsome Indian wife, made a striking appearance on television and—as Humphrey explained it—would appeal to all those forces of the insurgency who had to be brought back into the party. Thus the choice was Harris.

Harris was more than the scrub-weed traditional Western liberal once classified by Eastern conservatives as sons-of-the-wild-jackass. A muscular man from Oklahoma, a sharecropper's son, vigorous, hard-working, he was of that breed of devout American liberals who at this stage in history turn almost automatically to the New York intellectual center for guidance—as a decade earlier he would have turned to Cambridge. Harris called himself a populist (pronouncing it "popolist"), a word that was to become very fashionable in the spring of 1972. If pressed, he would admit to being an "ideological liberal," and thought his job as new chairman was to infuse the party with new ideas, new intellectual purpose, without losing the regulars. "We can't win without them," he said early in 1970.

It was up to Harris to implement the mandate for reform by appointing the two commissions authorized during the wild Tuesday night on the convention floor of 1968. For the first, the Commission on Rules, which would apportion delegates and review procedures for the convention of 1972, Harris made a straightforward establishment choice: Congressman James O'Hara of Michigan, a solid, progressive but hard-nosed urban liberal from a blue-collar suburb of Detroit.

The hot commission was obviously the Commission on Party Structure and Delegate Selection, more simply known as the Reform Commission. Senator Harold Hughes of Iowa—an intense, honest, ambitious man, yearning for the Presidency—ached to head it up. But Hughes was a dove who had abandoned Humphrey after the Chicago convention and never campaigned for him thereafter. Humphrey opposed Hughes. Much more agreeable was Senator George McGovern of South Dakota; no one considered McGovern a serious Presidential contender, but he was everyone's personal favorite. McGovern had been a protégé and neighbor of Hubert Humphrey when he first came to Washington; Robert Kennedy had called him "the most decent man in the Senate." McGovern was a scholar with a Ph.D. in American history; he was mild, gentle, lovable, had been with the insurgents at Chicago, yet campaigned manfully for Humphrey against Nixon in the fall. This was a good man, a trustworthy man, not dangerous—and so, on February 8th, 1969, George McGovern was named to head the Reform Commission, and McGovern promptly appointed Harold Hughes to be his vice-chairman.

If the two leaders of the Reform Commission and the fostering party chairman, Harris, gave the commission a decided tilt to the left at the top, the commission was by no means a revolutionary council. Of its twenty-eight members, most had supported Humphrey in 1968. Of the six who would become delegates themselves in 1972, four would support Ed Muskie, two Humphrey, none McGovern. The membership was spread nicely among regulars, Southerners and insurgents, with scattered places for such traditional allies as labor and academics (two members each). Of the twenty-eight, three were blacks, two Chicanos. But only three were women, and only one was under thirty (Vietnam Moratorium organizer David Mixner). If the commission had been a delegation to the 1972 convention, it would have had no chance of being seated under the standards it was about to establish.

Had all members of the Reform Commission taken its purpose with equal seriousness, the history of 1972 might have been written differently. Few full meetings were ever held. Relatively few regular or conservative members attended its meetings. I. W. Abel, head of the steelworkers' union and a commission member, never appeared at all— persuaded by George Meany, chief of the AFL/CIO, that the work was meaningless. The defense of the traditionalist cause and values lay chiefly with Will Davis of Texas, once Lyndon Johnson's lawyer, an able and eloquent man but on many of the most critical points clearly outnumbered. To those traditionalist Democrats who would later moan at Miami about the disaster the reforms had brought to their party, one was tempted to reply as Sultana Aisha had to her son, King Boabdil of the Moors, as he stood weeping on the Rock of Gibraltar when Ferdinand and Isabella finally ended Moslem dominion over Spanish Granada. "You do well to weep like a woman," said the Sultana to her son, "for what you could not defend like a man."

It was clear that this commission, like so many Washington commissions, was going to be run by its staff—and this was to be, as it soon also became clear, a runaway staff. The names of Eli Segal, Kenneth Bode, Robert Nelson might never achieve the fame of Roy Cohn and

David Schine, who directed Joe McCarthy's investigating subcommittee; or Robert Kennedy, once chief counsel to the Senate's Labor Rackets Committee. But the three grasped the essential reality of a commission —a commission is a collection of famous names, people too busy and important to pay attention to detail. A vigorous staff soon recognizes that in its accumulation of detail it is making policy.

The Reform Commission's staff was exceptionally vigorous, intelligent and dedicated. Chief counsel was Eli Segal. Segal, then twenty-five years old, a graduate of Brandeis and the University of Michigan Law School, had been blooded in combat in 1968 as Eugene McCarthy's lieutenant for the caucuses and conventions of non-primary states. Research director Ken Bode held a doctorate in political science, had studied at the University of South Dakota, had moved in 1968 from the McCarthy insurgency to become floor manager for George McGovern at the national convention. He was the best writer on the commission staff and was to wind up, with Segal, drafting most of its texts. Third in the triumvirate of major staff figures was Robert Nelson, staff director—a former South Dakota campaign manager and administrative aide to George McGovern. He would set in motion the hearings across the country from which, theoretically, the staff would bring to the commission the feel of what people were saying.

These men saw the commission as a crusade—behind entrenched positions, an establishment had led the country to war, denied the rights of blacks, clubbed their friends to insensibility in the streets of Chicago, choked off fair representation in a thousand backrooms and let happen those inequities of welfare and justice which, they felt, characterized America at the moment. They would make the party an instrument of justice. They were bright; and they were tough.

The problems to which these young men were addressing themselves were so immense as to bring humility to a council of philosophers, historians and elder statesmen. What was the role of a party in a modern society? What was the meaning of power? Do a party's rules carry greater authority than the laws enacted by legislatures of sovereign states? And who was entitled to vote within a party? At what level? Was a party a private association with clubmen's rules, or a public instrument of citizens to be defined with legal precision? And how does one ensure continuity within a party—the sense of persistent goals which cannot, without disaster, be changed every two years? Above all—how could the Democratic Party be made more open, more responsive to people?

To answer such questions, the staff set up national hearings around the country. "We didn't let the state parties choose the witnesses," said Nelson. "We went to the blacks, we went to the young, we went to the women." There were some seventeen national hearings, to listen to the voices of more than 500 witnesses; the transcripts of their testimony still lie waiting, largely unread, for exploration of the mood of America as it entered the 1970's. Such hearings were bound to arouse resentment among the party regulars. The Governors of Texas and Louisiana complained that they found out the commission was in their states only by reading the newspapers; on the other hand, blacks, Chicanos, local chapters of the insurgency never failed to get the word.

The hearings coincided with a time of trouble for Democratic big-city and state party organizations. Everywhere, the disbanded veterans of the 1968 Kennedy and McCarthy campaigns, with no Presidential war to enlist in for the next few years, were signing up for little guerrilla wars against local political establishments in Chicago, Los Angeles, Houston, New York, Boston. Presentations before the McGovern commission became a skirmish front in this war.

As the commission moved about the country, and as it grew, it became a training ground for many activists of 1972—most of them sooner or later winding up with McGovern. In Denver, a young lawyer named Gary Hart, a veteran of the Kennedy campaign, undertook to organize commission hearings there. He was to become McGovern's campaign manager. A McCarthy insurgent of 1968, Richard Stearns, then a twenty-four-year-old Rhodes Scholar, enlisted on the commission staff during vacation period as research assistant; he was to become chief delegate-accountant of the McGovern campaign. Commission counsel Eli Segal would enlist briefly in Harold Hughes's short try for the nomination, then finally move over to the McGovern campaign as master of its California and Credentials Committee operations in 1972. Applications from student volunteers poured in for the exciting work of exploration, and the Reform Commission's staff chose eighteen to be "summer interns," at the wage of $75 a week. (It should be noted that McGovern advanced $15,000 of his own money to finance their work.)

Armed with the authority of the commission, which in turn descended from the convention-in-turbulence of Tuesday-Wednesday in Chicago in 1968, the students could, and did, summon the veteran chieftains of the various state committees for explanations and accountings—and, eventually, compliance. Some old Democrats, particularly in the South, ignored the commission. Reform, they felt, should be left to reformers; their business was to govern. More of the regular organizations, however, did indeed accept the authority of the student outriders of the commission. That was the convention mandate; the press would style any opposition they might offer as the opposition of the "old guard," a term almost as killing as "racist." They knew, in their hearts, that there was indeed much wrong with the party and were convinced it was best to go along. They were like old alcoholics, drunk with power, listening sadly but seriously to young doctors who told them that, to survive, they must give up their alcohol—power.

So much was wrong with the Democratic Party of the United States, so many of its procedures had descended fossilized from the past, that the fresh voices of the brisk young staff came as the sound of Joshua's trumpet—and the walls of Jericho came tumbling down.

There was little debate in staff, or commission, on the great majority of proposed reforms. It was wrong, for example, flatly wrong, that a single Governor and state chairman could, as they did in two Southern states, name the entire state delegation to the national convention. It was wrong, flatly wrong, that the delegation-selection process should begin in the ward politics of some states—as in Massachusetts—fully three years before the Presidential campaign, before anyone knew what the issues (and who the candidates) might be. Proxy voting was wrong— a system under which, when a caucus was called, some local baron might pull out a list of absentees and slap down a paper majority which would outweigh the presence of concerned citizens gathered to vote. And wrong that a state committee, as in New York or Pennsylvania, could name one third of its state's entire delegation and in Illinois more than half. Again, wrong that a caucus at ward or precinct level should meet secretly, without notice, in a basement, parlor or backroom clubhouse and claim it spoke for all the community's Democrats. And again, wrong that a group of men who dominated a community could make a slate behind closed doors and offer it to the voters as their only choice of representatives. The list of procedural wrongs was thick. And as the staff drafted most of the new guidelines to correct old inequities, there could be, and was, little opposition.

There were, however, two larger matters of a philosophical nature —the problem of the unit rule, and the problem of quotas.

The issue of the unit rule, more popularly known as the winner-take-all rule, engaged the question of minority political representation: At what point should majority rule clamp down on an entire delegation and compel a minority of differing political views to vote against conscience or constituency? For most veterans of the McCarthy campaign of 1968 (which included Vice-Chairman Senator Hughes and much of the staff) the most galling memory of that year was their frustration in state after state where their workers had won a third or more of the votes at state conventions—and then seen their efforts frustrated by a majority faction which seized all, or nearly all, of the state's national-convention vote. Guided by a perceptive paper from Professor Alexander M. Bickel of the Yale Law School, a consultant to the commission, the commission "urged" but did not "require" that political minorities be protected against winner-take-all systems under which a faction with a majority of votes at a convention or in a primary could claim all of the delegates. It did, however, in the convention states, require that at least 75 percent of the delegation be chosen from districts and not by the convention at large. Thus in effect, for the convention states, the Commission had curbed the winner-take-all principle of delegate selection.

But the expression of minority political opinion was more difficult to codify in a state with primaries—and here the former McCarthy people were impassioned. In 1968 their slate of 174 delegates in California had run within four percentage points of Robert Kennedy's slate—yet Kennedy, under California's winner-take-all law, had won all of California's 174 delegates that year. Should the new rules outlaw California's state law? Fred Dutton, one of the most persuasive reformers on the commission, was, however, a Californian—he cherished his state's tradition, custom and power. Under his influence, the commission was persuaded that winner-take-all should be outlawed in caucus-and-convention states, but not in primary states—of which California was, incomparably, the most important. The states would be "urged" to give minority representation to differing political views in their primaries; but the commission only recommended that the convention of 1972 "require" such representation in future conventions. So it was passed —thus preparing the way for the great California controversy of 1972's Democratic convention.

All in all, the commission's discussion of representation of minority political views at the national convention had resulted in a great step forward. But then there was the matter of quotas.

And here we must pause. Until it came to discuss quotas, the Reform Commission could only be seen as a prodigious exercise in intelligence; its work was of the same order of thoughtfulness as had produced the American Constitution—a successful effort to look at the reality of the times and bring the logic of change to what time had worn out. As the Reform Commission moved on, however, to consider quotas, it was to plunge over a political cliff to disaster. It was to misread the culture of America.

The controversy over winner-take-all, or the unit rule, had pivoted on the representation of *political* minorities—men and women of specific political views denied their right to be heard in a national forum. The controversy over quotas, though never publicly called that, concerned itself with the rights of non-political minorities—special groups defined racially, ethnically, biologically.

American civic texts have until only recently chosen to ignore as too complicated and too sensitive the study of the reality of the separate races, separate communities, separate ethnic heritages that make up America. An old New Deal politician once compared the mingling of races and communities in America to the mysterious way in which a centipede walks. "If you asked a centipede whether he lifts leg 53 be-

fore leg 54 or before leg 55, he'd have a nervous breakdown; he does it
by instinct. Let God paralyze anybody who tries to ask that question
about our system." What the Reform Commission now set about was
not only to ask but to define just how biological and racial minorities as
such should be included in the political system. It was a question never
before considered in any society—and in trying to solve it, the Reform
Commission set the country's politics on the road to 1972, an election
in which race, community and ethnic differences were abraded as never
before in American history.

No better episode occurs to me in my political memories to illustrate how a liberating idea changes to become an intellectual prison than
the story of how ideas came to lock in the quota controversy within the
Democratic Party. The great advances of the nation under the Democratic Party had always rested on the ability of a liberal Democratic
President to coerce to his support a hundred-odd white Representatives
and twenty-odd white Senators from the South. These men provided the
indispensable Congressional base for all major creative domestic legislation. But Southern whites feared blacks—while Northern blacks in the
postwar world more and more began to provide the Democrats with
the critical popular votes for the Presidency in the big states where elections are decided.

Thus a contradiction.

The contradiction had been growing at least since the election of
1948, but it had broken through the concrete of tradition only at the
Atlantic City convention of the Democrats in 1964. There, as Lyndon
Johnson stage-managed his acclamation, the only disturbance he could
not taffy over was that created by the Mississippi Freedom Democratic
Party. The regular Mississippi Democratic Party, from Governor on
down to sheriffs and judges, had systematically abused the black population of that state. Among the documented forms of exclusion of blacks
from politics in Mississippi were not only conventional social pressure
but, at local levels, flogging, beating, torment of the body and spirit,
and even murder. Thus in 1964 a Freedom Democratic Party delegation
from Mississippi had arrived in Atlantic City to protest to the national
party that blacks had been totally excluded from the political process in
its state. The convention, under Johnson's guidance, tossed the blacks a
sop—and a promise. The sop was that two honorary Freedom Party
delegates—one black, one white—might be seated on the floor of the
convention in a place separate from the regular Mississippi whites. The
promise was much more important, for it was to be kept. In all future
conventions any state Democratic delegation which *excluded* blacks
could not be seated in the party's national convention. And by 1968, in
the shrieking of Chicago, the legal promise of 1964 had been kept by

driving out the entire white Mississippi regular delegation, and by dismissing half of the Georgia whites, to replace them with blacks. However great the cost to it in the South, the national Democratic Party was taking the high road.

The liberating idea in 1964 had been clear: Blacks must not be excluded from the political process, no matter what the pain to tradition. What the Reform Commission was about to do in 1969 was to take this idea and make a prison of it: Certain specific groups *must* be included, must be guaranteed their mathematical proportion of representation and legally, while all other groups must fend for themselves. Specifically, as the commission interpreted its vague mandate, the party must open itself to blacks, to women and to youth, not by striking at exclusion but by insisting on inclusion. Women, of course, were not a minority group, since they made up 52 percent of the population. Youth was a transitional biological state difficult to define. How were these three groups to be pegged, legally, into the structure of the party with guarantees to which no others were entitled?

Thus, the question was clearly posed when the commission assembled for its final session (twenty of its twenty-seven members present) at an all-day meeting in a hearing room of the Senate Office Building on November 18th, 1969. They began by discussing their own authority; and the staff assured the members that they had the authority of the convention to do anything they wanted. In effect, said staff members, they were the arm and instrument of the decisions taken on Wild Tuesday in Chicago, not merely advisers to the next convention. From there they moved to start at the top of the draft Guidelines, Section A-1, entitled "Discrimination on the basis of race, color, creed, or national origin." Will Davis, the professional lawyer, wanted some precision in the language, and since the term "requires" is more precise than the suggested draft wording "calls upon," it was agreed that on these guidelines, A-1 and A-2, this commission would "require" the party to follow the guidelines.

Then to the first decision—on blacks. It was Austin Ranney, professor of political science at the University of Wisconsin, who set the quota idea in motion, though before the day was out, and consistently ever since, he has expressed his abhorrence of quotas. The transcript of the meeting reads:

> RANNEY: . . . our fellow black Democrats feel that something more is needed than a no discrimination rule. . . . I want to suggest . . . that the Commission at the very least urge . . . that there be included as members of the delegation, adequate, fair, whatever the word may be, representation of minority groups in the population.

MC GOVERN: I should advise you, Professor Ranney, that
we discussed this matter at some length at the September meeting. The Commission, as I recall it, unanimously decided after
some discussion that it was not feasible to go on record for a
quota system.

RANNEY: . . . I think that we would like to at least urge
. . . that members of minority groups be adequately, fairly,
whatever, . . . represented.

[SENATOR] BAYH: . . . If we leave it there then I'm not
sure we've moved anyplace. [We should take] the professor's
motion . . . and add two or three words to sort of give guidelines saying that to meet this requirement there should be some
reasonable relationship between the representation of delegates and the representation of the minority group in the population of the state in question.

When the fateful vote on the wording came up, the vote carried
ten to nine for the Bayh-Ranney proposition.

By the time that vote had been taken, others had begun to feel
that the same guarantee given blacks should be given to women and
youth. Chief among those who wanted to extend categorical enfran-
chisement to the two other groups was Fred Dutton, one of the party's
leading political theorists, and later one of McGovern's senior strategists.

DUTTON: There is no reason why our national convention shouldn't have 50% women, 10 or 15% young people.

Others supported Dutton's proposal, chiefly the three women on
the commission, none of them by any means radical, but fighting for
their bloc, as women, to get what the blacks had won.

Perhaps the most lucid critic of what was going on was the commission's second academic member, Professor Samuel Beer of Harvard's
Department of Government.

BEER: I'd like to speak out against Fred Dutton's proposal. . . . what we're doing here is usurping the function of
the voters themselves. . . . It's not for us to say to the voters
of a state you've got to elect 50% women. If the voters want
75% women or 75% men, it's up to them. . . . I think it would
be a great mistake and would make us look really ridiculous
and would never work if we tried to say that you must have
proportionate representation of young people and women in
your conventions.

DUTTON: . . . As far as the idea being ridiculous, I can't think of anything more attractive or a better way to get votes with media politics than to have half of that convention floor in 1972 made up of women. . . . we're talking about winning elections, we've got to provide the symbols . . . which will activate women . . . activate young people, which will appeal to them, and this is a tangible device for doing just that.

BEER: Mr. Chairman . . . our charge is to clean up this process and make sure that people have full and free access to it. Our charge is not to decide what the outcome is supposed to be. . . .

VOICE [unidentified, probably George Mitchell, National Committeeman from Maine]: . . . whatever the record, whatever this hearing may say, and I don't know who's going to transcribe this and plow through the whole thing, isn't it correct to say that anybody reading the words, "bearing a reasonable relation to the presence of the group in the population" must interpret that to be some sort of quota?

RANNEY [who had now changed from his earlier insistence on something strong to force the inclusion of blacks]: I have the feeling, with Senator Bayh's assistance, I opened Pandora's box here. . . . I think we ought to recognize [that] if we pass this motion now we're going to a quota system. . . . How can we . . . give proportional representation to political views while making sure that there is adequate representation of blacks, women, youth . . . ?

DAVIS: I've waited for it to be said, but it hasn't been said. We don't have any evidence at all like we have in the black situation of discrimination against either women or youth because of the fact that they are women or young.

The commission argued heatedly about what constitutes discrimination against blacks, against women, against youth, and whether the party could impose rules on all its units down to state and precinct level deciding exactly how its organs should be constituted.

BAYH: If the national convention tells a state party that it requires it to include all of these people, you're going to do it. That's all.

DAVIS: That's my point right there. That's what I say. Suppose that state convention does not want to include all these people in the various break-ups that you're laying down these rules for?

BAYH: [It lies] with the Credentials Committee to kick you out, that's all.

DAVIS: That's the point. And I say this commission doesn't have the power to require that sort of a delegation make-up.

MC GOVERN: All right. Those in favor of that [Dutton's] proposition, please raise their right hand. All right, 13 in favor. Those opposed. . . . the proposition is adopted then by a vote of 13 to 7.

Thus, then, all state Democratic parties were required to take "affirmative steps to encourage . . . representation of minority groups on the national convention delegation in reasonable relationship to the group's presence in the population of the states." The same encouragement was required for women and for "young people—defined as people of not more than 30 nor less than 18 years of age." No one defined what "reasonable" meant, nor what minorities other than blacks would be so protected.

To take the edge off such language, a footnote was added to the final published text which read, "It is the understanding of the Commission that this is not to be accomplished by the mandatory imposition of quotas." Will Davis remarked that "They won't buy that in Texas"; and George Mitchell of Maine warned that the footnote wouldn't help.

But the Reform Commission had spoken. It had not only spoken, it had set in motion a dynamic of logic which was inescapable. The names and faces on the commission changed over the next year; the chairman who succeeded George McGovern was Congressman Donald M. Fraser of Minnesota, and it was Fraser who finally buttoned down what the new guidelines meant in terms of party statute. In a letter to all state party officials, he explained the exact impact of what the commission had done. "We believe," he said, in a letter circulated on November 29th, 1971, by the Democratic National Committee, "that state parties should be on notice that whenever the proportion of women, minorities, and young people in a delegation offered for seating in Miami is less than the proportion of these groups in the total population, and the delegation is challenged on the ground that Guidelines A-1 and A-2 were not complied with, such a challenge will constitute a prima facie showing of violation of the Guidelines; and the state Democratic party along with the challenged delegation has the burden of showing that the state party took full and affirmative action . . . to achieve such representation . . . and effective action." Whatever pious preachments to the contrary, the Reform Commission had imposed in fact on the national

Democratic Party a quota system to which its Credentials Committee could hold state parties to account.

One should say at once, before passing on, that the mechanics of quotas, the stipulations of blacks, women and youth in precise proportions, had little effect on the primary campaigns and the triumph of George McGovern at the Democratic convention. That he won on his own by dynamics we shall describe later.

But the idea of quotas, the concept itself which McGovern supported, was to be one of the major factors in the wrecking of his campaign and the triumph of Richard Nixon. Somewhere, somehow, without adequate public attention or debate, the liberating idea which had inspirited the Democratic Party for so long had become a trap.

Quotas decided no primaries and no elections—but the symbolism of the idea was too overpowering to ignore. It touched the roots of American culture, and the campaign of 1972 was to become one of those events in American history which can be described as cultural watersheds as well as political happenings. For many liberals, the experience was to be heartbreaking. The beautiful Liberal Idea of the previous half-century had grown old and hardened into a Liberal Theology which terrified millions of its old clients.

From the founding of the country on, the central instinct and pride of the American liberal has been to keep opportunity for individuals open. For two centuries the wars of American liberals—against King George, against the banks, against the slaveholders, against the railways, against the trusts, against the bosses—have reflected a doctrine which is more than politics, a doctrine which is of the essence of the culture of the nation: No man must be locked into or hammered into a category from which he has no opportunity to escape. He must not be locked in by the color of his skin or his racial genes; he must not be locked in by lack of educational opportunity; he must not be locked in by birth, or parentage, or age or poverty.

The quota idea was a wrench from this tradition. It set up stark categories within the political process; and the voters must, whether they will or not, confirm those categories in selecting representatives. By setting up such categories and ignoring other categories, it inevitably excluded as well as included. By insisting on a fixed proportion of youth, for example, and ignoring a fixed proportion of the elderly, it excluded the old. By insisting on a fixed proportion of blacks, Indians or Spanish-speaking and ignoring, say, Italians, Poles, Irish, Jews, old-stock colonials, it restricted. It restricted for the highest of moral purposes buttressed by the history of the previous decade. The decade of the 1960's had convinced American liberals that government is the chief instrument of action and morality; that the government must move to its moral goals by "affirmative action"; and, further, what the government did could be measured by quantifiable results—whether in housing, or the sulfur-dioxide content of the air, or the mathematical proportions of black and white children in classrooms. Always previously, however, American liberals, who occupied the moral heights, had fulminated from the hills, clarifying in the public consciousness what was "right" or "wrong," leaving to the pragmatic politicians the translation of their moral values into programs of action. Somehow, by the end of the sixties these programs had themselves become values. However much the real world might fear liberal programs, it must submit because programs were morality, even after programs had gone wrong in visible practice.

The world of the 1960's—which the liberals had dominated in America—was changing so rapidly that by the beginning of the 1970's change had created a climate of schizophrenia in liberal thinking, almost a civil war among thinkers who came of the same tradition.

Always, since the time of Washington and Jefferson, three great permanent issues have dominated American politics—foreign policy; the clash of the races; and the managing of the economy. In the 1960's, however, a liberal administration had accepted the war in Vietnam— and its unfurling had then split liberals from top to bottom. Liberals had championed the Black Revolution—and been unable to cope with its results. Liberals had masterminded the great boom of the 1960's—and not foreseen its effect on manners and morals.

Each of these three great incubators of change in America deserves a quick appreciation for its impact on the Liberal Idea as it hardened into the Liberal Theology.

The war in Vietnam was the first war in American history which America was not to win. Despite its purpose, it was an illegal war— no Congress, as is its Constitutional duty, had ever voted to draft or send Americans to die in Vietnam. The draft had been designed for World War II, a total mobilization in a war in which Western civilization itself was at stake. The draft could not work in a war for which there was no consent, either of Congress or of public, and which required so little manpower that choice for service became a matter of fate, bad luck or trickery. There are great wars of national survival and lesser optional wars of national policy. No popular policy war can be fought without a clear cause, and since the cause of the Vietnam war was never made clear, it became, consequently, the most unpopular war in American history. All American history, all loyalties were fed into an adventure which became a hemorrhage of loyalties—of loyalty to the flag, of loyalty to laws, of loyalty to all rules. The war had been accepted by a leadership group which was, if anything, the most liberal in

American history—and had been repudiated by liberals with the same absolutist ferocity as their kin-in-spirit had accepted it.

The second incubator of change in the 1960's was the Black Revolution. It was not simply that blacks were moving into the big cities all across the nation where their political power could, finally, be delivered. Not simply that the number of black Representatives was to jump from 5 in Washington in 1960 to 12 in 1970 (and 15 in 1972), along with a black Senator from Massachusetts; or that the number of black mayors rose from 29 in 1968 to 86 in 1972, or that in 1972 there were 206 black state legislators, more than double the 94 in 1964. It was chiefly that the education and moral sense of the nation could no longer accept what had been done to black people over the years; and that the blacks, in the decade of the sixties, would simply not sit still either. They would riot, they would kill, they would burn in a series of inner-city holocausts.[4] Any sensible political leadership had to seek ways to appease their wrath —or, at the very least, to release blacks, as individuals, for opportunities open to all other Americans. A price had to be paid by the dominant white society; guilt insisted on it. But how much, and how?

The third incubator was prosperity. In the decade of the 1960's, the dollar value of the Gross National Product had gone from $500 billion a year in 1960 to almost $1,000 billion a year in 1970. The Kennedy-Johnson tax laws of 1963–1964 had stimulated the greatest boom in American history. The nation could fight a war, rebuild its cities, explore space, corset the country in concrete highways, clear ghettoes all at once—or so it seemed. Moreover, the prodigious boom of the 1960's had been engineered by American academic economists—then at the peak of their prestige—and not by businessmen, as had the boom of the 1920's. Production, or so it seemed, was no problem; the problem was distribution, and wise men could direct the flow of the economy to moral ends to make a safer, healthier, more noble human society. Subtly, this burst of production linked itself to another phenomenon— the development of the right of the individual as a consumer as equal to his obligation as a worker. In addition to his right to have a job, whether or not he did or could work, he had a right to consume; nor could he, as a consumer, any longer be bilked as he had been since the phrase *caveat emptor* was minted millennia ago. The new consumer-citizen had champions like Ralph Nader. But the era of prosperity had incubated rights that went further than consumption. The citizen of the new era had the means to explore his own individual instinct for self-expression, whether in his snowmobile shattering wilderness quiet, or collecting pornography, or dumping trash from his boat into clean coves, or in new habits of dress, taste for exotic foods, manners of expression. The ethos of rugged individualism which had served America well in its

[4] See *The Making of the President—1968*, pp. 199–210.

primitive past, now, with the fostering of prosperity, took on a new aspect of menace. All wanted the government to help them express themselves—and restrict others whose self-expression they found obnoxious.

All in all, the war, the Black Revolution, the prosperity were the main incubators of change in the Liberal Idea. Their effect could be summed up in three cardinal tenets of the Liberal Theology: (a) War Is Bad—and the American military was almost, if not quite, a criminal institution, wasteful and profligate of life and treasure; patriotism was the last refuge of scoundrels, and the adventure in Vietnam "immoral." (b) Black Is Good—and the demands of blacks on the general society must become, in the revision of priorities that would follow the end of the war, priority number one. And (c) since money comes easily under the modern managed economy, the belief that Money Solves All Problems, as in the rhetoric of hope, "If we can spend the money to reach the moon, we can spend the money to save our cities, solve cancer, purify our streams, cope with drugs, cleanse our ghettoes . . . etc., etc." These three tenets of the Theology were, in turn, harnessed to a political doctrine called Participation: If the people could be brought to participate in the political arena, and there freed to express their real needs, then politics would become, as it should be, the instrument of national good.

Thus, out of such thinking, there developed in the years between 1968 and 1972 a formless but very powerful action group within the Democratic Party that can only be called the Movement—a movement whose roots lay in the insurgency of 1968, had been strengthened and nursed by the reforms of 1969, and whose future, as one looked forward to 1972, was obscure, yet beckoning.

The Movement had its own sometimes brilliant, sometimes blind perception of the political dynamics of American life and the Democratic Party, and since these perceptions were later to explain both its triumphs and its disaster in 1972, one ought to go into them.

Women, for example.

Blacks had been accepted by all Democrats as a new political power force in the campaign of 1964. The insurgency of 1968 had ushered in a second new power force—the student mobilization against the war. The Movement now in 1972 embraced for the first time a third new historic power force—women.

The engagement of women in the politics of the 1960's, and their action in 1972, can be traced almost directly to the civil-rights movement of that decade—nor is it odd historically that this should be so. Historians of women's rights recall even today that at the World Conference on the Abolition of Slavery held in London in 1840, two of

America's great feminists, Elizabeth Cady Stanton and Lucy Mott, had been shunted to the galleries and forbidden participation by their own male white American companions-in-arms against slavery. From that event, say some, came the first Women's Rights Convention, held in 1848 in Seneca Falls, New York. So, similarly, in the 1960's, had come the spin-off of the women's movement from the vast upheaval of conscience occasioned by the revolt of the blacks. Though a Stokely Carmichael might say "the only position for a woman in SNCC is prone," many women could recognize that they, as women, suffered from the same kind of categorical social and structural exclusions and injuries that deprived blacks, too, of equal human rights.

Women had always been an active force in American politics; and such organizations as the League of Women Voters had an honor roll of achievement in Congress and state legislatures that ranked almost in the same category of demonstrated power as that of the AFL/CIO. But the League of Women Voters was a citizens' organization, of good citizens who happened to be women, urging good causes on government for the good of all. The newer organizations such as NOW (National Organization for Women) and the NWPC (National Women's Political Caucus) had a sharper cutting edge. There were simple legal inequities in the laws of America which denied women their equal rights—the newer organizations insisted that these be rectified, and further insisted that these could not be rectified unless women were, by category, given a share of power.[5]

Of all the demands of the newer women's organizations, none was a greater political perplexity than their most justified demand, abortion —a searing political issue in 1972. A man is given by nature control of his reproductive process; he may make love and walk away from the child with no guide to responsibility but his conscience. A woman who makes love and conceives is condemned by nature to suffer pain, sometimes death, and then, again by tradition, is compelled to care for the child. Should not a woman have control of her reproductive process as fully as a man? asked the women of the 1970's. All through history, men have made the laws which governed women's bodies; in America, in the seventies, this masculine authority was to be challenged for the first time; and in the challenge lay not only a biological imperative, but also a breach with the culture of some of America's most important communities.

[5] In state after state, women's rights to dispose of property are still limited. Credit is denied single women where credit is always available to single men. Prostitutes in New York can be jailed for three months; their clients can at most be penalized by imprisonment for fifteen days; one state jails women drunkards for three years, but men only for thirty days. A woman's right to share in the property of her spouse, when they are divorced, is everywhere limited, despite her years-long contribution to their joint wealth.

For the Movement there was no real perplexity about the matter of abortion—or any other of the demands of the new women's organizations. Right was right, morality and conscience were imperatives—and in this perception the Movement was able to bring into play a grassroots force and an energy hitherto untapped by any other leadership. Later, George McGovern's staff was to describe the mobilization of women in the primary campaigns of 1972 as "the Nylon Revolution," a phrase which the vocal leaders of women's movements hated. But the Nylon Revolution was a reality—and the Movement, in seeing how the talents, the dogged devotions, the energies, the spare time of thousands of American women could be brought to active politics and participation, committed itself to a brilliant pioneer adventure.

If the Movement's perception of both the grievances and the power of women was brilliant, its perceptions of other forces were blurred.

Labor, for example.

The Liberal Idea of the thirties had undertaken to legitimize the right of ordinary workingmen to organize in their unions and let the unions confront capital and industry as equals. Labor had made the most of this encouragement and had, over thirty years, hardened into giant bureaucracies, led by hard men who, year in, year out, supplied manpower, money and votes for Democratic candidates and expected measurable gratitude in return from the many they helped to elect.

Liberals took labor's votes for granted—and labor, in turn, took liberal goals as its own. No major social legislation has been passed in America for the past thirty years, from housing and Social Security to the Civil Rights Act of 1964, without labor doing the essential arm-twisting in Washington. The decade of the sixties had thus been unsettling to labor's leadership—the Liberal Cause had been labor's home, the Democratic Party its partner; but now the cause had passed on to other priorities and the party was being invaded by hostiles. Increasingly, the new intellectual leadership of the party was questioning the needs of labor, its thinking, above all, its personalities. On too many tongues, from too many university platforms, labor's leaders were being described as part of the establishment, and their style as "bossism." Eugene McCarthy had called them, in 1968, "old buffaloes." And the labor delegates to the 1968 convention had ordered up and worn on their lapels buffalo pins to announce their pride. Labor's leaders were sensitive. The new reforms had by 1972 given categorical representation to young people, to women, to blacks—but yielded no recognition at all, as a category, to men who work for a living. They were being taken for granted. Said Al Barkan, director of the AFL/CIO's political arm, COPE, early in 1972 as he examined the scenario about to unfold: "We aren't going to let these Harvard-Berkeley Camelots take over our party."

As with the case of the women's cause, so, too, in the case of labor more than political numbers was involved—cultural values were involved also. The Movement considered the war in Vietnam immoral, denied any honor to the men who served the call of the government to arms. But the men who fought the war in Vietnam were the hard-muscled youngsters of labor—the assembly-line workers, the dock men, the hard-hats, the teamster boys. Labor's leaders and labor's men had always followed the call of the flag; the Movement's theologians considered draft-dodgers and draft-bound alike equally innocent victims.

If the Movement's perception of the dynamics and force of labor was blurred, its misperception of the dynamics of big-city life was absolutely blind. The cities of America are where the crisis of American civilization is happening. If the cities' problems cannot be solved, then the civilization goes to ruins. The old Liberal Idea of the sixties had provoked many experimental approaches to city problems; most had been passed into legislation—and most had failed. The huge cities and metropolitan areas of America are systems of communities, places where kinship groups, ethnic groups, cultural groups all revolve around each other in a political pattern where traditionally the city provided the services necessary to all, yet left each group, each neighborhood, free to develop its own identity in its own way.

By the early 1970's it was clear that the Liberal-inspired programs of the Great Society had failed in the cities; they had been based on a political misreading of how those cities functioned, and what communities in those cities required for community survival. What had actually happened in the great cities of America in the 1960's, and was continuing to happen as America entered the seventies, mocked all the billions of dollars spent on programs to "save" them.

If the decade of the 1960's can appropriately be called the Decade That Gave Goodwill A Bad Name, it is not because of the Vietnam war—it is because of what distant goodwill has done to life in the big cities. All the programs had been advanced by Democratic thinkers practicing the best doctrine of the day; but theologians put doctrine above experience. The Movement insisted on more of the same for the seventies— and in the big cities, where the Democrats get their core votes, more-of-the-same frightened too many of the communities who were being driven from their homes.

The big cities were to have only one spokesman in the campaign of 1972—Mayor John Lindsay of New York; he lost instantly. From then on, the campaign of 1972 was to be fundamentally a campaign of small-town boys vying to direct the most urbanized and complicated society in the world. It was to begin with a clash between Edmund Muskie, born and raised in Rumford, Maine (population 7,000) and George McGovern, born in Avon, South Dakota (population several hundred), and raised in Mitchell, South Dakota (population 10,000).

McGovern emerged victor from this first clash and went on to rebuff the challenge of Hubert Humphrey, born in Wallace, South Dakota (population unknown), raised in Doland, South Dakota (population 481). McGovern then challenged Richard M. Nixon, born in Yorba Linda, California (population unknown), and raised in Whittier, California (population 8,000). Among these small-town boys, George McGovern was by far the most perfect expression of small-town virtues. Decent, brave, friendly, innocent of the rumble of the subway or the blare of the night radio through the apartment wall, willing to accept the wisdom of the Movement as revealed truth, he was nonetheless a very able technical politician.

It is with the story of George McGovern that the narrative tightens on the year 1972. First, he would have to become the mobilizer of the Movement's energies; with those he would have to win the nomination of the party; and with the nomination of the party he would have to capture the Presidency and executive power.

George McGovern had been running for the Presidency a long time before 1972 began, and studying the problem even longer. The idea, he told several newsmen, had come to him in the fall of 1962 in a hospital as, recovering from hepatitis, he read a book called *The Making of the President—1960*. The book, written in a romantic style, made a more serious impression than later books by the same author, which McGovern felt "missed the story." Yet this first story of how a Presidency was won seemed reasonable and simple.

McGovern set out on the adventure himself three weeks before the convention of 1968—to keep aglow the flare of conscience Robert Kennedy had lit in the spring of that year. But the McGovern candidacy of 1968 was more a candidacy of conscience, a witnessing of his deepest convictions about the war in Vietnam, than a planned strategy. He had left the convention in Chicago in 1968, after the riots and bloodshed, convinced, however, that if Humphrey could not be President that year, he, McGovern, might be in 1972. It was a decision he shared only with his wife and his South Dakota staff, but he was off and running, at least in his heart, from the moment the polls closed in November of 1968.

George McGovern held strong convictions. First and deepest of these was his feeling about the war in Vietnam—an immorality, a sin, a barbarism. But he was also a loyal party man. He had grown up in a Republican home in Mitchell, South Dakota; his father and mother were Republicans; he, too, was a Republican until, during the war, he had come to admire Franklin Roosevelt. Then, one day in the summer of 1952, while painting his house on a ladder, his radio beside him, he found himself tuned in on Adlai Stevenson's voice coming from the Chicago convention of the Democratic Party. John the Baptist called;

and getting down from the ladder, McGovern drove all through the next night to volunteer his services for Adlai.

More than Stevensonian rhetoric stirred George McGovern, however. He was also a professor of American history; he had written his doctoral thesis on the massacre of the coal miners in the Colorado Fuel-and-Iron strike of 1913–1914, in the club-and-bust days of American industrial warfare. The conviction was deep in him, from learning and by instinct, that, as he put it himself, "the engine of progress in our time in America is the Democratic Party," and that the enemy was the "special interests."

In early 1970 I came to call on him, as a probably serious candidate for the Presidency in 1972, to ask how he saw himself in the spectrum of the party's personalities and problems. He approached the subject with candor. He was not, he said, a fervent ideologue; he was not a Barry Goldwater. What lay most on his mind was the memory of the Chicago convention and what it had done to the party—and his fear of a third or a fourth party splitting off from and destroying it. The Reform Commission he was then heading, it seemed to him, was the best method of unifying the party; the Democrats could win only as a united party; the reforms he was pushing through were the only way of drawing back into the party the young, the women, the farmers, even the Wall Street brokers. The party had to be saved, the party had to have a cause, the party had to be pulled together with a mission.

He assessed himself, his chances and his personality. Of course he was going for the Presidency; he was beginning to assemble staff, names, lists. "I made a decision as soon as '68 was over that I was going to try again and I wouldn't wait until three weeks before the convention to do it. . . . I've been doing that for over a year. I've identified support, I've made some money, I've got a good local press." He'd been pushing issues: the war; the hunger issue—he had bulled through his food-stamp program in Congress; and hunger, the empty-belly issue, was developing strength in the black communities, drawing to him support from people like Jesse Jackson, Julian Bond, Coretta King, George Wiley of the National Welfare Rights Organization; and he was strongest of all at the universities. He could, he knew, if he wanted to, "scare hell out of Middle America . . . but I haven't got the inflammatory personality of Bobby Kennedy. I'm not as exciting, I use a low-key approach. If I waved my arms and hit the podium as hard as Hubert, I'd never make it. I can present liberal values in a conservative, restrained way. . . . I see myself as a politician of reconciliation."

Though the decision to run had been made by the McGoverns alone in 1969 out of moral conviction, the planning of how he should run, what perceptions should govern his national campaign, was a harder exercise; and so, on the last weekend of July, 1970, George McGovern began the actual planning of an adventure that anyone else would have considered preposterous.

On Saturday evening, July 25th, at his summer house, Cedar Point Farm, near St. Michael's, Maryland, eighty-four miles from Washington, he assembled those people who had come, either lately or over the years, to enjoy his trust. The Senator himself and his wife, Eleanor, of course, and his secretary, Patricia J. Donovan. Of his South Dakota staff, George Cunningham. Of what would later become his council of war, three—Professor Richard Wade of City University of New York, a major urban historian; Gary Hart, who had only a few weeks before left his law practice in Denver to open the three-man McGovern headquarters in a tawny Italian palazzo, catercorner from the Capitol in Washington; and that eloquent and talented young scholar Rick Stearns, whose Oxford thesis had dealt with the mechanisms of reform and the Democratic Party of the United States.

The group gathered early on Sunday morning in the living room, after Eleanor McGovern had cooked their breakfast, and they began to consider the timing of their announcement for an election more than two years away.

It was McGovern who led off—he was for an early announcement. If he waited until November, at least one or two other people might beat him to public attention. Lindsay, for example—Lindsay was recruiting all sorts of people, said McGovern, and why should he be building such an organization unless he planned to run for the Presidency? And if he ran as a Democrat, Lindsay would become, in McGovern's words, "the white hope of the more rational humane elements of the party."

But how early was early? Wade and Stearns were for waiting until after the 1970 elections. That would give McGovern time to hold several more press conferences as chairman of the Reform Commission before resigning, which he would have to do. Waiting would free McGovern for the campaign swings he might make in the fall elections of 1970, where he could accumulate political credit from candidates he befriended, and perhaps raise some money of his own. Hart pointed out the problem of the press. Every political writer in the country would *have* to write a column on the campaign, and they would concentrate on how serious McGovern was—does he have a staff, does the staff look as if it knows what it's doing? Staff and organization had to be built before announcement.

Thus, on the timing, McGovern was persuaded to make his formal announcement *after,* not *before,* the fall campaign—some time in mid-November. (Later the date was to be postponed again, because it seemed to the group that a November-December announcement would be lost in the Christmas-card mailings; but it would be nonetheless the earliest announcement of any major modern candidacy—as it turned out, January 18th, 1971.)

They moved then to a discussion of potential rivals. There were Muskie, "Scoop" Jackson, Humphrey. McGovern considered Muskie bland—he would not stand up under pressure. Humphrey, if re-elected in Minnesota, would probably squeeze Muskie out. If Muskie arrived at the convention, he would arrive wounded and bleeding; if Humphrey arrived as the chief contender, he would still bear the curse of the Vietnam War.

The worry came on the left. There were Harold Hughes, Fred Harris, possibly Ramsey Clark or John W. Gardner. There was the possibility that Eugene McCarthy would go again. McCarthy still had troops and could raise big money on Wall Street. Lindsay seemed the most formidable contender if he started early enough. George Wallace was not even mentioned at the meeting. Ted Kennedy's name, of course, entered into the discussion and McGovern assumed Kennedy would not run because of Chappaquiddick; but, in any event, with Kennedy in or out, he, McGovern, would stay in the race. "My one unique position," said McGovern, according to the minutes, "with reference to the potential competition, is to be to the left of them all, but to make clear to the party pols and organization Democrats that they're not going to find me leading a fourth party or my candidacy producing pickets outside the convention hall. [It's] conceivable that while I might be the most left-leaning candidate, I am also the most reconciling candidate."

Thus to a consideration of the route to the nomination. There was the classic corridor of the primaries. They would get into every one, but they would target five as key races—New Hampshire, Wisconsin, Nebraska, Oregon, California. Later, Massachusetts and New York were to be added to this list of prime strategic targets. In the early primaries McGovern would have to eliminate his rivals on the left; in the final round, Oregon, California, New York, he could win if the early successes drew the big money necessary to campaign in the big states.

Which led to a discussion of finances—they needed a finance chairman, either John Hechinger or Henry Kimelman. They ran through the names of a few big-money liberals: Max Palevsky, Martin Stone, Hechinger, Levitt from Wichita—if they could get twenty men like that to give or raise $10,000 each, they would have the seed money needed. (Later, of course, they were to go the direct-mail route and develop that into a fund-raising instrument which seems certain to influence the course of all campaigning in the future.)

They went on to discuss the publishing of a campaign biography—and discarded the idea; discussed names of newsmen as potential press secretaries; and toyed with a memorandum from Fred Dutton urging a television campaign of visuals and happenings throughout the next year.

The Senator urged everyone to be "alert to imaginative things he might do over the year to sustain interest and avoid boredom that could occur with a long candidacy."

The long, easy-going session had the languid quality of a July holiday weekend by the shore. Eleanor broke early to drive down to the supermarket for fruit and soda, and made sandwiches for lunch. In the afternoon, some went swimming and others wandered down to the water's edge to catch crabs. For dinner, they went out to a nearby inn that George McGovern favored. Stearns and Wade shared a room before driving back to Washington the next morning. Wade slept badly that night, his roommate recalls—the birds kept him up. Wade was not at home in the countryside—and his roommate said of him that Wade's idea of a bucolic retreat was sitting somewhere on a quiet curbstone. It would have been well if the group, as well as Wade himself, had taken him more seriously. He was to be typical of a handful of men of large learning and ideas assigned by command, or self-assigned, to problems of tactics. Of Wade's great lore of urban folk-ways and history he was to impart but little to the quality and concepts of the McGovern campaign. He was there at Cedar Point as a loyalist and tactician, not as a scholar; his assignment was to be New York, where later he made the professional politicians of that state look like amateurs.

No one recalls from this meeting, or any other meeting until far down the road, any discussion of themes—of what troubled America's cities, or how the candidate could reach them with new liberating or reassuring ideas. The themes of the McGovern campaign had been accepted as given—the themes of the Movement, the message of the Liberal Theology. The tactics of the campaign, until mid-1972, all flowed from this ground assumption—that the first objective was to seize control of the Movement, of its manpower and womanpower now adrift, without questioning its premises. "We would have to consolidate the left wing," is the way Stearns summed up the basic decision, or "preempt the left wing," as Hart phrased it. With these as premises and strategy, the McGovern group was beautifully positioned to explode its surprises in the primaries; but it was also fatally vulnerable to the claims, demands and pressure of the forces it sought to bring together. Much later, when the election of 1972 was all over, campaign director Frank Mankiewicz reflected on what he considered the basic mistake of the campaign. Mankiewicz did not use the word "blackmail," but he expressed succinctly what he had learned. "We were always subject to this pressure from the cause people," said Mankiewicz. "We reacted to every threat from women, or militants, or college groups. If I had to do it all over again, I'd learn when to tell them to go to hell."

*   *   *

To discern in the politics of 1970 the shape of the ultimate event of 1972 was difficult—particularly for Democrats.

The country was moving—but whether it was a crescendo of the moods and violence of the late 1960's or a diminuendo was more difficult to decide. The invasion of Cambodia and the bloody suppression of the student demonstration at Kent State University in Ohio had set the students on the march again. The drug culture was alarming all, and along with it the spread of pornography in many big cities. The women's-rights movement was finding and identifying its prophetesses. And the environment cause had swollen into the favorite sacred issue of all politicians, all TV networks, all writers, all good-willed people of any party.

Politically, for Democrats, the cause people seemed to be winning in whatever internal party fights could be identified. New Democrats, moderates, were winning fights in the South. The peace spokesmen, who had lined up behind McGovern and McCarthy in the Chicago convention, were winning statewide Democratic primaries—these included candidates for Governor in California (Unruh), Michigan (Levin), Ohio (Gilligan), Wisconsin (Lucey), Pennsylvania (Shapp)—running for office as Democratic standard-bearers in the first, seventh, sixth, sixteenth and third largest states of the Union. So, too, were peace candidates winning in notable Congressional primaries—in Manhattan, in Berkeley, in Denver, in Newton-Cambridge. The peace and cause candidates seemed to have found a new system of energy: in students, and in housewives, so much of whose time is their own, the Movement seemed to have developed the manpower equivalent of the old patronage rolls of machine politics. This new political leisure class could man telephones or hit the doorsteps with bodies and skills that overwhelmed both the numbers and the quality of their competitors within the old party.

More exciting, and more disturbing to some, was what these new forces of the Movement could do in states whose conventions and politics rest on the caucus system—for what they were doing nationwide was phenomenal. In Oklahoma County, seat of Oklahoma City, the anti-war county chairman packed his convention with a clear majority of activists. His convention wrote a party platform calling for legalized abortion, a timetable for withdrawal from Vietnam and reduced penalties for possession of marijuana. One candidate warned the convention that they were murdering candidates for the Senate and House in that hawk-and-Bible state. Replied a liberal delegate, "Any candidate we murder, let him be murdered."

During a lull at the Michigan state convention, a rump faction of liberals remaining on the floor amended the party's platform to include (in late August, 1970) a demand for withdrawal from Vietnam by Christmas, unconditional amnesty for draft evaders and "reparations" to Hanoi. Washington state was even more interesting—the caucus politics of that state opens both Republican and Democratic party conventions to alternate coups and countercoups by militants of the right and left. The John Birch Society had swept the Republican caucuses of 1964 for Barry Goldwater. In 1970 the Movement people arrived at the state Democratic convention in Washington with a clear majority of delegates. Their platform called not only for the inevitable timetable for withdrawal in Vietnam and unconditional amnesty for draft-evaders, but also for a moratorium on missile-building, nationalization of the railroads and the repudiation of any candidate belonging to an organization which excludes blacks—like the Elks. For good measure, the convention also endorsed a primary opponent against Senator Henry Jackson, one of the most popular Senators in his state's history.

The Movement, it was quite clear in mid-1970, was swinging heavy weight inside the party itself. All events and episodes seemed to confirm the strategy of those who had gathered at Cedar Point—that the country was on the move, and they must capture the movement.

But the voters themselves, if one analyzed what average voters thought by what they recorded at the polls, were not swept away. One could start in Washington, for example, where the Movement had seized the party mechanism and offered a rival to Henry Jackson. In the open Democratic primary on September 15th, Jackson won his renomination by 84.1 percent against 13.4 percent for the endorsee of the state convention; and then went on to crush his Republican opponent in November by 83.9 percent (793,722 to 152,481).

Even more perplexing were the final November results in the big-city Congressional races. Wherever in previously solid Democratic districts the most colorful messengers of the new theology had captured upset nominations from old regular Congressmen, the final Democratic results in November all fell off. In Denver, Colorado, the new Democratic peace nominee lost the previously solid Democratic seat in the 1st Colorado Congressional. In the 3rd Massachusetts Congressional, north of Boston (a mixed district of Catholic working class, Jewish middle class, student activists), Father Robert F. Drinan led his Republican rival by only 5 points where in 1968 the incumbent Democrat had led the Republican by 19 points. In the 7th California District (Berkeley–Bay Area), Ronald V. Dellums led the Republican by 14 points in 1970—as against 33 points for his predecessor in 1968. In the 19th New York, Bella S. Abzug won by 9 points—as against the 20-point margin by which her defeated regular rival in the primaries, Congressman Leonard Farbstein, had scored over a Republican in 1968. In Connecticut, Republican Lowell P. Weicker, Jr., scored a surprising Senate victory over an outstanding Democratic insurgent, Reverend Joseph Duffey, 443,000 to 360,000. It was to be noted that on the same day the repudiated outgoing Old Guard Democratic Senator, Thomas Dodd, scored 260,000 votes from old-line Democrats on an Independent line. The new politics, apparently, could mobilize for caucuses and primaries and win victories inside the party—but it lost force, in the strangest of ways, wherever it penetrated the heart of cities.

The old Liberal Idea held that the job of a politician was to be a craftsman. Liberals might denounce the politician over and over again for having compromised with morality in squalid, dirty backroom deals. But so long as the politician moved the state or the majority in the right direction toward a more humanitarian society, they left the pace of change to him. For the Democrat politicians who were elected to govern, the men who sought and won control of the power levers, the whole matter was a continuing riddle: You stayed on in power only by the accommodations to clashing groups that American life required—by accommodation to ethnic pride and street-learned savvy in big cities, by accommodation to contending economic forces in the nation, by accommodation to or ultimately confrontation with foreign powers in the big world beyond, which history insisted on. In 1970 the Liberal Theology drew new lines—men of morality must take over the party and operate it; politics was too important to be left to the craftsmen of accommodation. The theologians saw no riddle at all in the contrary dictates of morality and reality. Life must conform to high principles—what was morally right, they felt, must be politically sound.

Richard Nixon, who had been involved in politics longer than any of his rivals except Hubert Humphrey, had come, however, to the belief that this was not necessarily so. He, too, had begun to examine the lessons of 1970 and look forward to 1972.

CHAPTER THREE

===

THE VIEW FROM KEY BISCAYNE: BLUE COLLARS AND BREAD-AND-BUTTER

O N Saturday morning, November 7th, 1970—four days after the mid-term elections of that year—Richard Nixon called together in the wood-paneled living room of his Key Biscayne home in Florida his political high command: John Mitchell, Attorney General; H. R. Haldeman, John Ehrlichman, Robert Finch, Charles Colson; Donald Rumsfeld and Bryce Harlow.

They were there to talk politics—but no official of the Republican Party was invited. All through the campaign of 1972, this distance between the President and his Republican Party was to grow to create the paradox of Election Night two years later.

Among the matters the President wanted to talk about was just this problem of the party and its management. The party needed a new chairman; and the President began by suggesting his protégé of twenty-five years, Robert Finch. But Finch, a man once intrigued by politics, had grown over the years into another personality —someone absorbed by government itself, by its intellectual excitements and meaning to people. Finch flatly would not take the party chairmanship. What the party needed, said Finch, was a gut-fighter who would get out there and rough the Democrats; he himself, hoping someday to run for Governor of California as a Republican in that overwhelmingly Democratic state, would not take a post that required so vivid a partisanship. Nor, as they went around the room, would John Mitchell take the post; nor would Donald Rumsfeld. The President had perhaps expected such answers, but he felt that certainly Bryce Harlow would say yes. Harlow, a man of his own mind, an elegant wordsmith, a man of confidence, had, however, his own plans—he, too, flatly would not have it. None of the President's political men wanted to run his party. He would have to go outside this group to find a chairman.[1] Without anyone recognizing it, a decision had slipped by without decision. The President would run his campaign for re-election, the Republican Party would run another campaign, and, in the age of ticket-splitting, the results would become visible only two years thereafter.

Choice of a National Chairman was very far, however, from being the most important matter in this Presidential review. Subject number one was the campaign of 1972—which meant a look at the results of the 1970 election just over and what they told of the future. In the election, the party had lost twelve seats in the House, gained a net two seats in the Senate. Finch felt the results were mixed. Haldeman and Colson thought they were good. But others held contrary views. Mitchell, for one, had previously expressed the opinion that the President had acted in the 1970 campaign as if he had been "running for sheriff." Nor was Harlow pleased with the course of the campaign just finished. The party had shuttled Vice-President Agnew around the country as if he had been a mountain howitzer, shelling the enemy Democrats on the law-and-order issue with such rhetorical effect that he had become one of the chief entertainments in a drab year. "Power-pack Agnew," as Harlow later called him, had accomplished his job in three weeks and gone on to overkill; then, in the last three weeks of the campaign, the President had gone out on the stump (22 states, 17,241 miles in 23 days of campaigning) to exaggerate the job that Agnew had already accomplished. All were agreed that the coming 1972 campaign must be run otherwise. As later recalled by one of the group, "the decision was to get politics the hell out of the White House and across the street"; or, as it became apparent when the campaign unraveled, the President in 1972 would run as President, far above the battle, and leave nuts-and-bolts politicking to others.

More important even than ordinary politics was the President's own view of the nation. "It had been growing on him for two years," said Charles Colson, recalling, "but now he defined his constituency better than he'd ever done before." The President felt that there was a "new majority" growing in the country, and this new majority rested on reach-

[1] Two months later the choice of the President finally settled on Senator Robert J. Dole of Kansas, a handsome, dark-eyed, vigorous war veteran wounded in the Battle of the Bulge, a Republican as regular as the Stalwarts of 1912. Dole respected the President; the President did not reciprocate; the chairman of the Republican National Committee was never able to penetrate the White House palace guard. Later, wiser, in 1972 Dole could sum up the relationship between himself and the President in a story he ruefully enjoyed telling. After months of seeking an appointment with the President, Dole received a telephone call from one of those he calls "assistant presidents." The conversation, as Dole told it, went something like this: "Hey, Bob, do you still want to see the President?" Dole: "When?" Answer: "Tune in on Channel 9, he's coming up on the tube in ten minutes."

ing the blue-collar working people, above all on reaching the Catholics. "They live," said the President, as Colson recalls, "in the rings around the cities, they're a new middle class." The Buckley election in New York, felt the President, was not a fluke; there was an emerging blue-collar conservative vote that cared about the flag, about patriotism, that believed in the work ethic. Workingmen stood up in time of trouble, he felt. Most other blocs were relatively stable in their voting, but the widest political swings took place in just this new blue-collar middle class.

The group lingered over the conservative phenomenon and that week's victory of James Buckley in supposedly liberal New York state. Buckley, on a Conservative third-party ticket, had defeated two liberals for the U.S. Senate—Ottinger of the Democrats, Goodell of the Republicans. More significant was the rhythm moving the Buckley family's Conservative Party. In its first try, in 1962, it had won only 141,877 votes in New York; in 1966 its total rose to 510,023 statewide; then, in 1968, to 1,139,402; and this fall, 1970, with 2,139,000 votes, it had emerged victorious as a statewide third party. Buckley had sheared through the nerve ends of working people by sharpening matters of culture and law-and-order more sensitive than old-fashioned bread-and-butter issues. The President perceived the opening.

Even more illuminating is Donald Rumsfeld's recollection of the President's thinking at the Key Biscayne meeting: "I came away with the sense that he believed that some leaders who pretended to speak for a group were not really representative of it—all the young people weren't the same as the ones doing the criticism, and the ones who spoke for labor weren't the same as the workingman. He had this sense of what happened to LBJ, who was taken in by those at the top of society. His own role was *not* to make an agreement with the leaders of those institutions, but to reach *underneath* them regardless of any discord with the elites at the top. He was disappointed in the quality of middle-level leadership in the country—'They didn't stand up to the ball.' They're afraid to do the simple, unsophisticated things because the howls of a few critics make them smart. People who bow to that sort of criticism aren't good leaders. Nixon had this conscious willingness to go ahead— to accept the abuse, the opposition, the criticism of the verbal leaders, this charge that he isn't sensitive enough. The louder they yell, the better it would be for him—people are turned off by this leadership."

Politics occupied less than an hour and a half at the Key Biscayne meeting; the group talked of George Wallace and how much Wallace might hurt the President on his Southern flank. As for the Democrats— George McGovern was not even considered. The two main Democratic contenders, the group felt, were Ted Kennedy and Edmund Muskie— which made it more important than ever that the President reach for the Catholic vote. The Nixon victory of 1968 had been won by the Southern strategy, drafted by Strom Thurmond and fleshed out by Spiro Agnew; the victory of 1972 would have to be won by a Northern strategy. The advocate and architect of this Northern strategy—the reach for the ethnic, blue-collar, Catholic vote—would be Charles Colson, who had, in the year of John Kennedy's national triumph in 1960, managed Senator Leverett Saltonstall's campaign in Massachusetts and saved a Republican seat by exactly that strategy. Colson was to emerge from this meeting very large in the President's counsels, third only to John Mitchell and Bob Haldeman.

The meeting, which broke for lunch—on sandwiches of leftover steak—had begun between ten and eleven and lasted through the afternoon until five, moving from politics to the more serious matter of government: What programs should the President advance to Congress in 1971 to set the lines for 1972? How hard should they push revenue-sharing? What about the property tax? What shifts in the Cabinet were needed? And most of all, their memories still smarting from the experience at the polls that week, they talked about the economy. Unemployment had undone them at the polls in 1970; the economy was ailing, what could be done?

The President, though bored by economics, has a visceral appreciation of what jobs, prices and bread-and-butter issues mean in politics. Looking forward to 1972, he must prepare to grapple with such issues. Among the sharpest recalls of his experience is the campaign against John F. Kennedy in 1960, and how the economy affected that campaign. As early as 1959, Nixon, then Vice-President, recognized the political danger as the second Eisenhower recession began. He had pleaded, early, in the Cabinet for an easy-money, pump-priming policy to get the economy moving before the election of 1960. His only ally had been economist Arthur Burns, but the Eisenhower administration had waited until late spring to loosen credit. By then it had been too late, for pump-priming requires long lead-time; and Nixon had been compelled to campaign against Kennedy with unemployment rising all across the country in the fall. He had lost. He did not want to repeat that experience in 1972. Now, time was running against him once more. What the people needed, said Finch at the meeting, was any action, bold action, positive action to show that the government was actively leading—controlling events.

There was very little at that point in time, November of 1970, to demonstrate to the American people that their President did indeed have very active control of anything. He had been two years President; a substantial beginning had been made in foreign policy, but its spectacular fruits were not yet publicly visible; he had been directing an enormous withdrawal in Vietnam, but men were still fighting and dying;

he had begun to cut the Pentagon's manpower and budget—but the ending of the draft still seemed a long way off. Twice he had been repudiated by the Senate in major Supreme Court appointments; vital national-security bills had been carried only by the slimmest of margins; and even the most benevolent of his proposals, the national-welfare bill, was dying in Congress. All in all, his first two years could aptly be called an exercise in frustration.[2]

What most frustrated Richard Nixon was the contradiction between the nature of American government and the nature of his own mind. The Nixon mind is neat, disciplined, severely sequential, compulsively orderly. In foreign affairs, the power blocs Nixon dealt with came packaged in clean compartments of national sovereignties, defined interests, measurable forces. Both he and Kissinger, his adviser, could view the world stage almost as a chessboard, where a good, analytical mind could plan, move by move, to anticipated response.

But domestic affairs and the governing of America were entirely otherwise. The mind of Richard Nixon seeks, above all, to understand how things work; his imperative is to make things work. His love of sports, of football plays, of training programs, of charts, of space achievements, of the mechanics of politics all translate in conversation into that particularly American fascination with the working of things. But American national affairs are untidy, they work by pressure more than logic. Government-as-a-process has swollen through the postwar years into a large and cumbersome bloat; its lethargy, its sluggishness, its complications defy all Presidents. To Nixon it was a permanent aggravation. Over and over again, wherever, however, one tapped at the offices in the White House in the first two years, one found reflected in the conversation of the President's staff the President's major problem: How could he get a grip on things? How could he control the machinery itself?

Leonard Garment, who was then the President's White House scout in the area of civil rights and cultural affairs, described the climate in late 1970 thus: "Henry Kissinger's got an easy job—foreign policy is cerebral, and the President's at his best with abstractions. But domestic policy is a family affair, and Congress is sub-cortical. The question is: Can you get something done, can anyone get anything done with this Congress? . . . In foreign policy you get drama, triumph, resolution—crisis and resolution. So that in foreign policy Nixon can give the sense of leadership. But in domestic policy, there you have to deal with the whole jungle of home problems, with this hyper-neurotic country called America. So on the domestic scene you have to ask: What's critical?

---

[2] See *Nixon in the White House: The Frustration of Power* by Rowland Evans, Jr., and Robert D. Novak (New York: Random House, 1971) for a narrative of the President's problems in his first two years in office.

And you can only pick out one or two things that will affect the whole thing. There's no sharp nodule to fasten on until a new proposal or new machinery comes along, and the machinery that exists now doesn't grapple. The President feels you got to figure out a way to make the government operate—there's always this discrepancy between perceived needs and available resources—and how do you make the resources serve the needs when the formless things are as important as the big news events?"

Wherever one was admitted to those in the President's confidence, one caught the same mood. The President had received a black delegation early in his administration, led by the Reverend Ralph Abernathy and George Wiley; they were under the impression, remarked the President to John Ehrlichman later, that all he had to do was press the buttons of government and they worked. But the government did not work that way, and the President was concerned about the rhetoric and inflammation abroad in the land. "They're fed up with government," the President said to Ehrlichman—the government didn't respond, it cost too much, it didn't work.

Over and over again in his first two years in office, the President had probed for ways to come to grips with the governing of America at home—always frustrated. When he first came to office, he had appointed an Advisory Council on Executive Reorganization under the chairmanship of Roy Ash, of Litton Industries; but the council had delivered few tangible results. He had set up an Urban Affairs Council, and when that did not work, he created a Domestic Council under John Ehrlichman, to parallel the work of the National Security Council under Henry Kissinger. But domestic affairs were more complicated than foreign affairs.

Returning from Key Biscayne after the meeting with his counselors, he began work on his State-of-the-Union Message for 1971—the large design of measures which, if Congress approved, would position him as Statesman for the campaign of 1972. In the White House they called it the "Big Six" message, denoting the six great goals the President announced in January: First, the family-assistance program to bring order out of the chaos of American welfare programs. Second, even more startling from a Republican, a deficit budget called a "full-employment budget," to get the economy moving again. Third, an environment program. Fourth, a medical program with special insistence on cancer research and Federally aided medical insurance. Fifth, a program called revenue-sharing that came from his heart: "I reject the patronizing idea that government in Washington, D.C., is inevitably more wise, more honest and more efficient than government at the local or state level. . . . The idea that a bureaucratic elite in Washington knows best what is best for people everywhere . . . is really a contention that you cannot trust people to govern themselves. . . ." He would share, by this fifth proposal, the immense revenues of the Federal tax system with local governments and let them do as they wished with the money Washington gave, rather than binding them by Washington money to programs Washington insisted on. Finally, "the Sixth Great Goal is a complete reform of the Federal Government itself . . . ," and on into detail about total reorganization of the apparatus which in his first two years he could not make work.

The Big Six message was not only one of the fruits of the Key Biscayne meeting; it was the largest and most complete intellectual exploration in public of Richard Nixon's design for American government and how it could be made to work. It was, as the White House staff fondly called it, the blueprint of a "New American Revolution."

Thus, their frustration was only intensified when, after six days of desultory attention, the media abandoned discussion of Nixon's revolution—his proposals were too detailed, too technical, to sustain vivid political writing. Governmental housekeeping was a subject to be dismissed to Congress, where the New American Revolution was to die in committee and partisan debate.

More important, probably, was the effect of the reception on the President himself as the year wore on. Whatever he proposed to do "to make things work" (which was one of his favorite phrases) was apparently not to be taken seriously or was considered too boring or too partisan for the great national debate in which he might, in his own imagination, appear as Solon.

Whatever he had to do would have to be done as he was preparing to do what he must in foreign affairs—done all by himself, or by executive fiat. He, who so persistently had opposed the executive authority and central command of Washington, would be forced, paradoxically, to demand more of it than any other President of his times.

One should linger over the Big Six proposals put forward as politics entered 1971 and began to shape toward the election of 1972—not as matters of government but, since this is a book about politics, as matters of politics. The Big Six program, and its reception, speeded in Nixon's mind his identification of his adversaries—and of his own role. Obviously, there were two formidable adversaries blocking his access either to public opinion or to public action—the new "opinion establishment" of America's leading thinkers, and the old Congressional establishment, descended from the past. He would have to go over and above them, as he had already implied to his friends at Key Biscayne.

Of the "opinion establishment," little more can be said than that it was in revolt, and would be in revolt no matter who the President, against any President of the United States who did not bring about peace, justice, equality and prosperity immediately. And nothing more eloquent can be said than was to be found in the President's files even before he entered office, in a memorandum from Professor Daniel P. Moynihan of Harvard, who was to serve the President in his first two years of office. "In one form or another," Moynihan had written to the incoming President,

> all of the major domestic problems facing you derive from the erosion of the authority of the institutions of American society. This is a mysterious process of which the most that can be said is that once it starts, it tends not to stop. . . . American society has been so stable for so long that the prospect of instability has no very great meaning for us. (As I count there are but nine members of the United Nations that both existed as independent nations in 1914 and have not had their form of government changed by invasion or revolution since then.)
>   . . . Your task then, is clear: to restore the authority of American institutions. . . . [Johnson] in a sense . . . was the first American President to be toppled by a mob. No matter that it was a mob of college professors, millionaires, flower children, and Radcliffe girls. It was a mob that by 1968 had effectively *physically* separated the Presidency from the people. (You may recall that seeking to attend the funeral of Cardinal Spellman, Johnson slipped in the back door of the St. Patrick's Cathedral like a medieval felon seeking sanctuary.) . . . The leading cultural figures are going—or have gone—into opposition. . . . they take with them a vastly more numerous following of educated, middle-class persons, especially young ones, who share their feelings and who do not need the "straight" world. It is their pleasure to cause trouble, to be against.

The opposition of what Moynihan called "the leading cultural figures" had now, by early 1971, proven irrevocable. The President had presented a carefully thought-out series of proposals to Congress and the nation. They were, indeed, political—designed to win his re-election. But they were also substantive—designed to make the government work better. Yet the thinkers simply refused to take the thinking of the President seriously; they ignored his proposals; and this rankled.

Equally important as an adversary, it was clear by early 1971, was the Congress of the United States. Nixon would have been, in any event, a crippled President, entering office as he did with a generation-old record as hatchet-wielding Republican, facing a Congress controlled by the Democrats—243 to 192 in the House, 57 to 43 in the Senate. His White House staff, furthermore, had little Congressional experience or knowledge of the political process in Washington itself. They assumed that the President, as boss, gives orders and Congress must agree or disagree, somewhat like a board of directors in a corporation. But Congressmen, whether Republican or Democratic, love to be loved, and a political kiss or telephone call or White House invitation to breakfast is frequently more persuasive than any degree of logic. The Nixon liaison staff could find only surly support for new programs from its own Republicans on the Hill, who had been trained for decades "to snap at anything that moved"; and the Democrats were by definition in opposition to whatever "Dick the Knife" proposed. Among those of the President's Cabinet, only Secretary of Defense Melvin Laird understood the ways of the Hill and how vital is the massage of Congressional egos at every step of a program—Laird could move the defense bills through Congress, but in almost every other area the President's staff failed.

Even if Nixon could have mastered the kissing, honey and arm-twisting at which Lyndon Johnson had been so artful, he would have been in trouble with Congress. The President is a man of very definite ideas, and of these his philosophy of decentralization is cardinal. He had run, not only in 1968 but in every campaign of his long career, against Big Government, against the concentration of power in the United States in the city of Washington. But whenever any program for dispersing the power of Washington is forwarded to Congress, it runs into categorical institutional hostility on the Hill.

The underlying reality of American politics is that central national power is just as highly valued by the committees and subcommittees of Congress as it is by executive departments. The chairmen and sub-chairmen of key committees hold chunks of national power which are real. It matters little who runs the Select Committee of the House Beauty Shop, or the Committee to Regulate Parking, or the Committee on the House Restaurant. But the men who chair the committees on Banking and Currency, on Public Works, on the Armed Services, on Interior and Insular Affairs, the Senate Committee on Foreign Relations, or, in the House, the Ways and Means Committee, are liege lords of the realm. Political scientists identify in Washington examples of what they call an "Iron Triangle"—an interlocking three-way association between a well-financed lobby (whether it be in mining, education, highways, oil or other areas), the Congressional committee or subcommittee that makes laws on such subjects, and the bureaucracy in Washington which applies these laws. When these three—the committee, the lobby and the bureaucracy—in any given area all agree, and wash each other's hands with influence, information and favors, they are almost impervious to any executive or outside pressure. Within their jurisdictions, they control national power. To tamper with the structure of the Federal government, around which Congressional privileges and prerogatives have encrusted, is as impossible as to deny plumbers triple overtime on Sunday nights—or sedentary Air Force generals their flight pay, or franchise holders a continuation of their television licenses. If Mr. Nixon really wanted to make American government work differently than it had in the postwar world, his great adversary was there in Congress, even more potent than the "opinion establishment" which irritated him more in emotion.

This latent exasperation was to burst in the year 1971, provoking Richard Nixon to those strokes of bold and individual exercise of authority in the summer that were to lay the groundwork for his campaign of 1972. But just before the "Big Six" State-of-the-Union Message was to go to Congress, his thinking on the Presidency was still quite orthodox; and he discussed it at the close of one December day with a favorite speechwriter, William Safire, who had been laboring over an intractable passage on economics for Presidential signature. The President called Safire into his private working office across the street from the White House, in the Executive Office Building. Neatly spreading a towel on the ottoman before putting his feet up (Mr. Nixon likes to talk with friends with his feet on the desk, but these days he no longer puts a towel over his foot-rest), he was soon ready for other conversation, since both he and Safire lack passion for the abstractions of economics. Both seek to be plausible in economics, but it does not grab their attention as does politics. Safire, leading the President, asked about his favorite Presidents. Well, Mr. Nixon liked Andrew Jackson—Jackson took on the banks. He liked Lincoln—Lincoln took on slavery and the cause of the Union. He liked Grover Cleveland—Cleveland took on the Congress, and restored the power of the Presidency which had been lost by Andrew Johnson. And Teddy Roosevelt—he had taken on the trusts and vested interests. And Wilson—Wilson took on the Senate and the isolationists. And Franklin Roosevelt. The common denominator, said the President, was that they accepted controversy and they made things move, they wanted progress. "There's a role in life for men like McKinley, good men," said the President. But he, Nixon, didn't want to be like McKinley, nor like Eisenhower. He wanted to be a leader.

Few Presidents have looked less like a leader than did Richard Nixon as he began the third year of his first term in 1971.

He had come to a narrow election victory in 1968 at a moment when the chief stimulant of political emotion was the war in Vietnam and the clear urge of the American people was to find a President who could get them out of it. In his first two years in office, Nixon had begun the largest strategic retreat in American history, the only strategic retreat of American arms since George Washington had abandoned the cities of the Atlantic Seaboard to the British. His popular support in his first two years in office had rested chiefly on his policy in Vietnam—he was, he explained, training and preparing the South Vietnamese to defend themselves without American troops, and as he explained his policy, his public support had soared.

Now, in February and March of 1971, came a major testing of Nixon's program of Vietnamizing the war—the troops of South Vietnam would be sent across the border of Laos to cut the Ho Chi Minh Trail. On February 8th, 1971—to the accompaniment of one of the most bizarre press heraldings of all time—the offensive so conceived kicked off, stripped of every element of secrecy. And in two weeks disaster had overtaken the adventure. Penetrating enemy territory only eleven miles, then meeting resistance and massed artillery fire, the ARVN troops stalled, in some cases panicking, as soldiers scrambled to cling to the skids of United States helicopters sent to evacuate them. By mid-March it was clear that the blow which it had been hoped would settle the war then and there was more than a failure—it was a catastrophe. Did it mean there was no hope, ever, of the South Vietnamese fighting their own war and freeing America to be at peace again?

Simultaneously, spread across all television screens and newspapers was the trial of Lieutenant William L. Calley, Jr., at Fort Benning, Georgia. Day by day, a tale of horror unfolded. Three years earlier, on March 16th, 1968, so the transcript of the trial made clear, Lieutenant Calley of C Company of the 1st Battalion, 20th Infantry, 11th Light Infantry Brigade of the Americal Division, had been ordered to purge My-Lai, in the Communist-raddled strip of the panhandle of South Vietnam. Calley's platoon of 100 men had landed by helicopter at 7:30 A.M. and moved on target. No resistance was encountered, no hostile gunfire; the armed Viet Cong units that had been operating out of the village had fled. Nonetheless, Calley, then only twenty-four years old, had rounded up the remaining villagers, old men, women and children. Thirty were herded together and Calley gave orders to kill them. Another 100 villagers were herded to a ditch and these, too, were murdered, Calley firing at point-blank range, as he testified himself. Women with babes in arms were killed by single shots. Old men were clubbed to death. Wounded were dispatched, said one of the participants, "to put them . . . out of their misery."

As these events were described three years later in the spring of 1971, the national conscience vomited. The hidden beast in every man, *"das innere Schweinhund"* described by Kurt Schumacher in the Nazi nightmare, lurked within Americans, too.

Few episodes prickled more quickly into national controversy: Was Calley simply a pervert, a murderer in uniform, an individual gone mad? Or was he the expression of national sin, an instrument of a national

policy for which all had to share the blame? Should he be penned in jail
as a criminal and punished? Or should he be given leniency as an ignorant tool of higher, but blind, authority? The controversy disturbed even
the President—who ordered Calley removed from jail and confined to
barracks while he made up his mind; whereupon another controversy.

All in all, by mid-April, 1971, the Presidency of Richard M. Nixon
had reached its low point. His conduct of foreign affairs had always been
his strongest appeal to the electorate; his high point of approval in the
Gallup Poll had been reached in November of 1969, shortly after his first
major television speech promising orderly liquidation of the Vietnam war
—the approval rating had touched 68 percent. Now with the Laos offensive a failure, the Calley trial on all men's conscience, inflation steaming
while joblessness was rising—now Nixon's standing in the polls melted.
The Gallup Poll had held him at a 56-percent approval rating at the beginning of 1971; the same poll showed him at 51 percent in February,
50 percent in March, 49 percent in April. The Harris Poll consistently
paired the President against his chief Democratic rival, Edmund Muskie.
In January, Muskie led Nixon in the Harris Poll by 43 to 40; in February
by 44 to 39; and in April by an astonishing 47 to 39! In the spring
months of the year, Nixon's popularity had fallen to a lower level, as
measured by the Gallup Poll, than that of any President since Harry
Truman at a comparable point in his administration.

In April of that year, I had dinner in Washington at the home of
Caspar Weinberger, then Deputy Director of the Budget, along with
Budget Director George Shultz and Bob Haldeman. The mood was relaxed and convivial, but there was a somber undertone to the pleasant
evening. Two qualities were apparent: these men were under siege—and
they were calm. They agreed that this was the low point of their administration; their story was not getting across. Over and over again there
was the problem: how to come to grips with the government. How could
they control a Democratic Congress which denounced Pentagon expenditures, yet, according to them, appropriated $1.4 billion *more* for the
Pentagon than the President wanted? A Highway Administration that
was piling up more money than could possibly—or wisely—be spent on
highways? The inherited programs of the Johnson administration which
apparently could not be liquidated over the resistance of the bureaucracies and the popular lobbies? Haldeman recalled the Calley story, not
yet healed in the public mind. The President had called the Chairman
of the Joint Chiefs of Staff, Admiral Thomas H. Moorer, after the court-
martial verdict and ordered Calley returned from jail to quarters. "Yes,
sir," Moorer had replied. Then the President turned to Haldeman and
said, "Anyone else would have answered, 'Yes, but.' " He had control
over the armed services—but what more?

*   *   *

No problem in this exercise of "coming to grips" was, however, more politically explosive than that of bread-and-butter—how Americans made a living, how the economy should or must be managed. Failure in this area meant almost certainly that the President would be doomed in the 1972 election—and, by 1971, time was closing on his ability to act.

Quite clearly, the worth of the dollar was the background of political emotion as 1971 opened. But whatever was ailing the dollar was considered, at that moment, chiefly a domestic matter; Americans had always managed their own dollar. Only in midsummer would it become apparent that what ailed the dollar was the agony of an era that did not know how to die gracefully—that the dollar was cracking in the general crack-up of the postwar world far beyond the shores of America. For the moment, however, the unhappiness of Americans about their dollar —whether the soiled bills peeled out by the housewife at the supermarket check-out counter, or the endless digits in economists' calculations—was the underlying discontent against which all other episodes echoed.

Dollars—like marks, rubles, yen, pounds—are a way government has of issuing tickets for goods and services. This is an immensely delicate and complicated process, for when too many tickets are issued by government for limited services, space or command of goods, then orderly daily economic life becomes a mob action.

In the spring of 1971, the pressure for dollar-tickets was threatening to become just such a mob action. At the point of greatest commotion in this mob action were the clashes within government as city officials argued with state officials and both argued with Federal officials. The nation wanted services more than goods and the chief purveyor of services was local government. No city, however, any longer commanded the financial resources to meet the growing clamor for better health care, better police, better schools, better fire protection, increasing welfare payments. Government itself was demanding a larger and larger share of all earned dollars.

There followed in the jostle the conflict between the great unions and the giant corporations. Terrified by inflation, having watched generous union settlements melt in purchasing power as the value of the dollar itself melted, union leaders were entering 1971 crouched to leapfrog the great inflation with yet higher wage demands, demands that could be met only by huge price rises in the goods their workers made. The nation had just lived through the seventy-one-day General Motors strike, which had won auto workers a 20-percent increase spread over three years, but had squeezed automobile prices up an average of $153 each. A major building boom seemed to be coming, and the construction workers won, early in 1971, raises that astounded even the AFL/CIO powerhouse— in some cases three-year increases of 50 to 60 percent in hourly wage rates. Economic muscle prevailed—while assistant professors of philosophy could be had at salaries of $9,000 a year, electricians, plasterers, sheet-metal workers were demanding, and getting, $20,000 a year.

In this economic power struggle, the vast majority of ordinary unorganized people seemed helpless. For the first time in a decade, so reported economists, there had been no real gain in 1970 in the purchasing power of an average American family. Six percent of all Americans, as 1971 opened, were without work, the highest number in twelve years, 4,600,000 of them, spreading ripples of worry from their families through their communities. Moreover, as joblessness rose, prices went swinging wild—hamburger at ninety-one cents a pound, milk at thirty-two cents a quart, bread at thirty cents a loaf. For twenty-five years, ever since 1946, prices had gone up every year, with the single exception of 1949. But now they seemed about to sprint. The two-cent postage stamp of prewar years had gently risen to three, four, five, then six cents—now the new Postal Service announced it would go to eight cents in 1971. In New York, the nickel subway fare of the postwar years had already gone to thirty cents—and politicians talked of hiking it to fifty cents! And so all across the country—who was in charge?

Ever since Franklin D. Roosevelt, the American people have assumed that the President is, ultimately, in charge of the economy—of bread-and-butter, and of jobs. It was, thus, up to Mr. Nixon to do something—but there, again, his old convictions confronted new reality. His political and cultural faith still held firm for the values of hard work and striving, for the values of free private enterprise, for the sanctity of the balanced budget. The balanced budget was, to him, more than simple politics: "What's a balanced budget worth in terms of votes?" he once asked a White House aide. "Fifty thousand votes in a national election, that's all." But he was for a balanced budget because his tradition insisted on it—as it did on all the other orthodoxies of classical economics.

These orthodoxies, however, had been shaken in his first two years in office. His term had begun, at the height of the war boom, with an unemployment rate of only 3.5 percent and an inflation rate of 4 percent. His withdrawal from Vietnam, the liquidation of the Pentagon's manpower and war burdens, had thrown at least a million war-industry workers out of work. By 1970 his tight credit policies—interest rates on short-term government notes had reached 8 percent, highest since the Civil War—had thrown the world of finance into a tailspin, and the stock market into a panic. Investors had seen the Dow-Jones average peak at 985.21 a month before he took office—and had seen it sag to an eight-year low of 631.16 in May, 1970. By the old theories, economics works like a seesaw contraption: If unemployment goes up, prices go down. But the old theories simply were no longer working—both unemployment *and* prices were going up at the same time. This economic mystery still remains to be clarified, but its political implications were clear in 1970. Early that year, Nixon had told a group of Republican leaders that if he couldn't bring unemployment down below a rate of 5.5 percent, the Republicans would lose in the November elections. He had been right. Unemployment had reached a national level of 5.8 percent in November, 6 percent in December—and the Republicans had lost. Being right was small consolation.

Thus, with his Big Six message of January 1971, Nixon had taken a long step away from his past. As 1971 opened, he was no longer demanding an old orthodox "balanced budget"; he was presenting a "full-employment budget," one infused with the thinking of John Maynard Keynes, the British economist, who felt that one of the chief duties of government was so to adjust its budget, disregarding commercial banking principles, that, if necessary, a planned deficit would result in increased jobs, thus in increased prosperity. The problem was that Keynes, like his predecessor classical economists, had also been outdated in the vast shift in world affairs, the entrance into the world market of so many new forces and claimants, the social changes in Western society. It was obvious by midsummer of 1971 that not even the new Keynesian philosophy was having its anticipated effect on what concerns people most: how to make a living or get along on what they make.

Politics was involved here, politics of the most fundamental nature. "How can you say when a campaign begins?" said John Ehrlichman later. "There's no sharp demarcation line, you just glide into it. . . . The campaign of 1972 began just after the campaign of 1970, some time in 1971, when we were thinking about the State-of-the-Union Message for 1972. It had such heavy political overtones. . . . I remember one session in the Cabinet Room in July, 1971 . . ."

On July 23rd, 1971, there gathered in the Cabinet Room, from two to four in the afternoon, the President's commanders of government, as opposed to the President's lieutenants for politics: the President; John Mitchell, Attorney General; John Connally, Secretary of the Treasury; H. R. Haldeman, John Ehrlichman, Charles Colson; George Shultz and Caspar Weinberger, Director and Deputy Director of the Budget; and several staff personnel. They had assembled for what one of those present called "a conscious political look" at the future. The major briefing officer was Dr. Edwin L. Harper, a section chief in Ehrlichman's Domestic Council, but formerly a professor of the history of the American Presidency at Rutgers University in New Jersey. Harper is non-political and regards his job as a planning exercise in defining four- or five-year goals for the American government, and meshing these longer-range goals with the immediate next year's budget plans. This planning session, said Harper, was not to be an "answer session," but simply a definition for the President of what appeared to be the national problems so that he, the President, could set priorities and concentrate their energies on those problems Nixon, as President, felt he must deal with.

Harper had prepared flip charts and transparent overlays for the President's consideration in a rather ingenious manner—showing what the problems actually were, and also what the public-opinion polls told of how Americans perceived the problems. The problems covered a large range: from the corn blight which threatened that year to wipe out the corn crop (but did not), to the problems of the aged, of veterans, of welfare, of busing. There were the problems on the one hand. And, on the other hand, the public-opinion surveys, Gallup, Harris, Sindlinger, Burns Roper, showing how people perceived them.

When asked what the nation's problems were, people invariably told the polls that the war in Vietnam came first; then crime in the streets; then the national budget; then other matters. But when asked what bothered them, *personally,* they would come up with simpler matters: busing in schools, for example; or the cost of groceries; or how to get along on the paycheck. "There was this inconsistency in the results," said Weinberger; "they all wanted the government to spend less, but they wanted more services for themselves." "It all came down," said Ehrlichman, "to the fact that the overriding issue of 1972 would be the economy."

There it was again—the bread-and-butter issue.

Weinberger, one of whose reading hobbies has been English politics ever since his days as a Harvard undergraduate, had visited England shortly before its 1970 election, in which Edward Heath had confounded predictions by upsetting Prime Minister Harold Wilson. Weinberger observed that it was the sharp spurt in meat prices in the few weeks just before election which had undermined Wilson's lead in all the public-opinion polls and given Heath his victory. The President was caught by that observation and said, "We can't let that happen to us." Later Weinberger observed of the President, "He has these strong convictions like a balanced budget. But he won't ride his philosophy into an area called failure. . . . The simple fact was, and the President was certainly aware of it, and was finally convinced of it, that we couldn't have a do-nothing image. While the philosophy was right, the politics were wrong. So the only counsel was action. A vigorous, activist role was more important than content. Something had to be done to show the people the President was acting. . . ."

The time sequence must be recalled, at this point—eight days earlier the President had announced to the nation his soon-to-come voyage to China, the first visible demonstration of his planning in foreign affairs. The public applause, from both friends and hostile thinkers, had been near unanimous. The boldness of the stroke had given him his first good press reception during the administration. By himself, he had totally reversed the course of American diplomacy—and the nation applauded. Now, once again, he was approaching a similar opportunity—an act of boldness that might reverse a generation of American policy as well as his own earlier-expressed philosophy.

The events of the next three weeks—July 23rd to August 15th—were of a historic order. Politics at home dominated long-range decision. But the immediate thrust came from outside: The postwar world was repudiating the quarter-century reign of the American dollar over world trade. And with it the measure of gold itself. Only by casting a long glance back over history's story of monetary values can one grasp the magnitude of what was about to happen—and how, consciously or unconsciously, Richard Nixon under domestic pressure was about to undo so much of the larger history of the world outside.

This story—of what money is worth—was to end in one of those changes of folk perception which color every major development in American politics. But it could be explained only against the distant background of world trade, which Americans in their power had so long ignored, and which, they were to learn in the next few years, affected the cost of their meat, their gasoline, their coffee. And it began, certainly, with man's oldest and universal measure of value, gold.

From time immemorial, gold, the miser's metal, had been the measure of value of all things, from the bridal dowry to the price of cattle to the worth of land. Gold had reached its peak of authority, however, only in the nineteenth century, the high summer of Western expansion, when the imperial buccaneers of Europe financed the building of the United States and Latin America, subdued Africa, raided Asia and tied all world trade into a global mesh bound by golden strands sacred to commerce. The mythology of gold persisted almost unchallenged until the great Depression of the 1930's, when the gold standard of world bankers brought economic life in the West to despair in the streets. Bankers insisted that all exports and imports, all trading bills, all national currencies must be redeemed in gold—and if a nation could not pay gold for what it needed, then that nation and its people must hunger and go without. The anguish that so cruel a system brought to the world and the effort of nations to escape from its dictation were among the larger factors contributing to World War II.

So it was, then, during the great war against fascism, that the United States, at one of its crests of idealism, invited its allies in July, 1944, to a financial conference at Bretton Woods, New Hampshire, to plan a new, more civilized way of regulating world trade. And with the war over, the new blueprint of world trade was accepted not only by the victors, but was offered to and accepted by the vanquished powers, Germany and Japan.

One must grasp how far-reaching were these postwar agreements to understand how sweeping a change Nixon was now, in 1971, about to propose. In simplest terms, the agreements of the postwar world had tried to make free trade work by pegging the value of every other currency in the world to the U.S. dollar. Other nations' money might fluctuate in value with the tides of world trade, but they would fluctuate only in relation to each other, while at the center stood the U.S. dollar, rigid, its strength firmly socketed in gold. If anywhere in the world a trading firm could convert yen, francs, marks or pounds into dollars, then those dollars, as of yore, could be converted via their central banks into solid gold by draft on the United States.

The system worked magnificently, but it worked because of a condition that the rest of the world and the United States both misunderstood: the episode of American power. America had emerged from the war against fascism with such a passing dominance of world trade as no other power had ever known before. Whether it was food, meat, grain, computers, aircraft, machinery, medicinals, sulfur, metals, coal or electronics, the United States was incomparably supreme.

Not only was it supreme, it was generous. To help the rest of the world achieve a new trading stability, the United States not only gave away $45 billion in civilian aid (in addition to $100 billion in military aid), but down into the 1960's it continued to urge all other nations to compete with the United States in trading, invited them to learn American technologies, encouraged them to invade its home markets. So strong was America in those days that its overpowering investment in science and fundamental research was thrown open to the entire world. Uncle Sam sat like a winning poker player at the head of the table, giving away chips to the losers, even tipping his hand when necessary just to keep the game going.

Not until the late 1960's did it become obvious that something was going wrong with this game. For one thing, the brains, science and gift of innovation on which Americans had preened themselves were no longer a magic limited to America alone; others had penetrated and mastered the magic, too. Not only were such low-wage U.S. industries as shoes, textiles and garments now being imperiled by foreign competitors. So, too, was the U.S. steel industry—pressed by European and Japanese exports. So, too, was the proud aviation industry. So, too, was the electronics industry—and the United States, which had pioneered both radio and television, found its markets dominated by imports selling below any possibility of competition. By 1971 the manufacture of black-and-white television sets in the United States had all but ceased; and major U.S. manufacturers of radios and color sets were, in many instances, simply assemblers of Asian-made components. The same situation threatened the camera industry. Even more unsettling was the threat to the U.S. automobile industry, the most vigorous and quintessentially American industry. That industry had absorbed the first penetration of the German Volkswagen soon after the war; then absorbed the invasion of its markets by French, Italian and British products. But in 1971 it was being punished savagely by an exponential jump in imports of cheap Japanese automobiles. From an import total of 63,000 cars in 1966, the Japanese had pushed the total to 415,000 in 1970, and in early 1971 Japanese cars were entering at a rate of 700,000 a year! Imports were costing jobs, and foreign competition was becoming a prime concern of American labor.

The over-all story told itself in starker figures. Ever since 1893 the United States had always earned more by selling abroad than it paid out for what it bought. In 1964 its trading surplus had reached a peak of over $7 billion. Then, slowly, it began to shrink. By 1970, the second year of the Nixon administration, the trading balance had shrunk to $2.7 billion—$42.7 billion of American exports as against $40 billion of imports.

And then, in 1971, affairs turned as if on a hinge. In April, 1971, a morbid figure was posted—the first monthly deficit in trading balance in two years. Perhaps just a fluctuation. In May came a repeat—another deficit, the first two-month-in-a-row deficit in twenty-two years. In June came another deficit. In July, a fourth. And the Secretary of Commerce warned the nation that for the first time since the nation had ceased being a colony of European finance in the 1890's, it appeared that the United States would have a trade deficit for the whole year.

Already the speculators of the world had taken notice of what was happening. The United States had once held a gold hoard which, at its peak postwar high, reached $25 billion in glimmering, hard metal. That had dropped by mid-1971 to $10.5 billion. Now, as inflation surged in the United States, as cheap foreign imports flooded in, as foreign banks claimed redemption of hot dollars in cold gold, how long could the United States, from its shrinking hoard, afford to redeem dollars in gold, as the Bretton Woods conference had ordained?

A first ripple of panic had come in claims against the dollar in early May of 1971, and been overcome by concerted international action. Now, in late July and early August, renewed panic, stimulated by the American trade deficits, was proving irrepressible. Great American corporations with multi-national accounts were transferring huge sums from country to country, getting out of their own dollars into foreign currencies. International art dealers were, suddenly, refusing to accept payment for treasures in dollars and insisting on Swiss or German marks. In the first week of August, 1971, the Bank of France was forced to receive approximately $300 million dumped on it by French traders for redemption. On Friday of the following week the Belgian National Bank alone received $11 million of dumped dollars. The Bank of Japan was forced by its traders to cover first $600 million and then $690 million on successive days. And all these dollars, dumped by frightened traders on their own central banks, were claims on the rapidly shrinking gold stock of the United States. Later Mr. Nixon was to say that if he had not acted to save the dollar on the weekend of August 14th–15th, 1971, there would have been no dollar left to save.

On the second weekend of August he had to act. And if he were to act, the quality of his mind dictated that he should not go about matters piecemeal. All the counsel he had received over the previous six months was beginning to add up. If one were forced to perform major surgery on the American economy, it might just as well be very major; he should be bold.

Thus, on Friday, August 13th, Richard Nixon summoned an economic-political council to join him at Camp David on the next day: Secretary of the Treasury and Under Secretary for Monetary Affairs, John Connally and Paul Volcker. Assistant to the President for International Economic Affairs, Peter G. Peterson. The President's economic wise men: Paul McCracken, George Shultz, Arthur Burns. Haldeman and Ehrlichman, of course. And speechwriter William Safire, who would draft a statement to be made to the nation on Monday night.

But it became at once clear that Monday night would be too late for a statement—Under Secretary Volcker, a long, lean man who did the briefing on the monetary situation, reported ashen-faced that he had heard from the British Treaury that morning that it expected to be hit with redemptions of no less than $3 billion within the next week! If decision were delayed or postponed until Monday night, the gold stock of the United States might not outlast Monday. The United States could either be forced to repudiate its gold pledge or, by itself, on its own initiative, declare that the dollar was no longer redeemable in gold and that the age of gold was over.

Others spoke. John Connally, Secretary of the Treasury, was political: The inflation at home was becoming a disastrous political liability. Arthur Burns, Chairman of the Federal Reserve Board, spoke. Burns was one of Nixon's oldest friends, not only an outstanding economist but a man of politics and philosophy. He had observed publicly only a few weeks earlier that "the old rules no longer work"—a terse summing up of a thoughtful man's reflections on a quarter-century of economic change. He had embittered his old friend, the President, shortly before the meeting, by insisting that there must be an "incomes" policy in America, for the paradox of rising unemployment and rising prices defied all previous economic theory. Burns and the President had had a heated session only a few short weeks before, after Burns's public remarks, in which Burns had said to the President, "I'm the best friend you've got, you're drowning, I'm giving you the best advice I can." Nixon had not liked any of it—he had thought of Burns as a member of his political family.

Now, though, the interlocking of events had made the President ready not only to accept the advice of Burns, of Connally, of Peterson, of his action men on every domestic front—but ready to wrap up all their advice in one package, and that very evening.

At seven in the evening of Saturday, the all-day session broke up, with speechwriter William Safire directed to draft a speech in which the President would announce to the world the closing of "the gold window," the stanching of the dollar hemorrhage. Waking early Sunday, after working until three A.M., Safire went to deliver his draft to the typists— only to discover that the President had preceded him. The President had risen at four A.M., and written notes on both sides of three sheets of a yellow legal pad. He had then dictated into a dictaphone exactly how he felt the sequence of his notes should go, and delivered the dictagram to the typists at six A.M. The typists were ready with the President's raw copy when Safire arrived with his own draft at seven. And the President's own draft swept the board clean. From it, after Safire's refinement, he would deliver a statement to the nation on Sunday at 9:00 P.M. E.D.T. There would be no delay for Monday delivery.

The speech of August 15th, 1971, which the President holds to have been one of the six critical steps in his re-election, was, above all, political in the sense that politics is to do what the people want. The people were frightened about bread-and-butter and paychecks; he was about to act, and give leadership. Technically, it was a closely reasoned seven-point proposal.[3] Of these seven proposals, two lifted the speech far beyond politics into the realm of history.

The proposal that America stop redeeming its dollars with gold remains even now, two years later, too large to be evaluated with full historical perspective, except as another marker in the passage of the world from one era to another. If the United States, as the President declared, refused to yield an ounce of gold for $35, what then was any money worth? Anywhere. Did money have a real value, or only the value a government said it had? On the new quick-closing globe, how could merchants, or businessmen, or tourists, or students, or planners make contact

[3] The seven points, summarized, ran as follows: First, an investment credit tax for industry to galvanize efficient plant development, hence more jobs. Second, lifting the Federal excise tax of 7 percent on American automobiles, the country's queen industry. Third, as a sop to the liberals, an increase of $50 in personal tax exemptions. Fourth, a proposed $4.7 billion cut in Federal spending. Fifth, a ninety-day freeze on wages and prices. Sixth, an end to the free conversion of dollars into gold. Seventh, an additional 10-percent tax on imports.

with each other across national boundaries for exchange? The outside world had pressed the United States off gold, and thus off the world's most ancient measure of value. What would replace it?

The proposal to impose wage and price controls on American life was equally stunning. This was not simply a rupture with all past Republican philosophy, the businessman's ethic which held that free play of market forces brought, over the long run, the greatest good to the greatest number of people. It was a rupture with all American economic history, a rupture as great as that which Roosevelt, thirty-six years before, had forced on American thinking.

Roosevelt had curbed the free-enterprise system by insisting that the rules of investment, and hence the terms of American growth, must be brought under the control of a Federal agency. Now Nixon had gone even further. Americans had previously accepted price controls and wage controls during war. But Nixon advanced and imposed the right of the government to control even in peacetime the relationship of earnings, spendings, prices in every American family across the land. With this right, so boldly assumed, he had also assumed an inescapable responsibility for every future American government. Henceforth all American governments would have to face judgment by the people on the proper relationship of paycheck to the price tabulator at the supermarket. *"Rien ne dure que le provisoire,"* say the French—"Nothing lasts as long as the makeshift." Nixon had offered a makeshift, transitory response to a problem of bread-and-butter, because politically he could not do otherwise. The outside world and the inside politics had compelled him. But in so doing he had opened a new chapter of American history. The postwar world was thoroughly over, at home as abroad, at the meat counter as in Vietnam.

Nixon had acted. He had given the people a sense of "control" by their government. He had scored heavily by his action on China; he scored even more heavily by his decisions of August, 1971. Shortly, the polls of public opinion would turn up for him; and since a major boom was to follow his August decisions, good jobs and relatively stable prices would sustain the polls with popular approval. He would not have to campaign, as he had in 1960 and 1970, against rising economic distress. Of the three great traditional issues—foreign policy, economics and race —Nixon had now made positively clear where he stood on the first two; and he would, in due time, make clear where he stood on the third.

It was up to the Democrats, now, to deliver something as clear, as understandable, as the Nixon policies to the voters who would choose a President in 1972.

CHAPTER FOUR

THE DEMOCRATIC PRIMARIES: A PARTY IN SEARCH OF IDENTITY

THE idea of Presidential primary elections is so naturally tailored to the American experience in democracy that no one can name its father or date its origins—except that it was born before the turn of this century somewhere "out west," as a periodic wave of American restlessness came to crest in the Populist-Progressive movement. People, ordinary people—so ran the thought—should have the right to go into closed voting booths and there accept or repudiate the party bosses in naming the party's candidates to govern them.

American Progressives had already beaten this idea into the public law of various states when, in the first ten years of this century, four states vied for the honor of translating the idea of citizen participation *within* their party to the higher level of Presidential politics. Florida in 1901, Wisconsin in 1905, Pennsylvania in 1906, Oregon in 1910 were the first—and with the clash of Theodore Roosevelt and the Republican stalwarts in 1912, nine more states added the device of a Presidential primary to party politics.[1] But the device seemed little more than that, as local and ideological insurrectionaries for a generation thereafter explored the primaries as corridors to national power, and failed. The politics of Presidential power in both parties remained in the hands of established leadership—men who commanded local power, cross-country connections, money and alliances; men who could influence the press to create a climate of opinion, or control structures that could deliver votes.

[1] See James W. Davis, *Presidential Primaries: Road to the White House* (New York: Thomas Y. Crowell, 1967), an excellent account of primaries and their history.

Until 1952. And then, in that year, the campaign leaders of Dwight D. Eisenhower finally managed to ignite the real explosive in the concept of popular party primaries. Winning the New Hampshire primary against the established leadership of Robert Taft's conservatives, and then running second to Minnesota's Harold Stassen, the favorite son, by an astonishing write-in of 108,692 votes in that state, Eisenhower achieved a political momentum that carried him to the Republican convention and nomination in July. Ever since then the primaries have been the great *mano-a-mano* tournaments of election year, creating heroes and Presidents, leaving behind as victims some of the most famous names of their times, signaling hitherto unperceived underswellings in American life. It was in the West Virginia primary of 1960 that John F. Kennedy made a bonfire of the totems of anti-Catholic prejudice. The primaries of 1964 destroyed Barry Goldwater, by the exposure of his ideas across the nation. The primaries of 1968 forced the wind-down of the Vietnam war as first Eugene McCarthy, then Robert Kennedy illuminated the disgust of Americans with the war in Asia.

Primaries had already thus become, by 1972, one of the great drive engines of American politics—for a primary is a deed. All else in politics, except money, is words—comment, rhetoric, analysis, polls. But a primary victory is a fact. There is a hardness to such a fact, especially if the victory is a contested one. With the lift of such an event, a candidate can compel attention, build votes, change minds. It is the underdog's classic route to power in America.

In 1972, however, primaries were to be different—and more exciting than ever before. They were to stretch four months; they were to be crowded with some of the ablest fighters in party history; they were to unroll not as episodes, but as a continuum, punctuated by public tears, gunfire, triumphs and upheaval under new rules of power. At one time, no less than fifteen Democrats had announced their candidacies for the nomination of 1972, of whom at least twelve took themselves seriously. And of these, by the year's opening, at least six had to be taken seriously by everyone—namely, Edmund Muskie of Maine, George McGovern of South Dakota, Hubert Humphrey of Minnesota, John Lindsay of New York, Henry Jackson of Washington, and George Wallace of Alabama. Moreover, in 1972 no less than twenty-two states and the District of Columbia announced Presidential primaries, a third more than in 1968; and from those states would come slightly more than 60 percent of the delegates to the convention of 1972 as against only 40 percent in 1968. The season would stretch from the opener in New Hampshire on March 7th, through to New York on June 20th. And what had been conceived of, at the turn of the century, as a simple device to let people have their say within their party would become a continental confusion that defied any reasonable attempt to summarize procedures.[2]

There was to be, and with solid cause, a year-long outcry of the concerned that the new system, pure as was its intent, was in practice a denial of Americans' right of a clear choice between clear alternatives. Some advocated a single national primary; others advocated a series of regional primaries; others again advocated a series of primaries clustered not by regions, but by fixed monthly dates. The dominant opinion of most wise men agreed that the crazy, accidental, fragmented pattern of selecting candidates state by state, a different set of laws governing each state, could be made reasonable only by a single national law governing all primaries.

All such criticism was, of course, valid, and the need for a new national law inescapable. Yet when all was said, there remained in the bizarre primary process, as there remained in so many curious American institutions, a value which defied rigorous analysis. This value could be described most simply as the value of narrative instruction, which is the best kind of instruction. Primaries tell a story. They last for months, spotted with drama and clash, and as they move across the nation and the front pages, the story teaches the nation about the candidates. The physical-endurance contest strains them to the limit of their nerves and vitality, and the nation sees how they behave under stress. The candi-

[2] There were almost as many kinds of primary as there were primaries in 1972. Some (called "delegate primaries") actually elected the delegates. Some (called "preferential primaries") allowed the voters to indicate whom they would like their delegates to support at the convention. Some preferential primaries (called "binding") went further and obliged the delegates—however chosen—to support the specific candidates favored in the primary. Many states had both a delegate and a preferential primary.

In 1972 twenty-two states held primaries, and the variety of ways in which they did so was one of the more breathtaking displays of the ingenuity of political man. In South Dakota and California you voted all or nothing for a complete slate of delegates pledged to a single candidate. You could not tell from the ballot who the delegates were, only whom they would—en bloc—vote for at the convention. In New York, on the other hand, you voted by name for anywhere from four to eight individual delegates, with no clue on the ballot as to whom *they* would vote for.

In Oregon, candidates for delegate ran in one primary committed, it said on the ballot, to one or another of the Presidential candidates. But at the convention they would be obliged to vote, not for the candidate to whom they were committed, but to the winner of the separate preferential primary. In Rhode Island 143 candidates ran in a delegate primary committed mostly to Muskie, Humphrey and Jackson. None was committed to McGovern. But because McGovern won the preferential primary, he got to choose the entire delegation.

It was, ironically, the gymnastics of the Democratic New Mexico legislature, trying to design a primary to satisfy the Democratic guidelines, which deprived Richard Nixon of a unanimous vote for renomination in Miami Beach. By getting 6 percent of the New Mexico Republican primary vote, California Congressman Paul McCloskey earned one of the states' fourteen votes at the Republican convention. It was the only vote there which could not be cast for the President.

dates' choice of staff is tested, and the staffs' quality tested, too. Most of all, as the candidates prod and poke, seeking for nerve ends of response, the initial ping of applause from friendly audiences and the negative pong of derision from enemies tell them which issues touch nerves and what bothers people. Thus the nature of the Presidential contest slowly defines itself in the common talk of bars, shops, lunchrooms, breakfasts, parlors, cocktail parties, union meetings.

All this was to happen, as before, in the primary season of 1972, and the drama of individuals was to fascinate. Overriding even such individual dramas, however, was the towering drama of the Democratic Party itself, the nation's oldest and most vigorous political institution, bewildered by the decade of the seventies and groping for a new identity.

To understand the drama of the Democrats, one must simplify the fundamental story of American political life in the twentieth century— the history that baldly reveals that throughout the twentieth century the Democratic Party has been the chief vehicle of American action.

Foreshortened, the history of American parties as it came down to Americans, whether by schoolbook or by word of mouth, in the year 1972 read something like this: The century began with the last Republican President who believed in action—Theodore Roosevelt. Roosevelt believed in trust-busting, big navy, saving the land and the forests, winning wars. But after Teddy Roosevelt the spirit perished among Republicans; nothing happened again until Woodrow Wilson, Democrat, an action man—who broke up the money bosses, forced the big banks into a Federal Reserve System, put through railway retirement laws and a federal income tax, fought the Germans and won a war. Then followed three Republican Presidents—Harding, Coolidge and Hoover; again nothing happened. Then came Democrat Franklin Roosevelt—and Wall Street was tamed, unions were fostered, farms were saved, unemployed went back to work; Roosevelt fought the Germans, too, and he won. Action. Then came Harry Truman, Democrat; he moved on civil rights, launched the Marshall Plan and NATO, fought in Korea and all but won there. Action. Then came Dwight D. Eisenhower, Republican—and nothing happened. Then came Kennedy and Johnson—elegance and gusto. Missile crisis and test-ban treaty. Urban renewal and civil rights, tax reductions and the Great Society. Action.

Except that a good deal of the action in the 1960's had gone on in two places where the results had been disastrous—in Vietnam and the big cities of America.

Republicans, of course, would object to this description of American politics in the twentieth century. They would point out, first of all, that every one of the great action Presidents of the Democratic line— Wilson, Roosevelt, Truman, Johnson—had plunged America into a war.

They would point out, further, that Richard Nixon in the last six months of his third year had matched any of his predecessors in dramatic action and was accelerating his rhythm as the election approached.

Yet in the minds of Democratic leaders, and in the emotions of their constituency, their party remained the classic party of the people's action. In a perfect world, the Democratic primaries of 1972 would, therefore, have defined the course of action that the party should take. Kennedy had made the party's theme his personal call in the campaign of 1960, chanting, "I say this country must move again." But that was long ago. Now, in 1972, all Democratic candidates still wanted the country to move again, away from the direction of Richard Nixon—except that, collectively, they could not identify an agreed way to move, nor agree on the shape the party would give the nation if brought back to power. Action had made the Democrats almost everywhere the local majority party; and since action and change are always good themes, most Americans still habitually voted Democratic locally, as they would again for Senate and Congress in November of the Presidential year.

But when one tried to add up all the local Democratic majorities into a national majority, a national program, a national leader—how would it go?

One name was, of course, the commanding name in the Democratic Party as 1972 opened—Kennedy.

The name of Senator Edward M. Kennedy of Massachusetts, last of the great Kennedy brothers, imposed itself on all political conversation. He had been politically wounded in July of 1969 when, after a late-night party, he had taken the wrong turn on a dark road on the island of Chappaquiddick, plunged his automobile from a bridge, then left the scene of the accident; and the young lady he had been escorting had drowned. The incident scarred the Kennedy legend and his own career—but Teddy Kennedy remained one of the smartest politicians and, without challenge, the most romantic figure in his party. The nomination was his for the asking, at any time. Kennedy, however, was flatly honest about his intentions. Publicly and privately he told the same story: he was not about to run in 1972, he would not even attend the Democratic convention. He felt his education in foreign affairs, in domestic policy, was incomplete; he was content to remain in the Senate for four or eight more years, he said, "to get a handle on things." Only once did he privately waver. I called on him in late April, in Boston, at a moment when the Wallace surge in the primaries was rising. It was faintly conceivable, he said, that if it looked, at the convention, as though George Wallace might get the nomination, he would have to go down to the floor to oppose him—Wallace stood for everything against which his two brothers had fought. But even at the peak of the Wallace surge, this thought seemed remote to Kennedy. He did not want to run, would not run, would support the party's nominee whoever it was, except Wallace.

Only romantics and amateurs took a Kennedy candidacy in 1972 seriously. All realists, all practical politicians, almost all reporters and political writers agreed that, with Kennedy out of it, the leading Democratic candidate for the Presidency was Edmund Sixtus Muskie, junior Senator and ex-Governor of the State of Maine.

Everyone said so, and Muskie himself believed it. The polls showed it: In the Harris Poll, in January of 1972, Nixon ran 42, Muskie 42, Wallace 11. In the same poll, Nixon ran 46 against Humphrey's 37. Even if one cast all the various Democratic candidates into a trial free-for-all, as did the Gallup Poll in January, 1972, it came out: Muskie 32, Kennedy 27, Humphrey 17 (and George McGovern 3). For journalists like this writer, there was only the annoying problem of how to make Edmund Muskie, that grave, Lincolnesque man of goodwill, interesting—how to spin excitement out of a nomination story which he apparently had foreclosed.

Muskie's life was, of course, exciting if one examined it as American folklore. His father, a Polish immigrant named Stephen Marciszewski, had settled in Rumford, Maine, a paper-mill town of 7,000 people, before Ed Muskie was born. Ed Muskie remembered his father with that affection which comes later to sons when they begin to understand the sorrows and strivings of their parents. The elder Muskie had taught himself to read English; had been a good tailor; had never been on relief; he had held the family warm and sheltered together through the hard times with the help of his wife. But the Depression seared young Ed, and by the time he entered Bates College in Maine (the only one of the six Muskie children the family could afford to send to college) Ed was a Democrat, even before he could vote. In his senior year, at the graduation reception at Bates, as Senator Muskie recalled thirty years later, the college president, a pompous, old-style educator, singled out young Ed in the receiving line. His class had chosen Edmund Muskie class president—and the college president simply wanted to know whether it was true, as he had heard, that Ed Muskie was a Democrat. It was shocking. But it was true.

From Bates to Cornell Law School, on scholarship. From Cornell Law School, home to Maine to practice law for a year, then off to the Navy and war; and home again to hang out his shingle in Waterville, in a meager practice. So that when the local Democratic politicians came to ask him in 1946 to run for the legislature because they were looking for young war veterans, Muskie accepted, and won. And then on and up: to become a good Governor, with a balanced budget, a clean record. Then, to Washington as Senator, in the Democratic tidal wave of 1958.

Yet Muskie remained forever shaped by his Maine experience. If you ran as a Democrat in a Maine primary, you faced no serious opposition in your own party; you ran always so as not to scare the good Yankee Protestants on the Republican side. You ran as a middle-roader, as a responsible. The thing was to establish trust in you as a man, and then, in a good society, you won all your own Democrats, naturally, plus enough decent Republicans who trusted you to give you a majority. Muskie could say, out of his own life, "I have an ancestral belief in this system. I inherited it from my father. I'm a man of the center, but the center gradually moves left, and it's the Democratic Party that does it."

The political image of a moderate thus fitted naturally when Muskie was tailored for it as Hubert Humphrey's Vice-Presidential running-mate in the campaign of 1968—and hardened into public style when he was catapulted into front-runner for 1972 by his Election Eve speech in the mid-term elections of 1970. Nixon and Agnew had campaigned that fall against violence, against demonstrators, against drugs, against college youth, and the Republicans had set the President up for an extraordinarily poor telecast on Election Eve, at his shrillest. Muskie directly followed Nixon on the air, quiet, self-possessed, and accused Nixon and the Republicans of name-calling, slander and the questioning of Democrats' patriotism. "That is a lie," he said, and continued, ". . . the American people know it is a lie. . . . There is not time tonight to analyze and expose the torrent of falsehood and insinuation which has flooded this unfortunate campaign. . . . They really believe that if they can make you afraid enough, or angry enough, you can be tricked into voting against yourself. . . . There are only two kinds of politics . . . the politics of fear and the politics of trust. One says: you are encircled by monstrous dangers. . . . The other says: the world is a baffling and hazardous place, but it can be shaped to the will of men. . . . Thus in voting for the Democratic Party tomorrow you cast your vote for trust . . . for trusting your fellow citizens . . . and most of all for trust in yourself."

Underneath this image of the grave moderate were, however, two essential qualities not yet recognized by the public but more than casually troublesome to Muskie's staff. He had a tendency to emotional outburst; and an even graver disability—a lawyer-like, ponderous way of dealing with all issues and even the most trivial decisions.

His staff recognized these qualities as hazards. They enjoyed telling stories about Muskie. He disliked the press and could be quoted vividly describing the press's shortfalls. Muskie was a man of old moralities. Once when he was picketed at an early campaign meeting by a group of Gay Liberationists, he exploded to his staff: "Goddam it, if I've got to be nice to a bunch of sodomites to be elected President, then f--- it." At another time, the staff had supplied to him, unread in advance, a speech on Medicare to be delivered to a New York gathering of specialists in ileitis and gastritis. Muskie had struggled through the awful prose, making the worst of it, and then told his staff, "For God's sake, let the newspapermen know that I don't write that kind of stuff myself." He had a fine sense of humor which would become evident only on the downside of the campaign later.

What bothered his staff more was his almost abnormal insistence on thinking things through, a habit of taking many too many matters seriously. He could impress his advisers by absorbing a four-hour briefing on the intricacies of the SALT negotiations before his trip to Moscow, along with the exotic thinking that goes into maintaining the balance of terror, and then summarizing it with exact precision. But in answering public questions, he could not bring himself to the hard one-sentence response, followed by the thinking. Instead, he insisted always on answering a question by starting with the thinking, the pros and the cons, the balance of judgment as a judge would give it, then, finally, his conclusions—and the long, conditioned, legalistic answers turned off press, TV and college audiences. Nothing in the campaign, he felt, must trap him with a phrase, or a commitment, or an inflammation of emotion that would hobble him in governing once he was elected.

This sense of responsibility, this semi-governmental quality of caution and double-talk, conditioned all thinking at the Muskie headquarters in Washington, at 1972 K Street. Indeed, to embittered field workers of the Muskie campaign, the headquarters—which they called the Taj Mahal—was the greatest burden the campaign bore. The Taj Mahal staff absorbed more money each month (some salaries running as high as $40,000 a year) than George McGovern was spending on his entire nationwide campaign. The staff sounded like a government; its routine of approvals, intelligence, layers and levels of responsibility were, in fact, almost a government, with all the slow, cumbersome initialing of documents and proposals before action; and, indeed, its constituency was government, those Democrats across the nation who actually governed.

Already by the fall of 1971, headquarters had an issues staff and a speechwriting staff; it had a full-blown media staff; it had a youth division, a women's division, a black division. It had an organization staff headed by two of the best field operators in the business, John F. (Jack) English of New York and Mark Shields of Massachusetts. These two directors claimed personnel were already in place in each of the twenty-three primary states of the nation, and in most of the non-primary states, too. Superimposed on these staffs was a council of Democratic elder statesmen who advised the candidate on national policy at the highest level. The names of these statesmen glittered—Clark Clifford, adviser to Presidents Truman, Kennedy, Johnson; James Rowe, adviser to all these Presidents and Franklin D. Roosevelt as well; Averell Harriman, the country's most celebrated living diplomat, onetime Governor of New York; and others. "Headquarters was our enemy," said one of the field coordinators later; "no matter what proposal you sent in, the answer was always there'll be time to make that decision later."

Later, in the melancholy days of the Wisconson primary, Muskie on the stump would tell a Polish joke, without realizing how tightly it fitted his campaign. Two Polish workingmen, so the story ran, were working on a house. Says Mike to Joe, "Joe, listen, if you were going to build a house, would you start from the roof or the foundation?" Then Joe, after a moment's pause, says, "I think I'd start with the foundation." "If that's so," replies Mike, "then come down from the roof and let's start digging a foundation." The Muskie campaign was 90 percent up on the roof, while George McGovern was digging foundations.

The strategy of the campaign, as it had been conceived in the summer of 1971, in a working paper approved by Muskie just before Labor Day of that year, was called the "high-risk" strategy. Muskie would spend most of the fall of 1971 as a low-visibility candidate perfecting organization and raising money. Then, starting in 1972, he would enter not one, or several, or a half-dozen symbolic primaries—he would go for broke, entering them all, North, South and West. Admittedly, this was high-risk—high-risk in money; high-risk in candidate's time and physical strain; above all, the risk of spreading personnel and energy so thin across the country that none of the states along the long corridor could be adequately dealt with. Yet the rationale was simple: Muskie was a national candidate, a government candidate, a centrist—not an ideologue. He was a man for all people.

The operational tactics of the campaign fitted this strategy, and the name of the tactical game was "endorsements." All across the country the Democrats as a national party were a governing party; they controlled the state legislatures in California, Connecticut, Maryland, Massachusetts, Michigan, Pennsylvania, Missouri, Texas, Florida, the South; they held 29 of the 50 Governorships; they controlled all the big-city Mayoralties except Cleveland and Indianapolis. To line up such governing Democrats, with all their power, behind the moderate ex-Governor of Maine seemed the course of wisdom; and with enormous diligence and shrewdness, Muskie and staff went about their job.

By January of 1972, the parade of endorsements from the established leadership of the party had become so crowded that one of the chief problems was sequencing their dates with enough separation to get maximum press impact. In Missouri, a feud-ridden Democratic party had been so deftly courted that all three rival Democratic leaders, Senators Symington and Eagleton and Governor Warren Hearnes, had jointly agreed to support Muskie. "Neutrality is my enemy" was Muskie's selling pitch, as he urged the power-brokers to declare themselves now, when it was useful to him, not later when he had the nomination locked up. And so they came: Senators Tunney of California and Stevenson of Illinois; then came Governors Gilligan (Ohio), Ford (Kentucky), Curtis (Maine), Scott (North Carolina), Andrus (Idaho), Shapp (Pennsylvania), Rampton (Utah) and others. Then, Senators Hughes, McIntyre, Williams, Moss, Hart, Metcalf, Burdick, Church.

So, too, did many of the liberals of the 1968 insurrection: Anne Wexler and Joseph Duffey of Connecticut, Jack English and Harold Ickes of New York, Donald Peterson of Wisconsin, Stephen Reinhardt and Martin Stone of California. These were the pragmatic liberals— they wanted a winner who could beat Nixon, and Muskie seemed likeliest to do so.

Superficially, in January of 1972, the firepower lined up behind Muskie's candidacy seemed overwhelming. Labor, to be sure, was holding back—Humphrey and Jackson were clearly more to George Meany's taste. But labor was anything but hostile; Leonard Woodcock of the automobile workers as well as Jerry Wurf of the government workers were openly backing Muskie, and even the governing autocrat of the AFL/CIO was prepared to live with Muskie if the party picked him.

There was Polish power, too. The Polish immigration at the turn of the century had settled mostly on the shores of the Great Lakes and along the tracks of the Pennsylvania Railroad. Muskie was sensitive about using his Polish background; but his staff made full use of what they called "Polish charisma," scheduling him into screaming audiences in Buffalo, Toledo, Detroit, Pittsburgh, Chicago and Milwaukee. Of the first six primaries on the calendar, only one (Florida) failed to give him the edge either of Yankee regionalism (New Hampshire, Massachusetts) or a significant Polish element in the electorate (Wisconsin, Illinois, Pennsylvania).

So, as 1972 began and the battle lines hardened, Muskie's campaign seemed irresistible. He had solid financial backing, a large and experienced staff, the endorsement of the party's leading figures, the advice of the party sages, the affirmation of the nation's pollsters. But if Muskie was long at the bank and on the letterhead, he was short, depressingly short, in ideas. "To this day," said campaign coordinator Jack English after it was all over, "I don't know what the campaign was all about. We never had a theme." Berl Bernhard, staff director, explained it more precisely as 1972 began: "We aren't going to hit the issues, that could hurt him organizationally; we aren't going to reach for headlines." Muskie would be all things to all men—until he became President.

The campaign flowed from the personality of Edmund Muskie and his perception of the Americans. In December of 1971, one morning in

Boston we talked again. He was steadfast. The country was coming into a time of trouble; the country didn't trust Nixon; the problems were immense. ("That busing problem, now," he said, "there's a son-of-a-bitch. I don't know what the answer is.") But he, Muskie, knew where he was going. "The next President has got to have the confidence of the people to permit him to pose the hard choices. My first task in these primaries is to establish my own credibility. Whether I can deepen or broaden it—that's the real challenge. I've got primaries all over the nation, and our political strategy has got to be credibility. You can't force hard choices on them before the nomination. Eisenhower had trust, he was a war hero; he could have asked the American people to do anything and they would have done it. After the nomination, after they trust me, that's the time to make them bite on the bullet."

The slogans everywhere read the same: "Trusty Muskie." So did his primary speeches. There were hard times coming, he would say; we had to live together; Nixon had promised to bring us together, but we were still divided. Let us live together. "I remember when I was a Polish boy living on the other side of the railway tracks. . . . Today other people live on the other side of the railway tracks. . . . We are all Americans. . . ." And: "Hope . . . for two centuries America has represented hope. . . . It's hope that brought other people here." People would listen to a Muskie speech attentively as he began; then rustle and shuffle their feet; and their attention would wane. Trust, without substance, was difficult to sell.

And always, as Muskie campaigned through January and February, raising money at dinners, soliciting donations privately, stumping from coast to coast, editing and sifting the papers of his staff which poured on him in Presidential torrent—always there he was, trapped on the one hand by Richard Nixon, who was about to fly to China and then dominate the airwaves with that story, and on the other hand by George McGovern, who was plodding through the snows of New Hampshire, sniffing the aromas of shoe factories, shaking hands with the clerks in the stores, encouraging his volunteers. George McGovern would spend twenty-four days in New Hampshire before the primary; Muskie could give it only thirteen—for his was an all-state, all-risk campaign. Absence, thought Muskie, might cost him three or four percentile points in the New Hampshire primary—but what he lost there he would gain in Florida, where already he had twenty-six offices and had invested $375,000; or in Wisconsin, or Pennsylvania, or California.

Muskie had entered the year bolstered by local polls which set his mark at 65 percent of the New Hampshire vote, yet confronted by newspapermen who, accepting the victory as he did, were now off on the clinical questioning that so annoyed him. Would a vote of under 65 percent be a defeat? What did he set as his private victory mark? If he did under 60 percent, what would he do next?

Such questions were difficult to answer, for New Hampshire was changing as the nation changed and becoming unpredictable. There were three New Hampshires, really. New Hampshire north of the Merrimack and reaching to the Canadian border was still Yankee-Protestant-Republican, with pockets of Democratic votes only in university towns like Hanover, or French-Canadian mill-working towns like Berlin—that remained unchanged. Then there was Manchester and its suburbs, the industrial center of the state, where Democrats were Irish or French Catholics who worked hard, for low wages, in the mills and shoe and electronic factories. The blue-collar vote was unstable in 1972, but Manchester should be Muskie country. Then, finally, there was New Hampshire south of Manchester, reaching to the Massachusetts border— suburban country whose citizens, mostly educated middle-class, were newcomers from the Boston metropolis, tuned in to the Boston media and the national concern. If Muskie were to do well, he must do it in the north country and industrial Manchester; in changing suburbia George McGovern's volunteers were at their strongest.

The slippage of the Muskie lead in New Hampshire was first noticed in February. A virtuoso piece of one-man front-porch doorbell-ringing reporting by the Washington *Post*'s national correspondent David Broder was followed by a major poll of the Boston *Globe*—and both reported the same thing. People were willing to trust Muskie, but were asking, again and again, trust Muskie for what? What did he mean? What was he all about? And they were wavering. The slippage was thus already quite visible when an episode speeded it up. The Manchester *Union Leader,* practitioner of a style of knife-and-kill journalism that went out of fashion half a century ago in the rest of the country, is the primary daily paper of 40 percent of New Hampshire's population; it had been savaging Muskie for months before, in late February, it began on Muskie's outspoken wife, Jane, and followed with the publication of a spurious letter purportedly describing Muskie as laughing at a description of French Canadians ("Canucks") as New Hampshire blacks.

"That previous week," said Muskie after his campaign was all over, "I'd been down to Florida, then I flew to Idaho, then I flew to California, then I flew back to Washington to vote in the Senate, and I flew back to California, and then I flew into Manchester and I was hit with this 'Canuck' story. I'm tough physically, but no one could do that— it was a bitch of a day. The staff thought I should go down to the *Union Leader* to reply to that story. If I were going to do it again, I'd look for a campaign manager, a genius, a schedule-maker who has veto power over a candidate's own decisions. You got to have a czar. For Christ's sake, you got to pace yourself. I was just goddamned mad and choked up over my anger."

Whether it was a choke, or a cry, or a sobbing—there was Edmund Muskie, a week before the primary, front page on the nation's newspapers and carried on television, with snow falling on his curly hair as he stood on a flatbed truck outside the Manchester *Union Leader* offices, his voice breaking, emotion sweeping him, crying.[3] "It changed people's minds about me, of what kind of a guy I was," said Muskie later. "They were looking for a strong, steady man, and here I was weak. I doubt whether I'm a candidate who could ever have won in this country this year. I'm a man for a country looking for a healer, not a country in protest. I wasn't a protest candidate."

On March 7th, 1972, with the weather sub-zero along the Canadian border, cloudy and frigid down to the Boston border, New Hampshire voted. The vote was heavy, high and full of portent. The Republicans had risen in number by 10,000 voters from 1968 to 1972, casting about 118,000 votes, of which 67.9 percent were for Richard Nixon, the rest split between liberal (Paul N. McCloskey, Jr.) and conservative (John M. Ashbrook) splinter Republican rivals. But the Democratic vote had jumped by 35,000 to a total close to 95,000—and of these, Edmund Muskie had won only 46.4 percent and George McGovern 37.2 percent.

Neither candidate paused long enough to examine the voting breakdown, for the next day George McGovern was off by plane to Florida, and Edmund Muskie to a fund-raising gathering in New York to refuel his faltering campaign.

But analysis was instructive. In the white-collar suburban wards, in the small academic towns, McGovern had led Muskie by 48 percent to 37 percent. In the blue-collar wards, Edmund Muskie had balanced that figure with 48 percent to McGovern's 33 percent; in the smaller working-class factory towns—Nashua, Berlin, Dover, Rochester, Claremont

---

[3] Rarely has the instrument of television been able, without any preconceived political intent, to frame perspectives more strikingly than on Saturday night, February 26th, 1972. CBS Evening News opened with a brief report on a flood in West Virginia, and then shifted to some magnificent color camera work in China, where President Richard Nixon and Premier Chou En-lai were visiting fabled Hangchow. Dan Rather gave the hard news from China, Walter Cronkite gave the historic background all the way back to Marco Polo, and in this context of beauty and majesty there were Richard Nixon and Chou En-lai feeding goldfish from the moon bridge in smiles and amity. Then followed, after the commercial, Ed Muskie, as anchorman Roger Mudd in New York brought the audience back to the campaign trail at home. ". . . Senator Edmund Muskie," said Mudd, "today denounced William Loeb, the conservative publisher of the Manchester, New Hampshire, *Union Leader*, as a 'liar' and a 'gutless coward.'" After a few more words, the evening news cut to Ed Muskie on the flatbed truck crying, or choking up, but obviously in great distress as his voice broke in a denunciation of the man who had attacked his wife. The contrast between the President's management of great events in Asia and the Democratic candidate's disturbance over an unexplained slander in Manchester, New Hampshire, was sharp.

—Muskie had scored margins rising to 60 and 70 percent. It was in the largest mill city of all, Manchester and its circumference, that the Muskie campaign had collapsed—under the pounding of the Manchester *Union Leader,* his expected vote had eroded to a slim margin of 600 city-wide. On his home turf, in New England, in his first round in the open, Muskie had stumbled; nor did he know how to recover.

All candidates were bitter at the press in 1972, but few more so than Muskie. The press had proclaimed him the front-runner for months; they had given him New Hampshire by a two-to-one margin in advance. Now that he had carried the state by only 46 to 37 percent, he seemed to have let them down, and he was angry at their judgment. Having pegged him as the administered managerial candidate, newsmen pressed him with clinical political questions, which increasingly embittered him. "I never could find a way," he said, "to turn them off with a humorous answer. The day after Wisconsin, the first question CBS asked me was, 'Mr. Muskie, do you think you're through?' How do you answer that?"

There might have been in the next six weeks a moment of decision to bring about a sharper tactical focus to the campaign, a choice of which primaries to contest, which to abandon. But the campaign planning was too elaborate, too well publicized to permit a basic switch. Most of all, the zest had oozed out of the campaign, the exhilarating sense of the sure thing. Starved increasingly for money; harassed by McGovern's shrewd insistence on open disclosure of funds, which Muskie could not answer since he had raised so much of his money secretly from Republicans who despised Nixon and feared reprisal; unable to change posture except by a thematic jog to the left, and the coining of the in-house phrase "No More Mr. Nice Guy"—burdened with all these considerations, the Muskie campaign slowly wandered off to an aimless end. Muskie was to finish fourth in Florida; win in Illinois, without much credit from the press; finish fourth again in Wisconsin; and reach the end of the trail in Pennsylvania on April 25th. It was a week before his final withdrawal that he summed up his campaign in one of his better rueful jokes. Asked whether he thought he was in trouble, he said it reminded him of an old New England story: There was this fellow, stuck in the mud with his auto, who was asked by a wayfarer whether he was really stuck. "Well, you could say I was stuck," said the fellow, "if I was going anywhere."

Muskie was going nowhere. He had run as a man of the center, candidate of a party out of power, condemned by definition to attack in a year when targets of attack were obscure. "You have to appeal to people," he said once privately, expressing the inner conviction of a decent politician, "above their own private interests, with an overriding imperative that seems good for the whole country." But he could not give that imperative any romance, or pump into the center the vitality which had once moved the Democratic Party, and with it the nation, to a unity of high purpose.

Muskie's next immediate move after New Hampshire was to be Florida. But in Florida the disorientation of the Democratic Party was at its most vivid. Of all the states on the primary route, Florida was the least likely to give the old party a clear new identity of purpose—or a plurality to a candidate whose message was union and brotherhood.

Florida, like New Hampshire, was rushing through a change of its communities; and the twin demographic and political revolutions in that state told as much about the politics of America as the speeches or strategies of the candidates in the primary of March, 1972.

Thirty years before, Florida had counted less than two million people and ranked twenty-seventh on the roster of the Union in population; by 1970 it had grown to 6,789,443 people and ranked ninth. The South and the sunlands had been drawing migrants from the North and Midwest for years, but no state—not California, not Arizona, not Nevada—could match the explosion of newcomers that had changed the old Southern politics of Florida beyond containment. Superimposed on this population explosion, moreover, had come one of the genuine triumphs of the Liberal Idea of the thirties—the application to Florida's in-state politics of the Supreme Court's one-man-one-vote ruling which required state legislatures reasonably to represent districts in proportion to population. The ruling had transformed the character of Florida's backward legislature, and the spirit of change had been capped, in the mid-term elections of 1970, by the election of two authentically liberal and outstandingly intelligent young men as Governor (Reubin Askew) and Senator (Lawton Chiles).

Askew, in his first year in office, had reorganized the legislature; lobbied through an act requiring that banks and corporations pay an income tax; begun to appoint black people to the bench, to school commissions, to draft boards; and was launching a serious program to give the people of Florida control over their environment. Flat, palm-hummocked, low-lying, thoroughly polluted from north to south, sewage pouring from its swollen coastal cities unfiltered into the waters off its coast, Florida as much as any state in the Union required the protection of wise government. Even the most conservative Floridians who had grown rich on the land boom were frightened. "If we could build a wall around Florida," said a banker from Jacksonville, "and keep out any more people who want to move here, I'd vote for it." Supported by what is, with few exceptions, an excellent state press, the state was moving to become a national leader in environment control.

But the sun and the palms, the languor and the entrancement of its once turquoise-green waters generated the only political emotions that bound Floridians together.

Beyond that, Florida was split in a way that tempted every one of the eleven Democratic candidates in the primary race to split it further by the narrowest political appeals. North Florida, the panhandle, was Deep Southern by accent, tradition and landscape—an extension of Georgia and Alabama. Central Florida was transplanted Midwest. From Daytona Beach and Orlando across the waist of the peninsula to St. Petersburg and Sarasota was another culture, where conservative Republicans had established themselves as a political force a decade before. And from Palm Beach south to Key West was a civilization of transplants. To the Miami area had come Cubans who had fled Castro, and Puerto Ricans seeking work; Italians were present in substantial numbers in Miami; more important even than Cubans, Puerto Ricans and Italians were the Jews, both the very rich and the inexpressibly poor, who had fled New York, Chicago and Philadelphia. Add a statewide demographic component of the aging (Florida had the highest proportion of aged to its population—14.5 percent over sixty-five—of any state in the Union), a large component of blacks (15.5 percent of the population), a defense and space industry which stretched from Key West to Cape Kennedy and Pensacola, a speculative construction boom—and one had a panorama of groups and blocs which teased the calculations of each of the eleven Democratic candidates who proposed to split the primary vote—and make it meaningless.

There could be in a state so diverse and with so many candidates no overwhelming winner; thus, logic read that each candidate should seek his plurality by picking out his own slice in the political spectrum, hoping he could fatten it into the thickest.

Hubert Humphrey was entered here as a candidate for the first time in 1972. His target constituency was labor, blacks and Jews. He would go for them. Henry Jackson was making his first try here—he would fight to split the labor and Jewish vote with Humphrey, and then shoot also for the middle-class whites and the defense vote. McGovern was entered in what seemed a perfunctory and useless try for the youth and black vote. Representative Shirley Chisholm of New York was trying to split the black vote with Messrs. Humphrey, Lindsay, McGovern, and add a handful of women's-rights votes to her total. The Muskie vote had no strategy—it was a high-cost, head-of-the-table, white-middle-class vote, dependent entirely on his image of front-runner, the safe man. Muskie had been wounded by the press reporting of New Hampshire, and even more by the crying episode. ("We pleaded with the Washington office," said one of his Florida campaign managers, "to humanize the guy. We were running a campaign based on credibility and strength, but we wanted him to be human. And then, for Christ's sakes, you talk about making him human, but not this crying jag.")

Then, beyond these, were John Vliet Lindsay, Mayor of New York, and George Corley Wallace, Governor of Alabama—rival silhouettes of indignation. Together, they helped print the word "alienation" both on the Florida campaign and on every fashionable analysis of spring politics. They were polar extremes—and were in full revolt against the course of American civilization as they saw it moving. Lindsay understood what the word "alienation" meant. His responsibility for the world's greatest city had rubbed his nerve ends raw; he was running for President because the Federal government had alienated not only millions of the citizens of his city, but his conscience as Mayor, too. George Wallace could not express alienation as well as Lindsay—but he had a simple word for it. He called it "busing."

If there was any issue that disturbed Floridians beyond the sacred issue of environment, it was busing; and in January of 1972 they had been sharply stirred. In that month a Federal court decision had jabbed busing as an issue onto the national consciousness as dramatically as the Tet offensive had jabbed the Vietnam war into the campaign of 1968. The jabbing had not only pricked Floridians from the barrios of Cubans in Miami to the small towns of the piney-woods panhandle in the north. It had touched all Americans nationwide, wherever the race confrontation abraded nerves—from Pontiac, Michigan, to Canarsie, New York, to Compton, California. Nixon had recognized this concern even before he left for Peking to make peace and was planning to speak to the nation on this second most important issue as soon as he returned. (See Chapter Nine.)

The jab of busing had come, to be precise, early in January, 1972, in a decision handed down by Federal Judge Robert R. Merhige, Jr., of the Federal District Court in Richmond, Virginia, 1,000 miles away from Miami.

One must linger over Judge Merhige's decision, for it affected the entire nation and the delicate, complicated civilization of all its cities. Though it was grotesque that the issue of busing and big cities, so intimately connected with the future of America's city culture, should prove the mainspring of the Florida primary, it was in Florida that its impact was first felt.

Judge Merhige had presided over a complaint brought to him by the Legal Defense and Educational Fund of the National Association for the Advancement of Colored People against the School Board of Richmond, Virginia. In Richmond, the school population in 1950 had been approximately 60 percent white, 40 percent black. By 1972 the school population had shifted to approximately 70 percent black, 30 percent white. Parents of white children were sending their youngsters to private schools or suburban schools. Mathematically, it was impossible to distribute schoolchildren within the Richmond public schools in such a way that some schools would not be left with a majority of black children. In consequence thereof, ruled Judge Merhige, the two counties adjacent to Richmond must be compelled to ship their white pupils into central Richmond City until the racial mixture was correct. A superior governing morality infused his opinion—a "burden is upon the school board to erase the racial identity of schools, and this the [previous] plan has failed to do," he said. Children going to public schools must be moved or "bused," no matter where their residence or what their parents desired, until racial proportions were considered right. Judge Merhige, himself comfortably provided for by a Federal salary, sent his children to a private school not affected by his decision. But others must abide by it, not only in Richmond but in the two contiguous counties, Henrico and Chesterfield.

The Merhige decision, seen against the larger backdrop of the underlying campaign, was relevant, if questionable—but Judge Merhige was approaching the problem of the American city with a meat ax. A city is a corporation in the eyes of the law, an instrument of the state; if it does not do what the law interprets as correct, it may be compelled to do so; if municipal or county jurisdictions are obstacles to what courts consider progress, they may be overruled; and with them the autonomy or self-government of the communities in which people have gathered to live because they sought kinship or protection under the shelter of neighborhoods they chose. The Merhige decision ordained, in effect, that no city or county could plan the education of its own children in its own schools if the racial mixture of its pupils was challenged and sustained— its children might be used to adjust the racial composition of nearby communities.

The Merhige decision was another of those traumatic events, like the quota decision of the Reform Commission, which fix a landmark in the change of the Liberal Idea to the Liberal Theology. The Liberal Idea had, in the 1950's, broken the old system of Southern segregation; the Liberal Idea held the clean thought that no child should be excluded from a school system which he was otherwise entitled to enter simply because his skin was black. Separate racial school systems were wrong because they closed children off from each other by the difference of their races; they were lock-ups. The Liberal Idea had been sustained by the Supreme Court's watershed decision of 1954 (Brown vs. the Board of Education, Topeka, Kansas), which outlawed segregation by color. Almost twenty years had gone by since then, and the Idea had become Theology, coming full circle. By the Merhige decision, a child, if he were white, might be excluded from a neighborhood school in his community—as black children had once been excluded because they were black

—simply because his white skin was needed for a color composition in some distant school. Color was again the touchstone of exclusion or admittance. Left to stand, the Merhige decision might have affected local governments everywhere, as well as in Florida. At least four major cities in the decade of the 1960's had become majoritarian black—Gary (Indiana), Washington (D.C.), Newark (New Jersey), Atlanta (Georgia). But, according to the U.S. Office of Education, at least fifteen of the fifty-one largest cities in the United States had a majority of non-white pupils in their public elementary schools—not only Washington (93 percent black pupils), but also Chicago (56 percent), Detroit (64 percent), Philadelphia (61 percent), Baltimore (67 percent), Cleveland (57 percent), St. Louis (65 percent), Newark (72 percent), Oakland (57 percent). Such cities, by the Merhige decision, would have the right to reach out over municipal, county or community lines and conscript white children of the suburbs to be bused into central-city black areas because the arithmetic of color required it.

The Merhige decision of January was to be reversed on June 6th of 1972, thus effectively removing it as the possible Dred Scott decision of the fall campaign of 1972. But in Florida, as the candidates arrived in February and March, no one could tell whether the Merhige decision would become the law of the land or not. Parents, both black and white, were agitated by the problem, the issue of the month; and all previously planned strategies of the Presidential candidates had to adjust to the magnetic field of new emotions.

Already, ten days before the primary, there had been a school strike in liberal Dade County: not in the city of Miami itself but in the enclave of Auburndale, close by; and not by racist whites against blacks, but by Cubans against a new local busing ruling. Cuban parents, by community custom, do not like their teen-age girls to travel by public transportation to school, and had struck. In Palm Beach, local busing had resulted in a spurt of violence at schools. Discontent among both whites and blacks reflected itself in a sharp rise in high-school dropouts; white parents no longer insisted that their sons and daughters finish their courses in dangerous distant schools to which they were bused. Even the liberals of Palm Beach felt long-distance busing a mistake. In Jacksonville, where long-distance busing had come to an absurdity which moved some little children twenty-five miles in the morning and twenty-five miles back in the afternoon from school to home or home to school, race tensions had reached the point of explosion.

Against this scenery, there thus unfolded the carnival of the Florida primary—and in the noise, the confusion of voices, the crisscrossing of the state by the candidates' buses and planes, the drenching of the state in television and money, it gradually became apparent that the outcome of this campaign, for all the effort spent here, would be meaningless in settling either the nomination or the course of the party. Only much later was the last wild touch of irrelevance added to the Florida story. It was in Florida that the dirty-tricks team of the Nixon campaign apparently took to the field for the first time.[4] According to a Federal indictment of May, 1973, as far back as December 1, 1971, one Donald H. Segretti had paid $50 to twenty-five-year-old Robert Benz, president of the Tampa Young Republicans Club, to plan disruption of the Florida campaigns of Senators Muskie and Jackson. All that had come of that investment was several thousand letters on stationery simulating Senator Muskie's, mailed out three days before the Florida primaries. The fake letters accused Senators Jackson and Humphrey of assorted, and totally untrue, misdemeanors—running from homosexuality through bastardy to drunken driving with call girls. The stupidity that was later to climax in the Watergate affair showed here for the first time. How, in a state where the Democratic candidates were spending, collectively, close to $2,500,000 to reach the voters, could a few thousand letters have been, expected to affect the outcome? Along with the stupidity went a characteristic chiseler's cupidity. The mailing could have cost no more than a few hundred dollars—of the thousands of dollars paid to Segretti from secret cash campaign funds, how much must have been pocketed on the way?

Only the two symbolic candidates, Lindsay and Wallace, were worth following or reporting because they alone had messages that transcended the limits of Florida's primary.

Of John Lindsay's campaign, it may be said that rarely has so eloquent a spokesman for so profoundly important a cause presided over so blundering a political campaign.

Lindsay's cause was the case of the city in America. But those who pleaded John Lindsay's cause in Florida were not simply city people, they were Manhattan city people; and New York City Hall, under John Lindsay, had turned over its political operations to some of the most parochial pavement politicians of the time. Their planning, to be sure, was cursed by bad luck; their decision to begin their national campaign in Florida had been made before either the Merhige decision or George Wallace's entry into the race was announced; now they would have to face the busing issue in Florida with one eye on Florida emotions and another eye on the racial politics of New York, their home base. The Lindsay campaign as it took off seemed to be going several ways at once. Television experts, spending some $180,000 in what they considered, naïvely, to be a "media state," were presenting an open-shirted, white-

[4] See page 275.

collared, handsome man called John Lindsay as a fighter—but a fighter with the style and language of the middle class. His schedulers booked him for "visuals" along Florida's polluted bays and shores, which always brought him his best headlines—but seemed slightly embarrassed at exploiting what they considered a "soft" issue, a middle-class issue. The organization men of the campaign brought with them a style and technique developed in the crowded blocks and apartment houses of the Bronx, Brooklyn and Manhattan. Green grass was a novelty to most of them. "Did you ever try to deal with Florida people?" asked Sid Davidoff, the Marshal Ludendorff of Lindsay's storefront operations in the politics of concrete and tenement houses. "In New York a volunteer wheels her baby carriage into the club, brings her two kids and spends a couple of hours at the telephone for you. Here they play tennis in the afternoon! They have lawns they want to mow! They like to sit in the sun! They come by automobile and they need parking places! Have you ever tried to motivate them? They go swimming in the afternoon!" Storefront clubs would not work in Florida; and finally the Davidoff organizational effort became little more than an attempt to court, cozen or buy up the black vote, which, no matter what Lindsay's position on busing, he would have to split with Humphrey, McGovern and Chisholm.

And Lindsay himself, the most important element of the campaign, addressed himself chiefly to conscience.

One should speak generously of John Lindsay. To Florida he brought the inner torment of six years as Mayor of New York, as well as the exaggerated reputation of the city's breakdown that the national media had hung on him. John Lindsay had lived with street killings, and knew the statistics of what loose guns and Saturday-night specials were doing to his town. He had learned what sorrow, sadness and tragedy were milled through the abortion walk-ups of his city. He knew the havoc of drugs, the pestilence of mugging, the crackle of race tension; and the institutional poverty of a great city starved of money, reckoning that each raid on Hanoi cost as much as might renew a slum block in the South Bronx. Above all, he was convinced of his historic duty to bring an end to the exclusion of blacks in a white society. Out of it all, he had distilled an indignation of conscience and a ferocity of expression which overwhelmed good judgment. Compared to John Lindsay, even George McGovern was a man of compromise. McGovern favored abortion—but thought it was a matter to be left to state laws. Lindsay thought it was a matter of national policy—how could a national leader be neutral about abortion in Florida when each year 5,000 Florida women came to New York City for the abortions they could not legally seek at home? McGovern had gone along with the Scott-Mansfield compromise on busing now up before the Senate. John Lindsay was against the amendment—he was for busing, period! And so on.[5]

Of the brief Lindsay fling, I remember best an afternoon visit to Orlando, in Orange County, Florida, one of the most conservative counties in America. Some awful miscarriage of judgment by Manhattan advance men had provided Lindsay, who spoke against the band shell of Aeola Lake, with an entertainment come-on by the troupe of *Hair,* a rock musical then fading from its peak in New York. After the music and support of the cast of *Hair,* John Lindsay proceeded to deliver one of the finest speeches of his stump career. He was trying to explain to the people of Orange County, Florida, what the other life was like—the life of drugs, of crime, of the unhappy and unfortunate squeezed into their slums and tenements, their evening stroll in the moonlight a tempting of muggers, their sleep disturbed by sirens or by television blaring against adjacent walls, horizons limited to welfare or dishwashing. He told them one of the stories that haunt him, of how it is to be a mayor on the frontier of violence and trying to comfort in a hospital the widow of a policeman who has just been killed, shot by a black man. He had spent years in the "marble halls of Washington" as a Congressman, he said, but "any single night on the streets of New York teaches you what works and what doesn't work more than ten years in Congress." Only a mayor understands what it is to choose between building a library and a drug center. He was for busing. Wallacism had to be confronted. "What's dividing this country is fear, the legacy of race and poverty, the refusal of big government to make big institutions be accountable to the public for what they do." And "Governor Wallace is running around frightening people on the question of busing, on the question of fairness and rightness."

His blond hair, now on the verge of silvering, blew in the wind, and his long forelocks slipped over his brow as he spoke. The cast of *Hair* liked his speech, and one of them said to him when the speech was over, in awe and admiration, "Mayor, you've been radicalized!" Lindsay appreciated the comment, for, he acknowledged, no man could govern a big city in America today without being radicalized.

But the audience before him was unstirred. Apart from the students who applauded, the audience were family people of Orlando. And most family people had fled here from the North to escape just the scene

---

[5] The Scott-Mansfield Amendment, offered by Senate Majority Leader Mike Mansfield and Senate Minority Leader Hugh Scott, was an effort to stem rising anti-busing sentiment in Congress by offering a moderate proposal to curb the use of Federal funds for busing unless requested by local authorities; it stipulated further that Federal authorities be restrained from ordering busing if it impaired the health of a child or carried him away to a school inferior to his neighborhood school.

that John Lindsay was describing. If there was any fight left in them, it was to defend the sun and the quiet to which they had come to doze and dream far from sirens in the night. And here was Lindsay with his furious eloquence, bringing to these green lawns and tranquil places the nightmares of the shrill nights they had fled—and insisting that even the other liberals, McGovern, Humphrey, Jackson, who had voted for the Scott-Mansfield busing compromise in the Senate, were little different from George Wallace, who had turned his back on the blacks.

George Wallace would have been a national influence anyway in 1972, for he had a master grip on an issue; but the Florida campaign and John Lindsay made him larger than he had ever been before.

The little Governor of Alabama had been running for a long time and, like Hubert Humphrey and Richard M. Nixon, his successive national races and experience had both educated and changed him. The round, beetle-browed, dark face that used to poke up from behind the lectern was now mellowed, the lines were easier. The hair that used to curl out in a ducktail slicked back with brilliantine, like the cartoons of Senator Claghorn, was now neatly cut, if somewhat sprayed. Under the influence of his attractive new wife, Cornelia, he had shed the old undertaker's uniform—dark suit, narrow black necktie—of Southern courthouse politicians, and was garbed now in bright shirts, fashionable double-knit suits, broad colorful ties.

It was always amusing, in following George Wallace, to try to distinguish the old from the new. His rally style, for example, was old—the tub-thumping country music, this year led by Billy Grammer, star of the *Grand Ole Opry;* the guitar-playing; the flags on either side of him as he spoke; the glowering state troopers watching the crowd for violence; the singing; the pails which were passed around among the audience and which returned full of coins and bills. But the crowds were different—no longer overwhelmingly made up of the shirt-sleeved, blue-collared, surly men in whose midst one used to feel frequently on the threshold of violence. In 1972 the gas-station men in blue coveralls were still there, the workers with muscular biceps growling or grinning approval. But among them were men in neckties and white shirts, with the sour breath of office workers; women in housedresses with their babies; more young girls than ever; old ladies with their gray hair sprayed into a blueish set; and a mood as much of joviality as of anger. Other candidates labored over their advance work and prepared for rallies with skill, art and delegated manpower. George Wallace simply announced a rally—and the crowds turned up to hear the talking.

"Send Them a Message" was George Wallace's slogan in 1972, a more subtle slogan than that of 1968 ("Not a Dime's Worth of Difference") or his original message of 1962 ("Segregation Now, Segregation Tomorrow, Segregation Forever"). The message George Wallace was sending in 1972 was at last being heard against the experience of the 1960's—by people who had come to question whether government really knew what was good for them either in daily life at home or in war abroad.

Wallace could state the message with precision when forced into the thoughtful mode. Invited to express himself on the Op-Ed Page of *The New York Times,* for example, he delivered the clearest analysis of his campaign early in March:

> The American people are fed up with the interference of government. They want to be left alone. Once the Democratic party reflected true expressions of the rank-and-file citizens. They were its heart, the bulk of its strength and vitality. Long ago it became the party of the so-called intelligentsia. Where once it was the party of the people, along the way it lost contact with the working man and the businessman. It has been transformed into a party controlled by intellectual snobs. . . .

Ordinary people, however, did not come to hear the Governor talk this kind of talk; they came to hear one of their own talk ("He says what's on our minds," was the way they phrased it), and he passed the message along in country-boy talk, with a homespun quality reached only by Hubert Humphrey and Lyndon Johnson at their best. The message came in interchangeable parts, the order of the peeves and jabs transposed from night to night, rally to rally, but always calculated to pluck emotions the way Billy Grammer plucked strings on his guitar.

Nixon? Nixon was a "double-dealer, a two-timer, and a man who tells folks one thing and does another." The government in Washington was run by "bureaucrats, hypocrites, uninterested politicians," men who couldn't "even park their bicycles straight . . . briefcase-totin' bureaucrats," and "if you opened all their briefcases you'll find nothing in them but a peanut-butter sandwich." He was for patriotism and national defense, and called the Nixon trip to China one of the most disgraceful sellouts to Communism anyone'd ever seen. Wallace would rarely use the word "establishment," but the crowd understood whom he was talking about. The correspondents of *The New York Times,* "the CBS," "the NBC," "the ABC," when present in the audience, were friendly props off whom he could score. Above all, the courts: ". . . the judges . . . have just about ruined this country. . . . They don't hang their britches on the wall and go jump in 'em, they pull 'em on one leg at a time just like regular folks. And the people didn't elect them either, like they did me." The Senators in the race, including Mr. McGovern, Mr. Muskie, Mr. Humphrey and most of their staffs, who sent their children to private schools in Washington but still advocated busing, were "hypocrites. . . . Washington is the hypocrite capital of the world. . . . They're like a bunch of cats on a hot tin roof. They're a-hemmin' and a-hawin' and they're about to break out in St. Vitus Dance. . . ."

He, George Wallace, was for the average man. The average man was being gutted by government. Taxes were important in George Wallace's message. "The greatest thing that exists in the air today is the unfair tax structure and you had better give tax relief to the average man in this country and put it on the filthy rich in Wall Street, or you . . . might wind up short at the next election period in the United States."

But, above all: busing. Busing was what really got to the average man. "This senseless business of trifling with the health and safety of your child, regardless of his color, by busing him across state lines, and city lines and . . . into kingdom come—has got to go." (Cheers.) This was "social scheming" imposed by "anthropologists, zoologists and sociologists" (Wallace loved to draw out the word "sociologist"); "the common people" should come together and say, "Mr. Nixon, our children are precious to us, and we want a stop to this busing." Or, in another speech, ". . . in China, the President asked Mousey Tongue for advice on busing and Mousey Tongue said, 'I can't advise you on busing 'cause when I take a notion to bus 'em and they don't like it, I just bus 'em anyhow.' And that's just about the way they're doing it here." And, in peroration: "Busin' . . . it's the most atrocious, callous, cruel, asinine thing you can do for little children. . . . these pluperfect hypocrites who live over in Maryland or Virginia and they've got their children in a private school . . . tomorrow the chickens are coming home to roost. They gonna be sorry they bused your little children and had somethin' to do with it. So, my friends, you give 'em a good jolt tomorrow. You give 'em the St. Vitus Dance."

It was clear for the last three weeks before primary day that George Wallace would lead in the spread-eagle Florida primary. He had the north and panhandle country, the old Southern stock. But it might be close. Even so good a politician as Jon Moyle, Democratic State Chairman, had opined in January that "you'll be able to cover the difference between Wallace, Humphrey and Muskie with a quarter." But by afternoon of primary day it was obvious, from the voting turnout, that the north was voting heavily; and the north meant that George Wallace's lead was now certified.

The national press sat by the swimming pools of Miami, talking with the national candidates and their staffs, and the betting was casual— Wallace would get a few points more or less than 30 percent. George McGovern that day thought there was even a chance for Hubert Humphrey to outrun Wallace. But the results came in otherwise, flooding to tide in efficient network gathering shortly after seven. Wallace was getting 50 percent in the first scattered returns; the lead shrank in the first half-hour to 47 percent, then to the low 40's, and then stabilized at 42 percent. But the 42 percent had a profile—it was not simply the north and piney-woods rednecks that were voting for George Wallace. Wallace was winning statewide, even in liberal Dade County; in the precincts of the elderly Jews at the poorhouse of South Miami Beach he was running third after Hubert Humphrey and Henry Jackson; Wallace, it became obvious that night, was not just a Southern phenomenon—he was much more than a statewide Florida phenomenon. He was a national phenomenon and would remain so until shot, two months later, and removed by a would-be assassin's bullet from national consideration.

All the other candidates lost, with one exception.

Hubert Humphrey lost—once Vice-President of the United States, once national candidate for President, once champion of all the good of the Liberal Idea, he could draw no more than 18.6 percent for second place. Henry Jackson, sober, decent, moderate, with a rational position on busing and defense, came in third with 13 percent. Edmund Muskie, fourth, with 8.9 percent, was finished—in a divided state, cross-section of so many conflicts, he could find no echo either for trust or for unity. John Lindsay, having spent more than $400,000 and his heart and his reputation, was the biggest loser, with 7 percent.

Curiously enough, George McGovern, who had won only 6.2 percent of the vote, was, after Wallace, the biggest winner.

The McGovern men had planned with precision, and the foresight of their early months achieved exactly what they had planned: to split the far-left vote with John Lindsay. To have abandoned the Florida primary to Lindsay would have given Lindsay all the left, all the youth vote, much of the black vote—and have made Lindsay either number two or number three in the voting, and thus poised on a springboard to go on to Wisconsin and the later primaries as a substantial vote-getter in hostile country. By reducing Lindsay to fifth place, while content with sixth place for themselves, the McGovern planners were now in position to pull the set-piece breakthrough which they had planned for Wisconsin. Let Muskie go on to Illinois (where he would win); let Humphrey and Jackson go on to Wisconsin (where they would split the moderate vote). The McGovern planners were now ready to leapfrog Illinois and roll up the party from the left, in a progressive state where history and tradition moved in their favor.

CHAPTER FIVE

MCGOVERN'S ARMY

AMONG the men who reported the revolution in China years ago, it was accepted that by the time guerrilla forces surfaced in any province, political infection had metastasized there too deeply to be stopped. By the time regular troops formed up to cope, the infected province was already lost.

As the Democratic primaries now, in the early spring of 1972, moved on from Florida to Wisconsin, the Democratic regulars discovered a similar guerrilla presence too late. No other metaphor but that of a guerrilla army on the move can describe the upheaval that was to shake and change the entire Democratic Party in the next ten weeks, for the march of George McGovern in those ten weeks would go down as a classic in American political history. Its only parallel, the strike of Barry Goldwater in 1964, had been an internal coup within a party; but the insurrection of George McGovern was a national mobilization of irregulars—a masterpiece of partisan warfare, its troops living off the land, tapping veins of frustration everywhere; raising money locally as they rolled; their captains and lieutenants, young men without commissions or epaulets, commanding and creating a net of cells in storefronts, cellars, campuses, kitchens; youth and women organized; all of them recruiting, preaching, persuading, stirring to action hearts hitherto unstirred by politics.

Had they studied the political terrain of America, Mao or Giap would have approved the tactics and strategy of McGovern's army; and they would have understood more than most contemporary Americans what gave this army its hidden power. The army had an idea that could snare souls. The idea was that politics could bring peace and establish justice; and the soldiers of the idea were pure. Unlike most men in politics in the United States, whether labor or Chamber of Commerce leaders, whether black militants or real-estate magnates, whether farm spokesmen or city spokesmen, the new people of McGovern's army sought no specific gain or advantage for any special bloc, or for themselves personally. Not until later, when the inhalation of power became intoxicating, would they begin to paw the ground and butt others around as all men do when power begins to stir them. In the beginning they seemed to conceal in themselves a secret rhythm which excited another hidden rhythm in American politics. Whether this rhythm was a major one that could sweep the country or a rhythm limited to the hearing of the audience they courted, neither they nor anyone else could judge. But they were ready to march and give the call.

Winter headquarters in Washington gave no sense of the formidable capacity of this army. On a slope just two blocks southeast of the nation's Capitol in Washington, at 410 First Street, headquarters occupied a low-ceilinged back space between a liquor store and a takeout-sandwich grocery shop. Headquarters was open—it posted no guards and needed none, for the lights were on twenty-four hours a day as pony-tailed girls and blue-jeaned boys worked around the clock. Beaverboard partitions in the rear set off six cubicles where regional intelligence was coordinated; in the crowded back bullpen stretched long tables covered with mailings, pamphlets, stuffings, posters, cola cans, and the leavings of peanut-butter and tunafish sandwiches; and everywhere—files, lists, shoeboxes full of names. In the front, as one entered off an airless corridor, were the three offices of the high command—Gary Hart, campaign coordinator; Frank Mankiewicz, campaign director; and Richard Stearns, director of research and organizer of delegates in caucus states. No inter-office chain of memoranda or communications linked this command together as at Muskie or Humphrey headquarters. When Mankiewicz, Hart or Stearns wanted to talk with one another, they simply slid back a partition and called, or walked across the corridor and sat on the other's desk. Messengers and volunteers, field commanders home to report, housewives with babies, students on vacation, all wandered through the offices, finding work, or inventing work to do as they chose. A bubble of mirth embraced the headquarters; comradeship seemed to hold them all together, as once long ago a similar fraternal goodwill had held together the men I first met in the caves of Yenan when the Chinese Communists were developing their leadership in brotherhood and spreading it across their ravaged land.

It was more difficult to pinpoint the strength in the field—and in the field, on the guerrilla fighting fronts, the joviality faded into a hard combat mode to create out of gentle people types like Eugene Pokorny.

And it would be well to weave the pattern of the McGovern insurrection by starting with the thread of a Pokorny, before describing what such young men and women did in Wisconsin, in Massachusetts, in California, in New York.

*   *   *

By the time I arrived in Milwaukee, following the trail up from Florida to the primary rendezvous in Wisconsin which the calendar set for April 4th, 1972, Eugene Pokorny had already been at work building his base for almost a year and a half.

Pokorny was all of twenty-five—lean, pale with overwork, immaculate in diction and phrase, sandy hair surmounting a choirboy's face set off by an accountant's steel-rimmed eyeglasses. Pokorny had the ability to stand off and look at himself as a stranger might, and called himself a "gunslinger grass-roots organizer." He teased his own story as he told it—born a farm boy in Howells, Nebraska, where his father and the three boys farmed 600 acres of black bottomland. "You can put in that I walked to school every day carrying a lunch pail to a one-room country schoolhouse." He considered himself an agrarian populist by heritage, and "if you don't understand the agrarian populist tradition of Kansas, Nebraska and South Dakota, you aren't going to understand George McGovern," he added.

Pokorny had gone off to the University of Nebraska in 1964—the year campuses came apart with their first riots, the year of the Mississippi summer action, when civil rights made campus politics turn. Pokorny's experience traced the thinking of a decade. If he were to be involved in student politics as he wanted to be, he had to be involved in civil rights, the hot issue. From which, the next step: anyone who was into civil rights had to be into the anti-war movement; and by 1967 Pokorny was into the Committee of Concerned Democrats, organizing for Eugene McCarthy; and then on to the Chicago convention. A whole generation of American youth leaders was moving at the same time in the same direction—from free speech to civil rights, to the peace movement, to McCarthy (or Kennedy) and thus into politics. The decade of the 1920's had left its football heroes behind on the campus; but the decade of the sixties moved its campus political heroes on into national politics by the scores and the hundreds, where they proceeded to act.

When Pokorny left the violence of the Chicago convention of 1968 behind, he left behind Eugene McCarthy, too. Pokorny had no stomach for martyrdom. "I made a commitment to myself never again to make a commitment to liberal politics if they weren't going to work. I didn't want to remake the world—I wanted to make a contribution to it. Mc-Govern's not in it just to raise issues—McGovern's in it to win."

The card files in the Washington McGovern office had turned up Pokorny's name as early as 1970. By July the organizational touch of Gary Hart had reached out to tap Pokorny on his farm. And by November of 1970, two years before the election, Pokorny was driving across the bridge over the Mississippi into La Crosse, Wisconsin, visiting the state for the first time—with a road map and fifty names from the Hart file as his only diagram of entry to a state of 4,500,000 citizens.

"Names, names, names," said Pokorny in 1972. "I'm a fanatic on three-by-five cards." Over the past six years Americans have been furrowed by a hundred causes dividing "progressives" from "non-progressives"—causes of peace, of civil rights, of women's rights, of horror at nuclear menace, of conservation and environment, of political crusades. Such names exist on obscure lists everywhere—and the names do not fade away. The essence of Pokorny's work—as of all McGovern field tactics—was to find and develop such lists, file the names on three-by-fives, then find the faces behind the names and energize them. The message was simple: peace.

Thus Gene Pokorny all through 1971, living in the home of a McGovern loyalist in Milwaukee, dining as a boarder with the family and three children, and traveling to organize names. "Our first task," said Pokorny, "was to consolidate the left." Which meant, specifically, to energize what was left of the McCarthy insurgency that had swept Wisconsin in 1968. It meant meetings in Wausau and La Crosse and Kenosha and Madison and all across the state, of six or eight or ten people at someone's home, and committing them—"our people were committed in blood." Not students, for, in Pokorny's mind, students were ephemeral. Basically, he sought teachers, "peace freaks," and then, above all, in Pokorny's earnest words, intending no pun, "peace-minded, broad-based housewives."

There was little innocence about Pokorny as an organizer, as there was little innocence about McGovern's other Pokornys about the country. What innocence the McGovern guerrillas were to display would be political and historical, an ignorance about the outer world beyond the guerrilla theater in which they acted. When it came to organization, they were precise and masterful. To organize at the grass roots, doctrine had developed. In Pokorny's mind, organization required two essentials: first, the creation of an identified volunteer group, committed to precise work-assignment schedules and bound to precise end-point targets; and, second, a positive reinforcement schedule which would energize these volunteers by the visits or inspirational activity of a national leader who would give their daily drudgery a larger visionary meaning. In this the national organization backed him up. As far back as 1970, Pokorny had insisted on, and Gary Hart had agreed to, at least one three-day tour of Wisconsin by McGovern, the candidate, every ninety days.

The work had thus been going on for a long time before the national candidates and the reporters, arriving in Wisconsin to examine the condition of the Presidential race among Democrats, discovered the McGovern cells in full metastasis. By the last week in March, 1972, every one of Wisconsin's seventy-two counties had a McGovern volunteer nucleus; thirty-five to forty paid organizers (most of them paid $50 a week) had opened storefronts in some counties, housewives had opened their homes in others, to cover the state. Ten thousand unpaid volunteer workers were walking blocks and country roads, marking voters on precinct sheets in the familiar one-two-three-four patterns of preference indicating the degree of pressure to be exerted to bring them out on primary day. $232,000 had been spent in Wisconsin, the largest expenditure ($65,000) on an eight-page reprint in eighteen Wisconsin newspapers that reached 1,250,000 people in February.

By the end of March, Pokorny was cocked to go. For other candidates and their methods, Pokorny had scorn. Muskie had organized the state from the top down—a good half of all the state's Democratic legislators, county chairmen and executive committeemen had endorsed him. But Muskie had no troops at grass roots. And the threat from the left? "We've locked up the left," said Pokorny. McCarthy had nothing but two storefronts in Madison and Milwaukee. And Lindsay? Lindsay, thought Pokorny, had been trapped—he was being reported in his own "image" terms. The press was discussing not Lindsay's issues, but his political skills and the technique of his advance man, Jerry Bruno. Lindsay was still "skiing down Publicity Mountain," in Pokorny's term. "His people underestimate the intelligence of American voters more than any other candidate's. Can you imagine his going to sleep in a worker's home in Milwaukee on a sofa? To see how 'they' live?!"

Pokorny was a star. But there were other stars all across the country—Grandmaison in New Hampshire, Himmelman in Ohio, McKean in Massachusetts, Swerdlow in Pennsylvania, Rogoff in New York, Segal in California. Together they were a brotherhood, intoxicated with the latent eloquence of their own action, convinced that they had found the secret of changing politics, loyal to each other, above all loyal to their field commander, Gary Hart.

The thread from all the Pokornys in the field led back to Gary Hart, thirty-four years old, born in Ottawa, Kansas, a lawyer on leave from his law firm in Denver, Colorado.

Hart was a loose-limbed, bushy-haired, blue-eyed six-footer, dressed always in open-neck shirts (he was excluded from one of Miami's finest restaurants in July, during the Democratic convention, which he dominated, until he borrowed a necktie from management) and skin-fitting pants over slim cowboy thighs. Hart drew the eyes of every yearning maiden in the McGovern camp for two years—except that he was too busy with politics for romantic distraction. He walked with the ranging stride of an outdoorsman, the lope of a walker in the sun, and no crisis ever ruffled his good manners or caused any visible loss of temper.

Hart was the apotheosis of the professional amateur—the archetype of the new breed, and thus hero to all the field commanders. He had spent his undergraduate years at Bethany Nazarene College, in Oklahoma City, then gone on to Yale to work for his Ph.D. in philosophy, literature, religion, before shifting to Yale Law School. The Kennedy campaign of 1960 had first engaged his political attention as a student volunteer in New Haven; he graduated from law school in 1963, then found a job with Stewart Udall as a Department of Interior lawyer for two years. Thence, to open his own law practice in Denver, where he was practicing when the Robert Kennedy campaign of 1968 swept him up. He was thus already a veteran of the grass roots when, in 1969, he offered his services to the Reform Commission and then, a year later, to the McGovern campaign, which he joined full-time by June of 1970.

Had emotion or inclination taken Gary Hart into the Army or General Motors or the church, he would long since have been recognized with a star, a vice-presidency or a bishopric—for he loved organization and, with his experience in political campaigns of the 1960's, he had become a master. Hart had the critical knack of drawing the last ounce of exertion from staff without raising his voice, of recognizing an imaginative insight from below, of detecting talent and investing it with responsibility, then weaving it into a master plan. But his mildness was deceptive—he was a true believer. He was to develop, slowly, through 1972 into a shrewd and skillful infighter, as adept with the long knife, when necessary, as with the encouraging pat on the back. His chief weakness was one he shared with most of McGovern's top commanders: For all of his skill and subtlety in the machinery of a campaign, he was a primitive on the issues. He hated the war; McGovern hated the war; his heart belonged to McGovern—beyond that, Hart's attention was not distracted by any deeper contemplation of America and its problems. McGovern would think for the nation, once elected; his, Hart's, task was to organize the election of George McGovern.

It was Hart, more than anyone else, who gave the guerrilla formulation to the McGovern strategy. Resistant to all pressures from the field and from McGovern's friends and glamorous advisers, he thought of himself occasionally as the Kutuzov of *War and Peace*—McGovern's Kutuzov. "Kutuzov was under the same pressure to attack and win, to attack anywhere," said Hart in January of 1972, "but we're an insurgency. I believe we should attack and retreat, attack and retreat."

Hart's campaign plan had, by early 1972, discarded McGovern's own romantic notion that they should fight Edmund Muskie primary by primary, state after state, all across the nation. Hart had eliminated Florida, Rhode Island, West Virginia, Indiana, Michigan and a dozen other states from his resource-allocation plan. Hart's plan—and Hart controlled all money, all the candidate's time, all the field troops—was quite simple. The guerrillas would take on Muskie in distant New Hampshire first, to wound him. For this mountain campaign Hart had allocated in 1971 ten trips of the candidate's time, plus twenty-two days of campaigning in the pre-primary weeks of 1972 and $160,000. Florida he would pass except to cut up Lindsay. Wisconsin would be highest priority, with Massachusetts held by a shadow operation for development if Wisconsin was a win. In Wisconsin the troops would have Pokorny as commander, $200,000 of money, and engage in their first set-piece battle. Once Wisconsin was won, they would move the troop commanders into Massachusetts for a breakthrough. Then, hopefully, having by then eliminated the entire left and much of the center in Phase One of the primaries, McGovern's army could, by victory, acquire the money and momentum for Phase Two, of which California would be the climax. In that huge state the McGoverns would need perhaps $2,000,000; but that effort would transform the irregulars into line-of-battle frontal troops; and if they won in California, New York would fall by itself, as Shanghai fell of itself once Peking had been seized in 1949 in the revolution in Asia.

It was all organized in Hart's head better than anywhere else: the lists, the computerization of names; the mailings out of which they must get their money; the unknown gunslinger organizers who might do well here, there or elsewhere across the country; the candidate's precious time. But at the root lay organization. Personally gentle, organizationally Hart was inflexible. The campaign would move or falter on the loyalties he could count on from his field commanders, their willingness to perform the impossible if he said the impossible must be achieved. And to hold their loyalties, he must reciprocate with loyalty to them, however cruel his actions might seem later to Democratic leaders outside the magic circle of youth and insurrection. Hart loved his organization as a painter does his canvas—touching, retouching, refining, admiring his own art. And the organization loved Hart. Its leaders and troops were the campaign, they were the Coldstream Guards of the Movement. "Their trouble," later said Hugh Sidey, *Time*'s Washington correspondent, "was that they were all in love with each other, with doing their own thing."

If Hart was the inside man, Frank Mankiewicz was the outside man. Where Hart was earnest, Mankiewicz was merry. Where Hart was inflexible, Mankiewicz was elastic. Where Hart, to the press, was a freshman in politics, Mankiewicz was recognized varsity. In the McGovern campaign he was one of the few men who could not only laugh, but cause others to laugh. Mankiewicz was always a press favorite, even after many realized that Mankiewicz's loyalties to McGovern were as perfect as Hart's—and that, if necessary for McGovern's interests, he would lead them astray, as he felt he had to in the dispute over the South Carolina delegation at the Democratic convention later.

Mankiewicz, at forty-seven, was the old man of the command force. Dark, with pouched eyes, roguishly attractive, he brought a saving dash of cynicism to the dedicated purpose of his companions. Mankiewicz

had come by his politics quite naturally. His father, Herman Mankiewicz, had been not only one of the great wits of Hollywood and a
cinematic master (*Citizen Kane* was the elder Mankiewicz's creation),
but a man fascinated by politics, American history and its grotesqueries.

From his father Mankiewicz had inherited style, but his own politics was shaped by his time span. At nineteen, he had volunteered for
World War II, won three battle stars in the infantry, and regretted forever that on the day his patrol was to reconnoiter the advance on the
Elbe in May, 1945, his jeep had a flat tire and he missed making the
link-up with the Russians at Torgau which marked the end of the war
in Europe. From Europe, then, home to Hollywood, to study at the
University of California at Los Angeles (where among his classmates
were Bob Haldeman and John Ehrlichman, later of Richard Nixon's
White House staff); then to law school and a successful law practice
until, with the election of John F. Kennedy in 1960, he had volunteered for the Peace Corps.

The Peace Corps was a radicalizing experience for many, aerating
once more, as so often in the previous twenty years, the dilemma of
American foreign policy: Is American aid to be given to governments
who will use it for those below? Or given to those below who will use
it to shape government to their needs? In Latin America, where Mankiewicz served, he, too, was radicalized, believing that aid should go to
the destitute of the barrios rather than the governments which controlled them. His stand had brought him to the attention of Robert
Kennedy; in 1966 he had become Kennedy's press secretary; in 1968,
after Kennedy's assassination, he had served in George McGovern's
brief Presidential try; then become a Washington columnist, and his wit
and charm had made him one of fashionable Washington's favorite dinner guests.

"We Can't Go On Like This" is the way Mankiewicz phrased his
politics, for he had stopped trusting the purpose of American government, either Lyndon Johnson's, which he had served, or Richard
Nixon's, which he reported, either in Latin America or in Vietnam. And
thus, when George McGovern in the summer of 1971 asked him to
come aboard, he was willing, even if it cost him money. He had been
earning $60,000 a year as a columnist-commentator and accepted
$40,000 a year from McGovern—the highest salary paid anyone in the
campaign, and resented by others.

Mankiewicz loved McGovern, perhaps most because of the contrast in their backgrounds. McGovern had grown up in the land of silos,
grain elevators and broad fields, Mankiewicz in a land of swimming
pools, freeways and manicured green gardens. The sincerity of Mc-
Govern attracted Mankiewicz as the strength of unspoiled innocence.
Where Hart was always obedient to what he thought McGovern wished,

Mankiewicz was protective. Mankiewicz believed in the new politics and understood the movement ("Right from the Start" had been his formulation of McGovern's position on the war). But he understood the old, too. In talking to older, regular Democrats, Mankiewicz could offer a conversational familiarity with the game as they played it—the names of the cards, and the bidding conventions in public or private deal. If Gary Hart's field strategy worked and the big primary breakthrough came in Wisconsin, then all credit would have to go to Hart and Pokorny. But after the victory it would be Frank Mankiewicz who should know best how to use it.

Wisconsin was just as familiar a way-stop to the political tourist on the Presidential corridor as New Hampshire—but it, too, was changing. More than New Hamphire, not remotely as much as Florida, Wisconsin was undergoing the squeeze of the new seventies in all its stresses and strains. Wisconsin's population had grown, of course—by 12 percent to 4,500,000 people in the last decade. It was still the foremost dairy state in the union, but of its seventy-two counties, nineteen in the countryside had lost population. Wisconsin's postwar growth had come in the cities, and its industrial wealth had grown twice as fast as its farm income. In the cities one found the same changing phenomenon that spoke of the disease of urbanization—the desperate effort to save downtown Milwaukee with magnificent new speedways and cloverleafs, the same sparkling new center-city architecture which made downtown Milwaukee, like downtown Boston, almost unrecognizable to the returning visitor. But round and about center Milwaukee, the still-clean but shabby intermediate ring was dying; and beyond that, the suburbs with their magnificent supermarkets and shopping malls were sapping the center's vitality.

There was much more of tradition in Wisconsin than in Florida, for Wisconsin is a state of proud history; and this tradition was being mercilessly squeezed by change. Wisconsin is not a rich state; its per-capita income of $3,720 is well below the national average of $3,910. Yet it prided itself for almost seventy years on one of the most advanced systems of social legislation in the Union. Under the La Follette Progressives, Wisconsin had pioneered workmen's compensation, the regulation of railroads and utilities, a state income tax; it had endowed its people with an extraordinary educational system capped by a superb state university in Madison, as well as one of the finest health systems in the nation. This progressive tradition, in the age of inflation and rising expectations, ran, however, smack against another tradition: that of the homeowner. Settled by Yankee farmers in the south and German farmers in the north well before the Civil War, Wisconsin had absorbed Swedes, Danes, Norwegians and Poles by the scores of thousands, all of whom brought with them atavistic longings for homes and gardens of their own. Wisconsin was a homeowner's state—69 percent of its citizens lived in their own homes; but in the decade of the sixties the cost of their progressive tradition and legislation, their schools, hospitals and fine roads had begun to squeeze the homeowners. Property taxes had been rising and grinding, from $400 a year for an average home to $600 a year, to $700 a year, to 10 percent annually, in some cases, of assessed valuation. "You take the average retired worker," said Congressman Henry S. Reuss of Milwaukee's 5th District, "who's living on Social Security and a small pension. His total income is perhaps $4,000 a year. When you ask him for $600 a year annually in property tax on his home, you're driving him to the wall." The cost of conscience for Wisconsin's advanced social legislation thus came high. Alone among the Governors of the Union, Wisconsin's humanitarian Governor Patrick J. Lucey did not gag at the McGovern promise of $1,000 a year to every American. He had taken a pencil and figured out that welfare, Medicaid and other benefits to poor people already exceeded $1,000 a year for each of Wisconsin's needy.

The $1,000-a-year debate was, however, several months in the future. In Wisconsin the arriving national candidates found their issue prefabricated: the property tax. In Florida all had been forced to debate busing, in a blur of denunciation, praise, support, alarm. In Wisconsin the hot issue created another blur—everyone, but everyone, was against property taxes. Wallace and McGovern, Jackson and Lindsay, Humphrey and Muskie all lifted their voices in chorus against corporations, giveaways, tax loopholes, the rich, the businessman, in that most ancient of Democratic anthems, "Soak the Rich."

In such a blur, with no issue dividing the major candidates, each trying to scratch the others with slur and innuendo, victory would go to the candidate with the best organization—and that was without doubt McGovern's. Of the Wisconsin campaign, beyond the organization of the McGovern troops by Eugene Pokorny, there remains little narrative: only vignettes of memory.

§ Of Hubert Humphrey, indefatigable, a political figure who had survived from the pre-television age, barnstorming from dawn to dusk, handing out recipes for Muriel Humphrey's black bean soup ("Vim, Vigor, and Vitality," read the recipes handed out at shopping malls and street corners); cuddling black youngsters in the ghetto, driving his campaign managers to speechless vexation by his delays, because he liked talking to the black children. And everywhere he went, he called on Wisconsin to remember the past—he, Humphrey, had pioneered the test-ban treaty, the rural-electrification authority, workmen's compensation, Food for Peace, etc., etc. And none but the old remembering, while the young were already mobilized for McGovern.

§ Of the moment of recognition—a visit to Serb Hall on the south side of Milwaukee, an obligatory ethnic rendezvous for all candidates, where they must drink beer, bowl with the men, eat fish-fries and strange Slav foods and smile while doing so. All the major candidates were scheduled for a drop-by on Saturday before election, and, by accident, four of them arrived at once—Humphrey, Lindsay, Muskie and McGovern. One caught again that strange, impossible-to-describe political moment of mood and portent: John Lindsay, blond, tall, self-possessed, wandering the tables with no attention, interrupting the muscular workingmen and their wives in housedresses, as they ate, to shake hands and introduce himself. The Secret Service had already decided that Lindsay was not a serious candidate [1] and so the six-foot-three Lindsay, stripped of the one dubious official badge of candidacy, must stroll the strange tables accompanied only by his devoted five-foot-eight New York police detective, Pat Vecchio. Then, Muskie, arriving late—his large frame stooped, his head down, swathed in a melancholy he could not shake, to be ignored. And Humphrey, at table with a posse of recognizable Wisconsin ethnics, munching away at his fish with gusto, attended by cameras, TV lights and newsmen—until the moment of McGovern's arrival, when the magnetism passed, as if a conductor had pointed with his baton to the real candidate. Cameras, lights, newsmen had moved, click, by unspoken command, to bunch around the Senator from South Dakota, and fallen into the serpentine formation which, in any contemporary political jostle, marks the path that the star cuts through the crowd.

Here in Wisconsin the moving star was George McGovern.

§ And, finally, primary night—the snow falling in the streets of Milwaukee, turning to wet as it fell, and the evening news on every television set leading off not with the contest for the Presidency, but with the news from Vietnam. Everywhere, from Quangtri to Kontum to Anloc, the Viets were again on the offensive; the unending war was killing Americans again. How much or how little the coincidence of the new offensive affected Wisconson voting one cannot tell; perhaps very little, for the war had been going on for a long time and people had made up their minds about it. McGovern's troops had been in Wisconsin long before the start of the campaign, and they had pressed "Right from the Start" into the subconscious.

The returns were easy to report, but surprising. The vote was smaller than anticipated—1,415,000 rather than the predicted 1,500,000. But of the 1,128,000 who voted in the Democratic primary, George Mc-

---

[1] The Treasury Department had its own political formula for assigning Secret Service men to candidates. Announced candidates who drew at least 5 percent in the Harris or Gallup poll would be protected starting March 20th; so, too, would unannounced candidates drawing more than 20 percent. But not Lindsay. Lindsay declared that, in any event, he would reject such protection—it would spoil his New York style of campaigning.

Govern carried off 30 percent of the state vote for a clean sweep of the eleven delegates-at-large. He carried seven of the nine Congressional districts, losing only the 5th in Milwaukee (largely labor and black) and the western 7th with strong ties to Minnesota. The surprise lay in the night-long seesaw of votes for second place between Hubert Humphrey and George Wallace—for here in Wisconsin, with almost no formal campaign or organization, George Wallace was to come in second with 22 percent, to Humphrey's 21 percent. Fourth was Edmund Muskie, with 10 percent, harvesting not a single delegate in a state where in December he had led all polls—not even in the heavily Polish 4th Congressional could he outstrip McGovern. Fifth was Henry Jackson, and sixth was John Vliet Lindsay, who had come to the dusk end of the ski trail and withdrew that evening.

The Wisconsin campaign had been even duller and more confusing than the Florida primary—but now, at last, the polarizing process had begun to work. There were only three viable candidates left who might still identify what the Democratic Party meant in the election of 1972— Wallace, Humphrey and McGovern. Of these, clearly, George McGovern was the most important and one could now concentrate on his trail. This was not generally accepted yet. With Pennsylvania, Massachusetts and Ohio the next big-state contests to come, and Humphrey strongly favored in two, McGovern was not yet the front-runner. McGovern had finished off Muskie and Lindsay and the left was now all his. But the elimination of Muskie helped Humphrey, as did the deflation of Henry Jackson. Wisconsin had been the prime national focus of the McGovern campaign. That he could produce in Pennsylvania, Ohio, New Jersey and other states remained to be seen.

There was a last image I carried away from Wisconsin, one that teased my mind for meaning, weeks and weeks thereafter, as I followed George McGovern.

It had been snowing on primary night in Milwaukee; and on the way back and forth to the candidates' activity centers and the studios on the block of the Schroeder Hotel, I passed a dimly lit storefront. The sign read: "MC CARTHY FOR PRESIDENT." Curiosity pushed me in, and there hung huge evocative portraits of a past Eugene McCarthy, the same dark, brooding face that had pushed the party to turmoil here in Wisconsin four years ago. But curiosity slipped into melancholy—on the tables were piles of unused literature and pamphlets and several silent phones. Two forlorn young girls stood by. Otherwise, empty. The two girls made a brave show of it—yes, they did have volunteers; yes, they believed Eugene McCarthy was the best man for President; well, they had been expecting Senator McCarthy to come himself this weekend, and people were willing to come to meetings, but Senator McCarthy

had had another meeting in California and couldn't come. It seemed
cruel to press them with harder questions, for they were so downcast,
and I went on to the live contestants. On my way back, shortly after
eleven, I passed the storefront again: it was already closed and abandoned.

Four years earlier, at that hour on primary night all Milwaukee
had been Eugene McCarthy's stage. Pennants and street banners flut-
tered from buildings; thousands of students slept on bare floors all over
town, or danced in jubilee, and the Movement was celebrating one of
its greater triumphs. Eugene McCarthy, too, had been able to call up
with his morality a new force in politics—and the energy that responded
swept American foreign policy from its moorings. A political wave had
carried McCarthy to Milwaukee and his high moment in 1968. In 1972
another wave generated by the same moralities was carrying George
McGovern to national attention while Eugene McCarthy bobbed, unnoticed, like a cork left behind in the trough. McCarthy's suite that
night in 1968 had been a free and open place, with laughter and drinking, and later in the night the reading of much poetry, chiefly Yeats
and McCarthy's own, while the phones jangled with calls from across
the nation. McGovern's suite, in the crueler politics of 1972, was
guarded by Secret Service, guests were checked off a list of invitees by
stern scrutiny—but inside was the same gaiety, the same jangling of
telephones as the political switchboards of the nation responded.

Retrospection posed the question clearly: Could George McGovern
use his victory more shrewdly than Eugene McCarthy? More importantly—was George McGovern the creation of his movement, or its
creator? Would he come finally to bob unnoticed in the trough when
the wave passed—or could he master and harness the wave's energies?

In Massachusetts, where I went next for the April 25th primary,
the wave was overpowering, and the McGovern army was riding it.

A precision of movement and logistics had now begun to mark the
operation of the guerrillas. Hart had learned much; he had sped twenty
of his New Hampshire organizers after the March upset to Wisconsin,
to reinforce Pokorny's field organization. The day after the Wisconsin
victory, his field organization had flown sixty-two veteran grass-roots
organizers from Milwaukee to Boston. The day after the Wisconsin
primary, said John McKean, the twenty-three-year-old campaign chairman in Massachusetts, "our switchboard lit up like a Christmas tree."
In the four weeks before the primary day, thirty-six field headquarters
had been opened; and the students of Massachusetts, who by and large
had sat on their hands until spring, were now turning up in hundreds to
canvass. McGovern headquarters, overlooking Faneuil Hall in Boston's
market district, could spray facts and figures like an army briefing room:
3,000 student canvassers were in the streets ten days before the election;

8,000 volunteers would be ready to go across the state on primary day; Boston had been penetrated, each of its 256 precincts coded by priority numbers for voting-day volunteer get-out-the-vote drives in 80 percent of them; radio and television were functioning (of the campaign's state budget of $150,000, two thirds was invested in these media); and McGovern's army was deploying now not for the top place but for a clean majority.

There was, to be sure, no organized opposition. George Wallace was to appear in Massachusetts for a single day; Shirley Chisholm had a parochial presence in Boston's black wards. Humphrey had no organization—he was fighting in Pennsylvania the same day, hoping to eliminate Muskie finally in the Keystone State. And the Muskie men—who had led in the Massachusetts polls by 46 percent to 15 percent (Humphrey) to 11 percent (McGovern) as late as February 13th—were in collapse. Bales of Muskie literature were still piled up at the entry of Muskie's Boylston Street office on primary day, undelivered for lack of troops.

Massachusetts, of all the primary states, deserves a digression—for Massachusetts was, later in November, to be the sole state in the nation to resist the Nixon sweep. In Massachusetts the old politics of ward and patronage and the new ideological politics of the Movement had met and married.

Boston, Massachusetts' capital, is, to begin with, the most Democratic big city in the nation. Over the last four national elections, it has given the Democrats their largest percentage margins, larger than those of New York, Chicago, St. Louis, Detroit. With a larger proportion (15.3 percent) of its people on welfare than any other major city, it has an unshakably Democratic voting bloc of the destitute. To which must be added the loyalties of Irish-American and Italian-American voters who suck in ward politics with their mothers' milk, and a sizable Jewish vote.

Beyond Boston ran other factors for McGovern—an unemployment rate (7.8 percent) consistently higher than the national average (5.9 percent); an industry extraordinarily sensitive to national policies whether in trade or in defense; and the influence of the Kennedy family and the Massachusetts education complex, which, between them, had changed Massachusetts in forty years from one of the most reactionary to one of the most radical states of the Union. The Massachusetts education complex was not only one of the cradles of the national Liberal Theology but also the host of the largest voting bloc in the state—its 300,000-member campus proletariat overwhelmingly devout in the faith of the new theology, as large in impact on state voting as the auto workers in Michigan (597,566) or the mine workers in West Virginia (62,500). To the influence of this bloc had been added the influence of the Kennedy family. The advocacy first of Robert Kennedy, then of

Senator Edward Kennedy had given a social respectability to the peace cause—even among blue-collar workers, who in other states still react to their fathers' stories of dash-and-do in World Wars I and II.

Add a final factor—the Boston *Globe*—and one has the Massachusetts story. The *Globe* is a regional newspaper that now dominates Massachusetts politics as the Chicago *Tribune* once dominated Illinois politics and the Dallas *Morning News,* Texas. Owned by an old Yankee family, the Taylors, managed for over forty years by another Yankee family, the Winships, it is heavily staffed by some of the most romantic Irish writers and reporters in the country. Together their skills and their management have backed against the wall or eliminated most of their onetime rivals. Combining the morality of the old Abolitionists with the eloquence of Celtic radicalism, the *Globe* rivals the Washington *Post* as the most anti-Nixon paper in the country. Its national political coverage is high-minded, literary, gay and unabashedly partisan. Its local excellences are outstanding: a sports page which grips Massachusetts proles, and a hard, sharp reporting of the nitty-gritty deals in the murk of Massachusetts ward politics, a subject of excitement in Boston eclipsed only by their hockey team, the Bruins, and their basketball team, the Celtics. The *Globe,* in short, is the indispensable paper in Boston, and if the *Globe* found McGovern the indispensable man to beat Nixon—which it did—so, too, would Boston.

For McGovern and his planners, Massachusetts was an opportunity to break through to the blue-collar votes in Massachusetts working wards and factory towns. The campus proletariat was, of course, all his. No bulletin board in any college, apparently, carried any other notices but those of McGovern volunteers or rallies. McGovern ignored the campuses here to concentrate on the working towns, and his message was simple: The war was bad. Young men shouldn't have to fight wars that old men make; the money spent on war should be spent here at home to keep Massachusetts workers working. It wasn't the names of middle-class people that labeled in gold those city crossings which Boston calls squares. The names of the honored dead of recent wars in Charleston, East Boston, South Boston, Dorchester read more like O'Shaughnessy, Dolan, Santinelli, Kelly than the names like Otis, Butler, Wentworth on the markers that commemorate the Civil War. The Kennedys were against this war in Vietnam—so was McGovern. Nowhere else did he score with quite such power on blue-collar workers. This was a good guy, was the message of his volunteers; and "I guess we ought to give him a hand" came the response from working people.

On April 25th Massachusetts voted. And in the land of the Last Hurrah, it was McGovern all the way: McGovern—325,673 (52.7 percent); Muskie—131,709 (21.3 percent); Humphrey—48,929 (7.9 percent); Wallace—45,807 (7.4 percent). The Massachusetts ballot, printed in type as fine as the compact version of the *Oxford English Dictionary,* offered opportunity to vote in three places—statewide preference, local delegates, at-large delegates. All the forces of the Last Hurrah had been lined up for Muskie in midwinter and their names were the power of Massachusetts politics. On the ballot in the 8th Congressional District the name of Congressman Thomas ("Tip") O'Neill, majority leader of the House of Representatives, an old Kennedy stalwart, led the list for Muskie delegates to the national convention. McGovern's slate won by three to one. Late on voting night O'Neill called the *Globe* to find out how the balloting was going, and was told the running returns. "My God," said O'Neill, "do you mean my own district is going against me three to one?"

The Movement was rolling now, the wave was sweeping, the strategy was working. It had all been obscure four weeks before. The magic figure of nomination was 1,509 delegates out of 3,016; and McGovern had stood at 3 percent in the public polls in January. Now, in the aftermath of Massachusetts, there he was—clearly front-runner. Massachusetts had brought a clean sweep of 102 delegates, which added onto the 54 from Wisconsin and others to bring him to an unchallengeable figure of 238½, as against 127½ for Muskie and 77 each for Humphrey and George Wallace. Muskie was now, however, the day after the Massachusetts and Pennsylvania primaries, through. McGovern's rivals left in the field were only Humphrey and Wallace, and it was Humphrey he must bring low. Humphrey had won in Pennsylvania the same day McGovern had won in Massachusetts—but the headlines led with McGovern, and national attention was his.

Ohio's primary, with its 153 delegates, was to follow the Massachusetts primary by only a week. By now the McGovern army had acquired a flexibility, a command of its own instruments that allowed it to amplify set strategy with targets of opportunity. Two weeks before the Massachusetts primary the leadership had met in Washington to consider a polling survey by Pat Caddell. Caddell, a twenty-two-year old Harvard senior, was still preparing for his final examinations there, but concentrating in real life on his responsibilities as chief pollster of the McGovern campaign. To the numbers his bell-ringers brought back he added scholarship. He had been right for so many months in describing the aimlessness and alienation of American voters that, in the shaping of McGovern's strategy, he had reached a status just below that of Hart and Mankiewicz. Caddell had now just finished a survey of Ohio. The Muskie campaign, said the report, was collapsing; the support for Humphrey was "mushy." If the money for a last-minute raid into Ohio could be mounted, the volunteers could be ready to go. McGovern had come late to that Sunday meeting, and agreed with his staff. Money had now been found (for Howard Metzenbaum had guaranteed it), and Hart had organized the volunteers.

Victory night in Massachusetts was jubilation. The ballroom of the

Statler Hotel swarmed with students, sitting on the floor, hugging each other, yearning for the leader who came before them to quote Yeats and declare this "a victory for peace, not war." The band of St. Theresa's High School played standard melodies, but otherwise the scene was that of the Woodstock Festival, not politics as once practiced in the home of Big Jim Curley. From the ballroom, McGovern was off to a hangar at the East Boston airport which had been commandeered for a champagne breakfast to send off the striking force of roving guerrillas now grown to eighty-one strong, to repeat in Ohio what they had done in New Hampshire, Wisconsin, Massachusetts. Next week in that state, so long conceded to Humphrey, they were to generate an astonishing 480,320 votes (39.3 percent) as against the former Vice-President's 499,680 (41.4 percent), and claim 65 delegates out of Ohio's total of 153.

George McGovern was at this moment, however, lifting on his primary cruising run to another level of altitude. He had run thus far as a man of peace and conscience; but now, as front-runner, as a serious candidate for the American Presidency, his mind, his thoughts, his perspectives must come under a new kind of public analysis. Much more now had to be told about the man.

I had lunched two days before the Massachusetts primary with Frank Mankiewicz. Mankiewicz said he had warned his comrades that up to now they had enjoyed a free ride from the press, which loves underdogs. Now, said Mankiewicz, they had to expect a different kind of treatment. Mankiewicz was bothered—the campaign had to get an issues team organized, a group that could meet the kind of questions and opposition now certain to develop. "I'm going to pay attention to issues, and getting them organized, right after Ohio," he said.

But it was probably, by then, already too late.

The question occurred to all simultaneously after the Massachusetts primary—to press, to analysts, to Republicans, to other Democratic candidates: What did McGovern really think? How did he propose to govern America?

I had first met McGovern in the fall of 1964, when we were traveling on Hubert Humphrey's Vice-Presidential campaign. As we looked out the windows on the rolling Plains states below, he had talked gently, insistently, with eloquence and grasp on his home country beneath, which so obviously he loved. I had met him again at the Chicago convention in 1968, as a candidate himself, and had found him, after the riots, in a state of fury at the bloodshed he had seen from his windows at the Blackstone Hotel. I had come to see much more of him in 1971 and the early months of 1972; and the more one saw of him, the more baffling he became.

His mind baffled the caller more than his personality. The mind was absorptive, not provocative. There are two kinds of American politicians. Most are talkers (like Franklin D. Roosevelt and Lyndon Johnson) who take over a conversation to frustrate the questioner with a protective screen of banter, anecdote and ramble; but there are also the listeners who force the questioner to do the talking. McGovern was definitely a listener—one of the great listeners of all time. He enjoyed hearing other people talk about America, he loved new facts, new figures, would pull out a scrap of paper to jot down anything that struck his scholar's mind as interesting. Most who came away from a first talk with McGovern felt they had swayed him deeply. But talking to McGovern was all input on the visitor's side. After a while, those who saw him frequently came away wondering what George McGovern thought himself. Eugene McCarthy made the cruelest comment: "Talking with George McGovern," said the insurgent candidate of '68 of his replacement in '72, "is like eating a Chinese meal. An hour after it's over, you wonder whether you really ate anything."

One came away, finally, with the sense that it was not what George McGovern said, or committed himself to, in private that was important—but what George McGovern said in public, what adhered to his mind from all the conversations, reading and experience he had lived through. The mind was like a gravitational field which attracted and rearranged scattered iron shavings of fact about a hidden magnetic polarity within. And in George McGovern's mind the polarity was always that of Good and Evil. He was a virtuous man; he knew what was right and wrong. His mind, like Richard Nixon's, had a pragmatic knack of political organization; but, unlike Richard Nixon's, it accepted input only if it fitted the polarities of his previously fixed thinking.

The mind of George McGovern would make a fine subject of investigation someday for a historian trying to trace the forces of morality and piety which give American politics so much of its unique flavor. The moralists have been a central source of political energy in America from the dissenters who fled the Church of England for the colonies, through the Abolitionists whose conscience freed the slaves, to the Prohibitionists who forced the nation to give up drink because alcohol was the syrup of Satan. George McGovern, in tapping the moral energies of the Movement in 1972, traced back to these antecedents.

The rhetoric of morality and Scripture comes naturally to him. His father had been a coal miner before migrating to South Dakota to become a Methodist preacher and evangelist; and the evangelist lingered always in George McGovern, the son, born July 19th, 1922. George McGovern believed that all men were brothers. He had grown up in a state which still, in 1970, harbored only 1,600 black people (the smallest state percentage in the Union except for Vermont) and 760 Jews; in South Dakota, children played together, went to school together, celebrated Halloween and probably went to harvest dances together. Life in Mitchell, a small town of hard-working, friendly farmers and workers, gave no sense of the intricate life of the big cities, the inner kinship of neighborhoods and ethnic communities, the hard adjustments between groups that big-city politicians learn are the transactions necessary to make brotherhood work in a metropolis. And not until maturity would McGovern read a daily newspaper more sophisticated than the Sioux Falls *Argus-Leader*. All men alike are children of God, George Mc-Govern learned, in city or countryside alike, and politics must be at His service.

Educated at Dakota Wesleyan, McGovern was as fine and good a young man as went off to World War II against Nazism—and not simply to serve but to fly the truck horse of the big bombers, the clumsy, lumbering B-24, in which he wrote a hero's record. It took not only courage but skill to fly that plane, in the best of circumstances. The pilot sat in a seat high up in a plane built to haul bombs and take punishment and be a target, with little ability to maneuver; the pilot could never see his bomb load of 12,000 pounds drop, and had to take his plane on through flak and enemy fighters on sheer guts alone. McGovern came away from the war with a Distinguished Service Flying Cross and a loathing of what he had had to do.

From the war—back to school, studying first to be a preacher, then a historian, at Northwestern University. His doctoral thesis was a study of the savagery of great corporations to their workers a generation before, and it deepened a mind-set that led him, at the same time, to consider engaging seriously in Henry Wallace's Progressive candidacy of 1948. The thought mode was further deepened after his return to South Dakota to teach, when he joined in the Democratic Party's efforts to build an organization in that then overwhelmingly Republican state. The South Dakota Republican party was, even by Republican standards, one of the most backward Republican parties in any state of the Union—and corrupt as well. It was in South Dakota that McGovern perfected his campaign style. Years later, in mid-1972, Owen Donley of his original South Dakota team remarked, "He hasn't changed his style at all—he still runs as the only honest man in town."

What McGovern brought away from it all was a simple view of the universe, and an American phrasing of one of the universal cries of twentieth-century revolutionary politics: "Comrades, we have been betrayed"—the call that broke the Czar's army in 1917, the Weimar Republic in the thirties, the fabric of resistance of Chiang Kai-shek's forces in China. McGovern phrased the call in his own way, in spring, on the primary trail, with his denunciation of the establishment center: ". . . most Americans see the Establishment Center as an empty, decaying void that commands neither their confidence nor their love. It is the Establishment Center that has led us into the stupidest and cruelest war in all history. That war is a moral and political disaster—a terrible cancer eating away the soul of the nation. . . . The Establishment Center has constructed a vast military colossus based on the paychecks of the American worker. . . . It is the Establishment Center that has erected an unjust tax burden on the backs of American workers while 40 percent of the corporations paid no Federal income tax at all last year. I say that is an outrage. . . . I want this nation we all love to turn away from cursing and hatred and war to the blessings of hope and brotherhood and love. . . ." George McGovern believed, as simply as Barry Goldwater did before him, that the American government was the enemy of the American people.

The attack on the establishment—whatever it is—was the central cultural concept of the McGovern campaign. It came, however, with a corona of less important but more vivid cultural issues that made him one of the most luminous figures in the orthodoxy of the Movement. In part, the vivid quality of his lesser issues was forced on him by his enemies, in part by his own strategy. He had had to recruit his army and its troops from the most extreme of the peace groups and the young of the campus—and if their cultural values were not majority cultural values, nonetheless tactic demanded he pursue them. He had spoken at the Washington Moratorium in November, 1969, on a stand flanked nearby by the banners of the Viet Cong. He had pounded his way through a hundred campuses; student cheers and student applause gradually fashioned the style of his rhetoric. He was for amnesty—and on the campus, students shrilled with delight. He felt, and specifically stated, that abortion was a matter best left to state governments—but he left no doubt that he, personally, was for it. He was for black people, busing and integration—without qualification. He was for civilizing the extravagant penalties exacted in many states for the use of marijuana. The colleges took him to their hearts. To win the nomination at all, McGovern had to energize with his morality whatever clusters of women, students and cause people could be moved by morality to action in the primary states. With these, he might be able to seize control of the party; with control of the party he might win control of the government; and then morality could be imposed as national policy. Yet what he said and spoke in the spring months could not be limited to audiences of his choice. On the college campuses, within the circle of his faithful, he might be cheered as the voice of the future; in the tormented cities of America, however, after a decade of similar ringing high-minded proposals, he sounded like the voice of the past—more of the same, and frightening.

McGovern was thus already wrapped in an image of his own making by the time, in mid-passage of the primaries, the more serious writers of the press found it worthwhile to begin the definition of the hard, specific programs which the front-runner was offering to the nation as a would-be President.

And of these, it soon became clear, three were primordial.

His first issue was peace. On the issue of war and peace, McGovern did his own thinking and could explain it with easy clarity. "The war against Communism is over," he said once to me, criticizing my story of 1968, "the challenge to the free world from Communism is no longer relevant. We're entering a new era, and the Kennedy challenge of 1960 is pretty hollow now. Somehow we have to settle down and live with them . . . there has to be an easing off of our reliance on power; too much reliance on power weakens a society." McGovern was for accords with China, with Russia, with the whole Communist world. But so, too, of course, was Nixon—and from February (when Nixon went to Peking just before the New Hampshire primary) until May (when the President went to Moscow just before the California primary), all the while that McGovern preached accommodation, live-and-let-live with Communism, there, on the tube of television, was the President of the United States practicing what McGovern preached.

This first issue, peace, hung on the Vietnam war. But the moralist in McGovern could describe the war only in terms of black and white. If Americans themselves were not criminals, then at least they supported a government run by criminals. America, he felt, sustained a corrupt clique in Saigon against a peace-loving regime in Hanoi; and McGovern's terms for ending the war, however he put them, were simple: to surrender, to ask only the return of our prisoners, in return for which he would liquidate the government a Democratic President had established six years before in Saigon. McGovern's phrases, pulsing with indignation, could reach pure demagoguery, as, for example, "Our government would rather burn down schoolhouses and schoolchildren in Asia than build schools for Americans at home," or "The Nixon bombing policy on Indochina is the most barbaric action that any country has committed since Hitler's effort to exterminate Jews in Germany in the 1930's," or "He's playing politics with the lives of American soldiers and with American prisoners rotting in their cells in Hanoi. He's putting his own political selfish interest ahead of the welfare of these young Americans. . . ."

The anguish of Americans over the war in Vietnam, the shame of soul and impotence, was a nationwide political datum. It was heightened, further, by events which in 1972 visibly transformed the war into a macabre anachronism of the postwar era. The war had been accepted to prevent the thrust of Communist expansion, centered, as was believed then, in Peking, from sweeping all of Southeast Asia. But in February of 1972 Nixon had flown to Peking and made peace with the center of Asian Communism. Why, then, the continuing war? Or, rather: How to get out of it? It was a stupidity of colossal dimensions that American policy wrestled with. For McGovern, however, the root cause was not American stupidity, but American criminality.

From this advocacy of peace, his strongest issue, flowed McGovern's Issue Number Two: the defense budget.

The McGovern defense paper, a fifty-six-page document, was the fall and winter homework of a young lawyer in McGovern's office, thirty-one-year-old, South Dakota-trained John Holum, a prairie student of defense policy. The Pentagon had, to be sure, slipped into ponderous unmanageability; it was fighting a war, moreover, with one of the most stupid leaderships in American military history; and this leadership was accepted with docile servility by both House and Senate Armed Services Committees. Holum's solution, an extraordinary flight of one man's imagination, was, simply, to take the chopper to the Pentagon budget and slash its $87.3 billion total in fiscal '72 by 37 percent to $54.8 billion in 1975—the savings to go to social welfare at home. As the thesis of a young Ph.D. student it would have been outstanding. But Holum was tackling the most complicated problem of American survival, and his action recommendations as a package did not make sense: the United States Navy would be reduced to six carriers. Military manpower would be cut from 2,500,000 to 1,750,000, lower than the days preceding Pearl Harbor. America's missile defenses would be unilaterally cut, without bargaining for balancing cuts with the Soviet Union. Politically, too, it was vulnerable to the attack of local politicians and union leaders from the aircraft industry of Long Island to the electronics industries of Los Angeles.

If the defense program of George McGovern had John Holum as its identifiable father, if it had the rational control of one mind exerting itself to bring order out of a stack of handouts and newspaper clippings, the same could not be said of the McGovern economics program.

The McGovern economics program was Great Issue Number Three. But the "thousand-dollar giveaway," as it came to be known, which was to haunt McGovern all through the year, was an orphan. No one ever, throughout the campaign, wanted to acknowledge fatherhood.

It had come about gradually during the early days of guerrilla planning. In August of 1971 a group of seven distinguished professorial economists had met in the East Manhattan town house of Blair Clark, Eugene McCarthy's 1968 campaign manager. They gathered at three in the afternoon and the session ran for six hours as they discussed the inequity of the American tax system, the need to redistribute income and the problem of balance of payments. "McGovern," said Clark, "behaved like a student at a seminar. He sat by the fireplace and took notes—they were bullshitting him so outrageously I was amazed. It wasn't a dialogue. He was a sponge. He asked respectful questions—but he never challenged them." McGovern could not stay to hear the end of the discussion, for he had to leave early that evening—his staff had arranged a meeting with Matthew J. Troy, Jr., the new leader of the Queens County Democrats of New York City, the first big-city political mechanic of note who had responded to the charisma of the Senator from South Dakota. But before he left, McGovern invited the eminent economists to send in more papers, more ideas, more data to his headquarters for some basic new policy on incomes.

Political tactic set the timetable of the issues. McGovern's campaign drudged along with little press attention in 1971. In early January, 1972, his plan therefore called for headline-catching statements on issues to engage that press attention. The Holum paper on national defense was almost ready (to be released on January 19th). But first would come the major domestic statement on economics and social justice. Thus, the task fell to Gordon Weil, a personality who generated much rancor within the McGovern campaign, but a most serious and earnest man. It was up to Weil to paste up all the ideas of the academics into one major paper on how wealth might be redistributed in America, and have it ready in time for the "issues phase" of the early campaign. For two full evenings, after his other exhausting work was done, Weil labored, putting together the ideas that had come into McGovern headquarters; and what came out was the famous Ames, Iowa, speech of January 13th, 1972, delivered to a college audience, ignored by the national press—but a speech which was to acquire a survival quality easily equal to Barry Goldwater's casual statement in January of 1964 that he could see no usefulness in Social Security.

The Ames, Iowa, speech was a long, loose ramble which McGovern and Weil presented not as a blueprint but rather as "suggestions" or "options" that, as President, McGovern might offer to Congress for debate. It was a collection of random thoughts on the fractured and deformed tax structure that has calcified in the postwar years about the interests of every special group of pleaders. It attacked the special treatment of capital gains; the oil depletion tax; the inheritance tax; the depreciation taxes. It proposed sweeping tax reforms that would close all loopholes, gut the rich, comfort the middle class and sustain the poor.

Of its specifics, two proposals achieved an exuberant vitality of their own. The first was a new taxation of inheritances—no individual in America would be allowed to receive, either in gifts from his family during their lifetimes or on their death, an inheritance larger than half a million dollars. Half a million dollars is about the value of a good family farm in the Midwest these days, and larger than a good many small businesses. In an age of inflation, half a million is one of the targets that hallucinate millions of ordinary people whose dreams toy with similar sums as they toss abed. ("Do you realize what this does to a life-insurance salesman?" cried John Bailey, Connecticut Democratic State Chairman. "We've got lots of life-insurance salesmen here in the party—

it can cripple them.") It was a truly revolutionary scheme. It would, said one academic economist, create an American capitalism without capitalists. More importantly, in the words of Richard Dougherty, McGovern's press spokesman, "it would wipe out the dream factor—every slob in the street thinks that if he hits the lottery big, he may be able to leave half a million to his family; it wipes out dreams."

More explosive even than the legacy stipulation of the Ames program was, however, the "demogrant" program. The demogrant program was McGovern's approach in economics to the problem of good and evil, and it was the best Gordon Weil could make out of all the confusing suggestions he had received from the academics. Quite simply, the demogrant program promised $1,000 a year to every man, woman and child in America, from Henry Ford and Jean Paul Getty to each unwed mother with her out-of-wedlock children in the city slum.

In the higher arithmetic of American economic thinking, the $1,000-a-head demogrant program is not nearly as bizarre as it was later made to seem. Variously called incomes equalization, negative income tax, family assistance, it reflects a thinking that all civilized leaders, mayors of big cities, Congressmen of both houses have for years accepted: the fact that the poor are ever with us and, in a big-city civilization, must be taken care of.

The ways of taking care of the poor are infinite, but the tax laws and appropriations required are complicated; and for over a decade now the matter of income redistribution has been under debate in America. Indeed, at the moment of the launching of McGovern's demogrant program, the Nixon administration had been fighting for almost three years for a minimum family grant of $1,600 a year (later raised to $2,400 a year); the Democrats on the Hill had been fighting for a minimum grant of $3,000 to $4,000 a year; and George McGovern himself had sponsored a bill, submitted by the National Welfare Rights Organization, to guarantee every family $6,500 a year. All these bills, however, were based on people's need, as were all the other contraptions of thought that had grown up in the 1960's to take care of the needy: food stamps, Medicare, scholarships, manpower training. The new McGovern demogrant program was, however, divorced from need. On the surface it appeared like the purest biblical utopianism. Everyone, but everyone, would get a minimum $1,000 a year from the Federal government—and then the government would tax back enough from the comfortable above a certain gross income to make up for what it paid to the poor.

So far, so good. But what kind of new taxes? On whom would they fall? How much would new taxes hurt *you* in excess of the $1,000 a year you would get in the mail from the Feds? Would it begin to hurt only those who made over $25,000 a year? Or would it hurt as far down as $12,000 a year, which is what a blue-collar worker with a working wife ordinarily takes in?

The trouble was that no one on McGovern's staff knew—not McGovern himself, not his speechwriters, and certainly not the academics who had fed their thoughts into the campaign and now fled from any intellectual sponsorship of their godchild as presented by Gordon Weil. Later Maurice Stans, finance chairman of the Republican campaign, would find the McGovern proposals on inheritance, demogrants and income tax one of the finest devices available for raising money from the terrified rich. Stans would brandish before very rich contributors the embossed Senate bill S3378, the McGovern-sponsored $6,500-a-year family guarantee (which McGovern now repudiated), as if he were presenting a high explosive that would blow them, and their fortunes, to doom.

But long before Stans and the Republicans got to work on the $1,000-a-year "giveaway," Hubert Humphrey had preceded them in the California primary, where he was about to make his last electoral stand in Presidential politics.

It was not so much that Hubert Humphrey was old at sixty-one— the vitality, the bounce, the lyric, copper-bell quality of his voice were still there.

But by 1972 Hubert Humphrey had been part of the scenery too long, as long as Richard M. Nixon—and he had become to the young and the press a political cartoon.

If Hubert were a woman, summed up an old friend, he would probably boast the largest pair of mammary glands in American motherhood. At his political bosom had suckled all the humanitarian causes of America for a third of a century. Friend of the workingman and his union leaders; of the farmer and the general storekeeper; of the soybean planter and the cotton chopper; of the sheepman and the cattle rancher; of the Masons and the Catholics; of the blacks and the Jews; of the aging and the students—Hubert Humphrey in the postwar world had attached his name to every cause labeled Progress in America. When he talked of his record—his sponsorship of civil rights, of Food for Peace, of nuclear disarmament, of student loans, of Medicare and Medicaid, of minimum wages, of Social Security, of rural electrification—one leaned forward, listening, half expecting Humphrey to tell how he had helped Ben Franklin invent electricity.

But the old record which Humphrey so often trumpeted was now advanced in a melancholy recall. Others had stolen his credit, he mourned; his children bore the name of false parents. With a receptive audience, like the aging Jews in the palm-fringed poorhouses of South Miami Beach during the Florida primary, Humphrey's lamentation could become folk art. After a list of all his bills, proposals, innovations to help the aged, to fatten Social Security for working people, coupled with the attack on those rivals who now grabbed credit for what he had nursed into law, Humphrey would continue before such an audience of the forlorn and the abandoned: "You know what I mean. The children, they grow up and go away. Everyone says what fine children they are, everyone takes credit for them, the way they act, the way they talk. But they don't remember their parents any more. . . . Only the parents remember how they stayed up late at night sewing the children's clothes, getting them ready for school, how the children came in late for lunch, and always expected *you* to be there to feed them, or take care of them when they were hurt. . . . People forget their parents in politics, too." And the aging Jews, like the aging blacks, and the aging everywhere, nodded their heads—they remembered, they understood.

Humphrey might some future day go down in American history as one of the greater Senators, like Clay or Webster or Norris, when his career was summed up. For the young of 1972, however, he was a man of the war, Lyndon Johnson's Vice-President. For most of the middle-aged, he shimmered with schmaltz. But over the same years of American politics that had spanned the career of Richard M. Nixon, whenever dream and reality had confronted each other, Humphrey had embraced the dream, Nixon the reality. Now, by historic irony, in June of 1972 in the California primary, at the end of his twelve-year pursuit of the Presidency, it would be left to Humphrey, the dreamer, to shove the reality of American life and government as it really was against the new dreamer and preacher of 1972, George McGovern, and thereby begin McGovern's destruction.

For Humphrey, the California primary was the end of the road on a last adventure which had somehow gone awry. It had begun in the fall of 1971 when a few political speculators had put up the money for an in-depth survey of voter opinion and had discovered how spongy was the support for Edmund Muskie. Obviously, the clash between the insurgency and the traditionalists which had broken out in Chicago in 1968 was about to repeat; and to many who feared the insurgency, if Muskie could not stop it, then the only alternative was Humphrey.

Early money was forthcoming from Humphrey's old sources. Labor's old alliance with Humphrey promised a working base; and there was all the past, the Humphrey record, the recognition value left from the 1968 campaign to buttress the try. Florida had been the first test— $550,000 had been spent there, a team of Florida "pros" hired to manage the campaign; but Humphrey had come in with only 18.6 percent of the vote. Wisconsin should have been Humphrey's—a neighbor state of Minnesota, it was conceded to Humphrey by the press as casually as New Hampshire had been to its neighbor, Muskie of Maine. $89,900 was spent in Wisconsin, as well as enormous physical vitality—but Humphrey finished third, after George McGovern and George Wallace, succeeding only in finally destroying by his presence the candidacy of Edmund Muskie.

Phase Two of the primary campaign had gone better. Humphrey had won Pennsylvania, against major efforts by Muskie, Wallace and McGovern. With the aid of the steelworkers' union in that state he had taken 35 percent of the vote, 57 of its 137 delegates chosen by districts. He had been hard pressed by McGovern in Ohio, but, with labor's backing, had taken 79 delegates there and won the statewide plurality. He had run and won against George Wallace in head-on contests in both Indiana and West Virginia. But then he had performed dismally in Michigan, a labor state, where he had every reason to hope for better than the 16 percent of the vote he finally drew. And had fared poorly in Nebraska in a head-to-head contest with McGovern. A major effort of McGovern's army had defeated him there, on May 9th, by 41 percent to 35 percent.

All in all, as Humphrey looked forward to California's primary scheduled for June 6th, he and his staff knew they were in trouble. His popular-vote totals were substantial, to be sure. In the primaries up through May 16th counting popular votes, Humphrey had scored 2,606,186, McGovern 2,183,533, George Wallace 3,334,914. But the delegate count was discouraging: McGovern now, after Nebraska, led by 560 delegates; Wallace, though eliminated by a bullet, held 324; Humphrey himself had only 311. On Tuesday, June 6th, four states would select a total of 415 delegate votes—of which, beyond comparison, California with its 271 delegates was the most important. "California is the ballgame," said Humphrey flatly, when asked what his chances were.

Looking forward into California was, for Humphrey, looking into the sunset. There he stood, Hubert Horatio Humphrey, the last defender of the center tradition of the Democratic Party against the insurgency; derided by the press, which had grown tired of him; stripped of his personal role as the party's dreamer by the preacher of 1972, George McGovern; and completely outgunned by the evangelist's organization.

The contrast in organization—Humphrey's and McGovern's—told much about the new politics and the old politics.

Of McGovern's army in California, one can almost say that it had reached that same perfect state of its art that the U.S. Bomber Command had achieved in 1945—and then gone on to overkill. One marveled: 283 storefront offices in place by election weekend; more than 500 out-of-state organizers dispatched to key localities; 10,000 volunteers walking precincts, ringing doorbells; precise polling was charting movements of voter sentiment; money and deployment followed the polling report of how the voters were moving. Two million homes would be

visited by primary day, perhaps 2,300,000. Three-by-five cards had
given way to print-out forms and computers. Electronic tapes of registered voters, purchased from the registration offices of each county, had
been cross-coded with other tapes of telephone numbers; had then been
sorted into print-outs of names (every individual name with its own number); been organized by print-out sheets in kits, on which volunteers
coded questions and responses. Storefronts gathered print-outs from
volunteer precinct walkers, then shipped them to regional headquarters;
from regional headquarters two trucks carried bales of print-out sheets
to computer centers; there the computer spat out and mailed a personalized form letter from George McGovern to each numbered respondent,
addressed to that voter's central concern as identified at the threshold by
a precinct walker: education, social security, the war, Israel, busing—
there were twelve letters in all. The guerrillas of New Hampshire and
Wisconsin had, in three months, become the most efficient technical apparatus ever fielded by any candidate in a primary. "I don't know," said
William Geberding, a political-science professor at UCLA. "I've been
telephoned three times myself this week by McGovern volunteers, and
a friend of mine has been telephoned four times. They may be doing
too much."

Humphrey's organization reflected another era—for, in contemporary terms, he commanded nothing he could call his own. Humphrey
had dealt always in the structured systems of power where friendly leaders could deliver what tradition or loyalty had long since packaged—
unions, ethnic blocs, farm groups, big-city machines. In California, so
large and so diffuse, Humphrey's strength rested on what manpower
labor could deliver, and how much money his friends could raise to reach
the unorganized by the media. Both were difficult.

The commander of the AFL/CIO's rescue squad in California was
Robert J. Keefe, a rising political quantity in the national labor organization. Said Keefe, talking of his dealings with California's labor leaders,
"We're doing all we can. But they're tired of Humphrey, he's been
around too long. They say, 'Oh, Goddamit, here he is broke again, we've
been pulling his chestnuts out of the fire for years.' All he's got going for
him here is what we're putting out for him—our mailings, our membership lists. But we have to piggyback him on local campaigns. Wherever
we back a local candidate in the primary, we'll pack Hubert in on top."
Keefe, like most labor leaders, likes to march in the front rank of a
parade that includes other elements, too; union leaders become embarrassed, discouraged or surly when they find that the parade consists
only of themselves. And Keefe was thoroughly discouraged. "What are
you going to say about a campaign when you go into headquarters in
the morning and the biggest question is how are we going to get $280

in cash, *now,* or else our staff gets tossed out of their motel rooms this afternoon?"

Keefe's problem—money—written with several additional zeros at the end of the digits, was the desperate problem of the Humphrey campaign in California, and lay squarely on the desk of the late Eugene Wyman, the campaign treasurer.[2] From Wyman's desk the picture looked even bleaker than it did from Keefe's. Wyman's efforts around the country had raised, and seen spent, over $2,000,000 nationwide for the Humphrey campaign before California. The money had come in large chunks, and had gone—where, no one knew, for bookkeeping was never a strong element in a Humphrey campaign. Now the McGovern camp, riding the tide of victory, had $2,000,000 to spend in California alone, plus the organization that Gary Hart had seeded across the state as early as June of 1971. For the last effort of Humphrey in the climactic California primary Wyman had managed to hold on to $400,000. And then, about ten days before his final media push, he had been wakened one morning by a telephone call from Washington—Humphrey's Washington headquarters was not only $1,000,000 in debt; it was all but in the sheriff's hands. If, somehow, Wyman could not send $250,000 immediately to Washington, headquarters might be padlocked; and those who had been writing checks for campaign expenses against deficit balances might be carried off to jail—that day. There was no question about what must be done; and most of the money squirreled away for Humphrey's California campaign, along with the vital television exposure it was to purchase, evaporated.

Without money, without organization, without press support, something else had to be added to the Humphrey campaign—an idea.

The idea, as it occurred to Wyman and William Connell, Humphrey's long-time personal aide, was quite simple. Up to now, by the polling analyses, McGovern had been winning primaries simply on the

[2] Eugene Wyman, who died after the campaign was over, was not only an outstandingly pleasant and effective man, but, had he lived, would have been seen as a transitional figure in a large historic phenomenon. Wyman had come to prominence nationally because he was a natural expression of California's rise to imperial status in the political community. In political terms, California had been a provincial state until the 1960's—a capital-import state. Eastern politicians pumped money into California campaigns and did their best to manipulate them. By 1972, however, California had become a political capital-export state. Like New York, Texas and Illinois, California had become a state whose very rich invested in candidacies in every other state of the Union. In September, 1972, a lunch (in San Francisco) and a dinner (in Los Angeles) raised more than $2,000,000 from California Republicans in a single day—as against slightly more than $1,600,000 raised by Republicans in New York on the previous evening. On the Democratic side, the unchallenged champion money-raiser was Wyman, an outgoing, warmhearted Beverly Hills lawyer, known to Democrats from Maine to Alaska as a man who could always raise the extra $10,000 needed to keep the Liberal Idea well nourished.

message of decency, trust and peace. Yet the voters, it appeared, did not know what McGovern really stood for. McGovern should be made to explain himself. California was a polyglot state, its Democrats even more split than its Republicans. California Democrats are a West Coast melting pot: Mexican-Americans; blacks; Indians; Orientals; Italians; Jews who might be made to worry about McGovern's obscure views on Israel; transplanted Southern Democrats, "ridge-runners" who might be made to worry about busing. And, above all, working people. Though in California working people wear sport shirts rather than blue collars, they worry about the same grocery and social issues that plague industrial workers everywhere—such as jobs and welfare. Defense is the state's chief employer, and McGovern's call for huge defense cuts sounded like less jobs for Californians on the line. McGovern wanted a more generous welfare system; most working people were suspicious about the sound of the proposal. Up to now McGovern had been winning primaries as Mr. Good Guy, the man who was "Right from the Start." Humphrey—so Wyman and Connell decided—must destroy that image, and expose what exactly McGovern was. In short, Humphrey must stop competing in the role of Mr. Dreamer; he must become Mr. Practical.

The simple solution offered by Wyman and Connell was that Humphrey should challenge George McGovern to debate the issues. Before a free television audience which they lacked the money to buy, Humphrey might, in the give-and-take of debate, force McGovern to define his proposals sharply and thus show the audience where McGovern stood. Humphrey approved the Wyman-Connell plan in Washington; by May 18th McGovern accepted; on May 28th, nine days before the primary, would come the first of three debates.

As the debates began, it stood in the polls that McGovern would carry California. Pat Caddell's private poll for McGovern, a serious study, indicated the margin might go as high as 15 points. The most respected California public poll, the Field Poll, held a week before election that the sweep would go as high as 20 points—McGovern 46, Humphrey 26, the rest scattered.

Sunday of the debate, Humphrey gathered his advisers at the Beverly Hilton Hotel. Their course was clear, all agreed—Humphrey must go on the attack as soon as the screen lit up, and hit the McGovern slogan of "Right from the Start." He must score immediately and throw McGovern off balance. McGovern had voted for the Tonkin Gulf Resolution in 1964, as had everyone else. Humphrey must say we had all been wrong on Vietnam, McGovern included. And then he must attack again: on defense. And then attack again: on welfare. Attack—all the way.

McGovern's briefing session was held at the Hyatt House, with eighteen people present to offer advice. McGovern, at ease on a chaise-

longue, his shoeless stockinged feet stretched out, entertained them first
with an anecdote. Yesterday had been Hubert's sixty-first birthday and
he had called his old friend to wish him well. Hubert had told him he
wasn't feeling very well, he had a stomachache and a fever. "Maybe
it's all those mean things you've been saying about me, Hubert, that's
giving you the bellyache," was McGovern's amiable recall of the conversation. And Hubert had answered, "I really don't like saying those
mean things, they don't go down very well."

McGovern now invited discussion, and as his advisers talked, he
listened, then would sum up. On defense policy it was quite clear that
McGovern knew more than anyone on his staff—of the capability of
nuclear submarines, of the situation in the Mediterranean, of the use of
bombers. It came then to the welfare problem, and McGovern inquired,
now in June, what kind of figure he ought to use in the debate. One was
first impressed, then disconcerted, as the conversation went on:

How many people would benefit from the welfare scheme, asks Mc-
Govern—we used to say 80 percent, now we're saying 50 percent, what
figure should we use? A babble of response from his advisers, but no
answer. Frank Mankiewicz breaks in, having read Humphrey's speeches,
"Humphrey's going to say that everyone who gets under $12,000 a year
in this country gets relief, and everyone over $12,000 a year pays for it."
McGovern: How many people in this country earn over $12,000 a year?
Again a babble of answers . . . a hundred million? No one knows. Ted
Van Dyk offers mildly the thought that a lot of people hope someday to
make *more* than $12,000 a year. Well, says McGovern, maybe we
ought to say that those who make between $12,000 and $25,000 a year
will pay a "slightly higher tax." Someone offers the figure of $21 a year
more. The figure pleases McGovern. And the advisers and economists
in the room break into discussion until McGovern says, "I like that figure. Twenty-one bucks a year more at $20,000 a year. I'll stick to
that." Then, after that, "Just for my own peace of mind, what's the estimated cost to the budget of my $1,000 proposal?" Someone offers the
figure of $30 billion. Someone else challenges it. Someone else says it
doesn't cost anything because it's simply a transfer of funds. No one
knows. McGovern sums it up—he thinks he'll say that it would be
awfully hard to devise a welfare program worse than the one we have
now. All nod in agreement, and Frank Mankiewicz, his square chin
stuck out, slaps on a kicker: "If we get hit, let's take it straight—let's
say, yes, the very rich and the powerful will have to pay more."

On to other matters for the debate: politics, the power brokers,
what about Wallace? George McGovern: "Oh, Wallace—if elected, I'll
name him Ambassador to South Africa." (Laughter.) On to busing.
McGovern is worried about busing. Frankly, he thinks he made a poor
performance in Michigan on busing—he waffled. What's our position on

busing? Again—a conflict of figures. Someone says that Walter Mondale has stated that 43 percent of all American kids are already bused to school; and someone else says no, the figure is 65 percent. Busing trails off into no answer. Pat Caddell raises several points—Humphrey is perceived in California as too strident, he hurts himself with his stridency; McGovern must play it cool. His (McGovern's) problem, according to Caddell, is that 20 percent of the pollees see him as a radical. McGovern mildly responds: "You mean the idea is they think I'm too radical?"

The California debates were watershed events in the campaign, for their impact on McGovern's image. Three veteran correspondents—Messrs. David Schoumacher of CBS, David Broder of the Washington *Post,* and George Herman of CBS—had agreed they would keep this first debate off the clinical details of campaigning and focus their questions on the issues; thus they delivered television at its finest.

The debate opened with Humphrey glowering and McGovern glowing, and McGovern scored first with a poetic passage about when he "was a boy growing up in South Dakota . . . every person I know loved this country and was proud of it." Then Humphrey, punching, moved in, as planned. "I believe that Senator McGovern, while having a very catchy phrase . . . 'McGovern Right from the Start,' that there are many times you will find that it was not right from the start, but wrong from the start. We were both wrong on Vietnam. Senator McGovern is wrong on Israel. Senator McGovern has been wrong on unemployment compensation . . . on labor law and on the two or three great issues here in California; on his massive unrealistic . . . welfare program. On taxation he is contradictory and inconsistent. He is wrong on defense cuts. I think they will cut into the muscle, into the very fiber of our national security."

McGovern froze and pedaled water for a few minutes. (I dined with McGovern the next night and he explained himself. Hubert had been his friend; he had never expected such ferocity of attack from a friend. And Hubert, it had seemed, was crying. McGovern was unfamiliar with Humphrey's vulnerability to the brilliant lights of television, and the watering of Humphrey's eyes seemed to indicate some deep distress in an old friend who, though now a rival, was still cherished.)

On air, McGovern was the more attractive man, soothing as he went. But Humphrey, in a state where defense industries sustain life, was unrelenting: "Senator McGovern . . . says, halt the Minute Man procurement, halt the Poseidon procurement, halt the B-1 Prototype. Phase out 230 of our 530 strategic bombers. Reduce aircraft carrier force from 15 to 6. Reduce our naval air squadrons to 80 percent. Halt all naval surface shipbuilding. Reduce the number of cruisers from 230 to 130. Reduce the number of submarines by 11. . . . When you . . . reduce the total number of forces 66,000 below what we had pre-Pearl

Harbor, you are not talking about just removing waste . . . you are cutting into the very fiber and the muscle of the defense establishment."

From defense to welfare. Welfare had by now confused all reporters covering McGovern, and Schoumacher of CBS asked, "As you know, reporters covering you have been trying for quite some time to get a price tag on your welfare bill. . . . Can you tell us today how much it will cost?" McGovern: "There is no way, Mr. Schoumacher, that you can make an exact estimate on this proposal." Schoumacher: ". . . you are asking us to accept a program that you can't tell us how much it's going to cost?" McGovern: "That is exactly right. There is no way to estimate the cost of this program other than to say there is no net cost to the Treasury at all. . . . Every American who is earning $12,000 a year or less would profit. . . . Above that figure, up to an income of $20,000, it might cost him another $21 a year in taxes to support this program."

Mr. McGovern did not know what his welfare proposal would cost, and Mr. Humphrey bore in: "I took a look at it right here in California. A secretary working in San Francisco making $8,000, a single person, and there are thousands, millions of single people in this country, would have an increase in his or her taxes, under Senator McGovern's welfare proposal, of $567." McGovern: "That is simply not true." Humphrey: "It is true. A family that makes $12,000, a family of four, would have a $409 increase." And so on.

To those watching in the studio, Caddell's analysis of the Humphrey personality seemed correct—Humphrey was strident, harsh, pushing. McGovern, so it seemed, was the nicer guy. To Humphrey's old loyalists, the debate was upsetting—Humphrey, said some of his old supporters later, had seemed so "mean." Humphrey was to change his style later, saying, "The first debate was rock and roll. The second debate we did a waltz. The third debate was free for all." But at the hard level in the first debate, where people were trying to make up their minds, it was Humphrey who had scored, not McGovern. He had asked the hard questions; McGovern had given soft answers. And the echoing observation that lingers in this correspondent's mind came from Ted Van Dyk, then high in McGovern's councils, who had watched all three networks at once during the debate. It was CBS that had carried the debate—McGovern versus Humphrey. That same afternoon the other networks were carrying Mr. Nixon out of Moscow—Nixon versus Brezhnev. Van Dyk, comparing the two shows, had thought that the President had looked very impressive—more impressive than either Democratic candidate.

The debates on television, especially the first debate, had been seen by very few, for on Sunday of Memorial Day weekend California was playing at the beach. A quick UPI survey by telephone of 120 homes had found 70 people out; of those who replied, only 20 had watched the debate; and only 9 of these claimed to have been influenced. Yet time was about to go to work and catch up. The local press, then the national press would spread word of the debate the next morning; talk would begin; the substance of the debate would be translated down to a few simple phrases. Wherever it was that Californians gathered to talk politics, they would be talking the next week of what the candidates had said; and with the talk would come an erosion of the McGovern lead—first in California, then nationwide. He had stood in the first week of June closer to Nixon in the Gallup Poll than ever before. From California on, that margin would widen and never approach parity again.

The California vote was slow coming in on the night of June 6th. McGovern led in the early totals; but in the key-precinct analysis of CBS and NBC it was much closer—far closer than the Field Poll's twenty points, even closer than Caddell's fifteen points. In general, the army had performed magnificently. McGovern was strong in northern California, surprisingly strong in conservative San Diego County, running far ahead in the Central Valley, which had been Eugene Pokorny's California field command. But the vote was breaking badly against McGovern in working-class areas—above all, in Los Angeles, where one third of California votes. Here in the Los Angeles metropolis Wyman had invested what little media money Humphrey had left to give McGovern his only opposition on air in the state. In the aerospace areas of Burbank and in blue-collar Huntington Park, Humphrey was running between two and three to one over McGovern in working-class precincts. He was splitting the black and Chicano vote in urban Los Angeles, despite McGovern's enticing welfare proposal for the poor. And in the lower-middle-class Jewish precincts of the Fairfax district, Humphrey was running ahead by two and three to one.

It was not until three in the morning that the major networks decided McGovern had won, after all, by what turned out to be a five-point margin, 44.3 percent to 39.2 percent. And with this five-point margin, by the winner-take-all rules of the California primary, McGovern had won all 271 convention votes of the state. He had won in New Jersey that day, too—71 out of the 109 delegates available; he had won all of South Dakota's 17 votes and 10 of New Mexico's 18. The wound that Humphrey's savage California attack had opened in McGovern's campaign was not yet perceived as critical; and now, in the week after the California victory, McGovern could count 975 sure delegate votes out of the 1,509 necessary to nominate. There was only New York left to go, with its 278-person delegation, the largest in the nation; but in New York the old order had collapsed and the state waited for mop-up by McGovern's army.

*   *   *

Had New York's primary happened early, rather than last on the calendar of spring events, it would have become a political legend rather than what it remains now, a cameo of near-perfect performance in the cabinet of memories of McGovern's army.

The McGovern campaign in New York provided all the local astonishments that the army had provided everywhere—and surpassed most. Its campaign coordinator, Edward Rogoff, a Columbia University undergraduate, was a full twenty years old. When one talked to him, a generation was swept away. He had been born during the Korean War. When he was eleven, his mother had kept him home from school with a cold one day and that Friday, November 22nd, 1963, he had been introduced to politics on television watching the story of John F. Kennedy's assassination. Politics, for him, began there. As a teen-age volunteer and canvasser, he said, he'd never been "in a campaign that wasn't computerized." And he knew his work—by primary day 215 McGovern Clubs had been opened across the Empire State, with 30,000 volunteers canvassing, and 12,000 manning each election-district poll.

The over-all Empire State campaign had been the responsibility of Professor Richard Wade, the American historian. His architecture, too, was near-perfect. A single advertisement in *The New York Times* in January of 1971 had begun it; Wade had rented a three-room suite in a hotel to receive the response mail—$9,000 and 2,500 names had come in reply. 1971 had been slow, but by the end of that year Wade, out of his name lists, had put together nuclear groups in the city suburbs where Eugene McCarthy had been strongest in 1968; had closed slowly on the city itself, to capture its Reform Democratic Clubs; had, all in all, spent only $112,000 by mid-April of 1972 when his net of alliances, volunteers and organizers had fielded full slates of delegates in 37 of 39 New York Congressional districts. And by then, in fact, two months before the primary day, the campaign for New York was over.

It is not demeaning to the work of an outstanding academic historian and an energetic boy, however, to say that theirs was not the story. The story in New York was much larger—it was that of collapse, the end of an era, the dissolution of what had once been the greatest state Democratic party in the Union. "Power was lying there in the streets," said Edward Costikyan, the most thoughtful leader the New York County Democrats had ever had, "it was in fragments. All they had to do was to come in and pick it up."

One had come into New York time and again during the long winter and spring campaign, marveling always at the city's splendor, at the towers that rose through the haze on the drive in from the airport, at the arches of its bridges, above all, at the vitality which is its essence. But the vitality of New York City, so long the political capital of the Democratic Party, lay not in its politics—it lay in Wall Street; or in its midtown cultural center; or on the waterfront; or in the creative community of images, film, stage, fashion. Politically, however, New York City was a land of pavement peasants, with peasant leaders. Politicians from all over the nation passed through New York in a continual parade, raiding its rich liberals for money and courting its masters of national publicity for exposure. But New York City politicians were to be despised—they not only possessed no power, they did not understand it.

In New York State, Democrats outnumbered Republicans by four to three, with a margin of 1,000,000. But there was no Democratic party any longer. In the state that once boasted of Al Smith, Franklin Roosevelt and Herbert Lehman, the Democratic party has in twenty years managed to elect only two major statewide candidates—Averell Harriman in 1954 and Robert Kennedy in 1964—a record equaled by the Democrats of Republican Vermont. The Democrats in 1972 were not only split, but so split by race, greed, sectarianism, culture and ethnic heritage as to make definition impossible. Broadly, there were the regulars: pockets of fossil chieftains in a few counties—Buffalo, Albany, Brooklyn, Bronx—led in the largest cities by incompetent predators. In New York City the predators were no longer even able to collect their own graft; and the bureaucracy, despite all of John Lindsay's efforts from above, looted on its own, not even sharing with the old regulars. Against them, broadly, there stood the reformers—the reformers had come into being in the 1950's, inspired by Adlai Stevenson and the cause of peace; they had fought the old regulars with an unprecedented street gallantry, succeeded over the years in simplifying the mechanisms of party procedure, and begun slowly to purify New York's backward, often corrupt courts. But as the reformers had triumphed in the districts, they had fallen into a schismatic, ideological sectarianism. With enormous vehemence they could debate in their clubs all the emotional causes of the day, civil rights, pollution, women's rights, gay rights, above all, peace and the Vietnam War—all things except the cause and future of New York itself. Reformers and regulars alike were devoid of ideas or purpose, except those pumped into them from above or outside.

McGovern's leaders—above all, Wade—had seen the power vacuum; they had moved first to field and file a delegate slate and control the reform wing; it was part of the grand strategy of rolling up the party from the left. The regulars had hung back, leaning toward Muskie but unwilling to make a commitment too early. "We're scavengers," said Meade Esposito, the regular leader of Brooklyn, to Lester Hyman, one of Muskie's early recruiters. "We'll take what we can get in patronage, but we've got to be with the strength." New York's regulars had waited for the outcome of the primaries to see who would emerge with the strength and then throw in their own supposed weight. What emerged, of course, was McGovern—but by then it was too late for the regulars to climb aboard. If McGovern had pre-empted the left, the left had also pre-empted McGovern.

The vote on June 20th, thus, was foreordained. One could only note anomalies; in the 26th Congressional District, where Averell Harriman was running, he was defeated by a nineteen-year-old sophomore from New Paltz College. Across the state, only one regular machine managed to elect a slate—in Albany, where eighty-seven-year-old Daniel P. O'Connell was still the boss; he had won with a slate whose top three members exceeded in combined age the total age of all eight McGovern rivals. All in all, McGovern won 230 of the 248 delegates contested at the polls in New York; 30 more would be chosen by the State Democratic Committee and he would be entitled to 91 percent of those, to give him a total which, at the convention, would come to 256 of the state's 278 votes. The intricate, yet iron-clad reform rules governed the McGovern delegation. The delegation, after adjustments were made, would be 44 percent women (as against 9 percent in 1968); 23 percent young (as against 1 percent); 10 percent black (as against 8 percent); 6 percent Puerto Rican (as against 2 percent). Wrote Frank Lynn in *The New York Times,* "Four years ago, the roster of the New York delegation to the Democratic National Convention read like a 'Who's Who' in the state party. This year the delegation that will leave for Miami Beach . . . might be more appropriately put in the 'Who's That' category. . . . Some of the biggest names in the state Democratic party . . . will be watching the convention on television . . . State Controller Arthur Levitt, City Controller Abraham D. Beame, the Democratic legislative leaders . . . James Farley . . . former Governor Averell Harriman, former Mayor Robert F. Wagner . . . the Brooklyn, Bronx, Manhattan Democratic leaders . . ." The list might have gone on from there by listing a full score great statesmen, ambassadors, Cabinet members who had helped shape the postwar world for the Democratic Party, who lived now in New York and had been wrinkled off by their party—but the obvious absent names were enough to underscore the discontinuity, the rupture of past from present.

No more than 15 percent of New York's Democrats had voted in the state's Democratic primary. What the other 85 percent meant to do with their votes, no one could guess. Neither the regulars nor the reformers controlled these other votes; they were a state of mind, and could be gripped only by someone who understood that mind. From this point on, that state of mind, not the delegates, was the target.

Mr. McGovern appeared in the Windsor Room of the Hotel Biltmore for forty-five minutes on the night of his last primary victory. A gold button was required for admittance, and the room was thronged with very rich contributors and the very celebrated in journalism and the arts. McGovern had been hard at work that day, flying to New Orleans to attend the conference of mayors and solicit support; Mayor Daley of Chicago had, that day, said about President Nixon's policy in Vietnam, "I may be old-fashioned, but I'll support the President; he knows more than we do." Now, with his nomination locked up, with his army triumphant, McGovern would have to deal with this mentality not only in Chicago and New York, but in all the big cities across the country. As McGovern strolled out of his victory party after the last primary, he remarked, "I've been running for so long, I don't know what I'm going to do tomorrow." He would, he told his friends, sit still for three days and think about strategy.

Within the Democratic Party, no political strategy had been more astonishingly successful than his in recent times. He had raided it, now dominated it. The final seizure would come in Miami. At that point the strategy would have to be tested publicly beyond the house of the party in the broad nation outside. The nature of that changing nation and its problems had been freshly defined by the United States Census in 1970. The results of that census were just becoming available with a message that politicians could ignore only at their peril.

CHAPTER SIX

THE WEB OF NUMBERS:
A MESSAGE FROM
THE CENSUS TO POLITICS

THE sixties had yet to fade off into the seventies when I realized that somehow, subtly, "the numbers" were changing my way of thinking—I was trapped in a web of numbers.

The realization came to me when I recognized that I was waiting for Thursday—"Bloody Thursday." Every Thursday evening my television screen would strike out at me with the numbers on Vietnam: 168 killed, 212 wounded, 13 missing. Or: 207 killed, 400 wounded, 19 missing. Or: 45 killed, 102 wounded, 7 missing. I would stay home Thursdays to catch the numbers on death, then turn off; and my mood, my political thinking would be warped, one way or another, for the weekend.

My emotions, I found, were being shaped by statistics. Numbers were doing it to me. At the beginning of each month would come the unemployment figures—up to 5.8 percent, down to 5.4 percent, up to 6.0 percent, all seasonally adjusted to affect my mood, like air-conditioning. A week later would come the price-index figures—these were always worse, and my mood went up or down depending on whether things were getting worse faster or slower. Prices were up 0.7 percent in a bad month, up 0.4 in a good month. Then would come crime figures; and housing figures; and export-import figures; trade-balance figures; school figures; divorce figures; finally Gross National Product figures, and these always baffled me. What were they? What did they measure? In whose web was I caught?

Statistics had once been a clearly marked area of scholarship, where economists, sociologists and planners held intellectual squatter's rights. Now the numbers were a new staple of journalism. The Bloody Thursday figures fitted into the middle pages of the newspapers, as did the numbers on traffic, schools and tobacco use. But the high-impact figures —unemployment, prices, crime—were front-page news everywhere, as well as natural stories for the television evening news.

Slowly, one tried to explore the numbers, for they had become the fashionable way for politicians to demonstrate a grip on reality. And one learned that there are real numbers and phony numbers.

The FBI numbers on crime, for example, were phony. No one could tell from them how grave the menace of domestic violence was to American civilization. FBI figures were bad not because the FBI was lying, but simply because it did not control its figures. National figures were put together by adding local figures collected by corrupt or efficient, slothful or diligent local police forces. If a fairly effective police force, like New York City's, collected its figures honestly, it made New York seem like Death Capital of the nation. If a city like Dallas slapped its figures together haphazardly, Dallas glowed by contrast. And the reputations of both cities affected their politics. But national figures on crime were meaningless. Statisticians had an acronym for such figures: GIGO—Garbage In, Garbage Out.

On the other hand, wherever the Census of the United States certified data, the numbers had to be taken seriously, for the Census made a formidable effort to be accurate. Each month, for example, in whatever week falls the 19th day of the month, the Bureau of Census sends out 1,500 canvassers who in the five days of that week must conduct interviews in 50,000 households in 450 specific areas, asking who is at work in the family, who is seeking but cannot find work. Daily, their sheets are mailed to twelve regional data centers for coding. The tapes are then sent to the national processing center at Jeffersonville, Indiana, which by the weekend is ready to fly processed data to Washington. The Census Bureau meets the plane at the airport and rushes the data to the only four men in the Bureau permitted to work on them. By Monday, some time between nine and eleven, the Census telephones the Bureau of Labor Statistics, which sends two couriers, who must be personally known to the men delivering the data, and the couriers carry the information to the BLS analysts, who work in secret for another week. Up to this point, all unemployment data are as secret as CIA messages—fortunes can be made in the market with advance information; not even the President or the Director of the Census has access to the data. Then, finally, the following Monday, the BLS announces what has happened—how many are working, how many are jobless, whether things are getting better or worse. And with the news, if there is a sharp break up or down, the national mood changes. The stock market soars or plunges, bureaucrats and Congressmen gloat or shudder; Governors, Mayors, labor leaders, academics weave the figures through their speeches; perspectives change.

There is history behind the unemployment figures as there is behind all the major series of numbers the Federal, state and local governments put out. In the Depression of the early 1930's no one knew even vaguely how many Americans were unemployed—was it 5,000,000, 10,000,000 or 15,000,000? And without the measure of the problem, the government could only fumble for solutions. It was the WPA which, in the Depression, first assigned unemployed scholars to work on a realistic facsimile of this information; and from their research came the concept of the Employment Act of 1946; and then the further collection and refinement of figures until the statistocracy of the United States became the world's leading producer of social numbers.

By 1972, numbers had become part of the political culture, picked over by officials, scholars, businessmen, public-relations experts, all of them brothers in a new Jesuitry, skilled—in mimicry of the old—at making the worse appear the better numbers. Were 12 killed in Vietnam in a week 12 too many, and hence evidence of a failure of policy? Or was that number—down from an average 300 a week four years earlier —the evidence of progress and disengagement? Which of two equally accurate numerical statements should a politician use: that more than 100 people receiving over $200,000 a year in income paid absolutely no taxes at all? Or that of the 15,300 people making that much or more, 15,200 of them paid 44 percent, or an average of $177,000 each, to the Federal tax system?

Or, when talking about Black Progress, do you point out that the average black family income rose almost 50 percent in the previous decade, faster than white family income? Or that white families still average 39 percent more a year than black? Or how does one handle figures that strike at the belly—is the alarmist correct because, factually, beef costs more in the United States than ever before in history? Or are the complementary figures on consumption more relevant—in 1972, Americans ate nearly 88 pounds of beef and veal a year; in 1962, only 71 pounds; and in 1929, at the peak of the then-prosperity, only 50 pounds. Are the demand-and-consumption figures more operative, or the price-rise figures more indicative of what is happening?

Behind every table of figures lies a pattern, a concept, an idea of what someone sought to measure. But do old mind patterns, by which numbers are customarily arranged, still measure today's America?

For example, in the largest pattern of all, the Gross National Product, whose numbers are estimated quarterly—is it a valid over-all measure of national well-being? How can numbers measure well-being if the concept of well-being itself changes from decade to decade? The concept of a national measurement of the Gross National Product was imposed in February, 1946, when the thinking of the postwar world impelled Congress to pass its first Full Employment Act, creating a

Council of Economic Advisers that would, in turn, decree the Gross National Product as a measuring figure.

"I was one of the key figures pressing for it then," says Bertram Gross, professor in the Urban Affairs Department of Hunter College, New York. "Who knew then that pushing for growth would distort all human values and priorities? I'm against growthmanship now. . . . The concept of national accounting, this measuring technique, came out of mercantilism; you can trace it from Colbert, through Condorcet, through Keynes. . . . It leaves out the measuring of national resources entirely. Progress came in the old thinking by conquest of national resources, exploiting nature—the more you took out of the ground, the richer you were. But, really, are you richer if you have less coal, or oil, or copper in the ground at the end of the year? . . . Do you value the environment as an asset to be preserved, or something you cannibalize for accounting purposes? . . . And how do you measure household work, the time the woman puts in her house? Or household investment in equipment and appliances—it's larger than industrial capital in our country by a margin of seven to five. GNP is a concept that worked for a certain time period. It doesn't work in a pre-industrial society, because it can't measure the large amount of non-market activities. And again, in this society of ours, this super-industrial society—we're in a period where growth can't be measured by GNP, because our growth is already largely in the non-market references."

In short—was our way of looking at ourselves obsolete? What were we measuring when we measured America? And how much of the heat of political debate came from measures that were misread? Or measures that no longer fitted? Was politics trapped by numbers that came from the thinking of the postwar world, which thus imprisoned the thinking for tomorrow? Or did the numbers themselves describe the new American post-industrial world, providing American data for the pioneer of new social theory—as the data of the British census, a century before, had provided the data for the metaphysics of Karl Marx?

Whatever the philosophic answer, there was no other way to begin an understanding of the campaign of 1972 except to explore the data of the national census which underlay the campaign—the Census of 1970.

One enormous fact dominated the Census figures, pushing through all its tables and indices—the collective decline of the American city, its anguish and turbulence. The postwar world had left the cities behind and gutted their industry and vitality. This story was to be almost entirely ignored in the Presidential campaign of 1972, giving it a quality of domestic irrelevance unmatched since the 1920's.

To make the Census tell what happened to the city, one had to go first to the gross data.

On April 1, 1970, so reported the Census, the population of the United States was 203,000,000. It had grown from 179,000,000 people in 1960 by 24,000,000 citizens (almost half the population of Great Britain), and would grow further at 3,000,000 a year to reach 210,000,000 people by voting day of 1972. This growth was the second largest growth in numbers in American history—but, contrariwise, in percentages the numbers had grown by only 13.3 percent, the smallest percentage growth in American history except for the Depression decade. The United States was growing, yet its growth was shrinking.

To sift the story of the city out of these figures, one had to start with the past, the countryside and the farm. At the beginning of the Republic, only 5 percent of Americans had lived in cities. Now in 1970 the proportion was reversed—only 5 percent lived on farms. As recently as fifty years before, in 1920, 40 percent of all Americans had still actually lived and worked on farms. The old song of World War I had been more accurate in predicting the future than it knew: "How Ya Gonna Keep 'Em Down on the Farm, After They've Seen Paree?" The answer since then, decade after decade, had come in continuing flight; and in the decade of the 1960's more people fled the farm to the city than ever before. In 1960, 15,635,000 Americans had still lived and worked on farms. But, said the Census of 1970, 40 percent of those had fled in the next ten years, leaving behind only 9,700,000! [1]

With the shift, however, had come only the vaguest effort of political imagination to catch up with what this movement of men and women had done to America's heritage of cultural values. The ethos of rural America had held that a man's individual effort made all the difference—his trying hard controlled his rewards. If you plowed deep and sowed with care, you harvested richly; if you worked diligently, you could clear timber and enjoy lush fields, or clear rock and have good pasture. But in the city this ethos no longer necessarily works. Individual effort in the city is webbed with other people's efforts in giant organizations; in the American city, as in the Communist world, your position of leverage in your organization can determine your reward as much as your effort; and the leverage of your group in politics determines what it gets as much as the group's needs. Yet the old cultural values of farm and countryside, no matter what the Census told of reality, still persisted in 1972—not only the ethos of individual striving, but its kindlier memories of neighborliness, friendship, charity. Of all the Presidential can-

[1] If one separated black from white, the black figures were even more startling. In April, 1960, 2,500,000 black Americans still lived on farms. By April, 1970, 60 percent (!) had fled, leaving behind only 900,000 black farmers, sharecroppers and peons to perplex Afro-American historians with their memories.

didates, only one, John Lindsay of New York, seemed to grasp that American cities were ungovernable by old cultural values.

The figures of the 1970 Census seemed to indicate that the movement of Americans from countryside to metropolitan center was irreversible. Of all America's 3,124 counties in 1970, 2,169 had witnessed a net out-migration of their people. Of these, 1,367 showed not only net out-movement but an actual net loss in over-all population; of these, again, some two thirds had been losing population for thirty years, and some for half a century; and three states—North and South Dakota and West Virginia—had net over-all losses in population.

A map published by the Census Bureau in varying shades of red and blue—red for loss, blue for gain—showed the movement graphically. In terms of mileage and space, red dominated the map. Like an inverted triangle, the red of the emptying interior spaces of the country ran south from a broad base on the Canadian border, narrowing as it pushed down through the Plains states west of the Mississippi, throwing off red spurs east in Appalachia and the old Black Belt of the South, then reaching a pointed wedge at the Gulf in Texas.

The growth counties in America were equally clear. The 955 counties that gained by internal migration were found mostly in the city clusters that the Census lists as the 243 Standard Metropolitan Statistical Areas of the United States (SMSA's)—those vast belts of touching cities, towns and suburbs which now create the dominant form of American civilization. And the new figures said:

§ 85 percent of the nation's population growth had come in these metropolitan areas—and within them, 80 percent of the gain had come in their suburban rings.

§ Almost three quarters (73.5 percent) of all living Americans lived in these urban clusters; the clusters fringed the shores of the lakes and the oceans, and the figures said that more than half of all Americans now lived within fifty miles of the oceans or the Great Lakes. The clusters merged into larger megalopolises; of these the largest was the 450-mile belt from Boston to Washington, where lived 36,200,000 people, one sixth of the nation.

§ Put another way: Three quarters of all Americans lived on 1.5 percent of the nation's land. Only 53,000,000 out of the 203,000,000 Americans could be described as living in the rural areas that covered the other 98.5 percent of America's stretch.

§ In this changing pattern of American life, the West had replaced the Northeast as the most urbanized area of the country (by 82.9 percent to 80.4 percent); California was the most urbanized state in the Union, with 93 percent of all its people living in Standard Metropolitan Statistical Areas. By contrast, only three states were still unspotted by such an SMSA—Wyoming, Alaska, Vermont.

As for life within these great clusters, even the serious analysts and scholars of the Census Bureau worried about the definitions underlying their collections of numbers. "What is a suburb now?" asked one of the Census Bureau's demographers when I pressed him for a definition. "We used to define a suburb as a place where people live who commute to work in the city. But now more people work in the suburbs than work in the city, jobs are growing faster there than in the city, the factories are leaving the central cities, but they want to stay in a metropolitan area."

No one could define a suburb any longer by function except to say that it was a satellite community in a ring of other such communities around a desperate central-core city which provided the key services for the entire metropolitan area, delivered its culture, entertainment and thinking, and fed and housed the area's poor on welfare. But the center city no longer provided the jobs for the poor, the illiterate, the unfortunate, the untrained by which, historically, it had grown great. The cities were left with the glories and the debris of a civilization ending.

Neither the Census nor any other figures could describe that macabre phenomenon of decay and fear which spread like cancer spots in half a dozen great American cities. The South Bronx in New York, for example, had become a two-by-four-mile human cesspool comparable only to Calcutta—wild dogs roamed it, drug addicts haunted it; by day and by night it was a place of peril, or, in the words of Dr. Harold Wise, founder of the Martin Luther King, Jr. Health Center there, it was "a necropolis—a city of death." An abandoned hospital, its windows broken, its doors unhinged, reported by its silence that the city had simply been unable to provide police protection necessary for health care in the most underprivileged health area in any big city in the country. Tenements in street after street were boarded up; open lots glittered with broken glass and stank of refuse. Here lived 400,000 people, 65 percent Puerto Ricans and other Hispanics, the rest mostly black—and the whites withdrew farther and farther north as the spreading tentacles of decay and violence urged them out. There seemed to be no way for urban civilization to make the life of these people better; and the phenomenon was repeated, on a lesser scale, in Boston, in Philadelphia, in Detroit, in St. Louis.

The Census of 1970 could only deliver numbers which people might interpret as they wished. For example: Of the twenty largest cities in the country, nine had gained population in the decade of the sixties, eleven had lost population. But if one sorted out such numbers, two gainers among the nine winners were special cases: New York, which had gone up by 1.1 percent, from a population of 7,781,984 to 7,867,760 by the special magic of its unquenchable vitality; and Indianapolis, which had risen, statistically, by an incredible 56 percent, from 476,258 to 744,624, by a technical change of jurisdictional count. When one eliminated these two special cases from the winning column, the figures on cities slowly took on a strange clarity: Every single major city of the North and East had lost population—Chicago, Philadelphia, Detroit, Cleveland, Boston, Washington, Milwaukee, etc. And every single winner—Los Angeles, Houston, Dallas, San Antonio, Phoenix—was in the Southwest.

These numbers represented gross movement; but within them was the most important political story in America: White people, in millions, were leaving the big cities of the North and East; black people and Spanish-speaking people were replacing them. No national politician could examine such figures candidly or openly without instantly exposing himself to the corrosive charge of racism and prejudice. The civil-rights programs of the sixties had delivered much of honor and vast achievement; but they had placed the burden of progress on the people of the big cities; and wherever white people, caught in the clutch of such inexorable programs, could find a way out, they were fleeing the solutions imposed on them.

Politics phrased the race confrontation in America in 1972 as "busing." But "busing" was only a gingerly way of talking about the largest emotional and social problem of domestic life: How would the two races of the country live together in peace? Would blacks eventually dominate the big cities of the North, whites surrounding them in the suburbs to make of the SMSA's huge bull's-eyes of black and white? Should the civil-rights theories of the sixties be pressed further, even if those theories required constitutional reorganization of all the cities and metropolitan areas of the country? Mr. Nixon said, quite clearly, no. Mr. McGovern's position was obscure. And neither could derive any guidance for the future from the figures of the 1970 Census.

The Census noted that black people numbered 22,600,000 of America's 203,000,000, 11 percent of the national total.

Then it added neutrally: "In the Central Cities of the 12 largest SMSA's, the black population increased 37 percent, while that of the whites dropped 13 percent." It provided other material for thought, but entirely avoided opinion or projection.

If one started examining Census numbers of black and white, one had to begin, historically, in the South—the onetime land of slavery.

The new South of 1970, for the first time in a century, was gaining population by net in-migration—not only such traditional gainers as Florida and Texas, but also such states as Georgia, Alabama, North Carolina, Virginia. The net in-migration to those states, however, was a migration of whites—whites passing on their way south the counterflow of blacks to the cities of the North, the whites surpassing blacks by substantial numbers in their contrary flights.

The dimensions of the internal migration of the black people in the United States have been equaled in American history only by the migration here of the Irish in the depopulation of Ireland in the middle nineteenth century, or by the migration of the Jews out of Eastern Europe at the turn of the nineteenth century. In 1940, 77 percent of all the black people in America had still lived in the South and were, in the eyes of Northerners, a rural Southern problem. By 1970, a generation later, 65 percent of American blacks lived in the industrial states of the North and West and had become in the eyes of most of the country a city problem. Moving at a rate of approximately 150,000 a year in the decade of the sixties, the 1,500,000 black migrants who left the South had pooled chiefly in five large states—New York, California, Michigan, Illinois and New Jersey; and, joining with the larger internal multiplication of the black communities already there, had increased black communities in a city like New York by 53 percent, Boston by 66 percent. Whether North or South, three out of five of all black people now clotted in the ghettoes of the central-core cities of a major metropolitan area. Indeed, the larger the city, the more densely blacks clustered there—by 1970, so the Census said, Negroes averaged 28 percent of the population of the central cities in metropolitan areas of 2,000,000 or larger.

Such figures, however, told little of the political or emotional impact on life in the big cities as the black movement proceeded. In 1960 only one major city had a black majority—Washington, the nation's capital. Now there were four such cities—Washington, Gary, Atlanta, Newark. And in metropolitan areas over half a million large, seven more core cities had black populations greater than 40 percent of their total. Of these seven (Detroit, Baltimore, St. Louis, New Orleans, Richmond, Savannah and Birmingham), only Birmingham was expected to keep its white majority through the next decade.

The blackening of the cities was rarely talked about in public political dialogue; but it was obsessive where mothers gathered in neighborhood parks, where men gathered at bars, where young couples talked with each other about apartment-hunting. On the common tongue, the whole phenomenon was styled "tipping": one block would go black; then another; then the neighborhood. In some inner cities, a major factory or mill would tip black, and young whites would look for work elsewhere. In this unspoken drama, it was the school system always that set off anxieties; if a local school tipped, the neighborhood would tip; if a city school system tipped, then ten or fifteen years later one could see the entire city beginning to tip. When politicians talked of "busing," they were obliquely talking, as everyone knew, of tipping. And tipping was a phenomenon limited not just to big-city neighborhoods.

When tipping began, even in small cities, it developed its own accelera-
tion. Of the ten cities in the U.S.A. with the highest percentage of black
population, no less than four were small California communities of less
than 50,000 population which had had white majorities in 1960 and
tipped by 1970—Compton (71 percent), Westmont (80.6 percent), Wil-
lowbrook (82.3 percent), Florence-Graham (56 percent).

Conscience, violence and determined government action had in the
sixties finally begun to open opportunities for some black people, and
numbers reflected that, too. Median Negro family income had risen by
50 percent in terms of constant dollars in the course of the sixties—to
$6,520 a year per family in 1970. Only 9 percent of black families had
earned more than $10,000 a year in 1960—by 1970, 24 percent earned
more than that. And *young* black families (those under thirty-five) were
now averaging $8,900 a year, or 91 percent of white income in the same
age group. Education of sorts was finally being delivered to American
blacks in the big cities—56 percent of all young black adults (between
twenty-five and twenty-nine years old) had completed high school, as
contrasted with 38 percent ten years earlier. By the fall of 1972, the
727,000 young blacks in college were more than double the number in
college in 1964—and they were 9 percent of all American college students; black illiteracy, counting those over fourteen years old, had
dropped in a decade from 7.5 percent to 3.6 percent.

Only imagination could bridge the gap between such numbers and
another more morbid set of numbers offered by the decade's change—
those on the break-up of black family life. Decade by decade, for twenty
years, the strain of life in central cities, and the alternative options offered
there had incubated the dissolution of the older disciplines of marriage
and family. In 1950, only 17 percent of black families had been headed
by mothers without husbands; by 1960 the figure had jumped to 22 percent; by 1970, despite the most intense efforts by the Federal government
to grip the problem, the figure had jumped again to 26.8 percent (and to
28.9 percent in 1971). White families in such condition—whether by
abandonment or tragedy—remained stable at 9 percent. Stated otherwise
—in 1960 the Census counted only 900,000 fatherless black families; by
1970 the number had risen to 1,600,000. And most of these lived in the
cities, on welfare. To be specific, in New York City the number had
grown from 81,000 to 127,000.

It was these broken black families as much as anything else that set
the politics of big cities in motion—for where they were thrust by poverty, or pooled by public housing, safety and tranquility broke down,
causing stable black families to flee from the danger areas of abandonment, crowding white families farther to the fringes of the central city.
Deprived by history of any opportunity to exercise discipline of their
own over their own community, the American blacks, who suffered most

from urban anarchy, could only turn via their newly educated leaders and newly independent black political figures to challenge all white politics. Government, they insisted, must do something to change the nature of the society they lived in since they could not do so themselves—and in 1970 such black leaders were at hand, men who proposed to use their leverage in conventional politics, as every other group had done before them, to advance what they considered the interests of their people.

By 1970 the social progress of the previous decade and the black concentration in the cities had opened political advancement on a realistic base to American Negroes for the first time in their history. The 5 black Congressmen of 1960 had multiplied to 12 black Congressmen in 1970 (and were to rise to 15 black Congressmen in 1972). A black Senator, the first since Reconstruction, had been elected in Massachusetts. Eighty-one black mayors had been elected (later, in 1972: eighty-six), among those the mayors of Cleveland, Newark, Gary (and Washington). The number of black state legislators had grown from 52 to 198 in 1970, local officeholders had multiplied to 1,567 (half of them in the South). And in such critical states as New York, Illinois, Pennsylvania, Michigan and California, caucuses of black officeholders had formed to get the maximum benefit from the explosive emotional issues for which they spoke.

It was this pressure—of growth, of migration, of family break-up—on a government and court system unable to find a new solution for the black condition which, second only to foreign policy and war, colored the politics of 1972. Within their own resources, the cities could not contain the blacks and other minority groups, or meet their problems except at the expense of older white communities which existed within the city.

The Census lumped all whites together. But these whites, under the pressure of black expansion within the city, had begun to cleave, too. Fancying themselves the victims of government which sacrificed their interests to blacks, they had begun to examine themselves as communities, as they had not since the days of their fathers' arrival. Once, as recently as 1960 with the election of John F. Kennedy as the first Catholic to reach the Presidency, it had been hoped that the final melting of the melting pot was under way. By 1972 that hope had turned out to be obviously illusory. Italians, Poles, Jews, Irish, Orientals, Puerto Ricans, Mexicans, even some Scandinavians were beginning to think of themselves as groups with identities and heritages of their own, and restlessly began to wonder how long their communities and heritages could persist in the meat-grinders of the metropolitan areas.

In the shorthand of the politics of 1972, all were lumped together as "ethnics."

*   *   *

Of the ethnics, the Census spoke obscurely, because Americans are less candid about their origins than about most matters.

The Census offered a bare-bone figure in 1970: Despite the growth of American population in the decade of the sixties, the number of Americans of "foreign stock" had apparently fallen: from 34,000,000 to 33,600,000. "Foreign stock" technically meant Americans who had themselves recently migrated here, or who had at least one immigrant parent. Seventy percent of this "foreign stock" was still European—but 30 percent of the new foreign stock was of other origin. Within the decade Mexican foreign stock had jumped by 34.7 percent, Chinese by 63 percent, other Orientals by 68 percent and Cuban stock by 352 percent.

These figures were, however, only the top layer of the ethnic strata of America—the identifiable layer of recent newcomers, with a special twist given such figures by the new immigration laws of 1965 inviting in hundreds of thousands of Orientals, Caribbeans, Colombians, Venezuelans. Beneath this layer of figures lay those of the mass migration of the turn of the century, choked off by the 1924 immigration act, which had by now created second-, third-, fourth-generation Americans whose origins the Census could pick up only by special surveys.

One such special survey had been made in 1969, as "ethnics" began to enter the common dialogue of politics. It was a disappointment. Americans are embarrassed to be asked at their doorstep "What are you?"—they like to think of themselves as Americans. Thus, the Special Survey on Ethnic Origin of November, 1969, could identify only those willing to talk about their origins. Of the then 200,000,000 Americans, the Survey could find only 75,000,000 willing to identify themselves by heritage. Germans and English led the list, with 19,000,000 each. Next came Irish, with 13,000,000. Then Spanish-speaking, with 9,000,000, then Italian, with 7,000,000. Then Polish, 4,000,000; and Russian, 2,000,000. The other 125,000,000 Americans (including 22,000,000 blacks) could not or did not want to be identified by heritage.

Yet the others were there: There were pockets of Swedes and Scandinavians somewhere in that mix, of Jews and French-Canadians, of Greeks, Swiss, Dutch, Czechs, Scots-Irish and half a dozen variants of the old white Protestants—as well as various kinds of blacks, each with a subtle, vital internal culture of its own. Only the antennae of politicians could pick up these varied cultural patterns, with their prides and fears; yet the demographic drama as these real, yet undefined communities mixed, joined, intermarried, had created the unique nature of American politics.

One should linger over the ethnic mix of Americans before going back to the numbers to understand how dramatically different Americans are from other nations—and how swiftly they are changing.

Until the Civil War, Americans were overwhelmingly Protestants of British stock, with a slight admixture of Germans and Irish—their values, customs, sports, laws, education all descended from Britain. Decade by decade since then, the old Colonial-stock Protestants have been shrinking in percentage. Their culture is still the matrix into which all other cultures fit, but this mortar, which cements the other cultures into the political tradition, grows always thinner. To give one striking example: Connecticut, the Nutmeg State, is considered a typically New England state, and this correspondent had so accepted it, until the dialogues of 1972. Stimulated by the new ethnic colloquy and by the Democratic debate over quotas, I asked Irwin J. Harrison of the Becker Poll in the spring of 1972 to run a shirt-tail question in Connecticut to one of his regular political polls: How many citizens of Connecticut could count as many as two of their four great-grandfathers as being born in Connecticut? The answer, I hoped, would tell me how many of the Nutmeg State's Yankees, who fought the Civil War, had left descendants behind in today's Connecticut. The survey came back reporting that only 2 percent (!) of the state's citizens could be sure that two of their four great-grandfathers had been born there a century earlier. In short, in Connecticut, once the most rigidly theological Protestant state of the Union (the Congregational Church in Connecticut was not disestablished until well into the nineteenth century), the Protestant Colonial stock had all but vanished. Here was the most decided minority in the state.

The English-descended Protestants had not vanished in anywhere near such striking proportions elsewhere in the Union—they had simply moved away from the big cities, moved away from the Northeast, held their own in the South and West, and from such areas and the suburbs they watched, with either cultural distaste or anxiety, what "others" were doing in the cities they had abandoned. As to who the "others" were, the Census gave an over-all unpublished figure when pressed to do so—insisting all the while that any such figures must be guesses. In the discussions of the new immigration law of 1965, the Bureau of Census had been required to prepare estimates of the origins of the 179,000,000 people in the United States in 1960. By 1972 their analysis of the population of 1960 was quite old—but it was the closest guess that one had to work with for the campaign of '72. The Census guessed that of the approximately 180,000,000 Americans of that time, people of British-Scots-Irish stock could be counted as 61,000,000, or one third of the total—still the largest ethnic component of American life, but now, definitely, only the largest minority among many minorities. Next, by their guess, followed the Germans, with an estimated 26,000,000; then the blacks, at that time 19,000,000; then the Irish with 17,000,000; then a mixture of people from the Slav countries—Poles, Russians, Yugoslavs, Czechs—totaling 12,600,000; then the Scandinavian family—Swedes, Norwegians, Finns, Danes—for 7,400,000; then Italians, for

7,400,000; then the French and Belgians for 4,000,000; and Dutch 3,000,000. To which must be added the loosely defined Spanish-speaking—9,000,000. And as a final yeast in the leaven: the American Jews, for whom the Census finds no category but who are estimated by the American Jewish Committee as 6,060,000—but their numbers are scattered indiscriminately through the other categories.

Since no real data exist on the geography or community involvement of ethnic groups in America,[2] no serious description can be made by anyone. What follows, therefore, is an impressionistic portrait of how ethnic groups fit into the American political jigsaw of the seventies, as might be described to a visitor from a distant land.

One must start with the largest minority, the old-stock Protestants. In the big cities of the North and East, such Protestants have vanished almost completely as a substantial voting group; their power in the cities of Chicago, Boston, Philadelphia, New York is more akin to that of the Manchu mandarins who governed the mass of Chinese for three centuries from enclaves of administrative residence. What splits exist in the Protestant mandarinate of the big cities are those of policy, of morality, of administration, of leadership rights or of economic interest. Moving west across the map from the Atlantic Seaboard, one begins to find the old-stock Protestants as a major voting force in upstate New York and Pennsylvania, and then, on the far side of the Appalachians, a continuing, sometimes overwhelming power group in small towns and suburbs. Old-stock Protestants vote, as most people do, their economic interests first; the general interest next; their ethnic interest last. They are registered predominantly as Republicans except in the South, where until recently they have registered overwhelmingly Democratic. Germans and Scandinavians are also generally believed to vote in the same pattern— by economic interest first, general interest next, lastly by ethnic interest or inheritance.

The Irish lie between the old-stock German-Scandinavian general-interest voters and the five major special-interest ethnic voting blocs. Suburban and assimilated Irish voters vote with the Protestants of the suburbs; the big-city Irish, ever diminishing, vote by ethnic inheritance.

The Big Five among the lesser ethnic blocs—the blacks, the Italians, the Chicanos, the Slavs and the Jews—vote by ethnic interest beyond all other interest. They are the weak; they are vulnerable; they vote for protection more than for hope. Any abbreviated description of these five voting ethnic blocs has to be a stereotyped distortion, for each one is split within. Yet, over the run of the sixties, one can see patterns in

[2] The best workaday running analysis of the data on ethnics in politics that I have found, and recommend, is *The Ethnic Factor—How America's Minorities Decide Elections,* by Mark R. Levy and Michael S. Kramer (New York: Simon and Schuster, 1972).

their voting. The most solidly Democratic voting bloc among this Big Five is the Spanish-speaking bloc; Spanish-speaking voters vote lightly— but they vote spectacularly Democratic, perhaps up to 90 percent. The next most solid Democratic voting bloc is the blacks, who, in the big cities, also vote 90 percent and up Democratic. (Since these two groups are at the bottom of the pecking order in American life, they sense their rivalry at the bottom and can, by deft political manipulation, sometimes be made to separate against each other.) Next most Democratic among voting blocs are the Jews, although the Jews are going through an internal diffusion of politics of their own, separating rich and poor Jews traumatically. Then follow the Italians and the Slavs.

The pattern of evolution of politics among these groups over the sixties runs like this: John F. Kennedy in 1960 did best with Mexican-Americans—getting 85 percent of their vote; next best with the blacks; then with the Jews, Italians and Slavs; he barely held his own Irish with him. Lyndon Johnson, running against Barry Goldwater, caught them all: Jews, Negroes, Slavs, Italians, Spanish-speaking, to make the landslide of 1964. In 1968 came a break in the patterns. Humphrey swept Jews, Chicanos and blacks—he had served them all in both substance and eloquence; but the drift away from the Democrats among Irish, Italians and Slavs was marked.

By 1972 each of these vulnerable ethnic communities was in turmoil. They seek, above all, protection—whether it be protection for jobs or seniority in the factories, for Italy or Israel, or for the tranquility of their neighborhoods. Among them, when stirred, the Minority Five ethnic blocs may cast as much as 30 percent of the national vote. In key states like New York, their vote may reach as high as 40 percent of the total.

These people of the Minority Five are metropolitan people; they live in the great cities and the suburban ring. There is no adequate map of these communities, and there can be none, not even a leopard-spot approximation, for most of them are mixed in texture. One finds a Parma, Ohio, just outside Cleveland, an overwhelmingly Slav satellite city; a Mount Vernon, New York, heavily Italian; a Beverly Hills, California, heavily Jewish. But most are vari-colored intertwining of racial strands, whose lawns and gardens and shopping centers all look alike, but for whom the thrusting menace is the growing black population of the inner city and the violence of the deprived. On the keyboard of their fears and hopes, politicians have always played campaign melodies. In 1972, more sensitive than ever before, the Americans of such communities were listening to what the politicians had to say. McGovern, in fact as well as in metaphor, read the numbers as black and white— and the whites, ethnic or not, gathered from his message that they must pay the price of the injustice and oppression which America's past delivered to America's present. Nixon, with longer experience in politics, read the ethnics as a threatened group—and promised protection.

If the story of the city and its suburbs was the chief drama traced in the 1970 Census' web of numbers, other substantial dramas in the numbers were useful in understanding the campaign of 1972.

§ After the city story came the youth story. There, on the age profile of Americans, like an orange passing down the throat of an ostrich, was the bulge made by the postwar baby boom. Americans between the ages of 14 and 24 had risen to 20 percent of the population, a larger percentage than in any decade since 1910. In 1960 there had been only 27,000,000 such young Americans; by 1970 there were 40,000,000 of them; and by 1972, so estimated the Census, 25,000,000 of them would be eligible to vote.

In examining the characteristics of these 25,000,000 new voters, one came across the education story.

Each decade in American life has a Sacred Issue to which all politicians must pay lip service. In the 1950's, the Sacred Issue had been Defense and Anti-Communism. In the 1970's, it seems certain that it will be the cause of Environment. In the 1960's, however, the Sacred Issue was Education—and the Census of 1970, reporting on youth, measured the mania for education which had swept American society in the previous decade.

It was clear that what most people spoke of as the generation gap was rather an education gap. For example: The Census said that 61 percent of all white college students came from homes where neither parent had ever been to college! And there were millions of such students. Of the 14,300,000 Americans between the ages of 18 and 21 (up 52 percent in absolute numbers from 1960), approximately a third, or 4,500,000, were in college. Of all those in the 20-to-24 age bracket, 23 percent were *still* in college, against a percentage of only 13 percent a decade earlier. Education had not neglected the others—of all youngsters of high-school age, 94 percent were still enrolled in high school. But there were differences among youth—those who left high school to go to work went to work at the hard trades; of the 16-to-19-year-old young men who had begun work, 56 percent were blue-collar workers; and an unidentified proportion more had been taken into the armed services, whose duties college youth largely escaped. Somewhere there would have to come a clash, or several clashes. Those in college, by the very numbers of the postwar baby boom, would have to jostle each other cruelly for the limited number of executive posts at the top; they had been trained, in the modern idiom of college education, for leadership, and they itched to command. But beneath them lay the proletarian youths of the big city, ethnics, blacks and majority-stock youths alike—

and these proles were not quite the same thing as the leadership youths. The one group wanted to lead; the other group resented this command.

It was impossible to draw their profile from the numbers, for education was more than schooling. The life-style of the young, their dress, their mobility, their dreams, their rhetoric, was entirely different from that of their parents. Television had changed their vision of right and wrong, of war and glory. They had grown up in the longest war of American history, the only war America was destined not to win. They were mobile people, more than any other identifiable group in history except the desert nomads. (Of those people 22 to 24 years old who were counted in 1970, no less than 45 percent had changed their address in the previous year.) Morever, the pill had changed their attitude to family life (in the single decade of the 1960's, for example, the number of children under 5 who had been born to college-educated women had dropped by 55 percent).

§ As for women, the Census had only such rudimentary measures as fertility, income and childbearing to measure the feminine dynamic of 1972 politics. The abstract concepts had not yet been developed to measure the role of women in the post-industrial society as individuals apart from their relationship to men.

What little numerical information there was, however, buttressed the eyeball observation of the liberation of women as individuals. Women were learning to live by themselves; for example—in 1972 the number of divorced women living alone was 66 for every 1,000 women living with husbands, up by 57 percent since 1960. (Indeed, singles, both male and female, were increasing at a phenomenal rate—one-person households in the United States had reached 11,100,000 out of a total household population of 66,700,000.) Women worked more. They accounted for no less than 30,000,000 jobholders (38 percent of the total work force) as against 22,000,000 only ten years earlier. Women waited longer to get married—in the decade of the sixties, the number of women under 24 who chose to remain unmarried had grown by one third. They wanted fewer children, said the Census: in a questionnaire of young women between the ages of 18 and 24, 70 percent responded that they expected to have two children at the most. And they were getting their way. Of all the numbers on women, the most critically important figure was the birth rate. In 1970, the birth rate had been 18.2 births per 1,000 population, a postwar low. The next year, in 1971, however, the birth rate was to drop to 17.2 per 1,000, the lowest in all American history.[3]

[3] Such figures fanned out when broken down by ethnics. Mexican-American women had the largest American families—an average of 4.4 children per woman. Black American women had an average of 3.6. At the low end of the fertility, or romance, scale were the figures on Italian and Jewish-American women. They averaged 2.4 children per woman, barely above the natural replacement level of 2.1 percent.

There were many other measures that graphed the emerging post-industrial society and the backdrop for the politics of 1972. But two more quick measures will have to suffice:

§ America was becoming a society where the definition of work was changing. The proportion of people who made things, who dug minerals, spun textiles, drove trucks, forged metal, assembled parts, was diminishing. Only 35 percent, or 27,791,000, of America's 78,600,000 workers actually made or moved things with their hands and muscle in 1970. The Census called these people, officially, "blue-collars." Most other American workers were called "white-collars," and the white-collars were rapidly increasing because America required services more than goods or food. "Take care of me, Daddy," was no longer a child's request— it was a social need in the complicated post-industrial world. Thus, the Census reported that in the decade of the 1960's, white-collar workers had grown from 43 percent of all jobholders in 1960 to 48 percent of the total job force, or 37,997,000, in 1970. If to this figure were added the figures of strictly old-fashioned service workers, like barbers, beauty-parlor operators, psychiatrists and housemaids [4] who came to an independent total of 9,712,000, then the proportion of American workers in service to those workers who hewed the wood, poured the metals, drilled for oil and harvested food and fiber had risen in the years of the sixties from 55 percent to 60 percent.

§ There was a last number to be separated out of the general employment numbers on how Americans made their living. It was a number overbearing in politics—the number of Americans who now worked for government.

The 1960's had been a decade of prosperity, but for none had it been a more prosperous decade than for those who worked in governments—Federal, state and local. Not only had their salaries, pension rights and fringe benefits increased far faster than for those who worked in private employment. So, too, had their numbers. In the decade of the sixties, they had risen from 7,859,000 to 12,320,637, by nearly 4,500,000 or somewhat more than 55 percent, in a population that had risen by only 13.3 percent. Government workers lived better than most average Americans and they weighed heavily on the budgets of others; at the county, village and municipal level, their demand on taxes had risen by more than 100 percent—from $22.6 billion in 1962 to $56.7 billion in 1971. George Wallace had a visceral sense of what was happening when he denounced the "pointy-headed bureaucrats" eating up the taxpayers' dollars; so did all the primary candidates in Wisconsin

---

[4] The plaint of the white middle-class housewife about the scarcity of servants was a very real one, according to the Census. The number of black and minority-group women willing to be domestics dropped in the sixties by 42 percent, from 898,000 to 520,000. White women willing to be domestics dropped also, but only by 29 percent, from 758,000 to 533,000.

when they discovered what a burden local services were putting on property taxes.

Government employees were now, like the academic staff men of the campuses, a constituency bloc, and, comparing government employees to self-employed, the contrast glared. Decade by decade, the number of Americans who worked for themselves had dwindled. But the drop in the self-employed in the decade of the 1960's was almost as spectacular as the drop in the farming population. In 1960, 15.7 percent of all American men had been self-employed, doing their own work, paying themselves out of their own enterprises, substantially more numerous than government employees. By 1970, however, that figure had dropped to 10.2 percent of American men. Meanwhile the figure of those employed by government had risen from one eighth of all working people to one sixth.

Government, by the end of the decade of the Great Society, had become obtrusive. In the post-industrial world, Americans needed government more than ever—to clean their air and water, to preserve natural beauty, to balance the economy and provide jobs, to build roads and protect the streets, to educate the young and heal the sick. But how far should government go? Was government to be judged, like other services, on cost and performance? Or was it to be judged by feel, by what it did or did not do that made daily life easier and more pleasant?

And with these questions about government, one had to leave the numbers provided by the Census and explore other numbers more relevant to the moods that were to underlie the campaign of 1972.

The campaign of 1972 was often to be compared with that of 1964, and with good reason. It was in the Goldwater-Johnson contest that the issue of government was first and most clearly raised. "Leaders of the present administration," said Goldwater, "conceive of government as master, not servant. Responsibility has shifted from the family to the bureaucrat; from the neighborhood to the arbitrary and distant agencies." To which Johnson had responded, "Government is not an enemy of the people. Government is the people themselves."

And the people, in 1964, had voted for Johnson and more government by a landslide.

Goldwater might have phrased what came next as, "You ain't seen nothing yet"—for after the landslide of 1964, the appetite, vision and reach of government expanded in a manner unprecedented in American history. Its visions were grandiose, its morality genuine, its goodwill robust.[5] But, for the social engineers of the Great Society, visions, moral-

---

[5] A typical example of the rhetoric at high noon in the Great Society might be Lyndon Johnson's presentation of the Model Cities program to Congress in January of 1966:

ity, goodwill were all ultimately measurable by numbers and statistics—both results and goals could be "quantified." Quantification was one of those legacies left to American thinking by the Second World War. In that war, American intellects performed with stunning success by imposing the logic of science on the whirlwind of combat, defining by the most sophisticated digital and numerical analyses the way combat energies should be managed. In the postwar world, social scientists, too, became intrigued with numbers—numbers on crime, numbers on black/white classroom ratios, numbers on suburban change, numbers on housing square-footage, numbers on unemployment and manpower. Such numbers defined shortfalls of achievement or morality; and dollars could provide solutions. The underlying assumption of the best postwar American thinking was that with enough dollars, and enough goodwill, and quantifiable goals, domestic problems could be solved with steady forward movement and a minimum of political discontent.[6]

But they could not. Education, for example, was a problem which did indeed require dollars, but which dollars alone could not solve in the political context of American communities. In no area had American government made a greater effort than in education. Federal funds had gone up from $1.7 billion in 1960 to $9.7 billion in 1972; local funds from $9.7 to $27.6 billion; over-all national spending for education from $24.7 to $86.1 billion. In no area had the approval and applause of intellectual leadership been greater. Left and right agreed that education was a Good Thing. Trying to describe the change in mood of American life in the years since the Depression, Frederick Lewis Allen had written in 1952, in *The Big Change,* that now, in the postwar world, "even the most conservative citizens wanted . . . bigger and better schools."

But exactly twenty years later, a parent in the East Flatbush section of Brooklyn, an orthodox Democratic-Liberal community, was quoted in *The New York Times* as saying, "For a long time it was hard to oppose a school per se. Schools were in the same category as mother-

---

"Today I have placed before the Congress and before you, the people of America, a new way of answering an ancient dream. That dream is of cities of promise, cities of hope, where it could truly be said, to every man his chance, to every man, regardless of his birth, his shining golden opportunity, to every man the right to live and to work and to be himself and to become whatever thing his manhood and his vision can combine to make him.

"The new way of answering that ancient dream is this:
—to rebuild where there is hopeless blight
—to renew where there is decay and ugliness
—to refresh the spirit of men and women that are growing weary with jobless anxiety
—to restore old communities and to bring forth new ones where children will be proud to say 'This is my home!' "

[6] For a thoroughly obsolete picture of the thinking of American intellectuals and their impact on government policy at the high noon of the Great Society, the reader is referred to a series called *The Action Intellectuals,* Spring 1947, *Life* Magazine, written by the author of this book in a season of disordered admiration.

hood. I grew up here. There's nothing special about this place, but it's good. And the school threatens that way of life." The school in question —Intermediate School 387—was to be built in a neighboring district at a site where it was certain to draw white students out of the East Flatbush community and tilt the precarious racial balance of the neighborhood. The morality of numbers imposed such transfers of children by color; but to the inhabitants of East Flatbush the numbers meant nothing; the school system had become a leverage by which a remorseless government, in the name of public interest, imposed its distant will on their home community. Said a Mrs. Elfie Haupt, executive secretary of the local school board, in February of 1971, "This community has been battered by their experiments. First there was open enrollment, then enclave zoning, then rezoning . . . , then pairing. . . . They never follow up with services, so the experiments fail. . . . They frighten people."

Across the country, whether in Flatbush, or South Boston, or Pontiac, or Dade County, or Richmond, or Los Angeles, this morality of numbers terrified people.

Public housing was another face of menace. By the broad measure, one could state simply that public-housing and public-road programs in the decade of the sixties tore down more houses of poor people, chiefly black, than they built. But where public housing was physically installed, it all too frequently brought disaster to the communities of reception. One of the national flagships of public-housing disaster was the famous Pruitt-Igoe project of thirty-three high-rise buildings in St. Louis, built by cost accountants, quantifying goodwill in maximum square-footage allocated to poor people—without ever inquiring what kind of poor people were going to live there. By early 1972 the $36,000,000 project, a showplace of the Great Society, had been so vandalized, so transformed into a place of private danger and random violence, that two of its eleven-story units had to be systematically demolished. But it was easier to erase such a public-housing project physically than to erase from the folk attitude the reputation of what public housing might bring to a quiet community in the way of social disorganization. By 1971 some twenty-five public-housing authorities in the country were described as being on the edge of bankruptcy. Opposition to public-housing projects had become nationwide. From Blackjack, Missouri, to Suffolk County, New York, citizens organized to keep planned housing out of their own communities. Appalled liberals called such opposition "racist"; but in community after community—Greensboro, North Carolina; Philadelphia; Flint, Michigan—middle-class blacks joined middle-class whites in court suits or public opposition to Federally funded projects that would implant in their own stable communities the social debris of the inner city.

If the mood in the early seventies was to reject, everywhere, housing planned or funded by public authority,[7] the hostility did not extend to the more colorful transformation of metropolitan America by private enterprise.

The shopping mall, for example. It was a phenomenon whose impact on American culture and commerce begged for the attention of social historians. No set of American artifacts will baffle future archeologists more than these impermanent temples of commerce. Archeologists will be unable to reconstruct adequately the sense of vibrant life they stimulated—the balloon-tagged cars in the huge parking lots, the lost children, the overspilling bins of plenty, the shopping lust which they were designed to celebrate—any more than they will be able to reconstruct the life and sound of the South Bronx. This correspondent, an inner-city man, found them in 1972 in every primary state, California, Wisconsin, Florida, Massachusetts, in a phase of development that made the early postwar supermarkets of Long Island and California a memory of pre-modern times. They were developing across the country like fantasy-land—the bulging warehouses of groceries, produce, clothing, appliances, surrounded by plazas and fountains, arcades of gourmet and cheese shops tucked away between the enclaves of giant corporate distributors; jewelry stores, fashion boutiques, gardening nooks, baby centers, movie houses, sometimes playhouses, banking booths, night clubs, restaurants, and even chapels and churches, accreting at these marketplaces where, as in medieval times, the suburban citizens found it most convenient to congregate. It could be argued and, indeed, was argued by liberal economists analyzing the tax system that such shopping centers or shopping malls were as much an expression of government intent as was public housing—investment in shopping centers, under the tax laws, was among the safest tax shelters that government permitted to people with high incomes. The government probably lost more money in remission of taxes to such investors than it paid out for public housing with tax dollars. But these temples of the merchandisers worked, and were embraced by suburbia, while public housing was abhorrent to them.

By 1971 there were over 13,000 shopping centers in the United States; in the next fifteen years their number, it was estimated, would more than double. And the inner cities might well tremble at what the numbers of the past decade forecast for the next. In 1958, the year before the first shopping center appeared outside Portland, Maine, its

---

[7] One of the first acts of the second Nixon administration, fulfilling what it saw as its mandate, was, in January, 1973, to suspend all new Federally funded public-housing projects across the nation. The program of Federal public housing had begun in 1949, blessed by Senator Robert Taft and opposed by then-Congressman Richard Nixon. It had built 800,000 housing units by the time Richard Nixon arrived in office; under his first administration more such housing was built than ever before in history, with the total now approaching 1,100,000 such units as old programs reach their end.

downtown businessmen had grossed $140,000,000; ten years later, with ten peripheral shopping centers in business, downtown Portland's business had fallen to $40,000,000. Other cities had less accurate measures —yet whether it was Janesville, Wisconsin, or Rochester, Minnesota, or Selma, Alabama (the last of whose three downtown department stores closed in 1972), the shopping centers of the suburban belt were destroying the central city, by draining it of its commercial vitality.

The flight from the city, from its laws, its taxes, its numerical definition of morality, expressed itself in many ways. For total security from the reach of government, however, nothing could beat the mobile home—with the house on wheels, one could escape not only the city, but the past. If a roving family did not like its trailer park, or the group life of the community it found in passage, it hitched up and moved on. From an almost unknown category of American life in 1960, the aging *wandervögel* of the mobile-home communities had grown to 6,000,000 in 1970. In 1960, only 103,700 mobile homes had been built in America; but mobile housing developed through the next decade into a golden growth industry that produced 415,000 in 1970 (and went on to an estimated 550,000 in 1972). Mobile-home owners—free from real-estate taxes, generally aging (average age: approximately fifty), fleeing violence, given the choice of new neighbors at every move until they found the right neighbors—had become a subculture in America.

The theme of flight could be explored in many other collections of data. For example, in the development of amusement parks. Many big-city amusement parks—the Luna Park at Coney Island, the Palisades Park of New Jersey—had begun to fold; they had become too edgy with tensions and frictions. But across the country, amusement centers which controlled and dominated their communities as their major industry were offering packaged escape and fantasy with such exuberant profit results that they had become investment blue chips. In 1960 there had been one Disneyland, in Anaheim, California; by 1972 it had received over 100,000,000 visitors—and its cheerful young public-relations officer, Ronald Ziegler, had graduated to become the stern public spokesman of Richard Nixon. Southern California by 1972 boasted the Lion Country Safari, Marineland, the Japanese Village and Deer Park, as well as the original Knotts Berry Farm. In Florida there was now a Disneyland East at Orlando. There was a vast new amusement park in Houston (Astroworld). Entrepreneurs in Chicago, Atlanta and Dallas and, doubtless, a dozen other cities were developing plans for even more glittering escape centers.

Two contrary impulses seemed to be vying in American life. Escape from government and constraint was one—escape from war, from draft, from cities, from taxes, from pressure. Sports were flourishing in America as never before, the great journalistic success of the magazine world

being *Sports Illustrated,* reaching its peak of profitability in the year
when its great sister magazine *Life* died for having rubbed America's
nose too hard in the reality of the times. Yet with the impulse of escape
from government came also the impulse of demand on government—for
cleaner air, for purer waters, for better services, for mass transportation,
for protection in the street from muggers and at the check-out counter
from commercial scoundrels.

Whatever the rhetoric of politics in 1972, it rang against a background of change. There could be no doubt that the candidates of 1972
were addressing a country different from that addressed by John F. Kennedy at his inaugural in 1961. "Ask not," John F. Kennedy had said,
"what your country can do for you—ask what you can do for your
country." Public spirit and social conscience had run low by 1972—a
war had worn out the spirit, and random experimentation had worn out
conscience. Few, except for the blacks and deprived, asked what the
country could do for them, and fewer still asked what they could do for
their country. Most, apparently, by mood and numbers, wanted their
country to leave them alone—and leave the rest of the world alone, too.
They wanted out of Vietnam, out of world affairs, out of the cities, out
of the web of numbers. Whether the mood was deep or transitory, accidental or historic, reversible or permanent—that was what the campaign
of 1972 was all about. Mr. McGovern persisted in the Lincolnian tradition of hoping an appeal to the better angels of people's nature might
summon them to new visions; Mr. Nixon proposed to deal with Americans as they are.

CHAPTER SEVEN

CONFRONTATION AT MIAMI

R ELENTLESSLY, through the sixties, the pressures of American life had been putting increasing strain on the conventions of the Democratic Party.

As recently as 1960, one could write of a Democratic convention as it used to be—a universe in itself, a nucleus of thirty or forty tough-minded power brokers, making decisions behind closed doors, while outside the thousands who swelled into the convention city made carnival. Tough, surly or corrupt as they might be, the old power brokers understood what gave the Democratic Party its unique power—its ability to absorb new groups, whether Irish, Italian, Jewish, black, ethnic or labor leaders. The national convention was the anteroom to national executive power.

Yet in the old days the new groups usually arrived disciplined under leaders who had a very pragmatic two-step view of the power process—first, to wring satisfaction for the needs of their clients from the party while, secondly, preserving the party's ability to impose its will on the nation.

1972 was to be a rupture of this two-step unwritten process of power. The closed universe of the old convention had cracked first at Atlantic City in 1964, when the blacks of Mississippi's Freedom Democratic Party forced their way into decision from the streets. It had come entirely apart in Chicago in 1968, when the bloody street confrontation of police and youth had cramped all decisions of power brokers in closed rooms. The reform rules of the McGovern Commission had been the consequence of the Chicago cataclysm—and thus the convention of 1972 was to be an effort to include in the convention process, at one gulp, by untried procedures, all the new claimant groups exerting the pressure of all the new ideas of the sixties, in the open presence of national television, which had now arrived at maturity. Above all, it was to be an "open" convention, all proceedings to be public—no matter what the effect on the November general election later.

The reporting of such a convention was to be difficult—for the old and familiar, the new and the strange would be clashing on uncharted terrain. And the impression this open convention made on America outside, in this new age of television, would be, politically, of as much weight in the campaign of 1972 as what anyone at the convention said or did.

The reform rules had, as we have seen, changed the fundamentals of delegate selection; they had also changed the housekeeping and ceremony of the convention. There would be no more circus demonstrations; favorite sons were to be severely inhibited; seconding speeches were to be limited; the traditional alphabetical roll-call abolished; seating arrangements would be done fairly.

Moreover, the reforms had altered the sequence of the political calendar in a way that created an awkward discontinuity in the repertorial treatment, and thus the public acceptance, of events. Traditionally, the three major committees that dominate a national convention—Platform, Rules and Credentials—had all met in the convention city a week before the opening gavel came down, and their proceedings had become fluid skirmish fronts as contending forces measured early strength in committee votes. Now the rules had changed the sequence and timing of the major committee meetings, so that the committees would gather in Washington at the end of June, to forward their decisions to all convention delegates ten days before they would meet in Miami.

Thus, then, in tracing the tangled beginning of the convention, one had to journey to Washington, where in the last week of June, 1972, the Platform Committee was to meet in the Statler and Mayflower hotels. Four years earlier, in 1968, the Platform Committee had sequestered its subcommittee on War and Peace in a closed upstairs dining room at the Stockyard Inn in Chicago. At that convention, delegates not accredited to the key subcommittee were ushered bodily out of the room; newspapermen clustered as close to the closed doors as the guards would permit and were driven away; rumor, gossip and calculated leak amplified and distorted the struggle between the hawks and the doves, and each successive wave of rumor set off another burst of riot and violence in the city outside. Now, in 1972—

"Forty years of experience in politics won't help you a bit to understand what's going on here," said Mark Ethridge to me as I entered the Mayflower Hotel's State Room. And he was right. The thrust of all the reform rules had been to make an "open" party—and "open" made all the difference. Women and students gathered with the men about fifteen little round tables, covered with gold cloths, as if at a banquet of some Parent-Teachers Association. Television cameras poked above the gathering from their tripods in the rear; benches and tables invited the press to participate and report. At the dais, chairing the meeting, sat Kenneth A. Gibson, the black Mayor of Newark, New Jersey, in shirt sleeves, commanding the group with a firm goodwill that embraced the hall. His affability soothed the Wallace delegates at their tables on the left, gentled the ladies who had come to write a blueprint of the State of God, calmed students outraged by what they considered any compromise with the Good and the True. The doors of the State Room were wide open; newspapermen and dignitaries all sauntered easily among the round tables; cheerfully and mildly Gibson cleared the floor from time to time when the babble became too great. Discussion was both serious and innocent, flavored, like a discussion in a political-science course in college, with the conviction that the world is there to be shaped afresh. Talk rambled; everyone had his or her say; women's voices outnumbered men's by three to one.

A draft platform had long since been put together as a composite of the proposals sucked up by grass-roots hearings across the country. On the floor in the Mayflower, these draft proposals were being massaged by new rhetoric, now and then amended by new phrases, intensely debated by earnest people. The idealistic outlines of the 26,000-word draft platform rose above the past, shimmering like a mirage of what America might be in the future. The theme was clear: The American people suffered from a sinister system of government that frustrated their benevolent nature; beyond the barrier and curse of the Vietnam War beckoned what might come about if the Democratic Party could be elected to implement the best of American goodwill. The platform included a laundry list of national reforms, both the best and the worst. It demanded peace, and a cut in arms; it called for massive income redistribution and a closing of tax loopholes; it demanded abolition of capital punishment and the outlawing of hand guns; it called for welfare reorganization, for abolition of Congressional seniority; it attacked the mania for highways, urged a national energy grid, proposed the transferability of industrial pensions. It included a sweeping demand for the abolition of the Electoral College, and called for the election of Presidents by direct popular vote (only four dissenters said nay when Gibson put the matter to a vote); insisted on the total reform of Congress ("I wonder if the young lady knows how Congress really works," said Congressman Jack Brinkley of Georgia, plaintively opposing a minor point). It promised an "equitable" distribution of all government posts between the sexes; it promised all peoples the right to explore their cultural heritage while simultaneously promising the blacks they might be bused away to any neighborhood to escape their ghetto.

The locus of power on the Platform Committee was clear. Power was controlled by the McGovern command, but was exercised with such melody and sensitivity as to make the full sessions of the committee seem like a waltz. Ben Wattenberg, an experienced political writer and the chief thinker of the forlorn Jackson campaign, sat on the fifteen-man drafting committee and regarded his role there as a sophisticated Greek watching the fall of Rome. He considered himself a hostage in McGovern's camp and observed the struggle within. "Their struggle," he said, "is between the wild wing and the mild wing; what they're doing is selling out their true believers on things like pot, amnesty and abortion. There won't be any riots in Miami because the people who rioted in Chicago are on the Platform Committee—they outnumber us by three or four to one." Then, as an after-comment, he added, "They just lost Michigan to the Republicans today, with their busing plank. No one seemed impressed by the fact that in Macomb County [a working-class suburb of Detroit] they voted against busing in a referendum last fall by fourteen to one."

The Rules Committee had met the same week, and one traced their spoor as another expression of the power contest. The Rules Committee had conceived of a party charter that would create a policy-making party superstructure and a mid-term national convention that would set goals for elected Democrats. Democratic Congressmen, hearing of the plan, had called a House caucus to consider what the new reformers proposed to do to them. Said Congressman Wayne L. Hays of Ohio, "The McGovern-O'Hara-Fraser commissions reformed us out of the Presidency, and now they're trying to reform us out of a party. Those 3,000 people [of the charter's newly proposed mid-term convention on policy] shouldn't run the party. . . . If they're going to run the party, let's abolish Congress and have them make the decisions. I was elected by the people of my district. Not by some packed caucus. I don't think those people represent the mainstream of the party." Added Congressman John H. Dent of Pennsylvania, who noted that only 18 of the 255 Democratic members of Congress were, up to that point, included in the approaching Democratic convention, "Right now, it's the damnedest mess. You've got quotas for everything—blacks, Chicanos, eighteen-year-olds. Pretty soon they'll want quotas for draft-dodgers." In the face of such opposition, the Rules Committee passed, dodging confrontation as it would until the end of the Miami convention.

It was at the Credentials Committee meeting, however, that power dropped all masks and stalked clear, flexing hard muscle. Reviewing the matter of credentials several weeks later, Lawrence O'Brien remarked, "Everyone can agree on rhetoric and words when you get to a thing like the platform. But when you're talking about credentials—credentials mean cold-stiff votes, and that's real power."

The power potential in the Credentials Committee had been misread by the McGovern commanders. From the California primary on, with the nomination touch-close, their national strategy had been to conciliate local opponents wherever state delegations were choosing members for assignment to the key committees. Gary Hart had passed the word to his people to be generous. McGovern wanted to control the Platform Committee, where the diagram of tomorrow's America would be written. Thus, ran the thinking, let places on the Credentials Committee be yielded to rivals to placate them.

It had been some time in May before McGovern's Democratic rivals realized that their power in their party was passing; and this realization had come first to the political thinkers of the AFL/CIO powerhouse. The Democratic Party was labor's home; if the title papers to the property were passing, then the first challenge must be to the legitimacy of the people who wished to inherit their property. Let McGovern's men pack the Rules and Platform committees; *they* would pack the Credentials Committee. From California came the prodding of Sigmund Arywitz, the AFL/CIO chief political operator there, underscoring an opportunity: Why should McGovern claim all of California's 271 votes when he had won only 44 percent of the vote in the primary? If Humphrey, Muskie, Jackson, the labor forces, the Southerners all joined in a coalition to challenge the California delegation, McGovern might yet be stopped. And the place to do so was in the Credentials Committee. Under the operations direction of Robert J. Keefe, the labor people had already begun to sift the arithmetic of the Credentials Committee. Of its 150 members, only 76 were necessary for a majority. Thus labor, leading the ABM (Anybody But McGovern) coalition, moved: In Ohio, where Humphrey had carried the state by only 2 percent of the vote, all six Ohio members of the Credentials Committee were chosen to oppose McGovern. In Texas, where McGovern had won 34 delegates out of 130, all five members of the committee, likewise hostile. In Minnesota, where McGovern had one third of the delegates, likewise hostile. Thus the shaping of the arithmetic.

The scene as it opened in the Cotillion Room of the Sheraton Park Hotel in Washington on June 27th did not visibly show the planning. The chairlady, Mrs. Patricia Roberts Harris, both black and feminine, had been chosen for her scrupulous impartiality. Austere, distinct of speech, neither a McGovern nor a coalition person, Mrs. Harris considered herself bound by duty to be immaculately fair. Frank Mankiewicz later styled her as "running a German kindergarten," but the crack of her gavel had authority. No less than eighty-two challenges had been offered for hearing, of which no less than twenty-nine were finally scheduled, all to be heard in a five-day period—and Mrs. Harris would brook no nonsense with so crowded a schedule. Of the challenges, three were major symbols: South Carolina's delegates would be challenged under the quota guidelines of reform for having too few women; California's would be challenged under the unit-rule guideline of reform for having played fast and loose with winner-take-all; Chicago's would be challenged for violating reform guidelines on slate-making.

First, South Carolina.

South Carolina immediately raises the problem of quotas and women. South Carolina Democrats have chosen only eight women (or 25 percent) among their thirty-two delegates; but in South Carolina, as elsewhere, women count a full 50 percent or more of the population. Does this mathematical disproportion show, all by itself, discrimination against women and non-compliance with the reform guidelines? The elected South Carolinians, speaking through a black spokesman, make a reasonable presentation of how they got there. Elections were open to all; women did actually run for delegates, but they lost. The voters freely chose this delegation, therefore it should be confirmed. The challengers rise. They begin their case with the improbable, symbolic, but real name of a Mrs. Wedlock. Mrs. Wedlock was a Democratic precinct councilwoman in South Carolina—but her mail from the party came addressed to *Mr.* Wedlock; this *proves* discrimination. Et cetera. There is no other solid evidence to prove discrimination in the Palmetto State, which has, by now, 31 percent black delegates in addition to its 25 percent women delegates. The vote of the Credentials Committee confirms reality—it decides women had a fair chance to run for office, the voters of South Carolina chose freely among candidates, the result was this delegation under challenge. The leader of the Women's Caucus floor fight for this particular challenge rises. She is Mrs. Brownie Ledbetter, tall, willowy, eloquent, wife of a political-science professor in Arkansas—and with unexpected traditional gallantry she moves that the decision be made unanimous, the losers, in the Democratic tradition, accepting the mandate of the majority. But the decision will be challenged by others in Miami.

§ Now comes the big one, California.

Only in the past week have the McGovern men realized the implication of Bob Keefe's arithmetic. Since no challenged delegation can vote on its own case, the chair will have to subtract the 10 California members of the Credentials Committee from the roll-call—to leave a total of only 140 eligible to vote. Of these 140, the ABM coalition can mobilize a majority.

Out there in California, McGovern has cleanly and fairly won the whole California delegation, for the law of California unequivocally states that whoever wins its primary wins all 271 delegates. Now the ABM coalition insists that the law of the sovereign state of California contradicts the new reform rules of the Democratic Party—since McGovern won only 44.3 percent of the vote, he is entitled only to 44.3 percent, or 120, of the delegates.

McGovern's people insist that you can't change the rules of the game once the game is over. "Bare-faced political hi-jacking" is what a Massachusetts delegate calls it. But appeals to reason are meaningless. The coalition insists that if McGovern wants the party to play under new rules, the new rules must apply everywhere. Speakers parade back and forth to microphones as Mrs. Harris gavels constantly for order, clearing staircases, scolding the press. The vote comes, clean: by 72 to 66 McGovern is to be deprived of 151 of the delegates fairly won in California, because the reform rules had, somehow, implied that a delegation bound by a unit rule can no longer sit in a Democratic convention. It is dirty; it is cold politics; a handful of people, manipulating a committee of 150 individuals, has denied the validity of the law and voting of California, a state of 20,000,000 people.

With quite an unaccustomed tone of rue, James Rowe, later that evening, summed it up. Rowe, a veteran of all the marches of the Liberal Idea since his boyhood in Montana, his studies at Harvard Law School under Frankfurter, his services as adviser to Roosevelt, Truman and Johnson, approved the coup—but had no delight in it. He tried to lift the California steal out of the frame of a simple caucus fight. "What you people don't realize," he said, "is that the majority of us Democrats don't like McGovern; and so long as we have any power left, we plan to use it."

§ The next day, Friday—Illinois.

The McGovern delegates had been caught off base by the California coup. They gathered Thursday afternoon upstairs on the seventh floor of the Sheraton Park, smarting and bitter. They had been chopped by a power play—tomorrow would come the Illinois challenge, the challenge to Mayor Richard Daley and his 58 Chicago delegates, men and women of the old politics. If the arithmetic had worked against McGovern by the exclusion of his 10 California committee members from voting on their own validity, now the arithmetic will work against the coalition by excluding Illinois' six delegates from voting on *their* validity. Vainly, Mankiewicz pleads for restraint—to kick Dick Daley, Mayor of Chicago, out of the convention jeopardizes the election in November. But the McGovern caucus is in fury. It has been scorched by a brazen exercise of numerical power; tomorrow it will retaliate against the Illinois delegation.

Bizarre as was the decision on California—that a committee of 140 could overturn the choice of 3,564,518 free voters—even more bizarre was the Friday decision on Illinois. The facts were quite simple. On March 21st the voters of Cook County, which is the city of Chicago and its suburbs, Mayor Daley's fief, had chosen 59 delegates hand-picked by Mayor Daley as *his* slate, over another 59 delegates offered by rival groups. The election had been open, the voters free to choose. Now the proposition offered by the McGovern people was that these were improper delegates—slated privately by Mayor Daley's machine before being offered to voters for public election, in violation of Guideline C-6. Moreover, the delegation thus elected was not adequately balanced with blacks or women or youth. And thus, as in California's case, the voters' decision must be rejected.

To replace the elected delegates of Cook County, the reformers offered others—chosen no one knew quite how. In the 1st Congressional District of Chicago, for example, a group of people had met at the home of one James Clement and decided that only ten of those present might vote for an alternate to Mayor Daley's slate; these ten had chosen 7 delegates, including the Reverend Jesse Jackson. This rival hand-picked alternate slate offered the exact proportion of women, blacks and youth required by the McGovern reform rules. Yet the elected slate in the 1st Congressional had been voted in by the people of Chicago and these had not. In one of the most effective political essays ever casually tossed off, Chicago *Daily News* columnist Mike Royko wrote an open letter to the reform leader, Alderman William Singer:

> . . . I just don't see where your delegation is representative of Chicago's Democrats. And that is what this thing is really all about. . . . About half of your delegates are women. About a third of your delegates are black. Many of them are young people. You even have a few Latin Americans. But as I looked over the names of your delegates, I saw something peculiar. . . . There's only one Italian there. Are you saying that only one out of every 59 Democratic votes cast in a Chicago election is cast by an Italian? And only three of your 59 have Polish names. . . . Your reforms have disenfranchised Chicago's white ethnic Democrats, which is a strange reform. . . . The other thing that bothers me about your delegation is that about half of it or more ran in the primary and got stomped. . . . Your people ran—and they should get credit for it—but they lost. . . . Your co-leader, Jesse the Jetstream, didn't make it to his local polling place. He's being hailed as a new political powerhouse and he couldn't deliver his own vote. Now they are delegates, having been declared so by themselves. . . . Anybody who would reform Chicago's Democratic Party by dropping the white ethnic would probably begin a diet by shooting himself in the stomach.

But no appeals to reason would prevail at the Sheraton Park. The coalition had brutalized McGovern on California and had voted absurdity on Thursday night. On Friday, virtue outraged, the McGovern people turned and brutalized the Illinois delegation. By a vote of 71 to

61, the elected delegates of the nation's second largest city were thrown out of their seats. Lapsing into the mood of his repertorial career, Frank Mankiewicz observed, "I think we may have lost Illinois tonight."

The first act of the convention having thus transpired in Washington, one paused at intermission to review the results, which were two.

First, the McGovern reform rules had bite. What bit most had been unintended—the diffusion and fragmentation of Americans by quotas either into races or into biological categories of sex and age. Previously, the reporter of conscience had been compelled by decency to glide over in print most race and ethnic differences. But now, since race was obviously a formal stipulation of the new politics, one could no longer conscientiously avoid such reporting, however racist it might seem. One could not avoid looking for blond hair, dark hair, curly hair; one could not avoid noting the dashiki-garbed and the turbaned heads. The old hypocrisy had been more civilized. But, whatever one's sympathies, how, now, could one avoid wondering what the political effect would be, on the television audience, of the sight of black people jumping and hugging each other with glee as Dick Daley was humiliated, or the sound of Spanish-speaking ladies jubilating over their triumph at this session.

Another more immediate matter had come clear, too. The numbers would determine the nomination at Miami. The most important numbers were the numbers of the California delegates—who would be allowed to vote for California? Then, the numbers on Illinois—who would be allowed to vote for Illinois? It was at all times difficult, even for those devoted to professional scrutiny, to keep the intricate numbers game of delegates, challenges and majorities clear in mind. For those beyond the tight focus of close-in reporting, it was all but impossible—and, thus, the introductory transactions in Washington could be only crudely translated to the public. The simple reality as it hardened out of Washington to the public was that the old politicians were brazenly trying to steal the duly elected California delegation from the McGoverns; and the McGoverns were trying to unseat the duly elected Chicago delegation and replace it with blacks, women and students. Something strange was going on.

It was thus on to Miami, for a game of Russian roulette, a one-day clash that would determine the technical politics of the nomination. That was to be the inside story, the traditional story, and for most of us in the press it was the story we had been trained for years to cover, like generals fighting the last war. But after the clash over the nomination would follow another story—the impression the nation would gather of the new, reformed Democratic Party. This impression on life outside would be far more important than the traditional behind-the-scenes story, but that was not yet perceived.

*   *   *

One returned thus to Miami, hot on the trail of the old story, trying to separate the familiar and old from the new and unshaped.

Miami Beach itself was familiar. The green waters still caressed the clean beaches from which the sun-bleached white hotels rose like latter-day Taj Mahals, inviting Americans to their everlasting love affair with the tropics. Miami Beach had changed little since 1968, when the Republicans met there, except that the open spaces that gave view of the ocean had shrunk to occasional narrow slits between newer condominiums and hotels which by now had become almost a solid rampart barring the passerby from entrance; and that prices had gone up—a drink at the bar had risen from $1.50 to $2 in four years.

Miami Beach has a paradoxical transience and permanence. Devoted to indulgence and vanity, its gaudy hotels lush, efficient and mirrored, it is made of plastic—untouched by what is poured into it, unmoved by its three million annual visitors, it receives all alike with the same smart efficiency and disgorges them in two-week batches with no mark left behind. Like plastic, it remains itself always, permanent until someday, like Atlantic City, it will shiver, crack and break up. The constant that Miami offers is service—solid, reliable service. If one can pay the price, if the credit card is validated at the desk or the outstretched palm wadded with bills, Miami Beach will deliver whatever is necessary for individuals or convention-goers, for politicians or insurance agents, for labor leaders or industrialists, for the aging rich or the aging poor—girls for racketeers, superb medicine for the ailing, fine food for gourmets, sandwiches for snackers, quiet for those who want quiet, noise for night-clubbers. For conventions, it delivers outstanding police service, a magnificent arena, easy buses, a superb daily newspaper and whatever else is required. But always it remains as sterile politically as glassware, each new gathering coloring it for a week, then passing on, leaving the receptacle unchanged.

So, now, in 1972, in the first ten days of July, the receptacle was filling with Democrats, diffusing themselves in a manner as puzzling to old convention-goers as the city itself was familiar.

A geographic pattern is always vital to an understanding of a convention city, and the pivot of this convention was unmistakable—the five-minute quarter-mile walk between the Doral and Fontainebleau hotels. North of this pivot was the familiar; south of the pivot was strange.

Somewhere north of the Doral-on-the-Ocean, running up Collins Avenue past the Carillon Hotel as far as the Americana Hotel beyond the 87th Street city limits, were domiciled all the great names of the Democratic Party which had once governed the United States. The famous diplomats of the past, led by Averell Harriman and Paul Nitze, sojourned here. The old power leaders, led by Barkan and Meany of the AFL/CIO, lived here. The headquarters of both Humphrey and Muskie were installed here. Southern delegations lived here, as did most of the old lobbyists.

South of the Fontainebleau Hotel, at 48th Street, began new country. Here, generally, were gathered the cause and caucus groups, the new voices come to press their issues on the delegates. Most of the young lived in the boardinghouses of the poor at South Miami Beach. The wilder among them, the roving gypsies on the outer fringe of the Movement, were encamped at Flamingo Park, living in half-shelters and pup tents, advocating peace, amnesty, abortion, gay liberation, tolerated by a supple policing that permitted pot, bare breasts or open fornication within the limits of the park.

Then, by far the most important were the women whose National Women's Political Caucus had taken over as headquarters the third floor of the derelict, sea-sprayed Betsy Ross Hotel. One might be amused by the high-octave span of women's voices gathered together, or the rooms with the unmade beds, half-unpacked suitcases, yogurt cartons, chests covered with blue-jeans and bras—but only briefly. The Betsy Ross Hotel was a power center. Mimeograph and Xerox machines spewed out leaflets in thousands of pink, yellow, green, blue sheets; the switchboard at the Betsy Ross Hotel jammed; fuses blew; and each night, after dark, couriers boarded the buses to travel north on Collins Avenue and persuade night clerks of the forty or more major hotels to stuff mailboxes or let them slip leaflets under delegates' doors. "WOMEN POWER 1972" remained stained on the Betsy Ross's third-floor carpet, in faded red paint, when the convention broke up; women power 1972 was real.

But the action, the old story, the conventional story, was all packed into the pivot area between the Doral and Fontainebleau hotels.

The Doral was the McGovern hotel. One could watch in the week before the convention opened as the Doral, one of the Beach's finer showplaces, changed character. One stood in the driveway and saw bellmen smoothly ushering out the middle-aged tourists, the Arnies and Madges, the Charleses and Sylvias, silver-haired men in their plastic patent shoes, covering outstretched palms with a last tip, their ladies of lavender-tinted gray hair and loose-fitting pants, pouting. Then, day by day, the arrival of the TV vans, with their mobile color units, to camp in the parking lot, and police, Secret Service, guards to post themselves conspicuously in place. And, finally, the arrival of the McGoverns themselves, the young in their chinos and levis, their awe at the splendor of the hotel giving way in hours to contempt for its culture until, by the weekend before the convention opened, the Doral had become just another bivouac of the guerrilla army.

The third floor of the Doral could have been, by that weekend, any hotel the troops had occupied in the six months of their long march.

At two-score desks, mimeograph machines rolled, typewriters clacked, the phones rang. A large table with jars of peanut butter, jelly and margarine and a huge urn of coffee fueled the volunteers. Habit patterns conformed to the old austerity—round-trip coach-fare tickets had brought them here from Washington or New York; the campaign paid for their rooms; but only $6 a day was allotted in cash for any food they might need beyond peanut butter and crackers, or for any laundry they could not do in the basins of their rooms. The hotel would provide no room service for volunteers, and place no long-distance calls, unless the volunteers could provide credit cards or cash on their own.

The guerrilla quality of the organization was somehow fading here at Miami; reality demanded tighter controls. "This room," read the sign over their base camp in the third-floor Valencia Room, "is not for reading, watching or waiting." Rank-and-file volunteers, able enough to have earned the right to come here, wore white buttons—but white buttons got them only to the third floor, or to their own room floors. To reach the sixteenth floor, where the hard tactical operations were conducted, required a red button. And to reach the seventeenth floor, which was the command floor, one needed a blue button. Conventions are always the same, with layer upon layer of temporary responsibilities and attendant perquisites. But for the McGovern young, their introduction to the necessary cruelty of hierarchy and its dignities was fresh and unpleasant. A barefoot, long-haired boy might be assigned to take a visitor as far as the sixteenth floor; at the entrance to the sixteenth, he would be dismissed by a contemporary proud of his red button, who led the visitor to the stairway to the seventeenth floor, where he, in turn, would be dismissed by a blue-button who cleared the visitor with the Secret Service men—none of whom were barefoot, all of whom wore neckties and, despite the heat, wore jackets at all times.

The seventeenth floor is command. Here are the suites of the candidate himself; of the finance leaders, Henry L. Kimelman and Morris Dees; of Mankiewicz, of Hart and of Rick Stearns.

Stearns is important. In any convention, with 40,000 or 50,000 people involved, there are no more than twenty or thirty who recognize where the action is, what the pressure points are. Of these, Rick Stearns, at the age of twenty-seven, is probably the key person in the weekend before the convention opens. Dark-haired, dark-eyed, lithe, self-possesed, he is the most fluent master of the language in the McGovern camp except for Mankiewicz. Stearns is part scholar still, part politician, not quite sure of his own role. Student politics had brought Stearns into the 1968 campaign, a very junior McCarthy volunteer in his native California, learning precinct maps and politics, from whence he had gone on to the Chicago convention. A scholarly pause had taken him to Ox-

ford as a Rhodes Scholar, where he had written a well-woven thesis on
the nominating processes in the American Democratic Party; he had
returned from Oxford as an academic specialist in nominating processes
to join the McGovern staff in May of 1970; and had become then the
numbers man of the delegate round-up, specializing in caucus states and
caucus-packing. In moments of relaxation, over a drink or at dinner, the
underthrust of his learning could carry his conversation to the uplands
of history—a comparison of the McGovern movement to the Methodist
revival in England in the eighteenth century, and from there to a splendid rumination on ethics, religion and politics; or to the sober view that
politics is only a way to get things done; most of the people in this Mc-
Govern campaign think that politics itself is the fun, said Stearns, "but
the real fun starts only after we get elected, after we start to change
things."

At the Doral Hotel, in the weekend before the convention, however,
Stearns is all function—the counting man of the McGovern headquarters. This problem of the count has been battled back and forth by lawyers and courts for ten days since the Credentials Committee meetings
in Washington. But, finally, the Supreme Court itself has decided—no
court can settle internal political disputes in the Democratic Party; to do
so would be to invade the "political thickets"; the party itself must decide its own rules, procedures, qualifications.

The central problem of the critical dispute is to decide what makes
a majority of this 1972 convention. The convention counts 3,016 votes.
Specifically, however, what will be a majority when the convention roll-
call comes to California? If McGovern can vote all the 271 delegates he
won in California, then he is virtually assured of nomination by the absolute majority of 1,509 on the first nominating roll-call. But if the
rip-off decision of the Credentials Committee is sustained by the convention, then he will be stripped of the 151 California votes handed over
to the coalition and now in dispute. Thus the question: How large a majority will it take to reverse the Credentials Committee by appeal? Should
it be an absolute majority of all delegates—1,509? Or should it be a
majority of those eligible to vote on the floor? And does this phrase
"eligible to vote" exclude the 120 certified California McGovernites as
well as the 151 in dispute?

The arithmetic of this inside story, on which may hang the nomination, is immensely complicated. But not at Stearns's desk. He has for
weeks been computerizing all delegates to the convention by nineteen
variable personal characteristics. He knows how many McGovern has
for certain; how many of the coalition delegates are wavering because
the California steal is too raw for their stomachs; how many more delegates can be reached if McGovern makes specific deals with their leaders. Stearns is quite confident. On his yellow pad he has marked in

blue 1,442 votes frozen for McGovern, another 187 coalition votes disturbed by conscience, a possible 106 more that can be reached by deals.

All weekend the pressure on these elastic numbers has been building and pulsing at the Doral-Fontainebleau pivot. At the Fontainebleau, National Committee Chairman Larry O'Brien must decide how he will arrange the arithmetic—who votes on which challenges, what constitutes a majority, what sequence of parliamentary maneuvers he will accept on Monday night for the sudden-death balloting on the credentials of members in dispute.

It is a moment of passage. What is about to follow is the final maneuver of the McGovern army, a virtuoso exercise in parliamentary tactic, the final investment prior, some would say, to the sacking of the Democratic Party. There are few real professionals in the battlefield of national conventions. The experience of a county or state party chairman in no way prepares him for the forces deployed, the maneuvers required or the overwhelming pressure of public attention at a quadrennial national convention. National conventions are like moon landings—there are too few contested conventions in a lifetime to train operational masters. Young men who devote themselves exclusively to a study of such conventions can achieve a grasp on their dynamics easily as complete as that of the so-called pros; and if rare opportunity offers them a chance to practice their study, they can make old pros look like stumblers. This opportunity was now offered Rick Stearns—and he was to mount a classic of convention warfare, a Battle of Tannenberg in which he was to be the young Hindenburg.

At 4:30 in the afternoon of Sunday, July 9th, the day before the convention is to meet, the command gathers in Gary Hart's suite on the seventeenth floor of the Doral. They are seven: two women, Anne Wexler and Jean Westwood; two of the field commanders, Eli Segal and Harold Himmelman; one black, Congressman Walter E. Fauntroy; Hart himself in gray denim pants, high cowboy boots, flower-blue open-necked shirt; and Rick Stearns. They are waiting for Frank Mankiewicz, who is attending the decisive meeting at the Fontainebleau Hotel in the bedroom of party counsel Joseph A. Califano, who is telling the staffs of all the contenders how Larry O'Brien, the chairman, plans to rule on votes, majorities, disputes.

Mankiewicz, in rumpled gray seersucker suit, bustles in, a smile erasing the fatigue lines of his face, ebullient. He starts repertorially, "Unless my brains have left me, we've just won California." Then, being unable to resist coloring the scene he has just left, ". . . it broke up with twenty-three out of twenty-four guys in the room rushing to the phone, all of them in a rage at Califano, and Max Kampelman [Humphrey's spokesman] shaking his finger. Kampelman was trembling with anger, saying to Califano, 'Joe, my principal instructs me to say that yours is a hostile act in response to intimidation and pressure.' "

Then to business, for no time can be wasted. Mankiewicz explains: O'Brien will rule that McGovern's 120 certified California delegates will be allowed to vote on the California challenge; but the 151 coalition Californians, under challenge themselves, will not. On all challenges, a majority will mean a majority of those present, eligible and voting. So far, simple. But the parliamentary complications are mind-boggling. The coalition will certainly appeal this ruling of the chair, and McGovern's people must be ready to sustain the chair. Their point of maximum strength will be on the California challenge—on that vote the 151 coalition Californians will be barred. But California is to be fifth on the agenda of appeals; and so strategy evolves. Nothing must give the coalition an opportunity to appeal or overturn the chair's ruling, and set a precedent, before the convention gets to California. The team must find a way to scuttle, compromise or eliminate all other challenges until California comes up.

Which raises the matter of South Carolina. South Carolina is not only first on the agenda of seating challenges, but it is the chosen battleground of the Women's Political Caucus, whose leaders wish to challenge the Credentials Committee's seating of 20 of 32 delegates from South Carolina. By the chair's ruling which Mankiewicz has just explained, a majority of those eligible to vote on this challenge is a majority of 1,499 (i.e., total delegate votes = 3,016; minus 20 disputed = total eligible, 2,996; divided by two for majority = 1,499). But supposing the floor majority for the women falls between this figure of 1,499 and the absolute majority of 1,509? And supposing then there is an appeal of the chair's ruling on what constitutes an absolute majority? What then? Has the coalition enough votes to overturn the chair's ruling on South Carolina and set a precedent for the later challenge on California—that decision must come by an absolute majority of all 1,509? The higher mathematics of the parliamentary conversation approaches Einsteinian complexity. But one point is clear: If the voting on South Carolina falls somewhere in the mystery zone of 1,499 to 1,509, there is peril.

"We can't afford to fall in that magic number zone," says someone. Comment, mutter. Nor can they afford to risk an appeal on the black-caucus challenge in Alabama or Georgia. It is obvious that the women's cause must be betrayed on the South Carolina challenge; all know that this will infuriate them. "We have 150 women out of our 1,500 votes who love women more than they love McGovern," warns Rick Stearns. "You mean," comes another voice, "we risk losing the blacks on Alabama, the women on South Carolina?" Another voice: "Our narrow interest is to see that we win California and Daley loses Illinois." Then

Eli Segal, summing it up: "This means we've got to balance the psychological cost of losing South Carolina against the need of carrying California."

The meeting moves easily, smoothly, to decision: How strictly can control of vote be exercised? How many McGovern votes can be persuaded to vote *against* the women's caucus in South Carolina so as to make sure, by defeat, that the critical challenge does not come up until California? "Let's get at least one delegation that can go both ways," says someone; then it becomes two or three delegations, four delegations they need that can go both ways. The Humphrey people are smart, they'll be tossing votes our way, we have to toss votes their way—we can't risk a floor appeal until California.

"This whole thing is bottomed on floor discipline," says Hart to Stearns, who is in command of the floor controls and floor captains. Stearns nods, quite unworried, like a wing commander confident of his flight's performance in combat. "Rick," repeats Hart quietly, "this means you'll be under intense pressure tomorrow night—we have to field a team with nineteen sophomores out of twenty-two on the squad, and we go up against Nebraska." Stearns nods again. They are all now giving advice to Stearns, who will be calling signals from the command wagon as his floor captains play basketball with the votes against Humphrey's men. "They've got to be drilled, Rick—in California they've got to follow Willie Brown, in New York they've got to follow Crangle."

So they are going to plan to lose on South Carolina, and the conversation turns to the politics of the outside world, and of television. "Well, if we're going to stake the organization on South Carolina, what'll we do if Walter Cronkite says on CBS it's a test of strength for McGovern and we're losing? What do we do about tipping Walter off?" and they play the game of how fully television should be informed of the maneuver. At this point, this observer decided to leave the room, being caught in a conflict of interests which might require him to spoil in public on air the game that was theirs to play.

Walking down from the Doral, back to the Fontainebleau, reflection on the meeting began to pucker into a question. There could be no doubt that the staff command was right—if McGovern was to be nominated, then the California vote was critical and the outcome on South Carolina would determine that. Besides, the women's caucus had no real case to present on South Carolina, except the case of power. Right was right, wrong was wrong; in scuttling the women on South Carolina the McGoverns were morally clean, just as they were in fighting for their rights in the battle on California. Yet, on the other hand, McGovern had promised the Women's Political Caucus just the day before that he would support them all the way on South Carolina. The women would be furious at the unfurling of events tomorrow and would scream betrayal—but who had betrayed them? No answer to that one except, in retrospect, thinking of other leaders like Richard Nixon or John F. Kennedy, it was curious that at this meeting no one had asked what McGovern himself wanted to do about the problem. The staff was making his decisions for him. Nixon or Kennedy would have controlled such a decision, one way or another, and Lyndon Johnson would have imposed himself down to the tiniest detail of the lady-sticking, with relish at the art of vote-manipulation. All three—Kennedy, Johnson, Nixon—knew how to play dirty; *their* staffs knew their leaders sometimes had to play dirty; but when a major dirty was under way, they usually made sure the leader knew of it. This evening McGovern had been absent; he would approve, of course, later. But the operation was under way.

As planned, so it happened the next evening, Monday, July 10th, opening night of the convention—the votes cast, recast, switched and planted; and the Women's Political Caucus challenge to the South Carolina delegation, which McGovern had pledged himself to support, went down in public view, to the mystification of most reporters and public commentators. So, too, was the black challenge on Alabama and Georgia compromised and swept from the agenda. Now, at midnight Monday, it was time for the California challenge which would determine the nomination. And I wandered back from the hall to the McGovern command wagons.

As I came in, they were still chuckling at the public ruse, the private triumph, the hidden-ball tricks of the game; Gene Pokorny was recapping, as after a good hard-fought game, "They threw forty votes our way in Ohio, so we had to toss in a few others. . . ." Frank Mankiewicz was still there, enjoying the scenery, watching the television sets, observing the floor, then, distressed by a McGovern demonstration he viewed on screen, he ordered, "Cut that demonstration." At which all eight young men at the telephones rose, seized their white instruments and passed the command to the floor. "Listen, Irving, this is Harold Himmelman. Two things: stop the demonstrations right now. And no adjournment until after Illinois."

When Mankiewicz had left, to be on the floor when his native California was voted on, one could observe that this operation center contained no one over the age of thirty. Four tables set in U-shape in the air-conditioned trailer wagon bore eight white phones, manned by eight young men. One had seen most of them operate all over the country—Pokorny, Segal, Smith, Clinton, O'Sullivan, Swerdlow, Himmelman. At the floor end of their phones now were much older people, of more presence and larger prestige, Governors, Senators, Congressmen, captains of a floor area of the convention. But the power to manipulate was here.

The master of the ballet is Stearns, as always relaxed and gently smiling, his sheet of projections before him, his vote count sure as, a few minutes before one o'clock in the morning, O'Brien's face on television says, "The clerk will call the roll."

California leads the roll this time—its 120 McGovern votes vote to unseat the 151 coalition votes. But the South Carolina delegation, seated by McGovern tactics, votes with the coalition ("Who cares?" says one of the table lieutenants). Stearns's sheet of estimates is the measure now, the lieutenants counting pluses or minuses from his estimate. Rhode Island is a break upward of 2 over their projection—all 22 to unseat the coalition ("Son of a bitch, got them all!"). Wyoming comes in at 4.4 ("Up one"). Indiana comes in at 33 ("Up one"). At Wisconsin's 55, the cry is "We're on our way, baby." Vermont comes in at 11 to unseat the coalition ("Up two," says someone, "we're going to cream them"). Then comes the second call of the roll for delegations which had passed. By Virginia, which comes in at 38½, it is all over. Stearns says: "We're going over 1,550. Get the word out, we're 38 ahead of absolute majority, the psychology is starting, get the word to the floor." The phones work; the command wagon presses the floor captains to stampede the rest of the balloting; the final vote is 1,618 to 1,238 to unseat the coalition's 151 California delegates and restore the seats to McGovern; which means that on Wednesday night's balloting the nomination of McGovern is assured.

There comes the anticipated after-test—the appeal to the chair on the nature of the majority just established, as Norman Bie, Jr., of Florida shouts, "This entire vote is contrary to the rules and done in contravention of two points of order." Stearns listens, comments, "Who would have thought that Hubert Humphrey's last hurrah would be a Wallace delegate from Florida making a point of order?" Then he snaps as commander, "Keep everybody in the hall, don't let anyone drift away." He is watching television, commanding the performance. "Get them ready to sustain the chair." Then, watching television, a minute or two later, "Turn them on."

Again comes the sense of ballet. The eight young men rise from their chairs as if drilled to rhythm; each puts a knee on his folding chair and lifts a white phone in a swooping motion. Each speaks to a floor captain who patrols one part of the floor to pass the word to other deputies. And it is all over. The chair is sustained—all California's 271 votes are seated for McGovern. One of the lieutenants snaps to his floor section: "Keep them there, keep them there, we're gonna seat Bill Singer's people in Illinois—all out!"

The smoothness of the performance is reminiscent of something past—of what? The phone in the back room is ringing, someone leaves to answer, then reports: George McGovern has just called from the Doral before going to sleep: "I just want to thank you. I want to thank everyone, Gary and Rick and Frank and Gene, for the magnificent job you've done. Well, it's been a great night for me, and we just had a little celebration, and I think I'll go to bed." The words are different, but the echo brings reminder. Back there in 1964, in San Francisco at the Cow Palace, Clifton White and Goldwater's argonauts had performed exactly the same ballet, exactly the same exercise, in a trailer wagon laid out on the same floor plan—and had received the same courteous message of thanks from the then prophet in his tower suite at the Mark Hopkins. Goldwater too had confused the politics of a nomination with the politics of American life.

A rule had now been demonstrated twice in a single decade: When a determined and intelligent group of people, energized by moral conviction, sets out to seize control of a major American national party at its convention, it can generally do so. But the impression the rest of the American people get of this seizure, and of its purpose, is as important as the control itself. This the Miami convention was to demonstrate once more.

The older and more experienced political reporters at Miami had, by professional obligation, to report the thread of action, in and out of the closed doors, from the floor, to the podium, to candidates' headquarters, for the record of events and for history. For them, with the events of Monday evening, the convention story was all but over. Hubert Humphrey would withdraw the next day, saying, "This has been a good fight. We've waged a good battle . . . we bow out now with a spirit of friendship and understanding, as a good Democrat." [1] Muskie would withdraw a few hours later, leaving only Henry Jackson to stand for the old tradition. For veteran reporters, the story was closed—except for the Eagleton affair, which would not balloon into its extravagant dimensions for another two weeks. But the younger and more impressionistic

[1] That evening Mr. Humphrey was his old self again in conversation with reporters: "I could become a bit bitter and cynical at times and I'm not going to let that happen. A lot of people that I think I've done a lot for didn't seem to know it. But the fact of politics is—even though I've pounded away at what is the record—it's the feel people have of you. It's different. The young blacks today are different than their parents, and they don't know too much about me. Lots of young people are the same way; they have very little sense of history. But that's true of every young generation. And I think that while it's difficult to take that—it's kind of a body blow, it's like getting hit in the solar plexus—you just have to know that's going to happen. And now I realize why a lot of Senators and Congressmen are really quite removed from what's going on. They really haven't had to be out here and mix it up. They haven't been touched up, they haven't been scarred up, and scratched up, which I think a campaign like this does to you. But I heal quickly. So it's a valuable experience."

reporters had the outside panorama to report—and the outside panorama, this time, was far more important than the indoor story.

What was happening in Miami had already happened across the
country; the convention was only the showcase of the forces McGovern
had mobilized from New Hampshire to California, in campus common
rooms, in the homes of mothers worried about their draft-age sons, in
the storefronts and parlors out of which McGovern's army had recruited
its troops. Now the army was marshaled in one place in the flesh; its
presence was the great story of Miami. And this presence, as told by
hordes of reporters, and displayed by television on millions of home
screens, would probably swing more votes than anything said or trans-
acted in the formal record.

The panorama began with the eye-sweep of the seating in the hall.
At Chicago in 1968, Lyndon Johnson and Dick Daley had, together,
arranged to seat the "troublemakers" of New York and California in
the rear of the Chicago Arena, squeezing together the delegates of
those unstable states in a symbolic pit out of which they could explode
only by demonstration. The luck of the draw—for in Miami the reform
had established seating by draw—and the results of the primaries, now
in 1972, set the stage differently. In the front rows, beneath the podium,
most inviting to television and thus the national view, sat the four most
erratic yet colorful and photogenic delegations ever sent to a national
convention—those of California, New York, Massachusetts and Rhode
Island. Between them, these four delegations, all more loyalist to Mc-
Govern than McGovern himself, held 673 delegate votes, or more than
a fifth of all on the floor. And since, as the lottery of seating had determined, the South Carolina delegation sat in front rows between California and New York, the opening of the convention with the challenge to
South Carolina drew the camera's eye to the contest down front; there,
the camera's eye, constantly sweeping and re-sweeping the floor, gave
the two big delegations the forestage of the scene.

The California delegation was the most colorful. California spokesmen had defended themselves earlier at the Credentials Committee as
having done more than any other state to meet the quota guidelines of
reform; they had accused the coalition of prejudice for attacking California's "overcompliance." "Overcompliance" was the California delegation's word for it. They had sent to the convention from a state where
minorities make up only 27 percent of the population a delegation 39
percent of whose delegates were minorities. The minorities invited the
best camera work: tall, high-cheekboned maidens, their black pigtails
stiff as Sitting Bull's in old monochromes; Japanese and Chinese youngsters with their delicately sculpted faces; blacks of every type—sturdy
responsibles, matrons in housedresses, intense bespectacled intellectuals.
Blacks were 19 percent of the delegation. Mexican-Americans were 17

percent. Women were 42 percent. The white males were young, dressed in open-neck floral shirts and tight-fitting pants; middle-aged white males were a decided minority. And of the total of 388 delegates and alternates, 89 were on welfare. Chief spokesmen of the delegation were the beautiful Shirley MacLaine and two extraordinarily capable blacks, Willie Brown and Yvonne Brathwaite. The California delegation had captured a mood in West-Coast Democratic politics, not its power structure.

The New York delegation sharpened the story. In the old days, New York's politicians, the cigar-smoking predators of the past, had arrived at conventions in dark suits, dark vests, pink-eyed and scowling. Each convinced of his own trivial importance, they drifted through the sessions with surly inattention to the proceedings, taking their places at the ballotings, waiting for word from the leadership, being barbered and manicured in the morning, boozing at night. The 1972 New York delegation was totally different—young, alert, earnest, dressed in slacks and casuals, they held their seats from opening to closing gavel, taking notes and reading documents. Among themselves they had already abolished Roberts' Rules of Order; elected not one but four chairmen; and the delegation's staff was relaying calls from New York to the floor, from parents whose young had hitchhiked down from Gotham to Miami to save money and had not called back—wanting to know whether their son, the delegate, had arrived safely.

One scanned the New York delegation for the old familiars. There was Joseph Crangle, the state chairman, in place. So was Matt Troy, the new Queens leader. One could recognize Arthur Schlesinger, the historian, and James Breslin, the romantic. But then? Then the only recognizable face was that of John Lindsay of New York, in the first row, towering above the others, like a tall blond captive in ancient Rome, surrounded by Mediterranean and African faces. Robert F. Wagner, his predecessor as mayor, had a functionary's title and a floor pass as a member of the party's soon-to-be-liquidated minorities division. Arthur Levitt, state controller, the Empire State's most consistent Democratic vote-getter, was not there. Averell Harriman, the greatest of all New York's Democrats since Franklin Roosevelt, sat in the gallery. "What kind of delegation is this?" growled George Meany, now president of the AFL/CIO, but once a plumber in the Bronx, where his roots still lay. "They've got six open fags and only three AFL/CIO people on that delegation! Representative?" John Lindsay, surveying the party he had chosen as his vehicle only eleven months before, said it more delicately: "This party seems to have an instinct for suicide."

One could focus one's thoughts best by moving from the personality of the solitary Lindsay to the other big-city mayors one normally sought on the floor. Except for Lindsay, they simply were not there. The

Democratic Party is a party that lives or dies in the big cities, and in 1972, of the twenty largest cities in the country, Democrats governed all but two (Cleveland and Indianapolis). Yet these Democratic mayors, whom the people had elected, were absent: Yorty of Los Angeles, Daley of Chicago, Alioto of San Francisco, White of Boston, Gribbs of Detroit, Rizzo of Philadelphia. Of the 255 Congressional Democrats only 30 were present.

The floor was the picture, and the picture told the nation its story—blacks, youth, women swirling around a podium at which only O'Brien occasionally gave them contact with a Democratic past. It was all new, all different—and the numbers behind the picture [2] measured the revolution within the party even better than the picture. There had been in 1968, at the Democratic convention, only 2.6 percent of delegates under thirty. Now there were 23 percent. There had been only 5.5 percent black. Now there were 15 percent. There had been only 13 percent women. Now there were 38 percent. The reforms had worked—insofar as they had brought this convention under new control. But they had to be tested against the emotions and reactions of the world outside, which, in the ultimate analysis, would determine the choice of leaders.

There were quite clearly two Democratic parties on the floor, and a third, far beyond Miami, watching. There was, for one, the old party which in most cities, many states and both Houses of Congress was responsible for the hard business of government. On the floor, even with the support of most of organized labor's leadership, this party was clearly outnumbered. Next came the new party, born in the insurgency of 1968 and brought to maturity by McGovern in 1972. This new party spoke in the high language of hope, promising so much that the old party of government could only be mute or negative in response. Beyond the convention hall, watching, was a third party of national Democrats—which could be described only as a state of mind among voters who for decades had thought of the Democrats simply as the party of the common man.

It was this state of mind that was probably most perplexed by the message the convention brought; for what captured its attention was not so much the decisions, the votes, the maneuvers as the pageantry of proceedings.

In the first night of action, Monday, the proceedings had been quite clear. McGovern had won California, had eliminated Mayor Daley, the nomination was his for the asking.

---

[2] The best demographic breakdown of the constituency and delegates at the Democratic National Convention is contained in an internally circulated handbook of CBS's political staff, edited by Martin Plissner, its political editor. The CBS handbook became in the week of the convention the source of all other analyses of convention composition, both for politicians and for press.

But from the second night on, the great struggle was not between the two contending formal factions but almost entirely within the forces of those who were assured that their man, McGovern, would be nominated. What was moving across camera was a family discussion within the dominant left wing concerning the platform, program and purpose to which it would bend the old Democratic Party. On most major matters, McGovern control could hold firm. It could hold firm, by the candidate's personal decision, against the welfare advocates who demanded a minimal $6,500 guaranteed income for the poor—a proposal McGovern had once sponsored and now considered unwise. It could hold firm against any softening of McGovern's solid support of busing. It could hold firm wherever it chose. But by the very philosophy of "participatory democracy" that had recruited its marchers, it could not impose discipline without first allowing debate. And open debate exposed for millions of Americans thoughts, ideas, proposals which had for decades been swept into the dark rooms of their culture and there locked up.

One could, for example, on the long evening session of Tuesday/Wednesday watch the parade of women across the podium. The women were forcing into politics matters never before publicly discussed at a national convention—for example, the laws of sex. Always hitherto, in all cultures, at all times in history, the fruit of a woman's coupling had been legislated by males, and most frequently by elderly males shriveled in the groin. These women at the podium, in the presence of the nation, now insisted they be allowed to control the fruit of their bodies. And the women who spoke were all the more disturbing for the fact that they were neither freaks nor neurotics, but healthy, full-bodied, intelligent women whose impact on consciousness was all the more revolutionary because it was so reasonable. Then came homosexuals to the microphone and camera, men openly demanding before the nation that the coupling of males be accepted not furtively, but as a natural and legal right. Then, on each side of every issue, the politics of the convention imposed a new pattern of speakers—each trio of advocates must include a man and a woman, a black and a white. Constantly, one knew, the McGovern command wagon was in control—its whips breaking up votes, commanding majorities on the "safe" side of such cultural issues as might alarm the traditional Democrats beyond the hall. But it was the parade itself that was important, the puncture of the past by new images. No matter how few or many people were tuned in at the wee hours of the morning to hear the endless talk, no matter how loyal were the Democrats who stayed watching to the end, the convention gave the sense of a movement rushing through and beyond the political and cultural limits all politicians had up to now accepted.

And over all, slowly, the weight of exhaustion pressed in. The exhaustion was a quality that neither press nor television could adequately transmit. The delegates had sat for almost nine hours, until 4:53 A.M., on Monday/Tuesday. They had sat for eleven hours on the night of Tuesday/Wednesday until 6:21 A.M. They had caucused, they had conspired, they had sought alliances, and been subject to the contrary pressures of conscience, self-interest and whip discipline. They had eaten cold chicken dinners, supplied by Colonel Sanders, then refilled after midnight at snack bars with hot dogs and orange juice. The fashionable parties that once left doilies of remembrance behind a big convention were ignored. Delegates, leadership, press, commentators all doggedly hung on and on at the convention hall, as the philosophy of open politics dictated that everyone have a say. Only the Democratic convention of 1924 had ever held a longer session than the convention of 1972— and that was at a moment when the blind, mechanical politicians of that era had locked on another cultural issue—Catholics against Ku Klux Klan—for which the party could then find no compromise.

Open politics is exhausting, for open passions tire the spirit; the executive mind avoids open politics, for executive decision requires another kind of energy. Thus of all those exhausted at the convention, none could possibly have been more exhausted than George Stanley McGovern, who for three days had been practicing simultaneously the roles of executive, politician and saint. The events of the next forty-eight hours, and even more of the next two weeks, can be understood only through the exhaustion of George McGovern.

On the Wednesday night of his nomination George McGovern had arrived back in his seventeenth-floor suite at the Doral Hotel, almost too tired to make sense. He had that afternoon, in his overcrowded schedule, made a statement to the wives of Vietnam war prisoners into which a speechwriter had written a statement that McGovern proposed, even after the end of the war which he promised, to keep American military forces stationed in Thailand. The statement had provoked a reaction from the outer fringe of the wild believers encamped at Flamingo Park; and now a small group of such fringe people had blockaded the downstairs lobby of the Doral Hotel. This particular demonstrating group was a portable protest package lifted out of the neighborhood ferment in Cambridge and North Boston, Massachusetts, where the great universities have generated a constantly fissioning community of roving dropouts and drifters. This revolving band of ex-students and academic demonstrators—recognizable as meaningless only to the Boston police and college reporters—led by a professor of philosophy, Hilary Putnam, had blockaded the entire ground-floor lobby of the Doral Hotel and closed all elevators except one guarded by the Secret Service for George McGovern's personal use. The demonstrators included SDS members, Progressive Labor Party members, the Revolutionary Communist Progressive Party, all brought together by their desire to tease the television cameras to further their own cause—the cause being peace at once, tomorrow. To which the twenty-year-old leader of the Workers Action Movement added the demand that George McGovern must come out for the thirty-hour week at forty hours' pay; and the gangly young leader of the Gay Liberationists demanded personal apology for slight from the candidate while leading the chant: "2-4-6-8, we don't overpopulate," changing it later to "3-5-7-9, Lesbians are mighty fine." McGovern students struggled with their erstwhile comrades of the student left to pull down the banners of the demonstrators lest television catch the sight and smear their cause with nonsense. Police and Secret Service stood by, itching to clear the lobby by force if only McGovern would give the word.

Under such circumstances, the evening of George McGovern's great triumph unrolled. To reach the candidate one had to climb on foot, floor by floor, up the stairwell from the ground to the seventeenth floor, an overheated column of winding steel stairs; on the eleventh-floor landing, earlier that afternoon, someone had vomited from exhaustion, and now the smell of vomit, wafted by the updraft of heat, accompanied one to the floor of the candidate.

The candidate, too tired to do more than cherish his family, had dined with his wife, their five children, two sons-in-law, two grandchildren. He had been too tired to do more than taste the beef stew prepared for him, and was now, at eight in the evening, being assailed by contrary advice. He must either go down to address, and thus disperse, the demonstrators; or remain beleaguered, as the candidate for the Presidency, by a handful of eccentrics in the lobby, demanding peace. The matter involved was the picture—the impact of pictures, live or still, that might show the nation the bloody clearing of the Doral Hotel on the night of nomination. McGovern, always reluctant to use force, decided he must go down to speak to the demonstrators and confirm to them his love of peace. And so he did, spoke well, then returned up the elevator and prepared to watch his nomination.

McGovern believes in open politics; and even on this night his suite is to be open to his in-laws; to what staff can be spared from the convention floor; to a dozen newsmen and photographers he has befriended or who have befriended him. They are all a demand on his kindliness and decency in personal relations, but he is too tired to be rude.

Assailed by questioners; by television interviewers; by photographers brought in by platoons, their camera shutters clicking like butterfly wings, McGovern works on his acceptance speech with a blue felt pen while the television set gives the dreary sound of some of the more uninspiring nominating addresses in the history of political conventions.

At 11:19 the roll-call starts, and McGovern lifts himself to a seat beside the television set to watch it. There is a sag to the jaw, and the face lines, which have been growing deeper, are now craggy. There are no surprises in the long roll-call, and, slowly relaxing, he begins to enjoy the rhetoric of announcement ("Delaware, the home of corporations, chemicals, chickens and charisma, casts . . ."). He laughs as former Governor Frank Morrison of Nebraska casts most of the state's votes for the man "who will bring a new glow around Mount Rushmore." At Washington's vote, with his lead mounting, he is relaxed enough to eat and is brought a bowl of Total, bananas and cream. He comes back for Utah's vote, and Utah's vote pleases him. He tells the story of Ward Clark, out there in South Dakota, waking up Walt Bryan, the National Committeeman of the state, the night of Harry Truman's election in 1948. Old Walt always went to sleep with a bottle of whiskey by his side, and Ward Clark woke up Walt that night, very late, because Utah was going for Truman, which meant that Dewey would be defeated; and old Walt, coming out of his stupor, said, "Utah? Utah? I always did like those Mormons." McGovern chuckles because this is the kind of low-voltage anecdote he enjoys. Then he pays serious attention to Illinois. Illinois, Dick Daley's state, comes up on roll-call at 11:58—30.5 for Jackson; then 119 for McGovern! And the nomination is mathematically, legally his.[3]

McGovern dreamwalks around the room; kisses his in-laws; shakes hands; then the phone is ringing in the other room. One call from Hubert Humphrey. Then Richard Nixon. Then Teddy Kennedy. The Kennedy phone call is the most important and takes a good while; no one knows what the Kennedy says.

But then there is so much more to do—other calls, staff calls, a party upstairs in the Starlight Room for big contributors, and the acceptance speech still to finish.

Beyond that, there is the Vice-Presidency. He has to make his choice the next day, but so far he has been too busy, too tired, too overwhelmed by events to think of what he will do if Teddy Kennedy says no once more, if the Kennedy really means what he has been saying publicly and privately all year long—that he is not going to run for anything this year.

So, just before going to bed, McGovern asks several of his staff to assemble the key members of the army's leadership, the veterans and the friends, early the next morning to screen Vice-Presidential names for him to consider when he gets up.

                              *   *   *

[3] The final tally of the Democratic nomination in 1972 read: McGovern, 1,715.35; Jackson, 534; Wallace, 385.7; Chisholm, 151.95; others 224.

An average of 17,800,000 American homes—approximately 71,000,000 people—tuned in each evening at prime time during the Democratic convention. The number rose slightly to a high of 18,800,000 homes on Wednesday during the balloting on the final nomination, and was in diminuendo on Thursday evening while the nation waited to hear what George McGovern had to say—prime-time listeners waiting between the hours of 9:30 and 11:30 were set by the Nielsen ratings as 17,400,000 homes. But they were not to see George McGovern in prime time. Normally, with the naming of a Vice-President, all else falls into place; ceremony on Thursday night proceeds with dispatch to guarantee the new nominee the attention of the nation at its prime listening time. Even at Chicago in 1968, with all the violence, bloodshed and dissension, the party had pulled itself together well enough to let Hubert Humphrey speak to the nation when the nation was ready to listen.

Not so at Miami in 1972, however—open politics dictated otherwise. The Vice-Presidential nominee, Senator Thomas F. Eagleton of Missouri, had been named rather late on Thursday afternoon but in good time to comply with the new rules; and, thus, when the session opened at 8:00 P.M. no immediate obstacles were apparent. There was, however, a first matter of business to dispose of—the compromise on the new charter for the Democratic Party. The original charter drafted by the reformers had proposed a total restructuring of the party and its National Committee; [4] it had been modified several times in the previous few weeks; even so, wise heads agreed it was too frightening and complicated a matter to put before the exhausted convention on the night of the nominee's acceptance. McGovern whips and old regulars agreed

---

[4] It has always been impossible, in less than full book-length form, to describe accurately the structure of American national parties. Wrote Martin Plissner of CBS, ". . . the national party apparatus has usually been a makeshift thing, headed by a part-time, unpaid official whose bills are normally paid by the Government (U.S. Congressmen and Senators are very popular for this reason) or the proceeds of some outside occupation. . . . In both parties, the National Committee has been traditionally an institution with very little clout, its chairman a person with even less. . . . One former Democratic National Committee official put it this way: 'No matter what happens in a presidential election, the Committee loses. If we don't elect a President we wind up broke. If we do elect him the really important political business is run from the White House.' "

The new charter worked out by the Reform Commission proposed to clarify the inner life of an American party for the first time. There would be a mid-term National Policy Conference of 3,900 delegates which should "consider and determine party policy and program." In addition, there would be a new National Committee of 334 members with vastly expanded authority. They would be capped by a new National Executive Council. But on top of all would be the new National Chairman elected for four years, in mid-term of the Presidency, by all 3,900 delegates to the Policy Conference, with a prestige equal to that of the party's national Presidential candidate. Moreover, only party "members" would be allowed to participate in the choice of the new bodies, and, the charter implied, membership would be dependent on dues-paying and specific enrollment, as in European parties.

that the matter should be postponed, referred to a special new reform commission to be established later. Not so, however, the New York delegation, wishing to seize the moment now when reform held the floor majority. For almost an hour, incomprehensibly, the New York delegation argued, caucused, demanded suspension of the rules to bring up a parochial matter of its own (its right to appoint eight of New York's eleven new National Committee members). The final vote to postpone was taken without the New York delegation's vote being recorded.

Then came the Vice-Presidential nomination to the agenda. Open politics now required another delay as six hopeless nominees for Vice-President insisted on pressing their symbolic or publicity causes from the podium, against McGovern's choice, Senator Thomas Eagleton. The Women's Political Caucus, deciding that this was their last chance to press their cause on the nation's attention, surfaced suddenly with the name of Frances (Sissy) Farenthold as rival to Thomas Eagleton, and the floor boiled with caucusing, whip-cracking, confusion as the roll-call started. It was late now, very late, 12:38 by the clock, and a silly giddiness swept the floor. Delegates vied in their ingenuity to insert the names of folk heroes of the new and old left on the roll: Ralph Nader, Benjamin Spock, the Berrigans, Cesar Chavez, Jerry Rubin—then several votes for Mao Tse-tung, two votes for CBS's Roger Mudd, a vote for Martha Mitchell, another for Archie Bunker—and on and on until finally, notwithstanding New York's 175 votes against Tom Eagleton, the Vice-Presidential nomination had been won by him with 1,741.81 votes against 1,274.19 for his scattered rivals.

Then, in a twinkling, the mood changed as Alabama's delegation called for the floor. Alabama's delegation was George Wallace's delegation, and now it offered to shift its votes to make Tom Eagleton its choice for Vice-President also. It was a graceful gesture—and the mood transformed itself to brotherhood. In the exhaustion, a pause ensued while the convention waited for the nominees to mount the rostrum— and Lawrence O'Brien ordered up music from the band. So they sang, and as they sang, they melted—they were all Democrats again ("Happy Days Are Here Again"); they were all Americans again ("America the Beautiful," "East Side, West Side, All Around the Town"); blacks started clapping in rhythm, whites joined them; ascending to the podium now were the heroes—Teddy Kennedy himself, just flown in from Massachusetts; and Hubert Humphrey, leading the candidate by the hand, as McGovern had led Hubert by the hand in 1968; and Ed Muskie, Shirley Chisholm, even Henry Jackson, all bowing to the audience, radiant, as the band played "Hail, Hail, the Gang's All Here."

Senator Kennedy spoke first, and they hushed to hear him, for he spoke well. Hubert Humphrey spoke briefly; this was no longer his business, but he was excellent. Then, the candidate.

Gaunt, beaded with sweat, his brow shining, the early-campaign dimple lines now cut into folds by weariness, George McGovern was about to have his moment. The moment was 2:48 in the morning. Even in California most people had gone to sleep; only in Guam, where it was still a quarter of six in the evening, was George McGovern speaking in prime time under the American flag. On the mainland, the audience for his speech had dropped from 17,400,000 homes to 3,600,000.[5] Yet he was speaking beautifully. He had sucked up from his experience in one of the longest campaigns in American history a knowledge of precisely those keys of emotion he himself could touch best, and the organ keys he played now were poetic and evangelical.

"With a full heart I accept your nomination," he began after the opening quips. *". . . My nomination is all the more precious in that it is the gift of the most open political process in our national history . . . the sweet harvest cultivated by tens of thousands of tireless volunteers— old and young. . . . This is a nomination of the people."*

Then to the ritual attack on the opposition: *". . . never underestimate the power of Richard Nixon to bring harmony to Democratic ranks. He is our unwitting unifier. . . . And all of us together are going to help him redeem the pledge he made ten years ago: Next year you won't have Richard Nixon to kick around any more."*

Then the address moved in to the biblical and poetic, which is McGovern's best style, and the podium became a pulpit.

"In Scripture and in the music of our children we are told: 'To everything there is a season, and a time to every purpose under heaven.' . . . This is the time for truth, not falsehood. . . . During four administrations of both parties, a terrible war has been charted behind closed doors. I want those doors opened, and I want that war closed. . . ."

Wild applause. Then the specific pledges. And the phrases, timetested in the primaries and the two years of campaigning.

"Within ninety days of my inauguration, every American soldier and every American prisoner will be . . . back home in America where they belong."

National security meant credibility. National security meant more schools. Meant better health care. Meant safety of the streets. Meant protecting the beauty of America: *". . . And if we someday choke on the pollution of our own air, there will be little consolation in leaving behind a dying continent ringed with steel."*

Jobs. Tax reform. Justice.

". . . together we will call America home to the founding ideals that nourished us in the beginning.

---

[5] By contrast, a month later when Richard Nixon delivered his acceptance speech, 20,100,000 homes were tuned in to hear him during the prime-time period.

"From secrecy and deception in high places, come home, America. . . .

"From the waste of idle hands to the joy of useful labor, come home, America."

He had been perfecting the call for almost a year and a half and had voiced it first in Indiana, in a college speech, a long time before, but now he was making the theme sing: Come Home. . . .

"From the prejudice of race and sex, come home, America. . . .

"Come home to the affirmation that we have a dream.

"Come home to the conviction that we can move our country forward.

"Come home to the belief that we can seek a newer world.

"And let us be joyful in that homecoming. . . . May God grant us the wisdom to cherish this good land and to meet the great challenge that beckons us home."

As McGovern finished, emotion swept out of the galleries, joined the emotion that rose from the floor and, magically, the song was there again—the old song which, in memory, has marked all American conventions when men are tired, or seek faith; the hall boomed to "Glory, Glory, Hallelujah." The gavel closed the convention, the lights began to go out; still they stood there swaying, regulars and reformers, white and black, and the "Battle Hymn of the Republic" went on; then it faded into other tunes, and they were singing "We Shall Overcome," the dirge chanted as if it were marching music.

It seemed barely possible, just faintly possible, in the exhaustion, the giddiness, the evangelical moment, that this George McGovern, the prophet, was indeed a serious candidate for the Presidency.

A college girl from Boston attending her first convention summed it up best writing to her father in New York of the last night. "Oh, Daddy," said her letter, "I want to trust again. I cried for Bobby Kennedy because he was willing to get his hands dirty. . . . I cried for Jack Kennedy, because if he had not died the life of the country might never have become what it did in the sixties. . . . If McGovern can only shape his people a little more, control them. . . . America is worth saving, South Dakota, Kansas City, Utah, Idaho, Oregon, Massachusetts, even maybe New York City . . . reviving, resurrecting, uniting. E Pluribus Unum, Shirley MacLaine said the same thing . . . I want to trust again. . . ."

They left the convention hall that night, all of them carried on song, all wanting to trust again. But the next day, Friday, with the convention over, trust began to crumble.

On Friday, July 14th, as the hotels disgorged the Democrats to the airports, the McGovern irregulars held in their possession what they considered to be the "machinery" of the national Democratic Party. Like rural insurrectionaries, as they moved into the city, they expected to find the levers of the switching yards, factories, power plants, telephone centrals abandoned by the possessing powers, to be theirs at command. And of these, the first command post to be occupied must be that of the Democratic National Committee. The Democratic National Committee was, of course, anything but that; it might more aptly be described as the central stationery-supply closet of the party—at most, a symbol. Which is what made the events of Friday, July 14th, immediately as preposterous as later they were to become tragic.

Traditionally, on the morning after a convention closes, the new candidate assembles the National Committee of his party, appoints a new chairman and instructs the committee in his will. The key action is the appointment of his new chairman—who, in any campaign, whether symbolically or for real, expresses the direction of the candidate.

For George McGovern, the choice on Friday morning, in his weariness, was exquisitely difficult; he had, in the course of his campaign, already offered, or promised, that chairmanship to no less than three different people—to Lawrence O'Brien, Pierre Salinger and Jean Westwood. Most candidates play this game on the road to nomination; but for the candidate of credibility it was more difficult.

All three were important symbolically, but of these the most important was Lawrence O'Brien. O'Brien had come out of the politics of Springfield, Massachusetts, than which there is no more hard-knuckled old-fashioned politics except possibly those of West Virginia, Indiana and Boston. Twenty years of experience—first as campaign manager for John F. Kennedy; then as Cabinet officer for LBJ; then as campaign manager for Hubert Humphrey in 1968; then as National Chairman—had, however, transformed the perception of O'Brien in the same way that experience earlier had transformed the perceptions of Al Smith in New York and Harry Truman in Washington. O'Brien, as well as they, had learned that politics, to thrive, must express what people want, and O'Brien, fundamentally, went along with the changes—trying to harness them to order as he went, irritated by what he called "the ultra-left liberals," yet aware that they spoke for something more important than the mechanics of the old politics could understand. O'Brien had learned much from the Chicago convention of 1968; and, in the old Democratic tradition, recognized then that new people had to be admitted to leadership if the party was to thrive. He had put all his authority behind the reform commissions of 1969 and 1970; and had begun during those years to lose his credit with older politicians who felt he was betraying them. He had widened the distance between himself and the old regulars in the week of the convention. His rulings, his decisions had been scrupulously fair, his management of the podium impeccable; the result had been disaster for his old friends among the regulars and the labor leaders who had hoped O'Brien would bend the rules, against what he considered honor, in their favor. He was now, in the eyes of the regulars, a renegade.

Twice in the week before, George McGovern had asked O'Brien to become his National Chairman of the Democratic Party. But O'Brien, as the neutral master of the convention, had cut McGovern off, feeling the offer at that point was in bad taste. Now, after the convention was over, O'Brien was finally free of the burden of fairness and was receptive to offer when McGovern invited him to lunch on Friday.

For over an hour, in his suite at the Doral, McGovern implored O'Brien to remain as National Chairman. O'Brien's recollection of the meeting is incomplete, the after-shock still traumatic. "He asked me and he asked me to become National Chairman. I raised all the objections and told him what I needed; but he wanted me; and then he went out to talk to his people . . . and when he came back . . . it's still unbelievable . . . I'd talked to my people, we agreed I had to take the offer . . . and when he came back, the offer just wasn't there . . . he wasn't offering it to me."

In previous circumstances, the party's nominee had imposed his views on his staff. But McGovern was not a man to impose decisions. He had left O'Brien to consult his closest staff—Hart, Mankiewicz, Westwood, Salinger, Kirby Jones, a few others. "I had no idea," later said Frank Mankiewicz, "what he'd done in the other room with Larry. He said he'd discussed the chairmanship. We assumed the question was still open. We didn't tell him to go screw Larry." What was at issue as the group talked, as they saw it, was the symbolism of an O'Brien appointment. "Rightly or wrongly," said Hart later, "the role of the new chairman had elevated itself into symbolism. Were we only to have been used to get McGovern the nomination, and then to be discarded as unneeded? Who was George McGovern? Was he just another politician?" For the group in the room, O'Brien, who had delivered the fairest convention ever held, was still a symbol of old politics. And, besides, McGovern had already promised the chairmanship to Jean Westwood. Westwood objected strongly to O'Brien. "I wouldn't say she was bawling," recalled Kirby Jones, "but she was teary, her voice choked up. She wanted it. And McGovern couldn't stand the personal anguish. That was always his problem, he didn't like to inflict hurt." Little more than a symbol was involved—but the symbol somehow touched on another symbol, the symbolic power of the regulars who might trust O'Brien. Through them the great X factor of the campaign—the state of mind of the traditionalists—could be reached. But, caught by conflicting commitments, McGovern chose Westwood. It was a hard decision; but it was made worse only a few minutes later by its explana-

tion, which raised for the first time, publicly, the root matter of Mc-
Govern's credibility.

At 2:30 in the afternoon, in the crowded Fontaine Room of the
Fontainebleau, there walk in, arm in arm, Lawrence O'Brien and George
McGovern. O'Brien is white-faced, but to the outer eye the pallor might
be that of exhaustion. They stride to the platform, and George McGovern makes a speech of fervid praise of O'Brien's performance. Then:
"I want to tell you as straightforwardly as I can that he has reached a
judgment that he will not stay on as the chairman of our party. I respect
his wishes. I regret it. But I respect those wishes."

There are at least ten people in the room who know this is simply
not true. O'Brien has been willing; since last night he has been willing
to run the party for George McGovern. Now O'Brien has been betrayed. The story must get out in a few days—and all the old politicians
of America will buzz when they learn that Larry, who left to join the
reform, has been betrayed by reform.

Thus, then, McGovern nominates Mrs. Jean Westwood as chairman of the party. All assent. And McGovern now nominates his choice
for vice-chairman—Pierre Salinger.

Pierre Salinger is another symbolic type. O'Brien has come from
an old past of pragmatism to become a hard-headed advocate of reform.
Salinger, still young, has moved in the other direction—as a college boy,
twenty years earlier, he had entered politics answering the call of Adlai
Stevenson, to make the party an instrument of morality as well as power.
Salinger has moved from reform to pragmatics, but the ideals of his
youth still govern him. Once press secretary to John F. Kennedy and
Lyndon Johnson at the White House, Salinger has also been a United
States Senator. Then, running for re-election in California in 1964, he
staked his campaign on the black cause against the advice of all
friends and counselors—demanding that Californians open all housing,
everywhere, to their black fellow citizens. In 1964, the year of the
Johnson landslide, Salinger was the only Democratic political figure to be defeated in a major state.

Thus the next ten minutes are grotesque. Only the official transcript
and the notes in this reporter's notebook insist that what followed actually happened. McGovern nominates Salinger. A hand rises from the
floor and is acknowledged—Charles Evers of Mississippi.

"Madam Chairman," he says, "inasmuch as we are going to try to
stay in line with the McGovern rules, I would . . . strongly urge that if
we are going to have a female chairman . . . I would like to place in
nomination a black man to be co-chairman or vice-chairman. . . . I
would like to place in nomination Mr. Basil Paterson of New York."

The applause booms out! This new Democratic National Committee is the creation of the new convention—women, blacks and youth, devout in their beliefs. They know nothing about Basil Paterson of New York, which is an irony. "Who is Basil Paterson?" comes an unidentified voice from the floor. In the quick thumbnail sketch of his record, there is no reflection whatsoever of the real quality of Basil Paterson. But this group will vote for Basil Paterson against Pierre Salinger simply because Paterson is black and Salinger is white, in their ignorance degrading both men. Now rises George McGovern and says, "I want it understood before this vote takes place that I regard Basil Paterson as one of the most distinguished and capable members of our party, and while I have suggested the name of Pierre Salinger, either one of these very able men would be perfectly acceptable to me and a great credit to our party."

Loud applause, roaring applause. But the rug has been pulled out from under Pierre Salinger, in public. Salinger, standing to the right of the platform, is in pain. He is already ill with backache from pacing the floor of the convention for three nights, eight and ten hours at a stretch, as one of George McGovern's floor managers. But he has been loyal to McGovern and has expected George McGovern to be loyal to him. Had history worked otherwise, had he been elected as champion of the Negro cause back in 1964, now as senior Senator from California in 1972, carrying the Kennedy aura, the glamour of the West, the clout of the nation's largest state, his ethnic background (half Jewish, half Catholic), he might well have been McGovern's runningmate. He has had McGovern's "personal commitment" for the chairmanship, but the commitment has been reduced to vice-chairmanship. Now this commitment too has been withdrawn. Salinger asks for the right to speak on the platform. He is quick, taking less than a minute, concluding, "I think I sensed the feeling of this committee and, therefore, I would like to withdraw my name from nomination and ask you to elect Mr. Paterson."

More applause.

Paterson is named vice-chairman to Jean Westwood, and the new Democratic Committee, after naming a white male as party treasurer, breaks up. McGovern must catch a plane back to Washington. O'Brien will make his own way there later that evening; Salinger decides to fly to the Kennedy compound at Hyannis Port to nurse his hurt. By afternoon the Democratic convention of 1972 is over, and Miami Beach begins to prepare for the Republicans three weeks later.

Yet there has been a shape to all of it, both inside and outside. The party had been purified both in public and in private; but there remained the difference between purity and reality. New people with new convictions now held the party; they had defeated the old in fair and decent combat on the floor; they had well expressed their purpose to the country; but they had also burned their bridges to the past, in procedure, in personnel, in philosophy and, finally, on Friday, to the key people who might have best explained their new philosophy to the millions who had so long found their political home in the Democratic Party.

"Come Home, America" still rang in one's ears from the last public proceeding. But no one had called "Come Home, Democrats," and the party beyond the hall was larger and more important than the delegates and committeemen who had made the old home, for so many, in one week, a disturbing place to be.

CHAPTER EIGHT

THE EAGLETON AFFAIR

THE way Americans choose Vice-Presidents has always been absurd—but never quite so absurd as in the Democratic exercise of 1972.

For seventeen of the past twenty-seven years, America had been governed by Presidents who made their entry to that office from the Vice-Presidency; Harry Truman came that way and history chose him to loose the atom bomb; Lyndon Johnson came that way and plunged the nation into the most disastrous war of its history. In the Vice-Presidency lies all the potential power of the Presidency itself—yet the choice is the most perfunctory and generally the most thoughtless in the entire American political system.

The traditional script in both parties reads the same: the Presidential candidate is nominated on Wednesday of convention week. His speech is usually unfinished at that point, and with the mantle of history being pleated for him, he insists on fussing with the speech once more, giving it that final gloss which will shimmer through time. The choosing of a Vice-President at this point is not only a bother to him—it is a curse. Matters never look quite the same to the principal candidate the night of his victory as they did when he arrived at the scene in full combat ardor. His defeated party rivals must now become tomorrow's allies; their supporters must be appeased; the half-promises, half-commitments he has given to friends on the way hang over him; the names he or his staff has floated to test public reaction have frozen into print. Concern about who could best govern the nation fades to the far corner of the tired mind. The immediate problem seems always to be who can best help carry the nation for the ticket in November; politics weighs more heavily than history.

All Presidential nominees for twenty years have handled the problem as their personalities shaped them.

Eisenhower, the conqueror of Europe, went to sleep in Chicago after defeating Robert Taft in 1952; with the calm of the veteran commander, he had told his staff to assemble the party leadership and get him a name for Vice-President. The leadership argued all night, then in exhaustion settled on the name of Richard M. Nixon—because he was young while Eisenhower was old, because he was conservative and Eisenhower liberal, because he was from California and Eisenhower from New York; and because, said Paul G. Hoffman, who was there, "we were all so very tired by that time." Eisenhower rarely questioned staff decisions and did not question this one. Richard Nixon, with a characteristic that later became familiar, made it quite clear that the contract was binding on both men; when the leadership two months later tried to dump him, and Tom Dewey telephoned asking him to withdraw from the ticket, Nixon replied that he had to get that word from Eisenhower himself—and that it was time for the chief to spit or get off the pot.

Stevenson, in 1956, left the decision to the convention, the only open choice of Vice-President in modern history—and thereby took Estes Kefauver to defeat with him, while preserving John F. Kennedy to run in 1960.

At his own convention in 1960 Kennedy was all master. He had been nominated late on Wednesday, enjoyed himself that night at a small party in his hideaway apartment, gone to bed for five hours of sleep, leaving his staff with the impression his choice would be either Senator Stuart Symington of Missouri or Senator Henry Jackson of Washington. He astounded the staff when, after deciding all alone, he told them the next morning his choice was Lyndon Johnson. His brother Robert opposed the choice; staff railed at him; friends tried to shake him; labor and Northern leaders were indignant. But Kennedy was stubborn—he needed Johnson for the election, and history would have to take care of itself. Besides—he did not plan to die.

Johnson, in 1964, enjoyed himself in the style of Caligula, toying with the convention, and teasing the television audience, before using his Presidential prerogative to choose Hubert Humphrey. And Nixon, in 1968, followed Eisenhower in style, leaving the choice to the conflicting groups of the party's leadership; then, when they deadlocked, and his own man, Robert Finch, refused the offer of Vice-Presidency, he selected Spiro T. Agnew over John Volpe as his runningmate. Agnew was the better political instrument for the tight border strategy Nixon planned to run.

In 1972, in the Democratic Party, the decision was to be neither solitary nor by a consensus of leadership. It was to be, in the style of McGovern's army, a participatory decision. Some twenty-plus people gathered on Thursday morning, July 13th, between 8:30 and 9:00 in a downstairs conference room at the Doral Hotel—all tired from overwork and celebration, some with only two or three hours' sleep, a good number hung-over, others with only a quick dip in the ocean at dawn to clear their sleep-starved minds.

Frank Mankiewicz was to chair the meeting, and earlier in the week, on Tuesday, Mankiewicz had discussed with McGovern the calling together of a small group—himself, Hart, Stearns, Salinger, Van Dyk, Wexler—to sift the choices. On Wednesday night after the nomination, McGovern had instructed other staff members to round up a full panel. "I showed up," said Mankiewicz, "and, Christ, there were about twenty-four people there. What was I going to do? The door would open and someone would say, 'George told me to show up here.' I was surprised someone from Gay Liberation didn't show up." The key women of the McGovern command were present—Shirley MacLaine, Anne Wexler, Jean Westwood; so, too, were the key blacks (Clay, Fauntroy, Martin); so, too, were the veterans (Caddell, Pokorny, Grandmaison, Segal, Himmelman); so, too, were the public-relations minds (Dutton, Dougherty, Jones, Salinger); so, too, was the general staff (Mankiewicz, Hart, Stearns, Weil); and others.

Time was already short, for McGovern required that they give him a choice of names by noon, to allow him time to check, clear, ponder or even seek an alternate—all of which had to be accomplished, under the new rules, by four in the afternoon. There were some forty to forty-five names in play at this point and, to simplify matters, it was agreed that no name would be discussed unless someone present was willing to make a hard pitch for the name. Mankiewicz was imaginative in his approach—his suggestions ranged from Father Theodore Hesburgh of Notre Dame to Walter Cronkite of CBS. Gary Hart, next in eminence, favored Kevin White, Mayor of Boston. Rick Stearns wanted Larry O'Brien. And all were very shortly dealing not in realities but, again, in symbols of reality. Of the masters of the new amateur professionalism, only three—Pierre Salinger, Frank Mankiewicz and Ted Van Dyk—had any large personal acquaintance with the men who govern America, out of whom choice is generally made. Van Dyk's own disillusion set in at the morning session: "It was frivolous," he recalls.

Of the six or seven names that emerged from the session for McGovern's consideration, the name of Kevin White, Mayor of Boston, led the list. There followed: Sargent Shriver (Pierre Salinger's choice); Senator Abraham Ribicoff of Connecticut (who had already turned down an offer of the slot from McGovern); Governor Patrick J. Lucey and Senator Gaylord Nelson of Wisconsin; and Senator Thomas F. Eagleton of Missouri. In the gathering of twenty-two people, no more than three had ever met either Kevin White or Tom Eagleton, and of those three, none had any real knowledge or experience or observation of their records.

Thus followed several hours of some confusion. All the names suggested to McGovern had to be forwarded for customary ritual clearance from various tribal chiefs. In the past such clearances had taken place with labor leaders, regional leaders or government leaders. Now the critical constituent groups were women and blacks, and Messrs. Hart, Mankiewicz, Salinger joined the candidate as he met in his suite with black leaders (Congressmen Clay and Fauntroy, Mayor Gibson, Yancey Martin) and women leaders (Delores Huerta, Elizabeth Carpenter, as well as Jean Westwood) to go over the final list of the morning's staff meeting. Salinger again made the case for Sargent Shriver: Shriver was a brother-in-law of the Kennedys and carried the glamour of the family; a man with a good war record; former Ambassador to France; first director of the Peace Corps and the Office of Economic Opportunity. The blacks approved Shriver strongly; McGovern tried to reach Shriver at his Washington office, discovered Shriver was in Moscow; so Shriver's name was dropped. Ms. Carpenter suggested her fellow Texan, Sissy Farenthold, but that had no support.

No one at that point had been assigned by anyone to do any kind of background check on any of the names mentioned. They were choosing a Vice-President—had they been choosing a field commander of the troops, they would have spent more time checking records. It was some time in the early-morning session that Gordon Weil had become disturbed; he had heard from Stearns that Eagleton's name was swathed in rumors of drinking problems; and he, Weil, knew nothing either of Eagleton or of Kevin White. Stearns, too tired to stay up any longer, had gone to sleep after the morning session. Weil had gone to his room and on his own initiative for an hour and a half, by telephone, had tried quickly to check out the backgrounds of both men. By the time Weil joined the clearance session in McGovern's suite, the prime name had become that of Kevin White. Weil reported that he had found no problems on White, a clean bill of health from all his hasty check sources. Did anyone care to hear about Eagleton? asked Weil. No one apparently cared to hear about Eagleton—his name had been put aside. Weil persisted anyway—he had found out that Eagleton was not an alcoholic; he had indeed been hospitalized, but the hospital had diagnosed Eagleton's problem as a technical medical problem of alcohol ingestion, not a drinking problem. But no one wanted to hear more about Eagleton.

By two in the afternoon, it was all but done. Mayor White had agreed. Stearns, who had gone to bed, was awakened and told to circulate immediately the necessary legal petitions required by the new reform rules. And George McGovern put through a final clearance call to Teddy Kennedy in Massachusetts. Kennedy's response startled McGovern. Kennedy was cool to Kevin White, he wanted time to "think it over." For McGovern, who had sought Kennedy for Vice-President for so long, it must have been as if, yes, there might be a Santa Claus. In all the secret trial polling Caddell had done for McGovern on putative Vice-Presidents, no name had helped his standing against Nixon except one: Kennedy. McGovern, standing alone against the President, in his trial heats was running 52/38 behind; but a McGovern-Kennedy ticket in the trial heats narrowed the gap against Nixon to 47/43! Did Kennedy's cryptic response mean that now he was reconsidering joining McGovern on the ticket? It was worth a wait to find out. In the meanwhile, news of Kevin White's choice was bringing opposition as it spread—chiefly from the Massachusetts delegation of McGovern arch-zealots, whose guru, Professor John Kenneth Galbraith, now reached the candidate with his most strenuous and, as usual, eloquent opposition to the choice; if White were chosen, the McGovern delegation from Massachusetts would feel itself repudiated.

Out, then, Kevin White—definitely.

At 2:30 the long-awaited return telephone call from Teddy Kennedy comes in. Kennedy thinks that Congressman Wilbur Mills, of Arkansas, would be a better choice than Kevin White. As for himself—for the uncountable last time, the Kennedy makes clear that he is not running for Vice-President this year with anyone. McGovern is now irritated with Kennedy and upset; time is closing on the four-o'clock deadline, and his mind turns to his old friend Senator Gaylord Nelson of Wisconsin, also on the approved list; and he tries to reach Nelson in Washington. Shortly after three, Nelson calls back—Nelson will under no circumstances accept the honor; he has promised his wife he will not go this route; but if McGovern was going the legislative way, so Nelson remembered saying, there was no more attractive and talented fellow around than Tom Eagleton of Missouri.[1]

Eagleton.

Eagleton is sixth on the list from the morning staff meeting. McGovern has met Eagleton personally only twice—once for forty-five minutes in the Senate steam-bath room, and once at a large dinner party in 1969 at Henry Kimelman's home. But symbolically Eagleton promises everything—Catholic; young; bright; witty; good connections with labor; big-city background; firm on law-and-order. The morning staff meeting had heard stories of an Eagleton drinking problem—but Weil has checked them out and knows the alcoholism story to be untrue. It is at this point 3:30, and in the living room of McGovern's suite are Gary Hart, Frank Mankiewicz, Fred Dutton, staff member Liz Stevens, others, none enthusiastic, all of them as exhausted as their leader, mildly acquiescent at the Eagleton name. At this point enters Charles Guggenheim, a genuine artist

[1] Two outstanding studies of the Eagleton affair are to be found in a series by Haynes Johnson in the Washington *Post,* December 3rd–6th, 1972, and a full-length essay by Loye Miller, Jr., of the Knight newspapers, in the December 8th, 1972, edition of the Miami *Herald.*

of political cinema, a McGovern favorite and media director of the campaign. Guggenheim is from Missouri and McGovern asks him about Eagleton's drinking problem; Guggenheim says there is no drinking problem and adds that he thinks Eagleton is a fine fellow. Whether at this point decision had been made, whether it came five minutes earlier or later, none of the tired memories can recall. But with some in the room still asking for more time to think it over, McGovern has placed a call to Eagleton's room; the phone rings; and it is Eagleton on the line.

Tom Eagleton had been in his suite at the Ivanhoe Hotel, two miles north of the Doral, all day. The Ivanhoe was the shelter of the Missouri delegation and its attendant press, and the Missouri press was now energized, as the Massachusetts, Texas, California, Illinois press had been in years before, by the thought that they held in their jurisdiction a possible national candidate whose career might flip their observations and writing to national attention. Tom Eagleton had thus found it prudent to stay in his suite rather than wait for word of his fate publicly down by the swimming pool where his old friends among newspapermen could badger him for reaction and for story.

There had been no Eagleton campaign at this convention—no posters, buttons, lobbying; Eagleton had even left behind in Washington his press aide, Mike Kelley. But Eagleton had known for several days that his name was in play—the press had said so, friends had told him so and logic insisted that he was a natural balance for a McGovern ticket.

There was, of course, the matter of his health—but that had been tucked away in some posterior pocket of memory. Mental disturbance is the second most common ailment, after the common cold, in American life; by some estimates, 25 percent of all Americans have, at one time or another, suffered gusts of mental depression, instability or incapability—moments when the ability to absorb strain is overwhelmed by too much of it—and most people recover. Yet mental illness still carries a stigma, like venereal disease—particularly among older Americans. And thus, many who have suffered mental illness, once they recover, do not talk about it, if possible conceal it and, gradually, forget about it. This is especially true of corporate executives and politicians.

Tom Eagleton had, in the past, concealed three serious rounds of mental illness; had, indeed, through his staff, deceived the press of Missouri when he ran for office there. He had been hospitalized three times: once in 1960, after running for Attorney General of Missouri and winning; once during the Christmas holidays of 1964; once more in 1966, out of total nervous exhaustion. He had on two occasions been given electro-shock treatment at Barnes Hospital in St. Louis and the Mayo Clinic in Minnesota, but the press had been told he was hospitalized for stomach trouble. The need for concealment was, however, by 1972 long past. Eagleton had learned the limits of the strain he could absorb, had learned, as he said later, "to pace himself," and had tucked away the memory of mental illness as completely as the memory of a broken leg. He had performed with distinction in all the offices he had won, and in the Senate, where he had arrived in 1969, he was recognized as a winner. He knew he was capable of action, was healed, full of zest for life.

No charge bothered Eagleton more in the next four weeks than the charge that he had deceived George McGovern. When George McGovern had called, shortly before four o'clock, Eagleton's room was full of staff, friends and friendly newsmen. McGovern's call was short and well reported, McGovern opening the conversation with his offer and Eagleton snapping back, "George, before you change your mind, I accept." Then, at the Doral end, in McGovern's suite Mankiewicz took the phone and asked whether Eagleton had any skeletons in his closet. Eagleton replied that he had none and, after more detailed questioning, later hotly disputed, turned the phone over to his administrative assistant, Douglas Bennet, who could brief Mankiewicz on the necessary biographical background for a press release. News was now spreading rapidly; strangers and more newsmen were bursting into Eagleton's room; Bennet remembers shushing the growing noise when a TV crew with beacon lights flaring burst in while he spoke to Mankiewicz. Eagleton remembers fleeing, seeking privacy from the TV camera, to his bedroom, where his wife was telephoning her parents with the good news—only to be followed into the bedroom by a St. Louis *Globe-Democrat* reporter and cameraman. In the instant mini-bedlam, privacy had evaporated, and with it any possibility of thoughtful reflection. Bizarre as had been the sequence of choice at the Doral, it would have been even more bizarre for an Eagleton or anyone else to have lifted the phone in such a crowded and public room and said in the pandemonium, "Listen . . . you should know . . . Tom's been hospitalized three times for nervous breakdown." In any event, as Eagleton kept telling visitors months later, "My health just wasn't on my mind, it wasn't on my mind, it was like a broken leg that healed." At no point during this or the next ten days was Eagleton dissembling to or concealing from George McGovern. At the charge of deception, the Eagleton staff still becomes bitter.

Yet the bitterness of the McGovern staff was understandable, too— they were grappling with a new kind of outer reality. And their information, and hence the problem, was coming to them in bits and pieces, jagged, disturbing, denying them the decision-making ability they had enjoyed but yesterday when they lived in, and controlled, their own tight little world.

* * *

Their tight little world was breaking up. The people whose personalities and ideals had been the protective shield of George McGovern's candidacy were undergoing the stress of power and the competition of those who collect around power. For days, press reports out of the convention had been speculating on staff shifts, the reorganization of the McGovern army for the electoral push. Nerves had been jangled; communications, trust and confidences within the old group were upset. Gordon Weil, who for over a year had traveled with the candidate as the custodian of his body and his day's time, was said to be on the way out. So, too, was Kirby Jones, who had served around the clock as press secretary in the hard times.

Thus, on the Thursday night of the acceptance speech and acclamation of the McGovern-Eagleton ticket, euphoria had been tinged with apprehension as the victors jostled for places on the podium. Then, the victorious ones had all gone back to McGovern's suite at the Doral for a short private celebration before mounting the staircase to the grander public victory celebration in the Doral's Starlight Room. Among the apprehensive and the moody was Gordon Weil, who, on the way upstairs, stopped Douglas Bennet and asked what was really true about the mixed rumors he had been hearing about Eagleton. Bennet replied that Eagleton had been so mentally exhausted after his 1960 campaign that he had put himself in a hospital to get help. At other times, until the day before, Weil might have gone directly to the candidate with the information; now he went to Mankiewicz and Hart to tell them immediately what he had just learned, in the room thronged with celebrants and contributors. Bennet joined them to discuss the problem. Mankiewicz, sleepless, but still creative, felt they could ride it out—if the question came up in the next few days, particularly on television, Eagleton could say simply that he had campaigned himself right into the hospital in 1960. But McGovern was not informed.

Yet the news was upsetting. It became more upsetting the next day. By this time Weil's separation from the candidate had become official; and without access to the candidate or a chance to say farewell, Weil had flown off from Miami alone. McGovern, unaware of the new development on Eagleton, had flown off shortly after three. By six o'clock Mankiewicz, preparing for a few days' vacation, was packing his bags at the now hollow Doral when Bennet called. This time Bennet offered the information that Eagleton had been hospitalized not once, but twice. In complete exhaustion, not wanting to break off his vacation—a mistake Mankiewicz readily admitted later—Mankiewicz asked Bennet to set up a telephone call the following day between Mankiewicz and Hart in the Virgin Islands and Eagleton in Washington. The call came at midnight, and while Mankiewicz talked, Gary Hart listened in. It was an unsatisfactory conversation; the memory of the Watergate bugging was fresh;

Republicans were bugging and wire-tapping Democratic lines. Mankiewicz asked, "Supposing Chuck Colson has the records before him and
he's going in to tell the President, what would he see?" Eagleton, in Mankiewicz's recollection, replied that he would see something like a report
on nervous exhaustion and melancholia. But such a conversation could
not be continued on an open line, and they agreed to meet privately for
breakfast on Thursday morning in Washington, when Mankiewicz and
Hart would be back.

Meanwhile, McGovern was not to be disturbed. The candidate
needed rest and refreshment of spirit. He was scheduled to depart from
Washington on Monday morning for his native South Dakota, where he
would spend his fiftieth birthday and rusticate in the Black Hills, near
Sylvan Lake, to think through the ideas, the re-staffing, the perspectives
of his campaign against Richard Nixon.

McGovern, in South Dakota, was thus still not aware of the crisis
when on Thursday morning Mankiewicz and Hart, back in Washington,
met Eagleton for their scheduled breakfast. By then matters were dramatically more serious. The switchboard at McGovern headquarters had
been taking anonymous calls for both Mankiewicz and Hart, messages
that Eagleton had a record of mental illness, including electro-shock
treatment and possibly worse. The Thursday breakfast brought out the
full story. When asked, Eagleton told all: there had been, actually, three
episodes of hospitalization; he had indeed been twice subjected to electro-
shock therapy; he still took occasional tranquillizers. The questioning was
rough. Eagleton offered to resign, or do anything else they wanted him
to do. Mankiewicz said no.

The decision was the candidate's. McGovern was interrupting his
South Dakota vacation to fly to Washington for a Senate vote that afternoon, and Mankiewicz and Hart would join the candidate for the flight
back to South Dakota the next day, Friday. It was on the plane going
back to South Dakota that McGovern learned from Hart and Mankiewicz
the full Eagleton story as they had pieced it together. McGovern said
nothing; but Eleanor, a tough-minded woman, was appalled. Saturday in
South Dakota was devoted to staff conferences as McGovern mulled the
matter over. Mankiewicz and Hart were both, by now, hardening in their
opinions. Hart considered McGovern attorney for the nation; the candidate had a responsibility for choosing the best man to succeed him as
President; unless the medical records of Eagleton's illness convinced him
that Eagleton was sound, McGovern should let Eagleton go. So Hart expressed himself.

Mankiewicz had become even more convinced that Eagleton should
go. There was, for one thing, a new development: Both the Knight newspapers and *Time* Magazine, Mankiewicz had learned, were on the trail
of Eagleton's past frailty; the story would not be the candidate's to pack-

age and manipulate as he wished; it was about to break. On Sunday evening, after Hart had returned to Washington, Mankiewicz went to McGovern's cabin alone and insisted, flatly, that Eagleton must go. It was necessary, Mankiewicz said, both politically and patriotically. Mc-Govern again made no comment. He listened. Said only that he was thinking about the problem; and preferred to wait until the next night, Monday, when Eagleton was scheduled to arrive at the lodge for direct conversation.

It was after midnight when Eagleton arrived—and, telephoning his arrival to McGovern, was invited by the candidate to bring his wife along to breakfast the next morning with both McGoverns.

With the two women present, breakfast was friendly and connubial. Eagleton had not brought with him the medical records which the McGovern staff had anticipated, but he was forthright and outgoing. Forty-five minutes were spent in the usual pleasantry of social dialogue when two couples meet for the first time; the next forty-five minutes were spent on the Eagleton problem. Foremost on McGovern's mind was the accuracy of the working memorandum the Knight newspapers had prepared to prod Mankiewicz into further revelation. The memorandum, despite several serious inaccuracies, was a reflection of genuinely diligent and responsible reporting. Eagleton again repeated the story of his troubles from Day One. McGovern was satisfied. The two candidates met next in restricted staff without wives; all decided that since the story was about to leak anyway, they might as well break it that afternoon at a press conference at the lodge.

The press conference began, after McGovern's opening remarks, with Eagleton telling his full story: " . . . on three occasions in my life I have voluntarily gone into hospitals as a result of nervous exhaustion and fatigue." It closed with George McGovern fielding questions from the press: "Tom Eagleton is fully qualified in mind, body and spirit to be the Vice-President of the United States and, if necessary, to take over the Presidency on a moment's notice." And if he had the choice to make all over again? "I wouldn't have hesitated one minute if I had known everything that Senator Eagleton said here today," McGovern replied.

With that, so far as George McGovern and Tom Eagleton were concerned, the issue had been opened, cleared and closed. Eagleton was off to California and Hawaii for a campaign swing; and McGovern could turn his attention to the unresolved problem of his campaign staff—confident that his prompt and open disposition of the Eagleton problem would earn him Brownie points for candor and decisiveness with the press and the public at large. Within forty-eight hours he would know better.

It was inevitable from the first unfolding of the news that Eagleton would be dropped from the ticket for the simplest of reasons: However competent, able or honest the Senator from Missouri, he had been hospitalized for mental strain—and American folklore had not yet learned to separate the degrees and different natures of mental illness. Presidents of the United States from Jackson and Lincoln through Wilson have been swept by stress and strain—some, like Wilson, collapsing completely, some, like Lincoln, moving through days of bleak despair to triumph. Yet in the folklore of older America, mental illness was a peril that bore the stigma of the deranged mind. And in a nuclear age, other considerations pressed: A pilot of SAC or the captain of a nuclear submarine would be invalidated by such a health record as Tom Eagleton's. Should Tom Eagleton then be propelled to a position where someday he might have command over them?

For a full day George McGovern held firm. On Wednesday night he gave his campaign its most memorable statement, that he was "1,000 percent for Tom Eagleton and I have no intention of dropping him from the ticket." The 1,000-percent phrase would haunt McGovern through Election Day, just as much as the event which produced it. It was possibly the most damaging single *faux pas* ever made by a Presidential candidate. That fatal phrase had hardly left McGovern's lips, however, when the events which would force him to repudiate it began. First the New York *Post,* the most rigidly liberal paper in that most liberal of major U.S. cities, pronounced sentence on Eagleton, calling for his resignation. Simultaneously, Queens County (New York) Democratic leader Matthew Troy, one of the very few party regulars who had backed McGovern even before the primaries, made known his views: "I have nine kids," said Troy, "I don't want to see them destroyed because some unstable person might become President." Then, Thursday, came the floating of an absolutely spurious story by Columnist Jack Anderson, who claimed to have proof that Eagleton had an arrest record of half a dozen charges of drunken and reckless driving. Simultaneously both the Washington *Post* and the Baltimore *Sun* were calling for Eagleton's resignation. Then came *The New York Times,* and *The New York Times* carried with it master influence over most of those liberals who contribute money to good causes like McGovern's. And by now McGovern, isolated from the centers of public opinion in Washington and New York, secluded at a summer lodge in mid-continent, was beginning to sense the pressure in the hundreds of letters and telegrams pouring in, the hundreds of calls jamming the hotel switchboard.

Some time on Thursday, decision firmed in George McGovern's mind. But then came again the familiar McGovern phenomenon—the man of goodwill unable to master the clean cruelty of necessary decision. Eagleton was now in campaign flight—to Los Angeles, to Hawaii, to San Francisco—cheered by enthusiastic crowds and bayed by the press, unable to shake the story or the questioning, harassed and embittered by renewed stories of his drinking; and mystified by reports of what was going on back at the ranch in South Dakota. Following Eagleton's course was like watching a chicken flopping around the barnyard, pursued by a little boy with a hatchet trying to chop its head off, the chicken bleeding and squawking as it went, the little boy upset by his inability to strike a clean blow.

Back at the ranch, McGovern's participatory staff was now in one of its full flights of confusion; but no one reading the stories out of South Dakota could be in any doubt that the staff's internal debate was moving sharply against Tom Eagleton. McGovern had tried to quench his aides' semi-public debate on Wednesday by scolding them to silence and issuing his 1,000-percent statement. By Thursday, however, he, too, was turning. On Friday morning he had penciled a new paragraph into a speech he was giving that day to South Dakota Democrats at Aberdeen—a vague statement that the skies were cloudy and while he made up his mind he asked for their prayers. This was a "signal," said McGovern to his staff. Then, lest the signal be misunderstood, the candidate wanted to make the signal clearer—and his press officer, Dick Dougherty, arranged that McGovern would dine in the common room of the lodge with the news correspondents, speaking first to Jules Witcover, then of the Los Angeles *Times,* a correspondent whose reliability is unquestioned and whose story would certainly reach Eagleton the next day in California, then to others as he table-hopped, making clear to all that he was reconsidering the Eagleton matter.

The signal was not at all clear to Tom Eagleton. That day, Friday, Eagleton had come back from Hawaii to the mainland after rousing crowds and rallies, and shortly before lunch he telephoned George McGovern from San Francisco. McGovern described to Eagleton the pressure on him, said he had "thirty editorials here in my hand which are against you." His people were worried. But he wanted to reassure Tom once more of his own stand: "Remember, Tom, I'm 1,000 percent for you." Eagleton went to bed in San Francisco that night at 10:00 P.M. while in South Dakota McGovern was just about to inform the press of his reconsideration of the nomination. "Why in hell," wrote Eagleton later, "did he have to table-hop? Why in the hell didn't he pick up the phone, call me collect if need be, and say 'Tom, it's over. There are too many imponderables in your candidacy. Your presence on the ticket jeopardizes my candidacy for the Presidency of the United States.'"

The signals were clearer on the East Coast. Money-raising at McGovern headquarters had been suspended as Henry Kimelman waited for the name of a new runningmate. The poster and button makers under contract to the campaign had decided to stop the run of McGovern-Eagleton posters and buttons until the situation was clarified. Democratic leaders across the nation now had the word Eagleton was to be dumped.

The press accepted it. Tom Eagleton alone did not get the message until Sunday, when it came to him publicly over the airwaves.

Eagleton had barnstormed back to Washington on Saturday from San Francisco, through his home state of Missouri, where he received a frenzied welcome, to the capital for his appearance on Sunday, July 30th, on the CBS telecast *Face the Nation*. At 1:00 P.M. he confronted a panel of inquisitors, and though faced on the panel with the unexpected participation of Jack Anderson, who had spread the drunk-driving stories about him, he performed admirably. But driving home, after taping another show for CBS, he learned that on the rival NBC telecast, *Meet the Press*, Jean Westwood and Basil Paterson, the new chairpersons of the Democratic National Committee, had dumped him publicly. Mrs. Westwood had phrased it as what "a noble thing" it would be if Eagleton quit the ticket. It was quite clear from the report—as indeed it was so in fact—that Mrs. Westwood had spoken to McGovern and had received his approval of the remark. Eagleton had got the signal finally, and the signal in the words of his press secretary, Mike Kelley, was "Goodbye, Tom."

It was now time for the McGovern leadership to formalize its decision. During the four hectic days since Tuesday, the McGovern staff had come to the conclusion that, no matter what Tom Eagleton's personal merits, if he stayed, for the rest of the campaign Americans would be discussing mental health, not the issues McGovern wanted to talk about. The senior group met at George McGovern's home—the Senator and his wife, Gary Hart and Henry Kimelman early enough to watch the broadcasts, joined later by Frank Mankiewicz and Jean Westwood as soon as the broadcasts were over. With no dissent they agreed Eagleton must go and the announcement would be made formally the next night, Monday.

But first, before the public Monday meeting, there was a last courtesy to go through—McGovern would meet secretly that evening, Sunday, with Eagleton at the home of Henry Kimelman. Escorted by Secret Service, slipping away from the scrutiny of press and broadcasters, both arrived, Eagleton first, McGovern a bit later, and, having sent their respective staffs upstairs, began their only face-to-face private conversation shortly after ten in the evening.

Eagleton dictated his notes of the conversation when he returned home and then, some time later, transcribed them:

> Only now as I write this do I perceive the bloody irony of a situation wherein the two nominees of a major political party are alone together for the first time since their 45 minute respite in the Senate steam bath in the spring of 1969.

How does any conversation start under these circumstances? Cautiously to be sure.

George complimented me on my "Face The Nation" performance. I complimented him on Jean Westwood's hatchet job—and I used just those words—on "Meet The Press. . . ."

To this McGovern rejoined, "Tom, believe me I had no idea what she was going to say. Only this afternoon when she and Basil Paterson came by my house did I first learn of what she said."

"Don't shit me, George," I said. This was the first time in our recent political linkage that either of us had said to the other anything that was less than kind. George smirked. Not a smile of faint amusement. Not a frown of slight irritation. A smirk, that's what it was.

"All right, Tom, let's talk some facts. You tell me your facts, I'll tell you mine."

They talked on, Eagleton telling McGovern of the huge crowds his campaign trip had drawn during the week, the warm and human response, the support he had received from personalities like Mayor Alioto of San Francisco, the Governor of Hawaii, telephone calls of support from Senator Kennedy and Senate Majority Leader Mike Mansfield. McGovern listed the newspapers, the Senators, the Congressmen, the state chairmen and others who had called demanding Eagleton's withdrawal.

" 'I know Mondale is a good friend of yours and a close friend of mine,' " said McGovern. " 'He called me every day in South Dakota since the beginning of this health business. He has begged me to get you off the ticket. He feels that you will defeat the national ticket in Minnesota and that you will defeat him for re-election to the Senate.' "

Then McGovern added, " 'Tom, I know you've gone through hell this week, but so have I.'

"The conversation seemed to be rambling," read Eagleton's notes, "then I said, 'George, I am now no longer Tom Who. I am Tom Eagleton, suddenly a very well-known political figure. George, you may not win with me, but you can't win without me.' This time it was not a smirk. This time it was a look of incredulous disbelief. There was a pause. It seemed like eternity, but it couldn't be more than fifteen seconds. 'Tom, tell me what you feel in your heart,' he asked."

Eagleton made one last plea for his candidacy, feeling that this time he might have swayed McGovern. McGovern answered, " 'Tom, you're one hell of a guy. Let's go home and sleep on it.' " And then, each of them summoning his staff, they went their respective ways home.

Eagleton and McGovern met the next evening in the Marble Room of the Senate, with Senator Gaylord Nelson, a friend of both, present.

Two *pro forma* telephone calls were put through by McGovern to Eagleton's doctors, McGovern taking the calls alone in a corner. The bill of health was clean, said McGovern. The two then went on to discuss once more the pros and cons of Eagleton staying on the ticket. Finally, to avoid embarrassing Nelson by forcing him to cast the decisive vote, Eagleton said to McGovern, " 'George, if my presence on the ticket causes you any embarrassment, or hindrance, or an impediment, I'll step aside.' " McGovern said, " 'Yes.' " Nelson nodded. And the McGovern-Eagleton ticket was over.

Much more, however, had been lost to the Democratic ticket than Tom Eagleton. Lost was McGovern's reputation as a politician somehow different from the ordinary—a politician who would not, like others, do *anything* to get elected. McGovern by this time had already antagonized many Americans by his stand on issues. For the first time, after Eagleton, he would incur not merely antagonism but—far worse in politics—contempt for incompetence.

The reporting of the first two weeks of August was to raze to the ground George McGovern's reputation for candor and trust; more than that, it was to make him look like a fool. The first weeks of August are always the low passage of the summer news doldrums, when television's evening news shows scratch to fill their time and editors wrestle with making the front page attractive. And in this news vacuum stood McGovern—he was prey, and the press was on the hunt.

He "is beginning to remind us of those school teachers who couldn't keep the class," wrote columnist Tom Braden, onetime writing partner of Frank Mankiewicz, and more than indulgent to McGovern earlier in the campaign. "You can find them, even in college. Nice people, too. One looks back with sympathy and a sense of shame. But at the time—was it that they were too nice?—their classes were a shambles. The erasers flew when they turned their backs. . . ." A reporter, no matter how personally fond of McGovern, could do nothing else but report the events of the following weeks as either hilarious, pathetic or simply tragic. After all, the man was running for President, an office in which the quality of decision is all-important.

McGovern's search for a new runningmate had begun on Monday, even before the formal dismissal of Tom Eagleton that evening. He had flown to Louisiana that morning for the funeral of Senator Allen Ellender; flying back, he sat beside Senator Edward Kennedy and again, in a courtship that had become embarrassing to Kennedy, he pressed his suit, to be rebuffed again. Again the following day he pursued Kennedy; and still on Wednesday morning tried to enlist the Massachusetts Senator with an early-morning telephone call to Senator Abraham Ribicoff for intercession. When Ribicoff reported back that Kennedy was adamant in his refusal, McGovern pressed his case on Ribicoff; Ribicoff, who had already turned down McGovern at Miami, was equally firm—he was sixty-two years old; he was to remarry in a few days; he would have none of it. McGovern and Eleanor had dined the previous evening at the Jockey Club with Lawrence and Elva O'Brien. He had told the former party chairman that he was high on the list, that there was strong support for him all across the country; O'Brien, suspicious of all McGovern overtures after his Miami experience, admitted only to a mild interest in this one, and McGovern said he would get back to him. But now, with two refusals in three days, McGovern turned on Wednesday evening to his old patron Hubert Humphrey in a semi-public courtship on the Senate floor, later in a more private plea in the office of the Secretary of the Senate. McGovern pursued Humphrey again the next morning at breakfast, and by noon all three refusals were public, Humphrey's being the most colorful public statement: "Imagine Hubert Humphrey on that ticket. . . . [The press would say] poor old Hubert, he just had to get on. He just couldn't remain off. He smelled the sawdust again and there he's in the ring. Well, bull. . . . I don't need to be in the ring. I'm just not going to leave myself open to any more humiliating, debilitating exposure."

That day, Thursday, McGovern tried to reach Governor Reubin Askew of Florida, in Tallahassee, proffering the Vice-Presidency just before Askew left for vacation, and getting Askew's refusal from North Carolina in the afternoon. With Askew out, it was now four tries at bat and no connection. Matters were compounded further when McGovern informally met a group of reporters and acknowledged he had been turned down by Kennedy, Ribicoff and Humphrey, but insisted he had still a long list of people under consideration . . . names like Ralph Nader, Republican Jacob K. Javits, Public Citizen John W. Gardner. Moreover, he said, he was also considering blacks, Chicanos and women —a courtesy bow to his constituent groups, but preposterous as a serious statement to reporters invited to believe it. Finally, added George McGovern, he did not mean to be rushed in his choice this time—and yet the Democratic National Committee had been summoned to convene on Tuesday to rubber-stamp McGovern's new choice, and that deadline was only five days away.

By Thursday evening McGovern was working on his fifth choice: Edmund Muskie, to whose Washington home the candidate drove that night to make the offer personally. Muskie, whose cautious deliberation had amused the press and the McGovern staff through the spring months, was still cautiously deliberate—he would need, he told McGovern, a day to think it over. He would fly to his summer home in Kennebunk Beach, Maine, to talk it over with his wife and children, then give his reply on Saturday.

By now McGovern had learned from experience, and was seeking standbys. On Friday he spoke to Larry O'Brien again and, stipulating that Muskie was up in Maine considering the offer, said that Larry had high marks from everyone around the country; it would be "heart-warming" to Larry, said McGovern, to hear what people said about him, and if Ed Muskie turned down the offer, he might be back to O'Brien once more.

McGovern was also telephoning Sargent Shriver that day. Shriver had never yet been approached by anyone directly and regarded himself, ruefully, as always a political bridesmaid, never a bride. He had been "mentioned" as Vice-Presidential runningmate in 1964, 1968, now again in 1972, but never asked. This time McGovern was asking: If Muskie turned it down, would Shriver be willing to consider it? Shriver would. Shriver had already been checking his prospects. He had called Lyndon Johnson, who had urged him to accept if the offer came. He had called Dick Daley in Chicago for advice; Daley felt the main issue had to be jobs, that McGovern had to make clear he wanted to keep the country strong, that McGovern had to soft-pedal the abortion issue; Daley pledged all-out support in the November election ("I've never been neutral yet," Shriver remembers Daley saying, "I'm a Democrat"). Shriver checked finally with his brother-in-law, Senator Ted Kennedy, who had flown from Washington for a summer weekend at the Kennedy family compound at Hyannis Port. At dinner on Friday, Kennedy was quite sure the choice would come to Sarge the next day—Ed Muskie, said Kennedy, is talking to his wife in Maine, and the longer he waits, the less likely he is to say yes. Shriver asked whether he would be crossing Teddy's path if he accepted, would he be getting in his way. Kennedy said not at all—feel free to accept if you want.

The next morning Ed Muskie telephoned George McGovern to say he could not accept "for family reasons." McGovern's call to Shriver reached the Kennedy family compound while Shriver was playing tennis. You know, said McGovern when Shriver came to the phone, that Muskie's turned it down—would Sarge now be willing to consider the offer? Shriver allowed that he was honored, flattered, wanted to discuss it with his family and Teddy. But the answer was yes. McGovern, up against deadline again, but more deliberate this time, mentioned the impossibility of going through another Eagleton affair, and was there anything in Shriver's background he should know? Shriver thought briefly and replied that he had been cleared for health by the Navy, cleared by the FBI for service in the Kennedy administration, cleared again under Johnson, cleared again under Nixon—the only thing he could think of was a picture in the scatology-and-scandal weekly *The National Enquirer,* which had shown him dancing at a Paris night club with a beautiful young lady in hot pants; but the lady was an old friend of the family. McGovern laughed, and that was the end of it.

The new Democratic National Committee met at two P.M. on Tuesday, August 8th, in Washington's Sheraton Park Hotel to consider the choice of a Vice-Presidential nominee to replace Tom Eagleton. The hall, hung with bunting, enlivened by taped music, entertained a melancholy group. The marching songs of Miami had long faded, and the evangelical euphoria of McGovern's acceptance speech, that pilgrim's call to pilgrim's progress, had passed from memory. Security was light, the atmosphere easy, and the committee members and press mingled in the lobby with the other conventions proceeding at the Sheraton Park at the same time—of the American Massage and Therapy Association as well as the Interallied Confederation of Reserve Officers. After all the calls to unity, a humorous and charming appearance by Tom Eagleton, a stemwinder in the old tradition from Hubert Humphrey, a brief appearance by Larry O'Brien, appearances by Muskie and Kennedy, Sargent Shriver was formally nominated for Vice-President. After that Shriver spoke gaily and with gallantry about what lay ahead, and George McGovern, suddenly looking like the old pictures of William Jennings Bryan, closed the evening by calling on all good people "to reclaim this nation so freedom can truly ring again."

This time, proceedings had gone off in prime time, so that the nation could pay attention if it would. But the nation had become bored with pilgrim's progress, and the ratings were down to 10,240,000 homes.

Another index provoked even greater reflection. The editors of *Time* Magazine had, with apparently correct appreciation of the political importance of the new team offered by the Democratic Party, covered the newsstands of the nation that day with an issue that joined pictures of Sargent Shriver and George McGovern on the cover of their magazine. The newsstand sale of the magazine bombed; passersby ignored the story of McGovern/Shriver. The editor of *Newsweek,* Osborn Elliott, had, however, entertained an oblique intuition. Despite the public excitement over the Eagleton/Shriver/McGovern affair, he had decided to offer the nation an off-beat enticement: a cover story on Chinese acupuncture. For those who chose their news magazines on the run that August week, the winner was acupuncture over McGovern/Shriver by a landslide, and *Newsweek* sold the fourth highest quantity of magazines at the newsstand in all its forty-year history. The nation had tuned the Democrats out.

Reporting the Democratic campaign for the Presidency later, after mid-August, was to be assigned to reporting a revolving, continental wake.

In the weeks before the Republican convention, with the image of

George McGovern shattered, there was little more to do than examine one's conscience and observations, and puzzle out why so fundamentally decent a man as George McGovern had cut so grotesque a profile on the perception of so many of his countrymen.

Goodwill was at the heart of it, of course. Each speech, each phrase, each program of George McGovern came from a heart of charity. If political goodwill terrified the citizens of the big cities, who had had their bellyful of goodwill in the 1960's, this political goodwill was nonetheless understandable and honorable. It was the personal goodwill that was so baffling—the gentleness and the kindliness which resulted in such aberrations of character.

The thought had first come to me shortly after a trip to Florida at the beginning of the year—a journey with McGovern in January of 1972. He was then polling only 3 percent support among Democrats in the Gallup Poll and his candidacy was apparently hopeless. No large press corps then attended his comings and goings; none of the major news organs had yet assigned a permanent reporter to dog him full-time; and on this particular day his half-empty plane contained only a few Florida reporters plus Stewart Alsop of *Newsweek* and Tom Braden, the Washington *Post* columnist, men of large dimension in national journalism. The busing issue was, obviously, about to become the key issue in the Florida primary, so I approached George McGovern and began to talk about it. He was disturbed—did we have the right, he asked, to bus children across county lines, in and out of neighborhoods, at a time of such racial tension? Busing probably increased racial tension. What would I think if he came out against cross-county busing? I said it might turn the race upside down; and then McGovern summoned his black aide, Yancey Martin, and they discussed the matter once more. It was a long flight down the Florida coast that day as we prop-stopped from Jacksonville to Miami, and in the course of the flight both Alsop and Braden had individual conversations with the candidate. That night, cautiously comparing notes as reporters do, lifting the down cards one by one to make sure the other fellow has the same story, it was quite apparent that all three of us had heard identical ruminations from the candidate—and that this internal debate in McGovern's mind on busing was a major story. Alsop and Braden proceeded to print the story—as a rumination, not a decision, of a major personality.

Ten days later I was in Washington again and opened the Washington *Post* to read in its letters column a letter signed by George McGovern: "The report that I am considering opposing the school busing orders of federal courts, or the recent decision consolidating school districts in Richmond, Virginia, is totally without foundation. (Tom Braden column, January 25.) All my political life I have fought for the principle and the

practice of integrated schools. . . . I will not change that position regardless of the political cost. . . ."

What Stewart Alsop and Tom Braden had printed had been accurate; but if McGovern chose to deny the story, then, in the murky
morality of off-the-record confidences, he had the Fifth Freedom of the
politician to deny what he had said.

The incident might have slipped from memory except for the fact
that the same day I was visiting with Al Barkan, labor's chief political
attack-bomber, a straight shooter but rough-tongued man. McGovern's
name came up early in conversation, and Barkan fulminated instantly:
"The man is a deliberate liar." Barkan then passed on to other things,
and would not elaborate.

Now, in midsummer of the year, with McGovern's public credibility
shattered by the Eagleton affair, with the AFL/CIO refusing to endorse
a Democratic candidate for the first time in twenty years, it seemed important to find out why he so disturbed labor's leadership. After all—
McGovern had been labor's man in his early days; the AFL/CIO had
put up the dollars necessary to pay for the recount by which McGovern
first won election to the Senate (by 597 votes) in 1962; and the Senator's
voting record was excellent on labor's own annual score card.

As pieced together from conversations with Barkan and Lane Kirkland, two quite different figures in the ruling hierarchy of the AFL/CIO,
the story of the feud was at once complicated in its origin but simple in
result. It was complicated by the intricate mechanics of parliamentary
procedure in the Congress of the United States; the story went back to
1966, and concerned the twenty-year-old effort of the labor leaders to
repeal provision 14B of the Taft-Hartley Act of 1947. That Act had left
it to the state legislatures to permit or forbid unions to demand a union-
shop proviso in their contracts. The AFL/CIO had wished, for years, to
outlaw this restraint of state legislation and leave the union-shop proviso
to free bargaining. By 1966 the AFL/CIO could take its count of both
House and Senate and feel victory close. The House had already passed
labor's repealer of 14B; and in the Senate, AFL/CIO leaders counted
56 sure votes for their side—if only the votes could get to vote. Yet
whether the Senate could get to vote or not depended on Senator Everett
Dirksen of Illinois, who was conducting a filibuster to prevent a vote.
The filibuster could be choked off only by two thirds of the then Senate,
or 64. And labor's leadership was not angry at Dirksen—they understood
him. They were still angry in 1972 at George McGovern.

The reasons for their anger were as simple as the parliamentary
background was complicated. They had counted on George McGovern's
vote against filibuster. Barkan, who rarely descends from his eminence
for nitty-gritty lobbying, was assigned to see McGovern personally. Mc-
Govern assured him that on this cloture he would vote labor's way. A

few days later Barkan, informed by Senator Lee Metcalf of Montana that McGovern's vote was in doubt, checked again. McGovern assured Barkan that his vote was solid for cloture. To stiffen McGovern's promise, Barkan invited to Washington the head of South Dakota's own AFL/CIO, Francis McDonald. Again McGovern assured his home-state AFL/CIO leader he was voting right. "And McDonald was sitting right there in the gallery, watching," said Barkan, "when the roll-call came—and when McGovern voted against us, he went up out of his seat like you jabbed a pin in his butt."

"That doesn't happen in this town," said Lane Kirkland. Labor in America is rough; but by labor's code a deal is a deal, and a commitment is a commitment, the given word is bond. Labor supported McGovern again as Senator from South Dakota in 1968 and proposed to do so again in 1974—but for the Presidency in 1972, no, they did not trust him.

It went on like that in the doldrums of August, everyone examining McGovern's personality afresh in the weeks of Sirius. All examination hung on the critical word "commitment." McGovern was committed to a vision, to peace and brotherhood, and would certainly be willing to die for that vision; but his commitment to people, individually or to any group outside of the staff of his own army—this was another matter. All through the early weeks of August, stories of feud, clash and broken promises multiplied in McGovern headquarters—from minorities division to registration division, grievances puckered and personalities soured. Some charges were excusable as misunderstandings of intent; others could be explained as the normal grumbling that goes on when any necessary reorganization downgrades the old, elevates newcomers. But then, on August 17th, four days before the Republican convention opened in Miami Beach, came the Salinger affair.

The Salinger affair, too, had its roots on the Black Friday of July 14th—the day of the O'Brien affair, the unraveling of McGovern's commitment to Salinger on the vice-chairmanship, the first hint of the Eagleton breakdown. Only the exhaustion of the candidate and his staff could have incubated so many blunders on a single day.

Chapter One of his dismay had ended for Pierre Salinger with his repudiation by the candidate, and the Democratic National Committee, in favor of Basil Paterson. "I left that room as angry as I'd ever been in my life," said Salinger later. But, packing his bags and holding his tongue, he was off that afternoon to the shelter of Hyannis Port, Massachusetts, where Ethel Kennedy had invited him for the weekend. Salinger, worn out, his legs numb from the waist down after four consecutive days on his feet at the convention, retired early—and was in bed no more than ten minutes before Ethel Kennedy knocked to say that George McGovern was on the phone from Washington, to begin Chapter Two of dismay.

McGovern was apologizing again for what had happened earlier that day in Miami, and now asked Salinger to handle an important one for him. McGovern's staff had received word via David Dellinger, leader of the peace demonstrators in Chicago in 1968 and one of the chief contacts of North Vietnamese in the U.S.A., that the Hanoi government wanted McGovern to send a representative to talk to it. Would Salinger fly to Washington to be briefed by John Holum, who had been briefed by Dellinger, and then explore the matter? "I said OK," recalls Salinger, "but in my mind I saw it as an effort to win me back with an important assignment."

By Monday, Salinger was in Washington being briefed by Holum; by Tuesday, July 18th, he was in Paris, his home abroad, conferring with two members of the North Vietnamese delegation to the Paris peace talks.

It was a tricky matter—for an American to deal with an enemy during a war tests the legal limits of one of the oldest laws in American history, the Logan Act of 1799. For McGovern to be communicating with Hanoi via David Dellinger, one of the arch-symbols of street protest, was perilous. To intervene with the North Vietnamese at a moment when the American government was itself negotiating with them bordered on the unpatriotic. Yet, thought Salinger, if his trip to Hanoi could bring about the release of thirty or forty American prisoners of war, it might be worth it. But he cautioned the Hanoi delegates finally, "If there is any way you can make peace with the current administration, you should do so without regard to the political events in our country. Senator McGovern would prefer peace in Vietnam today to being President, if that is the choice." And then Salinger was off on vacation, first to the Riviera, then to Sardinia, and was not to see the North Vietnamese again until August 9th, when, over tea, the North Vietnamese told him no prisoners would be released. Thereupon Salinger canceled his exploratory trip to Hanoi, and by telephone reported to Mankiewicz in Washington that the mission had failed.

It was a week later that matters came apart. For, as Salinger was flying back to New York, the United Press International reported out of Paris that Salinger had been negotiating with the North Vietnamese on McGovern's instructions, and had urged them to settle for peace at once with Nixon. At the airport in New York, another agency reporter demanded confirmation. Salinger made no comment, drove directly to a hotel in New York and frantically tried to reach the McGovern headquarters, which he found in the same confusion as the day he had left Miami.

Reaching the traveling McGovern party in Illinois, he tried to find out from Fred Dutton, who answered the phone, what their common reaction should be to the leak. The Senator had just left the room, said

Dutton. "What's he going to say about the UPI story?" asked Salinger. "He's just gone out to deny it," replied Dutton; and the furious Salinger demanded that the Senator get back to him directly, personally, at once. When McGovern did call back fifteen minutes later, he was soothing. Yes, he had denied the tenor of the UPI story that he, McGovern, had sent Salinger to Paris to urge Hanoi to make peace with Nixon; but no, he had not denied that he had sent Salinger to Paris. Agreeing with Mc-Govern that they would put out a joint statement as soon as possible, Salinger waited until an announcement had been worded, and then talked to the clamorous press from a script which he believed to be a common base of understanding. Salinger then turned on his television set in New York to find out what McGovern had actually said earlier that morning about the Salinger mission. And then came the statement: "Pierre Salinger had no instructions whatsoever from me. He told me he was going to Paris and he said while he was there he might try to make some determinations of what was going on in the negotiations. But there wasn't the slightest instruction on my part to him." George McGovern had been caught again in apparent flirtation with the facts.

If Salinger that night was flabbergasted, the American public was only slightly less so. McGovern had been revealed to be secretly negotiating with Hanoi; first he had denied it, then confirmed it. He had been doing so in the interest of peace, of course, which was understandable— as understandable as his final removal of Eagleton two weeks before. But why the confusion? Why the initial reaction of deception? Harry Truman had said of the Presidency, if you can't stand the heat, get out of the kitchen. The heat of decision evidently upset George McGovern— and if one examined the nature of all the McGovern blunders, both before and after the convention, a pattern became evident.

Goodwill was the pattern of George McGovern's frailty. On public goodwill, on care for the sick and aged, on respect for the blacks and the youth and the women, on peace and tax equality—he was inflexible. It might—and did—worry Americans who were on the wrong side of this goodwill. But when it came to individuals, in the critical face-to-face decisions and interchange of personalities, the goodwill was a weakness. He could not dismiss, or fire, or sharply disagree, or impose his intent on people he personally liked. His kindness and gentleness would lead him to say almost anything to any individual in his pursuit of friendship, brotherhood and harmony; if, later, people were let down by reliance on his private commitments, it was to McGovern a sincere, an acute, a poignant sadness; but he must be true to his larger causes. To the public, insofar as it believed he meant his larger causes, he was divisive; and as his private commitments one by one came apart openly, the public questioned the largest thrust of his campaign—his credibility and competence.

George McGovern's course in the American mind could be traced best by the polls; for all polls agreed, even with aberrations for bias— the rival public polls, Harris and Gallup, the private polls, Republican and Democratic polls. The McGovern problem as traced by the polls had a neat two-part sequence, if one looked back to the beginning of the year. The first problem had been recognition: Who was George Mc- Govern? The triumphs of the McGovern army, the deeds wrought at the primaries, had cured that. By late spring he was recognized. And, thus, being recognized, the second part of public examination had begun: What did George McGovern stand for? Hubert Humphrey in California had tried to define that problem rigorously for the Democratic voters of Cal- ifornia; the effect of that primary could also be followed in the graphs.

At his peak of popularity in the polls, fresh from cross-country victories and entering California, George McGovern in May had closed the gap between himself and Richard Nixon to only 5 points—Nixon 40 percent, McGovern 35 percent, George Wallace 17 percent, so read the Harris Poll. The California primaries had been the first occasion for examining the man himself; and, though winning the California primary, McGovern had slipped in public scrutiny. After the California primary, the Harris Poll read: Nixon 45 percent, McGovern 33 percent, Wallace 17 percent. The matter of credibility had not yet set in, and the Demo- cratic convention, if it came off well, should give him an upswing, as traditionally it does to all victorious candidates. Instead of that, the spec- tacle of the new politics at Miami Beach had thrust the polls the other way. Now, losing support as he gained recognition, McGovern had come out of the Eagleton affair and the convention in a straight man-to-man poll-testing at 34 percent against Nixon's 57 percent, with 9 percent un- decided. McGovern was now 23 percentage points behind Nixon in the pollsters' measure of public opinion—the largest gap between Democrats and Republicans since public-polling had been perfected. And yet to come were the Salinger affair and the Republican convention, which would widen the margin even further.

In the slow, languid days of summer when people flick the pages of the papers, watch their television through a cushion of beer, when, with- out recognizing their own unconscious urge to identification, they slowly try to identify the candidate of their choice, they were examining George McGovern—and he was slipping in their esteem more rapidly than any other candidate had ever done.

At a breakfast in the first week of August, Ted Van Dyk, who had been placed in charge of McGovern's disaster-prone issues desk, tried to define for a round table of Washington reporters what he held to be his candidate's fundamental appeal to the country. "Basically," said Van Dyk, "the people are going to have to decide from whom they would rather buy a used car. The campaign will be decided on the personality and the credibility of the candidates."

Two weeks later, on August 23rd, Ted Van Dyk was writing a confidential memorandum to George McGovern on where the campaign now stood:

> We had a meeting this morning in my office of those people primarily concerned with the issues effort in the campaign. . . . We were unanimous in our conclusions. Namely:
>
> (1) Our principal theme to date—namely, that McGovern is more trustworthy and credible than Nixon, both personally and across the key issues—has been defused by the unfortunate events of the past few weeks, i.e., Eagleton and aftermath, Salinger, the Hitler remark, the V.C. statement in your press backgrounder for last Sunday's newspapers. . . .
>
> (2) Our primary and perhaps only chance to win will lie in reclaiming those millions of traditional Democrats who are now undecided or leaning to Nixon. These Democrats, primarily in the big industrial states, are typically blue-collar, middle-minded and socially more conservative than our principal sources of support in the Democratic primaries.
>
> (3) These voters can only be reached by returning to the traditional Democratic themes. Namely, that the Democratic Party and George McGovern are good for ordinary people. . . .
>
> (4) Our principal theme from here on in . . . should be that George McGovern and the Democratic Party have supported Medicare, Social Security, decent wages and economic growth. They deeply care about the well-being of decent hard-working people. . . .
>
> (5) This theme can be illustrated in a multitude of ways —visits to assembly lines, bowling alleys, supermarket checkout counters, blue-collar shopping centers, plant cafeterias. . . .
>
> Summary: We urge that, from this point onward, you return to the traditional Democratic themes. . . . The traditional Democratic voter simply must come to feel again that you are deeply concerned about his homely everyday problems, such as *his* taxes, *his* job, *his* food prices where Richard Nixon and the Republicans have let him down.

Even more simply expressed, the struggle over George McGovern's campaign, raging at every level of confusion and mal-administration inside his campaign staff, could have been stated as "Come Home, George McGovern. Come Home to the Democratic Party." And Mr. Nixon and his Republicans were to preach that you can't come home again.

CHAPTER NINE

RICHARD NIXON'S CAMPAIGN: "OUT THERE"

I T was a cool summer in Washington, June and July happily skipping the steaming days that usually cook the city. The trees, in full leaf, gave the capital that blessing of green which no other American city matches. The gardens of Lafayette Park, lovely as ever, changed colors as the plantings changed; its new brick walks and the red brick reconstructions on either side of the park had mellowed; the older buildings were crisp and clean; pigeons cooed.

The early summer months invited one to stroll from appointment to appointment in downtown Washington, and it was easier than ever to report the Republican and Democratic commands on foot. Only a few blocks separated them. Once McGovern's headquarters had moved from the slope of Capitol Hill to the shabby honeycomb at the corner of 19th and K, one could make one's rounds in a ten- or fifteen-minute walk— from the White House to the Committee for the Re-Election of the President at the corner of 17th and Pennsylvania; from there to McGovern headquarters; from there to the Democratic National Committee at the Watergate.

Except that slowly one realized how much more than a ten-minute walk separated Republican and Democratic commands—it was a matter of culture that separated them.

It was difficult to identify or give the feel of this culture gap. The uniform at McGovern headquarters was slacks, bell-bottom trousers, sun-tans, open-necked shirts; on the grass embankment outside his headquarters, on a sunny day, students and volunteers ate quiche Lorraine, or beans and chili, or whatever the community's $2-a-plate special was that day. The lobby at lunchtime smelled like a college cafeteria. At the Republican Committee to Re-Elect, the uniform was the business suit, dark colors and pinstripes, 1950 Madison Avenue style, necktie neatly knotted, sideburns trimmed at mid-ear, and nothing more than coffee or Coca-Cola was served in the severe legal offices the Committee occupied. At McGovern headquarters, staffers followed the world-championship chess matches between Boris Spassky and Bobby Fischer, and some of the younger buffs brought chess sets to work on at lunchtime. At the Committee to Re-Elect, the Olympics were more important. At the White House, Ron Ziegler offered the thought that there was rub-off from the Olympics on politics—it stimulated patriotism.

"Patriotism" is an explosive word to use in American politics—but in trying to define the culture gap, one could not avoid it. At the White House, for the first time in any campaign, one noticed that the higher up the hierarchy one climbed, the more frequent were the American-flag lapel buttons. The President wore one, and so did those closest to him, all except Henry Kissinger. At the White House, the flag button was like a varsity letter—the first team flaunted it. At McGovern headquarters, the word itself, "patriotism," was a code word for intolerance, war, deception. McGovern's troops, in spirit and ethos, were just as patriotic as Nixon's; but they had grown up reading such books as *A Farewell to Arms,* and phrases like "peace with honor" actually did make them gag, as the President knew. Patriotism for the McGoverns was an emotion to be honored in the private places of one's heart. For the Republicans it was one of the main public thrusts of their campaign; never would the McGovern people acknowledge the right of the Republicans to explore it for political impact. Nor could they understand, or recognize, the dynamic of the family of terms that went with "patriotism"— "family life," "neighborhood schools," "American values." To them it all sounded like home-flag-and-mother.

When they discussed the Pentagon, Vietnam, the budget or welfare proposals, the two staffs used roughly the same figures and names, and complementary but antagonistic rhetoric. Yet, underneath it all, they were talking from the cultures of two entirely different Americas; style, purpose, values—all separated them. The McGovern people were always more sure of themselves and their rhetoric; the White House people were always defensive. The McGovern people were expansive, trusting, romantic; the White House people were wary, never quite sure that they were not being lured into ridicule, contempt or exposure. Though they controlled the government of the United States, the White House staff men regarded Washington as a hostile place.

The men at the White House were, at once, shy and cold; life in the capital had made them gun-shy of the vocalizers. The predominant idiom of Washington journalism was not their idiom, and the White House staff saw the gap in communications and dialogue as positively hostile, if not conspiratorial. Very few saw it for what it was: the cultural gap.

One or two could be amused, like William Safire, a connoisseur of language and its nuances. He chuckled over the gap—"Every time Nixon says it's time to stop running down America, we know it drives them right up the wall." Others were furious. "They own the word factory," said Victor Gold, then Agnew's press secretary, "they make the words. The White House tries to argue it out with them in their words—but they own the ammunition dump." And Pat Buchanan saw it even more vividly: "This hasn't been our town. They live in Georgetown, with their parties; they never invited us, they ignored us. We were the vanguard of Middle America and they were the liberal elite. It's a schism that's cultural, political, social, emotional. When we came in in 1968, they dominated all American society—the media, the Supreme Court, the bureaucracy, the foundations. They left us with our cities burning, and inflation going, our students rioting on the campus. And Nixon challenged all this. He rejected them outright, he challenged their assumptions."

Few at the White House, except Kissinger, any longer cared what the Washington press or the national press corps located in Washington said by early 1972. For, following their leader, they were no longer talking to Washington, or Manhattan, or Congress. Richard Nixon was talking over the heads of anything that might be called establishment— talking by television or by deed to the people beyond the Potomac and the Alleghenies, to the people that fashionable Washington usually called "Out There."

It was rare, at any time, to get a clear view when in Washington of what Richard Nixon was thinking; he had come, by 1972, to live behind a palisade of privacy more impenetrable than had any President of living memory. From behind this palisade he was not only directing a Presidential campaign, but toying with his opponents. As mysterious and complicated as was his inner personality, his politics and philosophy were so simple as to baffle the superior political analysis that sought in them some hidden sophistication.

By 1972 Richard Nixon had molded the Presidency to his own personality—or, more precisely, H. R. Haldeman had so molded it. The personality of Richard Nixon had been Haldeman's chief intellectual preoccupation for ten years; the President needed time to be by himself, to think matters through in his own way. Haldeman saw his function as giving it to him.

Over and over again, in any conversation with people in contact with the President, one was told how much this President craved solitude. He was short on small talk, and was awkward at it. He was impatient, and his mind was quick—he had a habit of hearing the first sentence of a visitor, then interrupting and finishing the visitor's thought quickly in his own words. He had a reflex fear of being quoted—particularly since in private his language was hard, stubborn, blunt. When he spoke for quotation, the strain of dressing his thoughts in public prose resulted usually in clichés or legalese.

Nixon liked conversations about real things. To lubricate social conversation with smiles or empty pleasantries or flattery was a burden to him. Candor was the private style. Once in 1968 I had been asked to his room on a night when the campaign cavalcade stopped in Indianapolis. His feet were up on a chair and he was wrestling with a paper that he said concerned the only problem for which he could see no solution at all. Vietnam? I asked. No, he said, the farm problem—I've got to make a speech next week in Des Moines on the farm problem; there's no solution I can see. From there Nixon went to politics, and then, when I said I could never be a politician, I could smile only three or four hours a day before I became a grouch, Nixon responded with a rare lifting of the curtain on his own personality. That's the hardest part, he said, shaking hands with them all day, smiling at them all day, and "sometimes at the end of the day when I'm smiling shaking hands, I really want to kick them."

By 1972 the people who reached him directly were almost exclusively those who talked of real things. With the departure of Professor Daniel P. Moynihan from the White House staff at the end of 1970, the last real conversational artist who could consistently lift the President out of his moods with anecdote, allusion and history had gone. Nixon still had Finch, to whom his relationship was that of an older brother; Finch could occasionally engage him with a longer philosophical view of things. His three favorite speechwriters—Safire, Price, Buchanan— could, *ex officio,* enjoy conversations with the President when he had to shift his mind from hard things and explain perspectives to them so that they could write for him the longer background thinking of the President. But these people the President used as sounding boards only when *he* wanted to sound off. The people who could reach him at their own initiative were men of hard conversation. John Connally or John Mitchell could always reach the President directly in 1972. But, generally, others waited until they were summoned by Haldeman—and then it was right to business.

The echo of professional conversation with Nixon by staff or government personnel brought one word repeatedly to mind: "tidy." Nixon would receive personnel, after having done his own thinking, with his long yellow legal pads already marked in points and sub-points like a syllabus of questions and answers. With outsiders he might occasionally let himself go in the rambling style once characteristic when his time was free of pressure; but usually now it would pull up short, with a summary, "There are three reasons for that—one . . . two . . . three. . . ."

The tidiness of mind surfaced in public sometimes in far-out statistical or symmetrical metaphors—as when, in meeting the Emperor of Japan at Anchorage, Alaska, he pointed out that they were met at a point absolutely equidistant from Tokyo and Washington; or as when, on the morning of his first inaugural, arriving with Agnew to meet Johnson and Humphrey, he observed that this was probably the first time in American history that four Vice-Presidents (Humphrey, Johnson, Nixon, Agnew) had stood in one place at the same time. He loved statistics, "the first," "the last," "the only," "the most historic" of visits, voyages, banquets, meetings, as if he had been brainwashed by listening to too many sportscasts.

But sometimes the tidiness of mind expressed itself in an outburst of temper—as when an orderly child, building a pile of blocks, flares at someone who tumbles them. The outburst of temper could sound like a snarl, as when his nomination of G. Harrold Carswell for the Supreme Court was rejected by the Senate. Nixon took no particular pride in the abominable staff work that had led to his commitment to Carswell's name—but Carswell was a piece in a symmetry of mind that required him to give the South recognition on the High Bench. Or his anger could be inexplicable at the moment—as was the violent White House reaction when columnist Jack Anderson produced papers revealing that Nixon had placed America on the losing side of the Bengali war between India and Pakistan. Nixon could not say so aloud, but he considered Pakistan an absolutely essential piece on the world chessboard, needed to reach a way into Red China. If he wanted to go Peking, Pakistan was a necessary springboard. He was furious at the disruption of his logical, but secret, planning.

The full nature of the Nixon mind was probably known only to three people, the three who saw him on a daily basis—Kissinger, Ehrlichman and Haldeman. With such people, the President had no need to conceal the clear tenacity of his thinking. With Kissinger alone the President could talk of the China problem in terms of Russia—of the delicate balance of fear in Asia which might give the United States an opening to make peace with both. With Ehrlichman, he could sit down to talk about the problems of the city and then cut through the guff and say, "All right, now we're talking about the Negro problem." But it was with Haldeman that the President was most at ease, Haldeman who could most easily put away his own pride of personality and become the President's instrument, the guardian of his broodings and his privacy.

There is always a Haldeman in any administration. Under Kennedy the name was Kenneth O'Donnell. Under Eisenhower, briefly, it was Sherman Adams; under Roosevelt it was Harry Hopkins. The function of such men goes back through time to the days when the title was chamberlain to the king. Some chamberlains are enlarged valets who arrange the king's time as others arrange his clothes and toiletries; others are the traffic managers at the crossroads of decision. Haldeman was the traffic manager; he decided what problems the President needed to pay attention to, whom the President needed to see, what documents or messages would move to his desk either for amusement or for necessity.

If Nixon were to be attacked, as he was, for being the most inaccessible President of modern times, which he was, it was Haldeman who was being attacked. And Haldeman could speak to the point.

"If you take the idea of an isolated President versus an accessible President, what do you mean? If you throw out all the crap, all the trivia, all the unnecessary, to provide him with time to think in finite limits—then in that sense isolation is necessary to provide accessibility. . . . Lyndon Johnson had really been isolated by his accessibility to everyone. . . .

"We started to build in free time—an hour or two a day for the President to be free. For the last year, we've kept Wednesday entirely free on the schedule so he can use Wednesdays on his own initiative. He knows on Monday and Tuesday that on Wednesday he can do whatever he wants to do—he can call in George Shultz to talk about taxes, or somebody else to talk about Congress or the Congo. Or he can even use Wednesdays just to sit there and read a book.

"Who should get in? Is it someone who's got a problem only the President can deal with? Or is it someone who's got input the President needs? Or is it someone who needs the President's time because it's helpful to *him,* not to the President? Of course you've got the symbolic meetings—that doesn't help him or help them do any better; and there's all the ceremonial stuff he has to do, from receiving diplomatic credentials to Miss America. . . . They all want to see the President. Do you want us to hang out a red flag saying welcome for ten hours a day? Abraham Lincoln used to do that. Should you hang out the welcome flag an hour a day? Or a week? Or a month? And then how do they get in? By age? By alphabet? You can't do it by Social Security number. . . .

"He needs input. And seeing people is not the only way, not necessarily the best way. Getting the facts, the opinions, the ideas, is input. How do you get the best opinions, the right facts, the new ideas? . . . The way to make him accessible is to isolate him from the trivia, and that's my job. . . ."

The way to understand Richard Nixon's campaign of 1972 was by beginning, as Haldeman suggested, to separate the trivia and the mechanics from the fundamentals which were of the President's decision alone.

"He wants things done," Haldeman had said in the fall of 1971, before the campaign got under way, "and he wants to know things are getting done; he's not interested in organization." To Republican Chairman Robert Dole, the President had conveyed a quite clear impression of Dole's function at the National Committee. Dole should get out there, the President told him at the beginning of 1971, make speeches, talk up, keep the party functionaries happy, do the housekeeping. But he should not bother the President with his problems; those should be cleared with either Haldeman or Mitchell. The Committee for the Re-Election of the President was equally mechanical, charged with running, in Haldeman's words, the "bumper-sticker end of the campaign"; it was to raise the money, spend it to get the message across in radio, TV, mailings, registrations. But neither committee was to be involved in ideas or planning above its station. Both committees together were an army led by corporals with no freedom to maneuver—energies with no place to go except at the direction of the White House. To break through to attention and ultimate reward of the White House, such corporals would have to be highly imaginative—the Watergate affair was ultimately to come from fevered imagination at the Committee to Re-Elect, spurred by ambition.

The fine points of political tactics and gamesmanship, once an obsession of Richard Nixon's, had by 1972 become a hobby. With a few people like Haldeman, Mitchell, Colson or Finch he might talk old-fashioned politics as in the old days—but on a one-to-one basis at unscheduled moments; or as a recreation, when the weather became hot, on a lazy late-afternoon cruise on the Presidential yacht, the *Sequoia*, which would sail down to Mount Vernon, where a helicopter picked up the party to return. The few invited to such afternoon talks on the *Sequoia* might get the telephone call as late as thirty minutes before the cruise departed, and then race the Presidential helicopter to the pier in frenzied fear that if their autos got caught in traffic they might miss the departure. But there were no more of those formal, long afternoon sessions of strategy over which Nixon, as candidate in 1960, had presided in his home on weekends.

The President's politics, which was the master politics of the campaign, moved on a higher level. It was conceptual, and reflected what he had learned from so many past campaigns: that to move people, to move groups or blocs, one's themes had to be spoken clearly or, better, acted out clearly. "He doesn't have to campaign," said Haldeman, "he doesn't have to establish his identity. He's been exposed for twenty-five years. Because of TV and his trip to China and the man on the moon, he's probably the best-known human being in the history of the world. For him to campaign would be counterproductive, superfluous." The campaign, in short, would be what the President said and did as President from the White House, not as candidate, and would be addressed to "Out There."

In the President's mind—just as in George McGovern's mind—the issue that most concerned the people Out There was the war in Vietnam and peace if it could be had. The operational concept that he had established early in the administration was to turn the war over to the Vietnamese. Democrats might denounce the President for "expanding" the war. Each charge made a news story for the day. But Out There the story Nixon was telling was clearer. Nixon had, within three weeks of coming to office, imposed on his Secretary of Defense, Melvin Laird, a politician to his fingertips, the command to get American troops out of Vietnam. Laird, within another five weeks, had imposed that will on the Pentagon, quelling a near-insurrection by the Chairman of the Joint Chiefs of Staff, and driven the military to establish a time-table of withdrawal. By 1972 the original 1969 print-out tables of withdrawal that Laird still flourished in the office of the Secretary of Defense were dirty, dog-eared and tattered, but the targets had been met. From 549,500 to 524,500 to 484,000 to 434,000 to 284,000 to 184,000, the number of troops had fallen to 139,000 as election year opened. In 1968 and early 1969 it was not uncommon for 300 Americans to be killed in a week; by midsummer of 1972 the average had fallen to 3 or 4. Out There, Nixon had promised to get the boys home; and for three years he had not missed a target date, or fallen short on the promise.

The conceptual approach of Nixon to foreign affairs was too grand, its results too successful by midsummer of 1972, to be appraised as mere "tidiness." What was more difficult to grasp through the haze of daily events was that Nixon had just as firm a conception of domestic politics as of foreign policy. He had been under observation by political reporters for twenty-five years and through almost all that time been reported as a tactician, the sly opportunist whom Democrats called "Tricky Dick." Yet Nixon's politics at home as abroad had been carefully thought out, was enunciated early, and would be sharpened for maximum tactical impact in 1972. Ninety percent of his campaign lay right there in his own skull; he had finally learned that ideas move people, concepts frame politics; had there been no Committee to Re-Elect at all, to translate policy to tactic, he would have done better.

He had begun with the peace issue as soon as elected in 1968. Bread-and-butter was the second issue, and he had addressed himself to that from midsummer 1971 on. The third of the triad of classic American issues was race, and he moved on that one cautiously at first, then more firmly, then flatly, bluntly, so that, for the first time in any modern campaign, a Presidential candidate made his position perfectly clear on the issue when the election pinched.

All through 1969 and 1970 the Democrats had tiptoed around the subject of race as delicately as possible until in February of 1971, finally accepting the reform rules, they had substituted "quotas" for philosophy. During the same period, however, Nixon, as President, had been forced to meet the issue of race as it was thrust at him by a series of court decisions; these decisions concerned the way people lived in the big cities, the inner life of their neighborhoods, where and how they sent their children to school. By late 1969 the working of the courts had made a response from him inescapable. "The neighborhood school," read, for example, one Federal court decision in Charlotte, North Carolina, "never prevented statutory racial segregation; it may not now validly be used to perpetuate segregation." The problem of race was moving from the traditional South to the North and the explosive big cities. Somehow the administration would have to position itself publicly—and in early 1970 the President decided to use the school issue for an unprecedented public philosophical statement on the nature of America's communities.

"We rolled that one around for six weeks," said Raymond Price, the thoughtful writer chosen by the President to handle the wording of his philosophy. "There were so many conversations with him for so long over how he felt about freedom and opportunity, and that closing passage on the 'free and open society' is my best effort to capture his ideas on paper."

Thus, then, as the Democrats groped their way to a position through 1970 and 1971, the President was ahead of them with his own concept, presented in a public statement on March 24th, 1970.

> The goal of this Administration is a free and open society. In saying this, I use the words "free" and "open" quite precisely.
>
> Freedom has two essential elements: the right to choose, and the ability to choose. The right to move out of a mid-city slum, for example, means little without the means of doing so. The right to apply for a good job means little without the skills that make it attainable. . . .
>
> Similarly an "open" society is one of open choice—and one in which the individual has the mobility to take advantage of those choices. . . . We cannot be free, and at the same time be required to fit our lives into prescribed places on a racial grid—whether segregated or integrated, and whether by some mathematical formula or by automatic assignment. . . .
>
> An open society does not have to be homogeneous, or even fully integrated. There is room within it for communities. Especially in a nation like America, it is natural and right that we have Italian or Irish or Negro or Norwegian neighborhoods; it is natural and right that members of those communities feel a sense of group identity and group pride.
>
> In terms of an open society, what matters is mobility: the right and the ability of each person to decide for himself where and how he wants to live, whether as part of the ethnic enclave or as part of the larger society—or, as many do, share the life of both. . . .

As we strive to make our schools places of equal educational opportunity, we should keep our eye fixed on this goal:
to achieve a set of conditions in which neither the laws nor
the institutions supported by law any longer draw an invidious
distinction based on race; and going one step further, we must
seek to repair the human damage wrought by past segregation. . . .

I am aware that there are many sincere Americans who
believe deeply in instant solutions, and who will say that my
approach does not go far enough fast enough. They feel that
the only way to bring about social justice is to integrate all
schools now, everywhere, no matter what the cost in the disruption of education. . . .

But, as for Mr. Nixon, he had positioned himself to move a year
and a half later, to translate his philosophy of the "Free and Open Society" into the roughhouse of street and kitchen debate on the issue of
"busing."

"Busing," said Leonard Garment, then the President's chief scout on
the civil-rights frontier, "went critical in the fall of 1971." A sequence of
cases on the court calendars of the nation had begun to move the ju-
diciary to what eventually peaked in the Merhige decision of January,
1972.[1] But Garment, like a distant early-warning signal station, had sent
a basic memorandum to the President, as well as to John Ehrlichman,
Elliott Richardson (then Secretary of HEW) and George Shultz in late
fall, pointing out the cases scheduled to come before the Federal courts
and the need for some Presidential decision before the matter "lit up."
The Supreme Court is incapable, reasoned Garment, of dealing in sudden social emotions; it is compelled to apply a legal remedy, no matter
how strained emotions of people have become. Now, in the fall, from
the conservatives, a demand came burgeoning for a Constitutional
amendment against busing; such an amendment, if it came to a vote on
the floor of Congress, would centralize American politics on the issue of
race for the rest of the year. The President must act. "There was this
upward curve of court action," said Garment. "We were moving from
abstraction to reality, and resistance was increasing. The courts were trying to sustain legal momentum—but civil rights had shifted, for ordinary people, from being an expression of freedom to a restriction of
their freedom. The key to leadership," continued Garment, "is knowing
what the speed limit of social change is. It's a question of what people
can digest in ten years, it's something the moral engineers don't understand. . . . Busing goes beyond schools and segregation—to all those
other areas where people feel threatened in seniority, prestige, identity,

[1] See pp. 86–87.

and begin to ask what are those bastards doing to us? And the President understands this better than any of the Democrats."

On the time calendar of 1972's politics, busing and China were issues that overlapped. While the President's mind was concentrated on the planning and the voyage to China in January and February of 1972, a first draft of a statement to Congress on busing was being prepared by Price and Garment. It was rejected by the President on his return from China as too soft. George Wallace was inflaming Florida on busing, it had "lit up" as a national issue and he wanted something stronger. He called, next, for a draft from William Safire, the fastest man at the keys in the White House and a centrist. "I wrote a conciliatory speech with a tough center," said Safire, "but I wasn't giving him what he wanted." Next up was Patrick Buchanan, the President's conservative writer, with what was described as a slam-bang draft. The President now urged Safire to weave in Buchanan's passages with his own; and after the fourth draft the President decided he would have to do it on his own. "In his gut," said Safire, "he believes forced busing is wrong," and thus, squarely, in his own language, on March 17th, 1972, came the President's message to Congress on busing—demanding that Congress drop the proposed anti-busing Constitutional amendment, that Congress set out other remedies for integration beyond the court-compelled busing by numbers. And lest the people Out There misread his message, he preceded it the night before with an appearance on air, saying in his own blunt words: "I am opposed to busing for the purpose of achieving racial balance in our schools. I have spoken out against busing scores of times over many years. And I believe most Americans—white and black—share that view. But what we need now is not just speaking out against more busing, we need action to stop it." The phrasing had the sound of a thump on the door. But it was clear. Nixon had positioned himself on the survival side of the big-city neighborhoods of the North, as well as the safe side of the white suburban strongholds.

Clarity, not eloquence, was the Presidential style as 1972 continued—crude, direct, addressed not to press or commentators, but over their heads to Out There.

Labor, blue-collars, ethnic groups, Catholics—all these were, in his opinion, his moving targets. Of his major substantive positions, his stands on busing and the war fitted the opinions and emotions of most of these groups quite neatly. The President's hard stand on Vietnam, his vocal patriotism, appealed not only to George Meany, chief of the AFL/CIO, always a hawk on Vietnam, but to the rank and file of labor who supply most of the combat manpower in the United States Army in any war the country fights.

But the third of his major substantive positions—the wage- and price-control measures of August, 1971—posed political difficulty. Wage controls had brought the instant hostile eruption of the patriarch Meany, and, ill-advised, Nixon had accepted the labor chieftain's blast as an opportunity. He would appeal, as was his general strategy, over the heads of labor's leaders to their rank and file—inflation was a faceless menace, and if Meany wanted to be the face of the menace, so be it. The clash with labor had peaked at a meeting of the AFL/CIO in Bal Harbour, Florida, in November of 1971, where the President had spoken in such a way as to appear clearly a divider of labor's loyalties. He had been booed and, so the White House insisted, treated with gross discourtesy.

1972 thus required an intense courting of labor. The year had begun with a statement in January by Al Barkan, chief of labor's Committee on Political Education, that labor's "primary political goal in 1972 [is] the defeat of Richard Nixon's bid for re-election." But already before that Richard Nixon had begun to reach for the blue-collars again by wooing the largest and most brutal of American unions, the International Brotherhood of Teamsters. The President had paid a fee to indecency by releasing from Federal prison the convicted former chief of the Teamsters, James Hoffa, two days before Christmas; and a few months later he was to receive the endorsement of the 2,500,000-member Teamster union. His fondness for the hard-hat construction workers had been made evident months before; he was to woo, and win, the support of uniformed policemen's and firemen's unions all across the country in the spring months; and as George McGovern grew ever larger in the spring months of 1972, Charles Colson was to begin the wooing of George Meany's staff in private conversations which would eventually help neutralize most of the AFL/CIO top leadership in the fall Presidential campaign.

With equal precision, the President was moving on ethnics, racial groups, above all, Catholics. Jewish leaders were invited to the White House to hear the President explain his Middle East policy. Mrs. Nixon was sent to give ceremonial greetings to Lithuanians. The President of Mexico, visiting the United States on a mission of state, was toured through Chicago, Texas, Los Angeles, in the areas where the Chicano vote might be impressed by Nixon's goodwill toward their mother country. For the Catholics, so urged Colson, two issues were parochially overriding: the support of their schools, and the public stance on abortion. In late 1971 the President journeyed to New York to tell a Catholic audience that it could count on his help to stay the closing of parochial schools, which all across America were closing simply for lack of money. He repeated the pledge formally in April, 1972, before the convention of the National Catholic Education Association in Philadelphia: "I am irrevocably committed to these propositions: America needs her non-public schools; that those non-public schools need help; that therefore we must and will find ways to provide that help."

And then, just a month later, he moved into the abortion controversy. The White House inner circle was overwhelmingly Protestant, with the spice and leaven of a few Jews and fewer Catholics. On this particular issue, abortion, which touches so many religious nerve ends, the staff's overwhelming advice to him was to be silent. Only Pat Buchanan (Catholic) and Chuck Colson (Protestant), a splinter minority among advisers, felt that the President should speak on this issue so sensitive to devout Catholics. And speak the President would: A month after the President's Philadelphia speech, Terence Cardinal Cooke of New York made public a letter from the President supporting his fight for repeal of New York's civilized abortion laws. "This is a matter for state decision outside Federal jurisdiction," wrote the President to the Cardinal, but, he added, "I would personally like to associate myself with the convictions you deeply feel and eloquently express."

The letter to Cardinal Cooke had been written in early May—at a time when George McGovern's army was reaching peak momentum; the McGoverns had run Hubert Humphrey a startling second in Ohio, and were on the march in the Nebraska primary. Traditional Democrats, now thoroughly alarmed, were firing back at McGovern's positions from every vantage, charging him with softness on amnesty, marijuana, abortion, and specifically directing their fire for maximum impact on Catholic voters. McGovern's position on abortion was, actually, to leave decision on that emotional matter to each state's legislature as it interpreted its state's position. But the fusillade of charge and countercharge disturbed Catholic emotions; and Nixon's statement comforted many.

The President's letter to the Cardinal could not have been more perfectly timed to define the difference of strategy and perception between himself and his Democratic rival—except that it became front-page news on Sunday, May 7th, 1972. And that day the front pages of the nation were dominated by more traumatic news: disaster in Vietnam. Mr. Nixon was secluded at Camp David with Henry Kissinger, and was telephoning his Secretary of State, William P. Rogers, to fly immediately home from Germany for an emergency session of the National Security Council.

Next day would be May 8th—a date circled in the President's own memory as one of the two hardest days of his first term.

By May 8th the largest of all the framing concepts of the Nixon campaign was shivering—the concept of "peace with honor." Now his attention must swing, with the unpredictable turbulence that events impose on a President's attention, from the rather enjoyable toying with and teasing of Democrats at home to the somber ultimate responsibility of history: keeping peace in the face of a determined and resolute enemy.

For eighteen years, in a way no historian can yet trace quite clearly, Vietnam had slowly grown to be the nightmare of American Presidents. It had begun as a place name on a distant map,[1] and been made artificially real by a fiction of the imagination of John Foster Dulles long ago. As Vice-President, Richard Nixon had sat through Cabinet sessions with Dulles, had never liked him (perhaps because Dulles so disdained the Vice-President), yet agreed on policy: that South Vietnam was a nation-for-real, a bastion that must be held against the surge of Asian Communism, and that some government must be maintained there which could resist Communism at any cost. The cost was to become apparent only in the administration of Lyndon Johnson—American troop commitment rising from 16,000 to 550,000; deaths mounting from two or three a week to hundreds and hundreds a week, until, by spring of 1972, they had mounted to more than 45,000 American dead. Expenditures rising to billions every month, reaching finally a minimum of $135 billion (without including an anticipated $50 billion in veterans' benefits), and setting off the inflation that was to ravage the American economy and crack the dollar.

For three years, since his election, Nixon's policy had been to get Americans out of combat, while equipping and training a South Vietnamese force to defend South Vietnam. By spring of 1972, secret and semi-secret negotiations to end the war had been going on in Paris between Henry Kissinger and Le Duc Tho of Hanoi's Politburo for thirty-two months. But they had developed a bleak clarity. North Vietnam would not give up its invasion of the Republic of South Vietnam until and unless that republic totally collapsed, or until and unless the United States government aided in removing the government of South Vietnam, replacing it with a coalition government amenable to Communist control. Until then there could be no cease-fire, no military agreement, no armistice and no return of America's prisoners of war.

The American appetite for war had long since been sated in Vietnam. From faculty club to student union, from bar to parlor, from Wall Street to Main Street, all wanted out of Vietnam. Opinion was divided only on how. Thus the country had separated into two real but unidentifiable opinion groups inhabiting both the formal Democratic and Republican parties: a group that wanted to get out immediately, at whatever cost, including acknowledgment of defeat, of which George McGovern was the leader. And a group that wanted to get out as fast as possible, provided it could have "peace with honor," which was the President's.

The merits of the American conception of honor and that of North Vietnam are best left for judgment by students of ethics. By the spring of 1972 the facts read thus: Serious negotiations between Henry Kis-

[1] See *The Making of the President—1968,* pp. 1–23.

singer and Le Duc Tho had been broken off the previous fall, when the
North Vietnamese had canceled a meeting scheduled for November 20th,
1971. Americans had tried to resume the talks, and finally been offered
a mid-March rendezvous; the Americans had suggested March 20th,
which the North Vietnamese had accepted. But then the North Vietnamese canceled that date and suggested April 15th; then accepted the
date of April 24th; then postponed the date to May 2nd—at which time,
finally, the chief American spokesman and the chief Hanoi spokesman
met face to face again.

By then, May 2nd, realities had changed. The North Vietnamese
were negotiating from a splendid diplomatic stance: superiority on the
field of battle. For months, while the negotiations had been postponed,
they had been secretly preparing the Easter offensive of 1972. By May
that Easter offensive was rolling, and on the northern front, where South
and North Vietnam are defined by the vague demilitarized zone of 1954,
the troops of the South Vietnamese Republic were in rout.

The eighty-mile stretch of beach along the South China Sea, from
the Ben-Hai River down through Quangtri and Hue to Danang, is today
unrecognizable to those who traveled that coast before World War II.
It was then a stretch of beauty, of thatched or red-tiled villages, poinset-
tias and other red flowers flaring in gardens staved off by bamboo wicker,
overleaved by banana trees, the coast flourishing with palms, the waters
shallow and blue, as remote from any American interest as an island in
the South Seas. By 1967, when last this correspondent flew over the remembered route, the landscape had been transformed. Pocked like the
lunar landscape with shell holes, its blossoms were the smoke plumes
of artillery and bombardment which seemed to go on around the clock,
night and day; its lesser villages were empty; and the fields around them,
streaked with the white stains of salt encrustation or the sere yellow of
wild growth, told that the peasants had fled in despair. War had visited
this place for longer, and with more savagery, than any other spot on the
globe; and it had become the central place of American involvement.

It was war again, at its fiercest, that dominated this distant coast-
line in May of 1972—and challenged Richard Nixon's planning. As the
Americans had withdrawn by the Nixon plan over the previous eighteen
months, the United States Marines had yielded this critical defense area
to South Vietnam's Third Infantry Division. The North Vietnamese had
measured the raggle-taggle Third Infantry; targeted on the little river
village of Quangtri, a provincial capital; then jolted through. The Third
Division had broken, panicked and fled. On radio, television and the
press around the world came the vivid story of disaster. "Thousands of
panicking South Vietnamese soldiers," wrote Sydney H. Schanberg of
The New York Times on May 2nd, "fled in confusion from Quangtri
Province today, streaming south down Route 1 like a rabble out of con-

trol. Commandeering civilian vehicles at rifle point, feigning non-existent injuries, carrying away C rations but not their ammunition, and hurling rocks at Western news photographers taking pictures of their flight, the Government troops of the Third Infantry Division ran from the fighting in one of the biggest retreats of the war. . . ." And the next day, "The fabric of Hue is disintegrating today, with at least 150,000 panic-stricken people fleeing south by truck and in flotillas of leaking sampans as the North Vietnamese push ever closer. . . . signs of anarchy began to permeate the city today. South Vietnamese Army runaways . . . were roaming through Hue today like armed gangsters—looting, intimidating and firing on those who displeased them."

The combat correspondent reports, as he must, the sight, smell, sound of what he sees from his jeep or where he trudges on foot. The larger picture can be seen only on maps in remote war rooms. And such maps posed Nixon's problem.

On the maps, in May of 1972, it was clear that the Hanoi Easter offensive was behind schedule. In the Tet offensive of 1968, with over 450,000 American troops engaged, Hanoi had moved faster and quicker. The North Vietnamese had, four years earlier, occupied the key city of Hue, murdering a reported 2,800 civilians after occupation, and been lodged behind Hue's crenelated walls for a month before American and South Vietnamese combat troops dug them out. In 1972, with only 65,000 American troops left, this Hanoi offensive had managed to seize only Quangtri. Hue still lay thirty-two miles south of the breakthrough, and Danang almost fifty miles south. But at Danang 14,000 American troops, with America's fighter-bombers and last combat punch, were endangered.

A decision was involved—at once diplomatic, political and military. Communist military doctrine has proven absolutely superior to Western military thinking at the level of irregular warfare. But Communist military thinking in frontal warfare is orthodox: It repeats over and over again the carefully planned, meticulously designed, short-range breakthrough, the coiled punch followed by the overwhelming jolt; it embraces little of the dash of punch-through, exploitation and far-ranging pre-planned mop-up sweep that characterizes American military thinking. Thus, in May, Quangtri had fallen to a classical Communist military jolt. Despite the reported panic at the point of contact, there was still a moment to think. What would happen next? If Russia or China had approved of another pre-planned jolt toward Danang, American troops would really be in danger. And so, acutely, would all of Nixon's three-year-long diplomacy. Could the battlefield be isolated, the next thrust restrained before it began? Was there enough fabric of South Vietnamese resistance to hold a line if the United States threw everything into a pre-cauterization of the next jolt? Would China or Russia intervene?

Bleak as was the situation in the field, perilous as the diplomatic consequences of escalation appeared, the gamble involved seemed even bleaker and more perilous when, during the week of disaster, Henry Kissinger met with Le Duc Tho, finally, in Paris. Le Duc Tho was in a classic negotiating posture of strength—his troops had just jolted through, his enemies were fleeing. "We were confronted," said Kissinger, "by the reading to us of the published Communist statement. It had taken us six months to set up the meeting and innumerable exchanges, and when we got there, what we heard could have been clipped from a newspaper and sent to us in the mail. . . . We were confronted with the fact that an opponent was insisting on continuing an all-out military offensive which he would stop only on terms that no American President can be asked to accept. . . ."

Kissinger returned to the United States on Tuesday; spent a few hours on the *Sequoia* with the President telling of his humiliation; flew to New York on Thursday night to address an audience of influence-makers in that city; went back to Washington; and joined the President for the weekend at Camp David.

Matters were now critical for Richard Nixon. The situation was not as cataclysmic as it appeared in the press and political debate, but it was nonetheless desperate in terms of decision. This jolt at Quangtri could be contained; but not many more could be contained; the jolting would stop only if, finally, an American negotiator could confront Le Duc Tho and, through him, the Hanoi Politburo with a counterbalance of terror and killing that might bring talk back to reality. On the one hand was the gross fact that the North Vietnamese had waited to initiate this round of peace talks until they held, momentarily, a superiority of killing. On the other hand—an American public disgusted with killing and eager for a negotiated settlement.

On Friday evening Nixon had gone to Camp David to think matters through. "The essence of this man is loneliness," Henry Kissinger had said once. Nixon was now very lonely as President. His architecture of peace had been neat, logical, diligently pursued; its capstone was to be his journey to Moscow, two weeks hence, just as its cornerstone had been his mission to Peking. If he responded now in the diplomacy of kill against kill, he might risk both capstone and cornerstone—as well as his re-election.

Few episodes, to my mind, reflect the quality of Richard Nixon's thinking better than his ruminations at Camp David as I heard him re-call them later. "There was no other choice on May 8th," he said, "and when you come down to saying you have no choice, you have to win. . . . I analyzed the situation. I determined I couldn't go to the U.S.S.R. if the

North Vietnamese offensive was continuing. If it continued, the summit would be a dismal failure, and they would have to treat me that way. If Russian tanks were rumbling down the streets of Hue while I was in the Kremlin . . . the American people wouldn't understand, only Brezhnev would understand. . . . We decided, and that was Haig's judgment, that mining [Haiphong] wouldn't be enough; that would be four or five months in taking effect, so we'd have to go all the way. I knew it would jeopardize the summit. I knew it would jeopardize the election. But by using power on a maximum basis, not escalating . . . it could stop their offensive, and then we could negotiate a deal on an equal basis. . . . We had some tough questions."

Nixon was back in Washington, Monday morning, May 8th, with his questions clear in mind. Pentagon generals had been conferring since seven that morning on the technical options available. They brought the options to a National Security Council meeting at the White House which lasted until noon. By two P.M. the President had given the orders for action. He called in, next, the house moderate of his speechwriting staff, Ray Price, to go over what he planned to say to the nation that evening, and showed him the draft he had written at Camp David. This time the draft was Nixon's alone. Later he called in the Congressional leaders and, meeting them in the Roosevelt Room, said, "Let me come directly to the point and tell you of a decision I have had to make." And at nine P.M. he was on air before the nation, telling of the decision.

Dressed in a blue suit, his face stern yet vigorous, he spoke slowly, enunciating his words clearly, his voice breaking with dryness only once or twice. He was balancing the kill-force of a nation tired of killing, against a concept called peace with honor.

"An American defeat in Vietnam," he said, "would encourage . . . aggression all over the world—aggression in which smaller nations, armed by their major allies, could be tempted to attack neighboring nations at will, in the Mid-East, in Europe, and other areas. World peace would be in grave jeopardy. . . .

"I have therefore concluded that Hanoi must be denied the weapons and supplies it needs to continue the aggression. . . .

"All entrances to North Vietnamese ports will be mined to prevent access to these ports and North Vietnamese naval operations from these ports. . . ."

The speech went on: The Navy would take appropriate measures to block off all of North Vietnam. The Air Force would be bombing all rail and road communications, as well as military targets in North Vietnam. Nixon was careful to hold out the olive branch to both China and Russia, to Russia especially. ("I particularly direct my comments tonight to the Soviet Union. . . . We do not ask you to sacrifice your principles or your friends. But neither should you permit Hanoi's intransigence to blot out the prospects we together have so patiently prepared. We . . . are on the threshold of a new relationship that can serve not only the interests of our two countries, but the cause of world peace. We are prepared to continue to build this relationship. The responsibility is yours if we fail to do so.") Then he signed off with an appeal for the support of the American people in his gamble. By this time American bombers and mine-layers were already in action, as they had been since two in the afternoon.

The bombing of Hanoi and Haiphong, the sealing of the ports, was an act of history, a dicing with war. But in the politics of 1972 no act more sharply confirmed Nixon's thinking about the nature of his campaign than the American response. Those who could speak or reach headlines or television were off instantly in denunciation the next day. McGovern: "This new escalation is reckless, unnecessary and unworkable . . . a flirtation with World War III." Kennedy: ". . . his decision is ominous and I think it is folly." Humphrey: ". . . filled with unpredictable danger." Muskie: "[He] is risking a major confrontration with the Soviet Union and with China and is jeopardizing the major security interests of the United States." Harold Hughes of Iowa: "A national tragedy." From a New York Congressman, Edward I. Koch: "The President is an international lawbreaker." One Democratic voice in support, Senator Gale W. McGee of Wyoming: "Under the conditions there was no other alternative than the one the President chose." Editorials, comment, commentators overwhelmingly against, at home and abroad, riots on campus, and demonstrations.

Except for one thing: the response from Out There. The Committee to Re-Elect had cranked up canned or stimulated support overnight —20,000 telegrams, with a backlog of 17,000 more undelivered; mail sacks laden with praise; telephone calls clogging the switchboards. But the President needed also more authentic expressions of opinion. The Republicans commissioned as early as Tuesday morning a reaction survey by the Opinion Research Corporation of Princeton. By evening its telephone poll of 702 respondents reported that three out of four of those called supported the President. On Tuesday and Wednesday, May 9th and 10th, Louis Harris threw a special survey force of his pollsters into the field—and reported that 59 percent of those polled supported the President, 24 percent disapproved, 17 percent were unsure. If it was kill or surrender, the American people would back their President on the kill side.

The bitterness that had been growing through the previous three years between President and opinion-makers was now hardened in concrete. "They were all against us," said one White House assistant, "the nets, and the press, and the savants, and the universities. They thought we were gambling with peace. Now there would be no summit conference in Moscow, a new rupture with Red China—we'd gambled it all away."

Mr. Nixon had gambled indeed—but not as a loser. He had won with American opinion Out There. And also on the world scene. There *was* to be a Moscow conference, despite the bombing of Hanoi and Haiphong. On Thursday, May 11th, three days after his speech, the President received Soviet Ambassador Anatoly F. Dobrynin and Nikolai S. Patolichev, Foreign Trade Minister, both members of the Russian Communist Party's Central Committee. The summit had not been canceled by the gamble. When asked whether the great summit meeting in Moscow would after all take place, Mr. Patolichev responded to the reporters, "I don't know why you asked this question. Have you any doubts?" The Russians apparently wanted peace as much as did the Americans.

By the weekend of May 13th the crisis in international affairs had been resolved. The mining of Haiphong had been the biggest gamble of all Mr. Nixon's diplomacy, and with its successful execution the grand theme of war and peace was safe.

What happened two days later, on May 15th, was not a gamble, but an accident. On May 15th, addressing an outdoor rally at Laurel, Maryland, George Wallace was shot by a madman, and thereby eliminated from the campaign. And with that elimination, the re-election of the President was finally, irrevocably, assured.

For two years George Wallace had haunted the planning of the White House. Whether public-approval ratings went up or down, whether Mr. Nixon went to China or reorganized the economy, his ratings in the major polls had stuck like a jammed needle at the same 43-percent-for-Nixon which the President had drawn in 1968. What jammed the needle was George Wallace, consistently picking up, whether in the Harris or the Gallup poll, from 9 percent to 13 percent of the American national vote.

"This entire strategy of ours," had said Robert Finch as late as March of 1972, "depends on whether or not George Wallace makes a run on his own." And it was not the strength of George Wallace in the South that bothered Finch so much as George Wallace's appeal in the North.

In the South, George Wallace's appeal had been fading for years until the Merhige decision of January. In 1970 Wallace had barely won his nomination for Governor in a run-off. In the words of Harry S. Dent, the President's point man for Dixieland, "Gangrene had set in for George Wallace until the courts resurrected him." Even after the Merhige decision, Dent professed to be unworried about the South—the President had kept his pledges to the Southern textile industry; had kept his commitments on new appointments to the Supreme Court; the Federal housing program in Southern low-wage, low-price construction areas was working smoothly, with spectacular results unrecognized by big-city newspapers whose communities could not be helped by the Federal housing programs; and the proposed revenue-sharing was the promise of a visit by Santa Claus to small Southern towns and big cities alike.

The South, plus the Rocky Mountain states, plus the farm states, promised the President between 182 and 227 of the 270 electoral votes needed to win. The President needed only two or three of the big industrial states to add to that total and his election would be guaranteed. Yet the President's men through winter and early spring were worried. As matters stood at the beginning of the year and well on into the spring, four or five states looked enormously chancy—California foremost among them, then Pennsylvania, Michigan and New York. If a Humphrey or a Muskie could carry off the Democratic nomination or if, even worse from the President's point of view, Ted Kennedy should accept it, then such a traditional Democratic challenger would be a major threat not only in California but all through the Northeast. It was here in the North, not the South, that the Nixon leaders feared the threat of George Wallace. Wallace had taken 11.8 percent of the Ohio vote in 1968, 10 percent in Michigan, 9 percent in New Jersey, 8 percent each in Illinois and Pennsylvania—and Humphrey had carried two of those states. With Wallace apparently stronger in the primaries of 1972 than he had ever been before, with the needle sticking at 43 percent of the vote for Nixon, the President was still vulnerable—until, of course, May 15th and the shooting. Then it was all over. Only the question of margin remained: whether the President could get that mandate for which his lonesome soul so longed, that landslide authority which might let him act with the largeness of the great Presidents of the past.

From May 15th on, from the White House point of view, it was only a mop-up operation—and the mop-up was the responsibility of the apparently efficient management of the Committee for the Re-Election of the President across the street. The Committee was shortly to be caught in what appeared at the time to be a minor police scandal—the bugging and wire-tapping of the Democratic National Committee's headquarters at the Watergate apartment-and-office complex.[2] Though annoying and irritating, the matter did not seem of major moment. The attention of the press was focused on the struggle within the Democratic Party, and

[2] See Chapter Eleven.

would be concentrated later on the Democratic convention and the Eagleton affair. The President's mind was focused, still, on foreign affairs and, insofar as he had time for detail, on the management of his own soon-to-come Republican convention in Miami.

Nixon had paid only fitful attention to the Democratic convention in July, but had stayed up long enough one evening in San Clemente to watch George McGovern's acceptance speech. Shortly thereafter he had gathered his speechwriters together and given them his analysis: On the plus side for George McGovern was the sense of openness and seriousness of the convention. But on the minus side were the "look of it," the ticket the Democrats had chosen, and the quotas. They'd tossed in Colonel Sanders, the chicken tycoon, to please the old folks, but they had given quotas to the young. And there was the "incredible blend of patter" in the McGovern speech, and the fact that he had not delivered it until three A.M. "The President was not unhappy about that speech," is the way one of his little group remembered his attitude.

As for Richard Nixon, his convention was to be different. It was, by force of circumstances, and had to be, a convention in name only. Had he wished, Richard Nixon might have accepted the nomination sitting in his office, receiving a delegation of party leaders before television and accepting the honor from their hands, as candidates did of yore.

Yet ceremonies are important, for they are punctuation marks in history as in life, and this ceremony of renomination would be as Richard Nixon wanted affairs to be—neat, tidy and punctual. There would be routine in the afternoon—"civic lessons for the people if anybody actually tunes in," was the way one stage-manager phrased it. And presentations for television in the evening—but on time.

The press corps rummaged through its closet of well-worn expressions to enliven the convention reporting, but nothing could enliven it. "Coronation" was the word that first came to mind, but that word comes to mind whenever a sitting President is renominated—it had been used for Eisenhower's 1956 renomination, and for Lyndon Johnson's convention of 1964. There followed then all the adjectives: dull, harmonious, controlled, listless, pleasant, torpid, jovial—above all, prim.

Two matters of historic substance briefly merited attention before the gavel fell at Miami on opening day, August 21st, 1972.

§ For twenty years, Republicans had gone before the nation promising in their platform to defend the nation from the might and power of labor bosses, praising the Taft-Hartley Act and the Landrum-Griffen bill as if they had been written into the Constitution. The Republican delegates on the Platform Committee wished, nostalgically, to include the old anti-labor rhetoric in their platform once again. It was an indulgence the White House would not permit this year; wooing the blue-collar labor vote was an overriding need. John Ehrlichman had been dispatched from the White House to oversee the Platform Committee; and, under his guidance, the Platform Committee renounced the Republican Party's long war with labor, making peace as it had with Red China and Red Russia, and went on to praise "the nation's labor unions for advancing the well-being not only of their members but also of our entire free-enterprise system. . . . We salute the statesmanship of the labor union movement." The old lions of the Republican right were allowed to roar at George McGovern's army in the old prose: "The National Democratic party has been seized by a radical clique which scorns our nation's past and would blight her future." It had taken a "convulsive leftward lurch." It would turn "back toward a nightmarish time in which the torch of free America was virtually snuffed out in a storm of violence and protest." The platform writers rejected McGovern's call as a "mish-mash of social experimentalism" and "fiscal extravaganzas" and "plaintive cries of 'come home America' echoing a new isolationism." But that was all that could be done to satisfy the old lions of the Republican right with red meat.

§ The second matter of substance concerned the young lions of the Republican future. Here, in a dispute over their own rules and reforms, from their various hotel rooms, young liberal Republicans, led by the ivory-tower men of the Ripon Society, matched wits with young conservative Republicans of the Young Americans for Freedom in an effort to sway the votes and opinions of their elders. The substance of their dispute was how votes should be allotted in the 1976 convention to delegates from large industrial (hence liberal) states as against delegates from the underpopulated (and intensely conservative) Mountain states. Computers whirled as various proposals were scanned by the bright young men of both left and right; but behind the figures and the cosmetics were the first two rival candidates for the Republican nomination of 1976—Spiro T. Agnew and Charles H. Percy, Senator from Illinois, momentary symbols of the conservative and liberal forces in the party. When, finally, revision of rules came to the floor for vote, the history of the Republican Party over the past decade was made quite clear. Conservatives cast 910 votes against 434 votes of the liberals. In 1968, conservatives had mustered 874 votes (for Nixon and Reagan factions) against 459 votes for liberals (Rockefeller). In 1964, they had cast 887 votes (for Goldwater) against 425 votes (for Scranton). The margin for the conservatives over liberals in the Republican Party seemed thus still frozen at a fairly consistent two to one. The Republican convention of 1972 was a conservatives' convention—as would be the convention of 1976 unless some liberal Republican, in the primaries, could upset it as McGovern had upset the Democratic in 1972.

Beyond that there were no matters of any moment to be decided at the Republican convention. Outside in the great nation beyond, George McGovern was that week weaving his unnoticed way, trying to conciliate Richard Daley, the Mayor of Chicago, whose delegates his people had thrown out; trying to conciliate Lyndon Johnson, whose war he had repudiated; trying to conciliate labor, which was irreconcilable. In the nation at large, as the Republicans met, the price of meat, both steaks and hamburger, had reached an all-time high; the energy crisis was beginning to pinch as day after day, in New York and other great cities, the utilities curtailed power delivery under the strain of air-conditioning demand in summer heat. But the living was easy, and no one paid mind.

There remain vignettes only of the Republican convention.

§ Vignettes of the floor scenery in the convention hall:

These were clean, neat people. This correspondent counted only three bearded delegates among Republicans, two of them from New York. And no long-hairs. What beards were visible were beards of photographers and newspapermen. The California delegation at the Republican convention, for example, was so different from the California delegation to the Democratic convention that it might have come not from a different state, but from a different country or different era—no cowboy boots, no open collars, no Indians, few blacks, no blue-jeaned girls. Republicans from California came from paintings by Norman Rockwell—stately, big-bosomed clubwomen; silver-haired men with pince-nez eyeglasses; one Oriental; a black woman, conspicuously seated on the aisle to catch the cameras; and the young men all looking as if they had showered and come in fresh, with neckties, from a workout with the track team. So, too, the Massachusetts delegation—Leverett Saltonstall, attending his tenth convention in forty years, haughty as a painting in the Boston Art Museum; Elliot Richardson, once overseer of Harvard, clean, surgical, attentive because it was his duty to be attentive; good Republican housewives from the Cape, the Berkshires and north of Boston, as much interested in gardening as in ecology.

Hugh Sidey of *Time* Magazine caught the mood thus: "These people were chips from the national foundation, the part of the country that goes on by itself no matter who is President. They don't dig ditches, or conceive the New Economics. They run the firms that build industrial plants and houses; they sell refrigerators, play pianos, bury the dead and straighten teeth. . . . Work . . . was for these people an answer to boredom, an elixir for unhappiness, a builder of slumping character and, of course, bank accounts."

Eric Sevareid of CBS caught it differently: "This week Miami Beach is Middletown U.S.A. Middle is an undramatic word, in sound and meaning. But it has to do with the center of gravity of America's collective affairs, the core that holds us together. . . . Certainly this Republican convention reflects the effort. This assemblage is middle class, middle aged, middle brow. And if there's a slight accent in its speech, it's middle west. . . . Republicans would like to think America really is a melting pot of all ethnic groups. Democrats are treating them like separate lumps at the bottom of the pot, but at the same time telling them to melt for the purposes of this campaign. . . . Republicans think the human animal needs quite a lot of direction and control for its own best interests. Liberal Democrats are more inclined to think he is the best judge of his own interests. If you pushed that to the extreme, as happens in many countries, you'd find that Republicans' deepest fear would be anarchy, Democrats' deepest fear would be the police state. . . . This is the convention of good feelings: not gay, not joyous, but contented, pleased with itself. As much gusto as you ever see from prudent, consciously respectable Americans. . . ."

§ Vignettes of the city as the Republicans occupied it:

The parties aboard the yachts; the clutter of private jet planes at the airport; the tours for the children; fashion shows and brunches for wives; Jimmy Hoffa, only a few months out of jail, appearing proudly at gatherings. And set against this spectrum of America, the demonstrators from another spectrum of America: the lean, hard-muscled Vietnam veterans sitting quietly in protest in the sun on the street paving before the Fontainebleau to protest the war; and yet another spectrum: the encampment in Flamingo Park, where pot was free, love was wild and young women exposed their breasts because they believed that doing their own thing was the best way of harming Richard Nixon.

§ And, then, the parade of characters across the rostrum of the convention floor. Richard Nixon had brought all his old adversaries to heel. He had reduced Ronald Reagan and had now invited Reagan to make one of the keynote speeches. Reagan was witty, gay, effective and plunged the shaft home hard ("Our traditional two-party system has become a three-party system—Republican, McGovern and Democrat. And, only the first two parties have a Presidential candidate in the coming election. Millions of patriotic Democrats were disenfranchised in the takeover of their convention. A former President of the United States became a non-person. His years in the service of the party and nation were unmentioned. . . ."). Then followed Barry Goldwater, seeming frail and aging on the high rostrum, talking for half an hour in one of his better speeches, no one listening, until suddenly in an outburst of old indignation, Goldwater intoned, "At this crucial point in our history we face something shocking, for the first time a candidate of one of our parties has already surrendered to an enemy before the election has even been held"—at which the delegates cheered and shouted, giving Barry their hearts again. Then, Nelson Rockefeller, who had so long tried to beat out Nixon's brains and credibility, rising to nominate the President for a second term: ". . . We need this man of action, this man of accomplishment, this man of experience, this man of courage, we need this man of faith in America . . . who has brought us to the threshold of peace. . . ."

At last, on Wednesday evening, at precisely prime time, 10:26, Richard Nixon moved to the light to make his fifth acceptance speech in twenty years. He had been around this track often enough to know the pace, and was hitting his adversary first with humor, then with scorn, before delivering the message.

Congratulating the delegates for choosing Spiro T. Agnew as Vice-President, he proceeded:

"I thought he was the best man for the job four years ago. I think he is the best man for the job today. And I'm not going to change my mind tomorrow." (Applause and laughter.)

Then, to another Democratic bleeding wound:

". . . the way to end discrimination against some is not to begin discrimination against others. Dividing Americans into quotas is totally alien to the American tradition. Americans don't want to be part of a quota—they want to be part of America.

". . . I ask everyone listening to me tonight—Democrats, Republicans and independents—to join our majority—not on the basis of the party label you wear in your lapel but . . . what you believe in your hearts. . . .

". . . I do not ask you to join our new majority because of what we have done in the past. . . . the choice in this election is not between radical change and no change. The choice . . . is between change that works and change that won't work. . . . It has become fashionable in recent years to point up what is wrong with our . . . American system. The critics contend it is so unfair, so corrupt, so unjust that we should tear it down and substitute something else in its place. I totally disagree. I believe in the American system. . . .

"Theirs is the politics of paternalism, where master planners in Washington make decisions for people. Ours is the politics of people— where people make decisions for themselves. . . . when you add up the cost of all the programs our opponents have proposed, you reach only one conclusion: they would destroy the system which has made America number one in the world economically. . . .

"Standing in this convention hall four years ago, I pledged to seek an honorable end to the war in Vietnam. . . . We have offered a ceasefire, a total withdrawal of all American forces, an exchange of all prisoners of war; internationally supervised free elections. . . .

"There are three things . . . that we have not and that we will not offer: We will never abandon our prisoners of war. . . . We will not join

*our enemies in imposing a communist government on our allies—the
17,000,000 people of South Vietnam. And we will never stain the honor
of the United States. . . .*

*"Let us always be sure that when the President of the United States
goes to the conference table he never has to negotiate from weakness. . . .*

*"I ask you, my fellow Americans, to join our new majority not just
in the cause of winning an election but in achieving a hope that mankind
has had since the beginning of civilization. Let us build a peace that our
children and all the children of the world can enjoy for generations to
come."*

It was neither to the audience of the faithful delegates at the convention, nor to the press, that Richard Nixon was talking. He was talking, as he had for months, and as he had designed his convention, to the
people Out There.

Out There, they had watched a series of pre-packaged film unroll
across screen like a child's story of a President's adventures—Richard
Nixon in the White House, Richard Nixon in Peking, Richard Nixon in
Moscow. An average of close to 20,000,000 American homes, or
60,000,000 people (29.30 by the Nielsen ratings), had watched these
shows, and the press corps on its benches at the convention had watched
with them.

Richard Clurman, once news director of the Time/Life news
services, remembered the hush that fell over the press as the films were
shown in the darkened convention hall. Normally, the press babbles and
is inattentive at canned presentations. This time, however, Clurman was
struck by a difference: "There were 3,000 guys in the press galleries—
and they all fell silent watching the Nixon film. It was cornball. But he
wasn't talking to them, he was talking to the people, and they ought to
be taking notes on it. There was this recognition that Nixon's world
wasn't our world—we were out of it."

Whether or not the reporters were out of it, Mr. Nixon did not propose to let them stay out. For his chief adversary in the next three
months was not George McGovern and McGovern's Democratic Party,
but the news media of America—and the culture they spoke for, which
so contradicted the culture for which he spoke, and on which he was to
found his victory.

CHAPTER TEN

POWER STRUGGLE: PRESIDENT VERSUS PRESS

W HAT lay at issue in 1972 between Richard Nixon, on the one hand, and the adversary press and media of America, on the other, was simple: it was power.

The power of the press in America is a primordial one. It sets the agenda of public discussion; and this sweeping political power is unrestrained by any law. It determines what people will talk and think about —an authority that in other nations is reserved for tyrants, priests, parties and mandarins.

No major act of the American Congress, no foreign adventure, no act of diplomacy, no great social reform can succeed in the United States unless the press prepares the public mind. And when the press seizes a great issue to thrust onto the agenda of talk, it moves action on its own— the cause of the environment, the cause of civil rights, the liquidation of the war in Vietnam, and, as climax, the Watergate affair were all set on the agenda, in first instance, by the press.

In a fundamental sense, today more than ever, the press challenges the Executive President, who, traditionally, believes his is the right to set the agenda of the nation's action. Power, said Karl Marx over a century ago, is control over the means of production; that phrase, said Arthur Schlesinger, Jr., recently, should be changed—power in America today is control of the means of communication.

And it was for this control that Richard Nixon warred with his enemies of the press all through the election year, and beyond.

One could best explain the nature of this struggle in 1972 by making an imaginary diagram of the American power structure at the turn of the century and comparing it to the American power structure as the postwar world came to its end.

In 1900, as William McKinley prepared for his second term, the American power structure could be described in pure Leninese. At the pinnacle of power was Wall Street—finance. Wall Street centralized American national action—it decided where mines would be opened, railways built, what immigrant labor should be imported, what technology developed. Wall Street set the agenda of national action without discussion. At a second level was the Congress of the United States—doing the will of the great financiers, enacting the necessary laws, repelling the raiders of prairie discontent. On a third level was the series of largely undistinguished men who until 1900 had held the figurehead office of President of the United States for thirty years; their chief power, beyond the expression of patriotic piety, was to deploy a minuscule professional army and navy against Indians and Spaniards. The American clergy exercised some moral power, best expressed in such issues of national political importance as temperance. Behind came all the other power ingredients—a decorative Supreme Court, the early labor unions, the corrupt big-city machines, the universities. Then the proprietary press—for the press was then a proprietorship, something owned by businessmen for making money.

By 1972 the power structure had entirely changed. The most important fall from power had happened to finance; businessmen might get fat, as they still did in 1972, by wheedling subsidies from national or state governments, but they were now a lobby that came hat-in-hand before a legislature and executive to whom once they had dictated. Labor, big labor, had risen to almost equal political power. The clergy had declined in power even more than big business. Congress, too, was a major loser in the power game—seventy years of domination by vigorous, aggressive Presidents had reduced its self-respect and, even more critically, the respect of the public. The Supreme Court had reached a peak of control over the national agenda in the 1960's; but its power was beginning to fade again as the seventies began. Universities were among the big gainers in the power hierarchy—universities now surpassed big business and big labor as centers of American innovation. But the two greatest gainers in the reorganized power structure were the Executive President and his adversary press, or, as one should more properly phrase it in modern America, the "press-television complex."

Both tried to operate under what they considered traditional rules, but American life had made that impossible.

What made it impossible was a number of things. The classical word-on-paper press was being concentrated into fewer and fewer hands, into news-gathering oligopolies.[1] Joining the word-on-paper press had come the infinitely more potent, even more concentrated power of the national television networks. And in both another change, more subtle but vital, was going on: a new appreciation by journalists themselves of their own role, their own responsibility, their own dignity. Once they had been hirelings of their proprietors, employed to articulate or con-

[1] See "The Rush to Chain Ownership," by Robert L. Bishop, in the *Columbia Journalism Review*, November/December, 1972.

solidate opinion or, at the very most, to entertain the masses with their reporting. At some point in the 1960's, however, they had begun to see themselves as creators of news—not the recorders, but the shapers, of events, with a self-constituted responsibility to history. The great men of this new journalism might, at a bar with their friends, nostalgically insist that they were reporters like the rest of the fellows; they might show their tattered press cards, reminisce about police stations they had covered from Paris to Kansas City, or recall the idiosyncrasies of the men they had worked for, from Roy Howard to old Hearst to Harry Luce. But they were not reporters any longer. In television, men like Cronkite, Sevareid, Chancellor, Smith had, and recognized, no responsibility to any boss or institution—duty bound them technically only to their deadlines, and conscience to their self-constituted responsibility to the American people. So, too, the senior national reporters still left free to describe the world as they saw it in the word-on-paper press. Concentration of press outlets made those journalists who still enjoyed a free outlet ever more powerful, and in their own eyes ever more responsible for values. The texture of their reporting had changed, too. Before World War II, the natural progression of a reporter's career had taken him from the sports shack to the political clubhouse; sportswriters had a flair for vivid copy and personalities, and such great artists as Heywood Broun and, later, James Reston were models for many others. Journalists who reached the summit of their profession after the war were, however, immensely more educated men than their predecessors, far more at home in the university seminar than at the police line-up or the football locker room. Their learning and their moralities made them a formidable group.

In the eyes of Richard Nixon and the administration, this concentration of power took on another cast. He could see, as every President before him saw, that somewhere in the press he would find a natural adversary. But within the new concentration of power, the significant heights of influence had been "seized" by men of a world-view, and of a culture, entirely alien to his own. These were the adversary press. Its luminaries not only questioned his exercise of power, as all great American journalists have done when examining a President. They questioned his own understanding of America; they questioned not only his actions but the quality of his mind, and his honor as a man. It was a question of who was closest in contact with the mood of the American people— the President or his adversary press? Neither would yield anything of respect to the other—and in Richard Nixon's first term the traditional bitterness on both sides approached paranoia.

Again, we must go back to sketch background.

All politics operates in an environment of public opinion. Any of

the great episodes of history, wherever one tries to trace the will of people bursting out from tyranny or police or dead tradition, can be understood only by trying to understand the talk of the times, how leaders
manipulated it, and what ideas and changing technologies conditioned
the way the talk spread. The oldest tradition of journalism is, for example, the style of Amos and Hosea—its rhetoric is still the easiest for
crusading journalists to master, as they emulate the prophets crying out
from the valleys of the desolate, hoping the voice can reach the fat and
the powerful on the hills of Jerusalem. The technology of the times of
Amos and Hosea was the range of the human voice, and the political
audience limited to the court of Kings Uzziah and Jeroboam. And for
millennia thereafter, journalists remained limited in the same way—to the
local community of politically involved, within the range of the human
voice or the local news sheet.

The modern age of journalism began in the United States at the
turn of the century—and with it the modern age of American politics,
responding at first slowly, then ever more rapidly, to the new audience
brought to political involvement by the changing technologies of news
delivery.

It is easiest to approach this change in journalism by glancing at the
commerce, structure and technology of 1900—for commerce and technology were, over the next two generations of American life, increasingly
to change the news-gathering business until in the 1960's it climaxed in
the explosive force of national television. A number of related develop-
ments had been maturing in the decades just before Theodore Roosevelt
became President. There was, first, the completion of the railway network, which linked America from coast to coast to provide manufacturers for the first time a continental market. Manufacturers, by 1900,
could ship stoves, furniture, oil, beer, machinery, timber, housewares
anywhere in the country. But to explore the reachable new market and
sell their wares, they needed a national advertising medium. Until the
turn of the century no such medium had been available. Local newspapers, when they carried what they called "foreign," or out-of-state,
advertising, printed ads for small package goods, like patent medicines
or books, that could be shipped easily. Now, with bulk goods coming
in, like washing machines, carpet sweepers, stoves, automobiles, all finally transportable, the manufacturers could deliver all across the country—if they could find a voice, a horn, a trumpet to tout their goods.

Technology had also made the horn ready. The development of the
high-speed rotary press which could spin off several million copies a
week had made mass printing possible. And coupled with this technical
magic was the development of the halftone photo-engraving process
which could illustrate text, and thus entrance the semi-literate native
Americans of the day as well as the immigrants who could read little or

no English. Publishers could now print, illustrate and circulate millions of magazines, and sell their pages to advertisers for huge sums—if only they could find editors with talent enough to capture the imagination of a whole nation.

The men the publishers found (and frequently the editor and the publisher were the same man) were editors of an entirely new breed. Editors of national magazines required a different eye span and thought frame from editors of newspapers. Their medium [2] was different, its audience larger—in fact, nationwide. For the first time, a breed of journalists was required who could think beyond the interests of New England, or the Midwest, or the Cotton Country, or the hometown. As they sat there in New York at their desks, the mind's eye of such men had to sweep the nation as, previously, only the mind's eye of a Wall Street financier or the President had done. Moreover, their time frame was different from the time frame of newspaper editors of the era. News until then had been just that—the record of what happened in the twenty-four-hour cycle. Newspapers reported what had happened yesterday. But for magazines, the time frame was what was *happening*—what had been happening last week, last month, the last three months, which would continue to be news, and relevant news, next week, next month, perhaps even next year. Newspapers captured only the event; magazines captured the swell and roll of events. Corruption of municipal governments was not just the local story of a sheriff caught dirty-handed yesterday accepting a bribe; corruption of municipal government was part of a nationwide phenomenon, a disease of the system, and it interested people everywhere. The trusts were not just local gougers—they were national monsters, whose purposes and plans could be made clear only by looking at them nationally; the despoliation of nature was a national problem, not a local offense. And these national problems, once they were identified and exposed and their cast of characters described as villains or heroes, made vivid national reading—as vivid in California as in Maine.

The magazines thrived, and as they thrived they changed American politics. The great writers and editors of the muckraking era of the 1900's—Lincoln Steffens, Frank Munsey, S. S. McClure, Upton Sinclair, Ida Tarbell, Ray Stannard Baker—are the ancestors of every important

---

[2] "Media" is a word invented by advertising agencies. Essentially, it is a phrase in the advertising man's sales pitch to manufacturers about the cost-effectiveness of their advertising dollar. A maker of goods has just so much money to be budgeted for reaching potential customers—and advertisers measure the reach in Cost-per-Thousand, or so many dollars per thousand of potential audience. "Media" is a quantitative, commercial term and measures the relative effectiveness of spending to reach such thousands via newspapers, magazines, radio, television, billboards or direct mail. "Media" is an outsider's term, and no journalist thinks of himself as a member of the media. The author will do his best to avoid the use of the word "media" in the rest of this book and refer to members of the news community by the old-fashioned word "newsmen."

investigative reporter since then. More than that—they and their editors, for the first time, jostled big business and the clergy for control of the national agenda, forcing politicians to respond to the concerns the "muck-rakers" had raised. In doing so, the muckrakers moved the nation to pass its first consumer legislation, its first environmental legislation, to control the money supply and banking system, create a first-class navy, reorganize its tax system.

The dominance of the magazine as the overbearing news-master of American thinking reached its apogee, perhaps, in 1940 when three publishers of the East, the masters of *Time* and *Life,* of *Look,* of the *Saturday Evening Post,* the dominant magazines of the day, created a man called Wendell Willkie, decided he should be the Republican nominee of that year—and then imposed him on that party. Few naked exercises of press power can compare to their feat except, perhaps, the imposition of John Garner as Vice-President on the Roosevelt ticket in 1932 by publisher William Randolph Hearst.

But by 1940 the predominance of the magazines was already threatened, for news had been freed from its bondage to the printed word, and had gone electronic. By 1940 Franklin Roosevelt had found that radio was the simplest direct appeal over a hostile printed press to the ears of the American people. Roosevelt learned to use radio not only artfully—for no Republican could match the ring of his silver tone on air—but also with trickery. Friends still recall his glee at the out-foxing of Thomas E. Dewey one evening on radio in the campaign of 1944. Roosevelt reserved time for a quarter-hour radio address on the National Broadcasting Company network; his rival booked the following fifteen minutes to exploit Roosevelt's listening audience for his reply. But Roosevelt spoke to clock time for only fourteen minutes—then left one full minute of paid time in dead silence after his remarks. The listeners frantically twiddled their dials, searching for sounds on other wave lengths; and the millions, who found other stations as they twiddled, were simply not there when the Republican candidate, Dewey, came on the air to speak.

Electronics are like that—subject to manipulation by experts in a way the printed press is not. But electronic journalism is more than that —it is the human voice, the human personality, there in the room with the listeners, supported by the most elaborate effort to gather all news, all information, all reality into ten-, fifteen- or thirty-minute time packages with incomparable impact on the individual mind. Television has a life and vitality of its own beyond manipulation. The Second World War lured the nation to radio—Edward R. Murrow intoning "This is London," or voice-casting from a bomber over Berlin; William L. Shirer broadcasting from Berlin and Compiègne. Radio was part of the home atmosphere from D-Day on; by 1960 radio had been multiplied by television; and by 1972 television was where American politics took place.

By 1972, 50,000,000 grown-up Americans sat down each evening to learn of their world as the massive resources of the three great networks delivered their three visions of that world in capsulized twenty-three-minute packages. Ninety-six percent of all American homes held TV sets. A Roper survey declared that 64 percent of all Americans now got most of their news from television, with radio, magazines and newspapers sharing the rest; and they trusted television by two to one over any other medium for credibility. And between this newest and most potent form of news delivery, on the one hand, and the President, on the other, was growing up an institutional hatred.

Richard Nixon never ignored television; had suffered at its hands; would continue to suffer. But by 1972 he had learned how to use the instrument against its masters. As President, he could conscript its time and the attention of its audience—the rules of the game required that when he went to China or to Moscow, television must show what he was doing; the rules of the game stipulated that if he chose to speak on an issue of state—Vietnam, prices, busing—he was news, and television had to give the news air. But though he could command the time of the instrument, he could never master, or even win to friendship, the personalities who controlled television for all the other evening hours of the year. There was the continuing adversary. "We came in talking togetherness," said Pat Buchanan in 1971, the President's sage and scout on the news front, "and now they attack us for divisiveness. But we can talk togetherness until we're blue in the face. It does no good if every night they see on the tube blacks attacking whites, or whites attacking blacks, students in demonstrations, picket lines, war riots. The tube is doing it, the tube is dividing us. The AP and the UPI put out a complete news service every day, and editors can pick and choose how they make up their front pages from what the wires bring in. But the networks lay down a half-hour news show that every station *has* to use all across the country. It's as if the AP put out one boiler-plate front page every morning which every single newspaper had to use unchanged."

It was the struggle over the agenda that bothered Buchanan—and over and over again the struggle between President and press came down to this struggle. Who controlled what went before the American people? Did a candidate—a Democratic candidate as well as Nixon, the Republican—have a right to expect that the newsmen would present what he said as he said it? Or did the newsmen have the right to choose what they thought was important in what he said? Who chose? Who decided what truth and news were, what people would talk about?

In November of 1969, Vice-President Spiro T. Agnew had made the administration's case public in one of the most masterful forensic efforts in recent public discourse:

"A small group of men, numbering perhaps no more than a dozen anchormen, commentators and executive producers, settle upon the twenty minutes or so of film and commentary that's to reach the public. . . . They decide what forty to fifty million Americans will learn of the day's events in the nation and in the world. . . . We do know that to a man these commentators and producers live and work in the geographical and intellectual confines of Washington, D.C., or New York City, the latter of which James Reston termed the most unrepresentative community in the entire United States. Both communities bask in their own provincialism, their own parochialism. We can deduce that these men read the same newspapers. They draw their political and social views from the same sources. Worse, they talk constantly to one another, thereby providing artificial reinforcement to their shared viewpoints."

Was authority in the press and in television really centered in the two cities of New York and Washington, where in truth, as Agnew described them, a limited, definable group had become the leadership elite of the news-gathering profession?

No conspiracy had concentrated this elite in the New York–Washington centers. Commerce and technology had done it, to create a change in American journalism as profound as had ushered in the muckrakers seventy years before—and even more unpredictable in result.

The figures did not really expose the nature of the change. Just before World War II, there had been 1,878 daily newspapers in the United States. By 1971 that number had fallen to 1,735—apparently no great change. What had changed, however, was proprietorship—great and powerful groups were gobbling up individual papers all across the country, linking them to one another and to radio-TV franchises. Local competition of daily newspapers had all but ceased in 1972; at the time of the muckrakers, 60 percent of all cities had enjoyed daily a choice of two or more rival newspapers; by 1972 that number had dwindled to 4 percent. Autopsy of the apparently small number of papers which had died was more significant. The most important of them had died in the large metropolitan centers of the nation where the city problem boiled and news competition had been keenest. Los Angeles, which had had four newspapers at the end of the war, had only two by 1972. Chicago had been a town where four proprietors divided the daily press; in 1972 Chicago still published four newspapers—but now only two proprietors controlled them. San Francisco had had four newspapers; by 1972 there were only two. In the Presidential year 1972, Newark, New Jersey, was to lose one of its last two daily newspapers.[3] Washing-

---

[3] The condition of press and public affairs in New Jersey can only be regarded as tragedy. New Jersey, the eighth largest state of the Union, had been deprived in the 1960's of its only VHF television franchise, thus leaving it the only state without a video outlet of its own. The death of the Newark *Evening News* closed down even further the ability of New Jersey's citizens to find out what

ton, the same year, was to lose the Washington *Daily News,* leaving the city's opinion and information to be divided between the Kauffmann-Noyes family (of the Washington *Star*) and the Graham family (of the Washington *Post*). Boston was to lose, in 1972, the Boston *Herald-Traveler,* having already long since lost the Boston *Transcript,* the *Record,* the *Post,* and remained now with the Boston *Globe* and the *Herald-American.*

Television—and, to a lesser extent, the craft unions—had been strangling the older forms of news delivery in the big cities. Television delivered the news quicker, more attractively, with more talented manpower than the older news-delivery system could afford. Television offered news sauced with a visual drama that words could not match; and drew off the advertising dollars, as well as the audience, which had sustained rival systems of news delivery. Television wrote the end of the general national magazine's hegemony over American thinking—in 1969 the old *Saturday Evening Post* had been scuttled; in 1971 *Look* Magazine died; in 1972 *Life* Magazine, that majestic creative force of photojournalism, was to die, ending the postwar world in American periodical journalism, too.

The geography of the newspapers that survived in the United States required entirely new definition. The need to make a profit and stay in business had sorted them into groups that could better be defined culturally or commercially than by regional, sectional or political interest. There were newspaper chains that published straight news to make money and were efficient at both—the Newhouse chain, the Cox papers, the Scripps-Howard, Knight, Gannett, Ridder chains, the Cowles papers, several papers in the Hearst chain. Such commercial chains accounted for 60 percent of the daily circulation of the country. There were also, across the country, simple, barefoot individual proprietorships whose ideas had changed little since the time of Warren Gamaliel Harding, himself a publisher, proprietor of the Marion, Ohio, *Star.* These spanned the right end of the opinion spectrum, from stovepipe-hat conservatism (like the Copley or the Pulliam papers) to the rock-throwing, pistol-packing Neanderthal quality of a paper like the Manchester *Union Leader,* which dominated New Hampshire.

The administration had little to worry about from the "proprietary" press which controlled so large a share of the country's daily circulation. Ninety-three percent of all papers that endorsed a candidate in 1972

---

is going on in their own communities. New Jersey's politics has come to rank among the most sordid, squalid and disgusting in the chronicles of state politics. Between the 1968 and 1972 Democratic conventions, no less than six members of the 1968 New Jersey delegation were convicted of felonies. Cursed with unmanageable problems of industry, race and suburbanization, none of its citizens can easily find out what is happening in New Jersey today. The state is a national sadness, the stamping ground of demagogues and ignorants.

endorsed Nixon—753 dailies, with 30,500,000 in circulation, supported him as against only 56, with 3,000,000 circulation, for McGovern. "Out There," where lay his spiritual home, Nixon was reported cleanly and fairly, in his own terms. The gentle rounds of Herbert G. Klein, Nixon's Director of Communications, were smoothly devoted to explaining to the press leaders of Out There what the Nixon Presidency was all about— and Klein was both persuasive and effective.

What neither Nixon nor Klein could reach or affect was a specific cluster of newspapers, all lumped together by them under the convenient rubric "Eastern Liberal Press." Geography contradicted the neatness of this rubric, however, for this crowning cluster was spread as far west as the Los Angeles *Times,* held a beachhead in Chicago with the Field papers, reached south to the Louisville *Courier-Journal,* as deep into the interior as the St. Louis *Post-Dispatch* and added these logotypes to the obvious Washington *Post, New York Times,* Boston *Globe* and Long Island *Newsday.*

All of these were immensely profitable newspapers. Having survived the competition of television, having established their community leaderships so solidly that nothing could shake their advertisers, they were immune to any hostile pressure except from their unions, or outright government legal persecution.

Yet an even more important characteristic marked them: All these great enemies of the Nixon administration were family-owned or family-controlled publications. And between this "baronial" press and the proprietary press is a difference of spirit far greater than that between a state teachers' college and an Ivy League university.

The newspaper families of the baronial press are the last great aristocracy in American life. If there is an elite in America, a truly self-recognizing *noblesse,* it is the great families who own and manage the outstanding daily publications of the nation.

One used to be able to see them all in the flesh in unforgettable display at *The New York Times's* annual reception on the tenth floor of its mausoleum at Times Square, when the Associated Press each spring gathers publishers from around the country for its annual meeting. The Sulzberger family would receive as befitted the Grand Dukes of Manhattan, Arthur Hays Sulzberger sitting in his chair, his consort, Iphigene, standing beside him, both nodding graciously and extending their hands to the other noble families of the realm as they strode proudly in. There were the great personages from out-country, the Grand Duchess of Los Angeles, Mrs. Norman Chandler; the Grand Duchess of Washington, Mrs. Philip L. Graham; there were the earls, counts, countesses of lesser but still courtly blood—the Taylors of Boston, the Binghams of Louisville, the Fields of Chicago, the Pulitzers of St. Louis, the Ridders of the Midwest. They were to be distinguished, by bearing and disposition, from those publishers who worked for powerful but publicly held commercial enterprises where family lineage was either absent or, like the Newhouses, too fresh in power to have acquired patina. As politicians and diplomats watched, the great family figures would circle, flanked by small courts of their own famous writers, stars or editors. If swords, costumes and decorations had been permitted, one might have transferred the personages to a levee at Versailles when the nobility of France was assembled in the Hall of Mirrors—and they would have been at home. And among such families, the proudest in carriage and bearing were those who had come to be bracketed as the "Eastern Liberal Press."

What characterizes these hereditary newspaper barons is something not too difficult to define—a sense of patrician responsibility, a sense of the past both of their own communities and of their nation, and an invulnerability to common fears, common pressures, the clamor of stockholders and advertisers that weaken the vigor of lesser publishers. They understand power better than most politicians; their families have outlived most political families, locally and nationally; they can make politicians—and, on many occasions, break them.

What follows from the pride of these publishers is, however, more subtle, more difficult to define and, in terms of the clash between them and Richard Nixon, the operational fact: They insist on their own concept of honor and style. The families that own the great newspapers of the Liberal Press have the taste, and the purse, for the finest newswriting; they invite from their staffs elegant, muscled, investigative reporting. In this field, they outclass all other newspapers; their quality is evident every day on their front pages; they have survived, and their competitors have perished, because of this quality. These families regard their star reporters as almost sacred—as great racing families regard their horses, horse-handlers and jockeys. Men and women are proud to work for such publishers; their reporters set the style for all other reporters everywhere who hope, someday, to have their prose appear in such newspapers. In a sense, the great organs of the Liberal Press have escaped from the direct control of the publishers who own them and belong to the journalists who operate them for the owners. There is no way the Nixon administration, or any other administration, can reach or influence their reporting, their assessment of the agenda of the nation's unfinished business, their challenge. They are independent not only of Mr. Nixon, but of all pressures except the internal self-criticism of their own communities. They live in a world of their own.

If, in the 1972 campaign, one had drawn up an imaginary hate-list at the White House, one would have had to rank an order somewhat like this: first, the Washington *Post;* second, the Columbia Broadcasting System; third, *The New York Times;* fourth, the Hanoi regime; fifth, the Saigon regime; sixth, American universities; seventh, the Indian government—and so on down the line until one came to George McGovern, the rival candidate, somewhere between tenth and twentieth. (Reviewing this imaginary list one day, a White House friend, who declared it to be preposterous, said to me: "You ought to get the Boston *Globe* in there somewhere—if it were important enough nationally. It's even worse than the New York *Post*—because it's better.")

The three top names on the imaginary hate-list deserve special examination.

The Washington *Post* had been a moribund conservative newspaper until purchased by financier Eugene Meyer in 1933. It had persisted with a feeble flicker of vitality and much deficit financing as a secondary newspaper until management passed in 1948 to Mr. Meyer's son-in-law, Philip Graham, who acquired control of *Newsweek* and invigorated both the newspaper and the magazine until they became major national forces. It was, however, only when direct authority passed to Mrs. Katharine Graham, on the death of Philip Graham, her husband, that the Washington *Post* acquired that exuberance of reporting which made it the chief enemy of Richard Nixon. Mrs. Graham, one of Washington's great hostesses, a shy and beautiful woman of enormous power, manages her empire as Queen Elizabeth managed England—by choosing vigorous men and sending them out on the Spanish Main with freebooters' privilege to seek targets of opportunity. The seadogs Katharine Graham chose when she took over her domain in 1964 were buccaneers of the caliber of Drake and Hawkins, men of quality who enjoyed a good fight. Her two chief admirals, Benjamin C. Bradlee, the executive editor of the Washington *Post,* and Osborn Elliott, editor of *Newsweek,* two Harvard men of the same generation, proceeded to recruit staffs of their own characteristic vitality and style, and, between them, helped change journalism in the sixties.

It is Bradlee and the Washington *Post* that concern us most here—for the Washington *Post* hates Richard Nixon, and Nixon hates the Washington *Post,* and they are locked like two scorpions in a bottle, determined to destroy each other. It was the *Post,* more out of zest for the hunt than any political malice, that made the Nixon administration its target. With gusto, total dedication and courage, its reporters made the Nixon administration their prey—and as they cried "Tally-Ho," the rest of the press pack followed. As the Washington *Post* uncovered the spoor of the Watergate scandal, word was relayed to Mrs. Graham that John Mitchell, the former Attorney General, had declared that "Kay Graham would find her t-t in a wringer" if her staff carried on. Mrs. Graham folded her arms, figuratively, over her bosom and supported her staff. It was for her a question of losing the loyalty of her troops, on the one hand, or perhaps, on the other hand, of being squeezed out of her substantial broadcasting properties by a hostile government. She chose in lonesome gallantry to support her staff, and the Watergate investigation went on.

The Columbia Broadcasting System, second on the imaginary hate-list of the Nixon administration, was another news-gathering institution which had acquired its own internal dynamic, subject to little more management control than cost-accounting. CBS was not to be compared to the baronial press in corporate structure—it had become a widely held public corporation, quoted daily on the New York Stock Exchange. But three men had made it great. Two of those were William S. Paley, chairman of the board, and Frank Stanton, its former president, who regarded the network as their own property, which it had long since ceased to be. The third man had been Edward R. Murrow, one of the great journalists of the twentieth century. Paley and Stanton had had their problems with Murrow's intractable integrity over many years; yet they had been proud of him. He was not only the chief decoration of their News and Public Affairs division, but also a spectacularly able organizer and chooser of other men. Murrow had created for himself, and for the broadcasters he chose, a position *vis-à-vis* management which held simply that management's only control was to fire them or cut them in pay; he and his broadcasting team could not be told what to say, or what the news meant. Murrow's professional fathership of names that came to be reference points in the history of television news reads like this: He had first employed Charles Collingwood and Howard K. Smith in Europe, fresh from Rhodes Scholarships. He had added to his staff Eric Sevareid, in Paris, at the age of twenty-seven. He had put to work in television Fred W. Friendly, at the age of thirty-two. He had been the original sponsor of William L. Shirer, David Schoenbrun, Chet Huntley and other still-glittering or once-famous names who created news television. Of the great men of television, only Walter Cronkite had not been moved forward by an assist from Murrow somewhere along the way.

But to all of them, as well as Cronkite, Murrow had bequeathed something more important than opportunity and fame: He had bequeathed a sense of conscience and importance with which neither management nor government might interfere. Murrow's concept of public advocacy had emboldened him to ignore timid management and launch the attack that destroyed Senator Joe McCarthy; he had spoken for blacks against government, for the poor against the landlords, for the hungry against the establishment. And at CBS, a huge corporation more vulnerable than most to government pressure and Washington reprisal, he had left behind a tradition that the reporting of news and public affairs was to be what its correspondents and producers wanted it to be, not what management sought to make it. Paley and Stanton honored this tradition. It was as inconceivable for them to lift the telephone and tell a Cronkite or a Sevareid what to say as, for example, for the Elector of Saxony to tell Johann Sebastian Bach how to compose his music or to play his tunes at the court's next chamber-music gathering. When they went on air, the CBS newscasters held absolute, unrestrained power.

There remained next on the imaginary hate-list the press organ most difficult to characterize—the most important of them, *The New York Times.*

The Nixon administration and its spokesmen insisted that they did not hate *The New York Times.* It is difficult for anyone to hate *The New York Times;* but *The New York Times,* the best newspaper in the world, is the major power force in American thinking—and it can kill, without malice, simply by a reflex of its muscles. Where the reporters of CBS and the Washington *Post* could be described as being out of the control of their proprietors, *The New York Times* could be described as being, in critical areas, out of the control of its own management, too. For the *Times* lives at the center of a closed loop—it lives in the Manhattan world of opinion makers, and it is impossible to say how much the Manhattan opinion makers influence the *Times,* and how much the *Times* influences the opinion makers.

The New York Times did not create this closed loop, nor does it even take pleasure in it. But the postwar world had been harsher to the daily press in New York than in any other metropolis. New York had boasted eleven daily newspapers just after the war. One by one, the postwar world had squeezed them out—first, local newspapers like the Brooklyn *Daily Eagle* and the Bronx *Home News,* leaving those multi-million boroughs as the largest communities in the nation without a voice of their own. The conservative *Sun* had died; the radical *PM* had died, as had its successor, the *Daily Compass;* so, too, had the *Daily Worker* and the *Daily Mirror.* In 1964, in the Goldwater-Johnson campaign, there still remained six major daily newspapers in New York—the *World-Telegram,* a Scripps-Howard paper; the *Journal-American,* a Hearst paper; the *Herald Tribune,* an ailing but distinguished baronial newspaper; the New York *Post;* the New York *Daily News;* and *The New York Times.* But television, its evening news and the demands of printing unions had wiped out half of the six, until by 1972 there remained only three—the *News,* the *Post* and the *Times*—of which the *Times* was clearly the greatest, with a power that no other newspaper in any other city even approached.

The New York Times is not the hometown newspaper of New York—New York is many hometowns, and the *Times* serves several of them; far more are served by the New York *Daily News.* But the

Times is the hometown newspaper of all men of government, all men of great affairs, all men and women who try to think. In the sociology of information it is assumed that any telephone call made between nine and noon anywhere in the executive belt between Boston and Washington is made between two parties both of whom have already read *The New York Times* and are speaking from the same shared body of information. Whether in finance, music, clothing industry, advertising, drama, business or politics, it is accepted that what is important to know has been printed that morning by *The New York Times*. The *Times* is the bulletin board not just for the city, but for the entire nation's idea and executive system. It is the bulletin board for book publishers, who decide what books may be incubated from its dispatches; it is the bulletin board for the editors of the great news magazines, who speed their correspondents to the scene of any story the *Times* unearths; it is the bulletin board of all three national television networks, whose evening news assignments, when not forced by events themselves, are shaped by ideas and reportage in the *Times*.

The power and the influence of *The New York Times* stem from its unchallenged supremacy in the art and craft of reporting. Reporting at the *Times* has since 1968 been under the jurisdiction of A. M. Rosenthal, its managing editor, once a superb reporter himself, who has continued, even after being pinned behind a desk, to salivate at the reading and printing of good reportorial copy. Supported by his publisher, Arthur Ochs Sulzberger, Rosenthal had by 1972 slowly supplemented a generation of older reporters with younger, more vigorous reporters who vied with the Washington *Post* team as the best in the country, and excelled it in depth of strength, specialization of coverage and, above all, in foreign correspondence. Whether it was news of Germany or China; of the environment or the Democratic Party; of City Hall or real estate; of Vietnam or Zionism; of the theater, the book business or Advertising Row—the reporting of *The New York Times* maintained for its proprietors and management the adjective its onetime patriarch Adolph Ochs had most savored: "indispensable." It was indispensable for anyone making an executive decision anywhere in the world; it was the first paper read at the White House; it was the second paper read in any foreign capital where airmail could carry it; it was the first paper read in any newspaper office or any television station anywhere in America, after the editor or producer had read the local papers.

But *The New York Times* was more than a great instrument for reporting news. It was also the most powerful voice in the national culture. Its critics of art, books, theater, music, movies, dance, its Sunday *Book Review* and cultural sections were to the cultural marketplace what the Dow Jones ticker is to Wall Street.

On the *Times,* as on most other publications, these departments deal in value judgments; and the values which dominate the *Times* are not those of "Out There." They are the values dominant in New York's centers of culture, values shared by the major university campuses. These values, as we have noted earlier, were strongly anti-war from 1967 on, highly tolerant of radical youth and black militancy, and in polar opposition to those of the President.

What was true of the *Times*'s critics was also true of its editorial writers. Their values and opinions, moreover, were given national circulation not only through the nationwide distribution of the *Times* itself, but through its syndicated news service to 221 client newspapers throughout the country which conveyed the generally liberal opinions of Tom Wicker, Anthony Lewis, and James Reston (along with those of the only consistent President well-wisher, C. L. Sulzberger, its chief foreign correspondent). The impact of the critical and editorial writers of the *Times,* piggy-backed across the nation on the *Times*'s indispensable hard reporting, was massive. And, in the eyes of the Nixon administration, formidable. What the Nixon administration found most offensive in the *Times* was not its provocative reporting, but its editorial reflection of the opinion industry of Manhattan.

For the Nixon administration, the Washington *Post* was a recognizable enemy, out to get it. *The New York Times* was different—it was the spreader of elusive values that completely contradicted the administration's own: the values of Manhattan, of the universities, of the opinion set, of the intellectuals—the subtle, corrosive values which had, somehow, taken over television's minds and, through television, set up the chief opposition the administration recognized in the campaign.

The values of Manhattan's *avant-garde,* and the university, television and opinion centers they influence, are matters for another book—on American intellectual history. In the campaign of 1972, however, those values were the values the administration saw itself as opposing: the judgment of all its performances against an unreachable perfection of attainment, the art critic's measure of all things by their symmetry of composition; the derivative intellectual scorn of men who profess a higher morality than those who must compromise with reality or settle for less than perfect in order to make things work now. Words are the fuel of politics. In 1972 the words of patriotism, honor, family, peace-and-quiet, law-and-order—as well as the blunter, harsher words that describe the cruel front of race clash in American communities—were essential dividers in the political contest between the liberal cause and the conservative cause.

Power is to liberals, said someone, what sex is to Puritans—liberals loathe it, yet lust for it; distrust it, yet itch for it. The key belief of liberal intellectuals, shared with conservatives, is that power, in the hands of any but their own kind, conceals a hidden wickedness. In the case of Richard Nixon, liberals were not only convinced of the hidden wickedness of his use of power, but affronted by his manners, his speech, his style. For years, thus, climaxing in 1972, Nixon felt himself relentlessly pursued by such intellectuals, who thereby displayed to their own friends and admirers their courage, their superior virtue, their pious orthodoxy. The election of 1972 as it unrolled outraged liberals—it proved that Richard Nixon read the mind of the country better than they, that he was closer to the country's throb. The tragedy was that, however great his achievements—and they were spectacular—his management of power in the place closest to him was flawed exactly as liberals expected it to be. A crime had been committed in his name, authorized by men of his choice. The unveiling of the Watergate scandal was on the way—and when it broke, it would entirely erase whatever credit balance was his in the proceedings between him and the Liberal Press.

We have thus the pattern of opinion in the campaign of 1972—a proprietary press across most of the country overwhelmingly in favor of Richard Nixon; a "Liberal Press" in several great metropolitan centers freed of the dictates of its proprietors; and an opinion center radiating out of New York, its ideas carried on the back of *The New York Times*'s indispensable reporting, and influencing at the center most of the major news magazines, all of the book publishers, all of the sectarian magazines of opinion and, most importantly of all, the world-view of the great national news networks.

The most apt political parallel for New York is to be found in Berlin of the 1920's. Berlin in the 1920's was the cultural center of the Western world—the place where great art developed, where theater exploded, where experimental writing was entertained, where the most bizarre political theories were given hearing. But Berlin could not capture the mind or culture of out-country Germany, where Germans listened to other voices. In 1972 New York could influence serious thinkers anywhere in the country; but it could not reach the thinking of the common people beyond the Alleghenies. For those in the towers and lofts of Manhattan, the thinking even of Queens County across the river from their windows was as remote as the thinking of Bavaria from Berlin in the twenties.

The President feigned indifference to the press and New York-based television networks. And, indeed, he behaved as he insisted he must—he must act by his own instincts and judgments, not heeding what the nets and liberals said. Yet a reporter could never rid himself of the realization that the hostility of the Liberal Press obsessed Nixon.

Across the street from the White House, in Rooms 122 to 127 of the Executive Office Building, there had been installed under the management of Dr. Lyndon (Mort) Allin, a political-science graduate of the University of Wisconsin, an elaborate center for press surveillance. There the White House view of the press was daily shaped; and the shape the press made of itself was, to the Nixon command, frightening. Each day a staff of four, assisted sometimes by eight volunteer clipping ladies on the top floor of the Executive Office Building, monitored, reported and clipped the news-and-opinion flow of the nation. News tickers clacked; video-tape monitors stood by to record the television news shows; newspapers and magazines piled up from all over the country, stacked on tables, desks, wastebaskets, shelves, until the offices looked like a paper-baling operation in a junk shop. And out of this each day Allin and his staff prepared for Pat Buchanan, who passed it on to the White House, a summary of what television was saying, what the wire nets were reporting, what the opinion magazines opined, what the columnists and commentators commented.

Each day the Allin scrutiny examined fifty key newspapers among the 1,700 dailies in the country. These included, of course, all the famous names of the notorious "Liberal Press." They also included what Allin described as "the stalwarts" which would be with Nixon "no matter what"—the Detroit *News,* the Dallas *Morning News,* the Chicago *Tribune,* the New York *Daily News,* minor newspapers in Jacksonville and Orlando, Florida. Then followed the "generally sympathetic newspapers" —the St. Louis *Globe-Democrat,* the Houston newspapers, the Fort Worth *Star-Telegram,* the Los Angeles *Herald-Examiner* and the San Francisco *Chronicle.* Then followed the neutral papers, which played the news straight from the wire services, but whose editorials and comment might go either way. And once below the top fifty newspapers of the country, support for the President grew overwhelmingly.

Apart from the country press, however, the view from the White House was dismal. The networks were all of them generally regarded as "bloody," with CBS the most hostile and, in White House eyes, ABC the most reasonable. The syndicated commentators and columnists were filed by name—forty of them—with their key dispatches all preserved for the record; the columnists were, of course, generally hostile. Worst of all, however, as seen from Allin's paper-barricaded lair, were the opinion periodicals.

The surveillance center received some forty-two major periodicals of opinion and reportage. They ranged from *Human Events* (hostile to Nixon from the right—*Human Events* believes Nixon is soft on Communism) to Manhattan's *Village Voice* and the *New York Review of Books* (hostile to Nixon from the left—they treat him as if he does not belong to the human race). In between came all the rest, the finest of

American thinking, intellectual conception and cultural values—*Time, Newsweek, Life, The New Yorker, Atlantic* and *Harper's; Saturday Review, New Republic, Nation, National Review;* the *Progressive, Intellectual Digest, Current, Kenyon Review, Partisan Review, Commentary, Ms., Esquire.* Of the forty-two opinion reviews received in 1972, two were published in Europe (the *Economist* in London, the weekly *Le Monde* in Paris); one was published in Wisconsin (the *Progressive*); and all the rest were published in the belt of resistance to Nixon—Boston (1), Washington (7) and New York (all the rest). Apart from the business magazines (*Dun's Review, Forbes, Business Week*) and the periodical stalwarts (*Reader's Digest, U.S. News & World Report*), the panorama with one exception—the *National Review*—ranged from distrust to suspicion to contempt to disgust. The nation's opinion makers, centered in the Boston–New York–Washington area, loathed the President.

Each day the Allin rooms summarized this vast outpouring of material for some thirty members of the White House staff, all of whom needed to be approved by H. R. Haldeman for receipt of distribution. Allin's staff worked around the clock, from seven in the morning until one the next morning. The top two pages of the report, prepared by Buchanan himself, who arrived at seven, always summarized the three evening news shows on television and whatever the major wire services said of note. Then followed twenty to thirty pages of summary of other television shows (*Today* or the CBS Morning News) and the gleanings from the fifty major newspapers. And on Mondays, to start the week, there was a special summary of the opinion journals and the commentators, a bitter dosage for the President. "I just don't understand," said Mort Allin after two years on the job, "how the hell he can sit there and take this shit day after day."

Mr. Nixon had passed, however, by 1972, well beyond any public sensitivity to news comment. He had, perhaps wistfully, hoped that his election in 1968 might cause some abatement in the relentlessness with which he had been pursued by the press for over twenty years. Now that he was President, perhaps they might treat him with the dignity the office suggested. But he was up against Hooker's Law of journalism. In another time of trouble, four centuries earlier, Bishop Hooker had written, without knowing it, the basic future code of American political journalism: "He that goeth about to persuade a multitude that they are not so well governed as they ought to be, shall never want for attentive or favorable hearers. . . . And . . . are taken for principal friends to the common benefit of all. . . . Whereas on the other side, if we maintain things that are established we have . . . to strive with a number of heavy prejudices . . . in the hearts of men, who think that herein we serve the time and speak in favor of the present state because thereby we either hold or seek preferment." The way of advancement in political journalism is not to praise but to attack, and Nixon was coming to office at a time, as we have seen, when American journalism, at least in the hands of its most eloquent practitioners, was passing from the reporting of events to interpretive or advocacy journalism; and when the variety of opinion was being more and more concentrated by technology to fewer and fewer voices.

The Liberal Press was doing its job, as it always had—but with relish. The press was, in Nixon's mind, frustrating him on Supreme Court appointments in 1969 and early 1970; the press was obscuring his effort to disengage in Vietnam, deriding it as deception. Nixon rammed through the first logical attempt to deal with environmental problems in 1970. It was ignored by the press. He was trying to engage Congress in a serious effort to reorganize national welfare programs— the press gave it only intermittent attention. At the beginning of 1971 he was preparing his Big Six proposals,[4] announcing the New American Revolution. More than thirty Washington columnists, commentators, bureau chiefs were invited to individual briefings by White House staffers; Congress was divided up into key contact groups; the President himself would attend four regional conferences of key editors and publishers; Cabinet members would brief editorial boards in their home cities. Nixon's staff and thinkers had worked hard over this system of proposals, but the dry administrative substance needed press resonance if it were to be made romantic enough for government action. The press resonance was not there. The New American Revolution rippled like a phrase in the wind for a few days, and then vanished—absolutely vanished.

There was never any concerted, planned-out response by the Nixon administration to what it considered press hostility. The President himself, by 1972, had completely tuned out the adversary press and television. They no longer influenced him. His adversaries had pursued him so relentlessly over so many years that whatever they said could be discounted as malice or fiction—even the Watergate affair. Which was tragedy. Others in the administration, however, had taken their cue from his mood. Vice-President Agnew had felt—with the President's approval —that the concentration of the press in hostile hands should be publicly denounced as a national peril, and so he did, starting in 1969. Attorney General John Mitchell had begun another counterattack by leading the way for innumerable assaults in court on the privacy of reporters' sources, which, if successful, might well undermine the First Amendment. He had followed, further, with the first attempt in American history to restrain newspapers by prior censorship when first *The New York Times,* then the Washington *Post* sought to publish the famous Pentagon Papers,

4 See Chapter Three.

stolen from government files by an individual but legitimately published as current, once made open. Others struck even more personally at specific administration enemies—as, for example, an FBI investigation of CBS correspondent Daniel Schorr in one of the most shameful attempts on record to intimidate a reporter into submission or moderation of tone. The Nixon administration had begun with formidable enemies in the press; it proceeded to imperil them by a counterattack in which their survival seemed at stake.

Mr. Nixon had by the beginning of 1972 arrived at a personal assessment of the problem. All his major impacts on the American people in his first term had been made by an appeal over the concentrated voices and influence of his very real enemy, the Eastern Liberal Press. His speech of November 3rd, 1969, on Vietnamization of the war, had been sneered at by his enemies—but had turned out to be a triumph, judged by the response of public opinion. His announcements of his trip to China, of wage-price controls in 1971, followed by his own trip to China in early 1972, convinced him that the critically important elements of the news-delivery system in America would bleach out all his thoughts except those expressed in fact and deed. Thus, his campaign of 1972 would be carried to the American people by leap-frogging the news system itself.

The Nixon campaign baffled the news system as few others had done before.

The leading candidate was simply unavailable for questioning.

He had given only eight formal press conferences in his first year in office; in 1970, the number had dropped to four; in 1971 he had moved up to nine press conferences; but in 1972, election year, he had dropped that number to seven. From Franklin Roosevelt on, Presidents had found the press conference the easiest, quickest way of reaching the news system and provoking reaction—they had averaged, until Nixon's time, from twenty-four to thirty-six press conferences a year. Richard Nixon reduced that average to seven. He preferred to reach the people directly, by TV and radio, with the pageantry of the Presidency in action.

1972 was a year when Nixon dominated the airwaves—Nixon from Peking, Nixon from Shanghai, Nixon from Moscow, Nixon from Kiev, Nixon from Hawaii, Nixon greeting foreign chiefs of state. For those who wanted more substance and less pageantry, Nixon had another channel—the campaign radio address. He had first experimented with radio in 1968 and had found paid half-hours, in terms of dollar cost, the most effective way of delivering a serious theme. By 1972 he had, thus, abandoned the telethon, the question-and-answer period, which had once been a staple of his campaigning. In 1972 he was to deliver no less than thirteen daytime radio addresses (plus one in the evening), usually on weekends. With sober, carefully prepared stands on the major issues as he saw them, he reached usually one to three million people per broadcast, and he provided with the texts the background material that the out-country press could digest as policy. If the nation wanted drama, there was the President on TV; if the editorialists demanded that issues be clarified, there were the radio speeches they could read. His public record and theoretical proposals were delivered to the American people better than any candidate's had been before.

But for newsmen, reporting the President was a chore. The news corps had grown in number as the number of newspapers in America shrank. By 1972 their number was almost self-defeating—graying veterans and college editors all jostled in a mob in which every second hand seemed to sprout a microphone, and the booms, cameras and sound poles of television crews clubbed any head not alert enough to duck in time. If one followed the President and was very lucky, one might be made a pool member, one of the revolving five men or women allowed to sit in the rear of Air Force One. There, occasionally some member of the White House inner staff might wander back to say hello and even vouchsafe real information. On the plane you might actually see the President—a newsman scrambling down the rear steps could alight in time to view the President as he came down the front steps of the plane. But the rest, the swollen horde that had now become the trail of all campaigns, were sentenced to the press buses.[5] And the press buses, two, three, sometimes four, would stretch a quarter-mile behind the President in procession, too far back for their passengers ever to see the man in the flesh, who was audible, if at all, only on the loudspeaker in the bus, from which the voice of a pool man up front might relay what was happening on the trip they were covering. It was easier to cover the President on campaign in 1972 by staying home and watching television with the rest of the people—which was the way the President wanted it.

Mr. Nixon had planned his strategy long before the nomination of George McGovern; the strategy ignored all Democratic candidacies as well as the conventional news-delivery system. But even had the Nixon strategy been planned with George McGovern as the intended victim, it could not have trapped his Democratic rival better. McGovern's philosophy of "open politics" was not merely verbal. It reflected the deep personal conviction of George McGovern and his entire staff, and was in turn reflected at every level of his campaign. It was reflected in the pleasant, companionable atmosphere of his plane, where he and his staff were almost always available for direct questioning, and where the cloth partition between the candidate's personal forward section and the

[5] A fresh view of press coverage of the 1972 campaign will be forthcoming in the fall of 1973 in a most entertaining book by Timothy Crouse called *The Boys on the Bus,* published by Random House.

large rear press section could always be breached by a smile. It was reflected even more in his Washington headquarters, where his staff had been trained to be straightforward with newsmen, and thus invited them to explore every crevice of privacy and report each rustle of discontent. The press covered McGovern with stifling thoroughness—partly because he invited it, partly because it was, as one reporter called it, "the only show in town." Analyzing his defeat, McGovern said bitterly, after the campaign was over, "I was subjected to the close, critical reporting that is a tradition in American politics. . . . Yet Mr. Nixon escaped a similar scrutiny. The press never really laid a glove on him, and they seldom told the people that he was hiding, or that his plans for the next four years were hidden. . . . Not a single reporter could gather the courage to ask a question about the bugging and burglary of the Democratic National Committee. . . ." The press was to make up for that shortfall in 1973—but by then it was too late to do George McGovern any good.

It is always easier to write of a campaign long after it is over than when it is going on. In October of 1972 it was quite clear: No candidate had ever more calculatedly set out to ignore the press or done it better than Richard Nixon; and no candidate who had ever set out to befriend newsmen had done worse than George McGovern. Richard Nixon had won hands down. Had his ministry of power in his own home been as successful as his ministry of power in the world abroad and the nation at large, he would have been positioned to tilt positively the battle between the American Executive and the adversary press in favor of the Executive, perhaps permanently.

But this was not to be. The Watergate scandal played only a secondary role in the campaign of 1972. With five clowns seized in a bungled burglary and wire-tapping, and two more held under suspicion, it seemed to be dismissable in June, 1972, as an excess of zeal or stupidity on the part of hustlers—except by those of the adversary press whose reputations and honor were on the line. Two young reporters of the Washington *Post,* at a level almost below the notice of management, had locked onto a simple police story. One of them, Bob Woodward, thirty years old, had left the Navy only two years before and had not yet enjoyed eighteen months of tasting the power of the press when, on June 20th, three days after the Watergate break-in, he learned from another *Post* reporter, Eugene Bachinski, that the police had seized two notebooks from the burglars containing White House telephone numbers that could be traced to E. Howard Hunt. Woodward set out immediately to find out what he could about Hunt. Three days later, twenty-nine-year-old Carl Bernstein, another reporter of the same paper, found that the source of $25,000 in cash paid to the burglars could be traced directly to the Committee to Re-Elect the President. And on October 25th both

young reporters, combining in what was to become a series of almost 200
articles by the next year, struck at the throne itself—alleging that H. R.
Haldeman, chamberlain to the sovereign, was implicated in a deed unprecedented in American politics. "It tightens your sphincter muscles,"
said Bradlee, executive editor of the Washington *Post,* as he described
the responsibility of an editor whose proprietor had given him authority
to place the entire reputation of her enterprise as well as her properties
and her fortune behind two young reporters whose charges seemed, to
the outside world, incredible.

It also tightened the sphincter muscles of the White House—but
that was to come later.

The story of Watergate was only one of a number of major stories
in the election of 1972. As it unraveled, it was to become a story of 1973
and would fit better, someday when all was known, into a story of the
use and abuse of power in a modern state. The elections of 1972 were
determined, basically, by the record Richard Nixon had written in the
understanding of his people—and his chief adversary was not George
McGovern, but that vanguard of the press which claimed it understood
and spoke for the people better than he did himself. On this immediate
level of contest, Richard Nixon won. The people preferred Richard
Nixon.

There was, however, the other level of contest—the ongoing fight
between the President and the press which an election could not settle:
control of the agenda. The Washington *Post,* followed by the Columbia
Broadcasting System, followed by *The New York Times,* had decided
they would place squarely on the agenda of public talk the matter of corruption in government and, specifically, corruption of power in the Nixon
campaign.

Once there, it could not be removed, and would become the tragic
Watergate story.

CHAPTER ELEVEN

THE WATERGATE AFFAIR

No simple logic yet embraces what is known as the Watergate affair. In the word "Watergate" are contained a family of events, a condition of morality and a system of acts, charges, allegations which, until those accused have had their chance to speak in court and be judged by law, defy final judgment.

Yet the story of Richard Nixon's re-election cannot be told without it. That election was not a traditional party contest between Republicans and Democrats. As presented to the people, it was an election of ideas—sharp-set, harshly contrasted—and of two personalities who spoke clearly of their directions. But underneath their claims it was a clash of cultures breaking away from the old common culture of comity and civil peace that had once bound Americans together. Watergate was born of two new cultures which saw Americans as enemies of each other. And since the Committee for the Re-Election of the President struck the decisive blow against the old common culture, it is the Committee to Re-Elect that concerns us here.

The Committee to Re-Elect was born of legitimate purpose, but was entrusted not only to men ignorant of American politics, but to amateurs who were among the most stupid and criminal operators in electoral history. Though after midsummer of 1972, under Clark Mac-Gregor, it became one of the most efficient vote-management organizations in recent history, its direction at genesis begins in yet unanswered riddles:

How, under MacGregor's predecessor as chairman, John Mitchell, could so great a stupidity have been conceived, for such trivial and profitless stakes as could be won by criminally invading and criminally wiretapping the Democratic National Committee at its Watergate offices?

And why should such an enterprise have been carried on at the end of May, when—with the elimination of George Wallace from the campaign, the successful gamble of the President in Vietnam, a blaze of triumph sure to rise from his trip to Russia—victory was assured? Why, at this moment, should so much have been risked in so squalid an adventure?

And, above all, what philosophy governed the men who were to be found guilty? What sort of men were they? Who gave them authority?

It is perhaps best to start with the personalities, and then go on to the philosophies which finally rocked the White House and American politics with scandal and taint that surpass, in American history, even the scandal of Teapot Dome or the grubbiness of the Grant administration.

One starts at the beginning, and with the supreme personality—that private and lonesome man Richard Nixon, one of the more able minds to occupy the Presidency in our time, a devout patriot, his personality already scorched by years of humiliation and roughhouse combat before his election to the Presidency in 1968 by 499,704 votes, an infinitesimal margin of 0.7 percent of the total vote cast.

By the week after that first victory, the view from Nixon's new eminence was not at all what he had long imagined it would be—that when the President calls, patriots respond. He sought to have Hubert Humphrey, his defeated rival, speak for the United States in the U.N.—Humphrey turned him down. He sought, as a gesture of bipartisan unity, to appoint Democratic Senator Henry Jackson as his Secretary of Defense—Jackson turned him down. He sought David Rockefeller as either Secretary of Defense or Secretary of the Treasury—David Rockefeller turned him down. He sought William Scranton as his Secretary of State—Scranton turned him down. He wanted Robert Finch to be his Attorney General. Finch refused. He wanted Daniel P. Moynihan of Harvard as his Secretary of Labor—the leaders of labor vetoed the choice.

Only a few months earlier, during the campaign of 1968 when his election seemed certain by a huge margin, he had described to me one evening on the road his concept of government. "I want two teams in the White House," he had said, "a big team, but also a young team." The big team—names like Governors Romney, Rockefeller, Scranton—would run the Cabinet. But he needed a young team, men between thirty and forty—"they learn awfully fast." He needed people who could move hard and fast. Haldeman, Buchanan, Price. Finch would certainly be in the Cabinet. What did I think of Henry Kissinger for foreign affairs? he asked. And he had Professor Glenn Olds, whom he described as a "brilliant man," at work on details of staffing the government. I was familiar with the work of Olds, a philosophy professor who had been conducting perhaps the most sophisticated screening of talent ever done for a Presidential candidate, heading a team dedicated to filling the Federal administrative structure with the best men America could offer.

But it was not, as it turned out after the election, to be that way at all. The entire pre-election screening of personnel conducted by Olds never reached Nixon. The big men would not join him. And, like all Presidents before him, he found that no single man's range of personal acquaintances was broad enough to give him the staff to fill the key leadership posts of American government. Truman, Eisenhower, Kennedy, Johnson had all rubbed against the same limitations before. And Nixon itched to work on problems—not personnel.

"I feel very frustrated about personnel," he said to me in the 1968–69 interregnum between election and inauguration. "I don't like to do it. I'm more an idea man. I like to leave personnel problems to Mitchell or Haldeman or others, but at the highest level I just have to do it myself, and there's a scarcity of personnel at the level I want." He mused that day, so my notes refresh my memory now, about the kind of people it takes to run the government of the United States. Businessmen? "Damn it, most businessmen aren't good at government. Some people go to the other extreme, get intellectuals—but intellectuals get torn to pieces in government at the levels they have to work at. Then they say, get politicians—but politicians, though they do have the necessary experience, they tend to be not imaginative enough. . . ." He wanted bright people, young people, people with ideas, people to whom he would give time to think. But always, in this and other interregnum talks, two people were uppermost in his trust and confidence—Haldeman and Mitchell. As for Mitchell, said Nixon two days after he had been inaugurated, after having come from a two-hour lunch with Mitchell, "I want no climate of fear in this country, no wire-tapping scare. He [Mitchell] will control that with an iron hand." And then, as in all other conversations, he went on to ideas, with that fascination he can exert when he talks of ideas. From the very beginning, the mind of the 37th President came to rest on abstractions, while the choice of men who would become his lesser instruments was left to people in whose personal loyalty he had absolute confidence.

Three years later, by early 1972, this requirement of personal loyalty had isolated the President—not only from his Cabinet but from much else: from Congress, from the press and television news system, from his own Republican Party. He was President; his intellectual energies were, above all, absorbed by foreign affairs. Those closest to him knew he was bored and irritated by small detail; and the atmosphere of the White House had become that of a court. The President wanted the ordinary things done. Those who moved forward, in his court and in his esteem, were those who got his will done and did not bother him with details.

Where court politics and national politics meshed, the rivalry for the President's ear was most acute—and a fascinating study. Closest to the President were John Mitchell and H. R. Haldeman—rivals since the campaign of 1968, when Mitchell had been the President's campaign manager, but Haldeman, his roving chamberlain, had been his personal manager. In the next echelon were Charles Colson, John Ehrlichman and Robert Finch. Then came others, attendant lords, thanes, scribes—

and then a vast gap, and after that, the leadership of the Republican Party.

Roughly, one could divide the courtiers into two groups: the hard and the gentle. The governing of America, which is a very tough country, requires both toughness and sensitivity. Richard Nixon can be very, very tough, and very sensitive, too; the personalities around him reflected this split in the spirit of the man. In one cluster around the President were the apparently gentle of spirit: Henry Kissinger, Robert Finch, Herbert Klein, Leonard Garment, John Ehrlichman, Caspar Weinberger, and speechwriters Safire and Price. In the other cluster were the apparently tough men: Bob Haldeman, Charles Colson, John Mitchell, John Connally, Pat Buchanan. Both groups included some honorable men and, as it turned out, some dishonorable men; but the tough and the gentle were anything but unified factions on principle, policy or politics.

All were contenders for the President's ear, where power was to be influenced. Haldeman and Ehrlichman, though very different personalities, always stood together as friends, and Ehrlichman, who had won direct access to the President's ear by 1972, was never at odds with Haldeman. They had been classmates at UCLA; while there, young Bob Haldeman had managed the unsuccessful campaign for student-body vice-president of pretty Jeanne Fisher—Ehrlichman's wife to be. Haldeman had drawn Ehrlichman into Nixonian politics as a campaign advance man. At the White House, Haldeman was interested, above all, in the mechanics and administration of the Presidency, uninterested in issues; Ehrlichman savored ideas, with a true appreciation for the long-range shape of American problems. Both Ehrlichman and Haldeman had been California friends of Robert Finch, too, but now, in power, they ruefully began to see their old friend as too soft for the tough decisions of the Presidency. Occasionally they referred to him as "the Pasadena Hamlet."

Then there was the antagonism between Charles Colson and John Mitchell. Colson had come, like Ehrlichman and many others, to the President's entourage under the sponsorship of Haldeman and had, by 1972, replaced Pat Moynihan as the President's favorite conversationalist. Colson's office was next to the President's hideaway in the Executive Office Building; occasionally, when political argument in his office grew too loud, he would put a warning finger over his mouth, shush the group and point to the wall beyond which, presumably, the President was at work. The gesture had weight; and as gossips at the White House peeked at the daily log of the President's phone calls, some days showed more calls from the President to Colson than to Haldeman.

Hardest of all the hard men around the President, by far, was John Mitchell. A man of aquiline nose, freckled and balding, he was as charming a conversationalist as one could meet—and at the same time as cold a personality as one ever encounters in politics. Mitchell was an effective lawyer, but a poor executive. More important, he was neither by training, temperament nor traditional code a politician. He was contemptuous of most politicians—his legal specialty had been the drafting and placement of public-interest bond issues, a skill which, though lucrative, scarcely teaches a man high respect for public officials. Among Republican politicians he was generally disliked—and had the reputation of never returning phone calls, which estranges politicians of importance. But Mitchell was bound into the President's affections as deeply as Haldeman or Finch. During the bitter years of Richard Nixon when, as an exile from politics, he practiced law in New York between 1963 and 1967, Mitchell's home in Rye was among those places warmest to him. There, Martha Mitchell played the gracious Southern hostess; there Nixon might join in the singing, as he liked to do, or bang the piano while Leonard Garment, another partner of the law firm, played along on the clarinet.

It was difficult at all times to keep the teams in the game of palace politics sorted out. Haldeman, Ehrlichman, appointments secretary Dwight Chapin and press secretary Ronald Ziegler came bunched as a group, clustered with Charles Colson—Haldeman men. Robert Finch was, obviously, being squeezed out in the power struggle—as was Finch's friend Herbert Klein, who understood the Washington press better than anyone else in the administration. Finch was as close to the President as ever, personally—but not on the day-to-day mechanics of politics as he had once been. Nixon had offered Finch the Vice-Presidency in 1968 and Finch had declined the honor, as well as, later, the Attorney Generalship, and sought to be Secretary of HEW. That, as it had turned out, was a mistake. The Secretary of HEW was caught between the statutes and constituencies of need he represented, on the one hand, and, on the other hand, policy decisions from the White House which governed all Cabinet departments. Power, in this administration, lay at the White House and Finch soon realized he should be back there at the center. By the time he returned, however, in 1970, he was out of the power contest. Although officially listed first on the White House staff as Counselor to the President, he was in fact anything but that. He was now an observer and commentator. It was Finch's hope that the Haldeman-Mitchell rivalry would offset the two men as checks and balances to each other in the 1972 campaign. Then, Mitchell, too, had his own men in the White House—chiefly John W. Dean III, legal counsel to the President, a handsome young lawyer who brought with him a somewhat tarnished record: he had been fired by a law firm in Washington for reputedly unethical conduct. All of these men, all of these groups had pieces of the action as the election of 1972 approached.

The President, as we have seen (Chapter Three), had decided in

Key Biscayne at the end of 1970 that he would stay out of the details of actual campaigning in 1972, concentrating on the issues and grand conceptual strategy. By 1971 a new formulation had thus been developed for managing and administering the campaign—there would be a special committee, a personalized committee for the President's campaign, across the street from the White House, entirely divorced from the Republican National Committee and the party. And when the time came in 1972, John Mitchell would direct that committee.

In accepting the management of the Committee, Mitchell laid down two stipulations. He insisted on the right to choose his successor as Attorney General—Richard Kleindienst. And he insisted on having absolute authority over the Committee. Translated baldly, this meant that he wanted Charles Colson out of his operation. "We wasted hours," said a friend of Mitchell's, "just trying to figure out how to foil Colson. Normally, John [Mitchell] could call the President directly about anyone and if John didn't like the guy, he'd be gone the next morning. Not with Chuck, though. Chuck was there to stay." Within the White House, others were uneasy about the choice of Mitchell. There was Haldeman for one—Haldeman, as the President's chamberlain, retained the right to interfere, question, reach into the Committee and find out what was going on; and anyone at the Committee in direct contact with Haldeman was wired into the top. Finch, for another, was wary of Mitchell—as early as March of 1972, long before the first bug was placed in the Watergate, Finch was quietly urging at the White House that Mitchell be relieved of chairmanship of the Committee and sent elsewhere.

Each of these major personalities in the campaign of 1972 thus had his own role, his own field team, his own ambition. Later, when the mythology of Watergate reached full flower in 1973, the theory of the grand conspiracy, to suborn and undermine both justice and democratic tradition, was to conceive of all these operations as if some diabolical band of planners had contrived one master adventure. But the campaign of 1972 from the Republican side was more like the backfield of a football team with no quarterback and four footballs to run with—every ball carrier racing off on his own play—and the coach, who understood best what the campaign was all about, was preoccupied with action elsewhere.

Colson, for example, was to develop his own intelligence system, jealously guarded from Mitchell's interference. Colson worked with labor and Catholic leaders, with public and private pollsters, introducing some of them to the President for conversations which the President enjoyed. He specialized in information on Democratic rivals—commissioning at one time a private poll on Edmund Muskie, compiling his own dossier on Edward Kennedy. Later in the campaign Colson masterminded what was called the "attack group"—early-morning sessions of the White House staff at which he choreographed the movements of Nixon campaign "surrogates" across the country, and orchestrated with enthusiastic malice their statements, attacks and ripostes designed to take air time and headlines from George McGovern and make McGovern look like a fool. Colson enjoyed his work. In August he wrote a memorandum to his staff: "I am totally unconcerned with anything other than getting the job done. If I bruise feelings or injure anyone's morale, I will be happy to make amends on the morning of November 8, assuming we have done our job and the results are evident. . . . Just so you understand me, let me point out that the statement in last week's UPI story that I was once reported to have said that 'I would walk over my grandmother if necessary' is absolutely accurate." Colson was tough—but he was very professional, and very much a lawyer, and very distrustful of John Mitchell. It would please him no little to see Mitchell in trouble. I saw Colson ten days after the story of the Watergate wire-tapping and bur- glary first broke in the press and he was in a state of apparent rage. "Idiots! . . . Idiots!" he expostulated. "Anybody who did that should have been sent to Siberia! Whoever heard about it should have fired them!" Colson was too much of a politician to believe that anything of value could be learned at the forlorn and hollow Democratic National Committee. His own intelligence net was far more effective—but he would not share what he learned with anyone except the President and Haldeman.

There was, next, another team running with its own ball in the murk—the so-called "dirty-tricks team," which moved on its own in the darkness. The dirty-tricks team of Chapin-Segretti-*et-alii* could not have functioned without the authorization of H. R. Haldeman— but how much Haldeman knew in detail of their tactics is, at this writing, still unclear. The dirty-tricks team is, of course, no recent innovation in American politics or, indeed, in any system of republican politics.[1] In the past decade, however, dirty tricks have moved from the ward clubhouses to the White House, reaching that level in 1964, when Lyn- don Johnson's men set out with glee and malice to harass Barry Goldwater. The Democrats called their group the Five O'Clock Club, and its men met in the White House in the afternoons to prepare what they called "negative advance" for Goldwater. Their purpose was to precede, accompany and follow Barry Goldwater's campaign tours with instant organized contradiction. Somehow they managed always to

---

[1] Dirty tricks, the spreading of lies and rumor, go back to the grass roots even of ancient Rome. The excavators of ancient Pompeii found, when they uncovered it from the ashes of Vesuvius, that Pompeii had been smothered and extinguished in the midst of a local election campaign. On the walls they bared, the archeolo- gists found campaign slogans: "VOTE FOR VATIUS, ALL THE WHOREMASTERS VOTE FOR HIM." "VOTE FOR VATIUS, ALL THE DRUNKS AND SLUG-A-BEDS VOTE FOR HIM." "VOTE FOR VATIUS—ALL THE WIFE-BEATERS ARE VOTING FOR HIM." The barren walls do not state, nor do the records show, whether Vatius' unnamed opponent won or lost the election before the eruption erased the city from history.

get Goldwater's advance schedules, speech drafts, internal planning, by means never exposed or investigated—and the Democratic troops were ready with counter-demonstrations and mischief around the country wherever Goldwater showed his person.

The campaign of 1972 now carried the dirty-tricks game further. There was always all that money available from the Finance Committee to Re-Elect; there was the temptation to find ingenious ways to use it. And so, passing beyond the dirty tricks of the Johnson men of 1964, the Nixon men did their best to pollute the Democratic primary contests of 1972 operating all across the country, reporting directly to Dwight Chapin, the President's appointments secretary, funded by Herbert W. Kalmbach, the President's personal lawyer in California. Again, one must separate the after-myth of the effect of such tricks from the record as it was at the time of the election. The myth now reads that the dirty-tricks department interfered in the Democratic primary campaign to manipulate those primaries so that the weakest of the Democrats, George McGovern, would emerge victorious. In this writer's opinion, the Chapin-Segretti dirty-tricks operation had the weight of a feather in the internal struggle of the Democratic Party. That contest was moved by far greater issues, and in that contest George McGovern won the cleanest of victories, by the strategy he had conceived, in the fairest of appeals, on his own.

One moves thus, in this assortment of Republican teams, from the mean and hard to the slippery and slithery, both familiar from past experience, to the novel; from the vicious to the criminal. And by this path to the Committee to Re-Elect, and the characters who crowded under its banner.

The title "Committee for the Re-Election of the President" had been suggested by New Yorkers who had liked the ring of Nelson Rockefeller's 1970 campaign slogan—"Elect Governor Rockefeller Governor." But the spirit, the political ethos, was Californian. "These guys from California," said F. Clifton White, who had grown up in New York State politics and captained the Goldwater coup of 1964, "don't understand a party structure. They don't understand precinct politics. Out there in California they change chairmen every two years. Nixon never lived through party politics." In California, ever since the days of the famous Whitaker-and-Baxter team, candidates have run not as party men but as public figures cast in roles by their public-relations men and tactical strategists. In Republican politics in California, particularly, the dictum runs that politics is too important to be left to politicians. The Committee's members reflected this peculiar disdain of formal party organization and members. Though selected from all over the country, they behaved in that spirit. "Don't waste your time over at the Republican National Committee," said one of the Re-Elect Committee's spokesmen to this reporter in friendly private advice. The Committee was not engaged in managing a party campaign—its purpose was single-minded: to re-elect the President, Nixon.

The Committee was conceived early in the spring of 1971 and announced formally in May of that year. Its prime purpose was to mobilize votes—to analyze and organize special-interest and ethnic groups, to register them, to set up subcommittees for them, to get out the mailings, to supervise the media and publicity operations. Its staff were those young Republicans the White House stalwarts regarded as the most promising of junior politicians. "We're staffing it with new troops, to blood them in action, to give them experience," one of the President's confidants expressed it. But for the young men chosen for the Committee's thirty-five separate divisions it was a showcase where those on the make could demonstrate their energy and skills, and the boss was always John Mitchell. "John Mitchell runs this committee with an iron hand," said DeVan L. Shumway, the Committee's spokesman, early in 1972, before Mitchell had come aboard officially, "we are only input."

Typical of these new troops, almost all of them amateurs in politics, was Jeb Stuart Magruder, aged thirty-seven, the man chosen to keep John Mitchell's chair warm as deputy chairman until Mitchell would take over in March, 1972. Magruder's clear brown eyes, his curly hair, his deference and courtesy, his eager-beaver desire to be helpful made one feel that if he had a tail, he would wag it. Magruder had campaigned in the past as an advance man in various Nixon campaigns; had subsequently settled in California; and had done fairly well merchandising cosmetics, facial tissues and hosiery. He had been recommended to the White House staff by a substantial California Republican contributor, Edward W. Carter, chief of the Broadway-Hale department stores, for whom he had once worked. Both Finch and Haldeman liked Magruder, and he moved at the third level through the White House staff, winding up as deputy to Herbert Klein, director of communications for the Nixon administration, before finally being sent across the street to Committee headquarters in the First National Bank Building at 1701 Pennsylvania Avenue until Mitchell could take over. Magruder had a disarming surface frankness. Explaining why he had been chosen, he said, "They were looking for a man that both Mitchell and Haldeman trusted, and they chose me." Here, then, he would make his mark—if he did well in the campaign, a sub-Cabinet post was surely his, perhaps a Cabinet post; he was on his way, and ambition spurred. He had worked long enough at the White House and the Executive Office Building to know that the primary imperative was to get things done.

The First National Bank Building housed not only the Committee to Re-Elect, but the Finance Committee to Re-Elect the President, an independent body under the leadership of Maurice Stans, a man devoted to Richard Nixon, whom he had served as Secretary of Commerce. Stans had been treasurer of the Nixon campaign in 1968, but in 1972 he was to outdo himself and write himself into the records as the all-time champion money-raiser of American politics. Stans had begun life as an accountant (he still looked like one—neat in dress, carefully groomed, gray of hair), and had become a California banker. He was the kind of man you would want to make out your income tax—trustworthy, intelligent, a man who knew exactly how far you could press the deductions or contributions before falling afoul of the law. As Secretary of Commerce he had performed with distinction in the first Nixon administration, both in domestic reorganization of the department and in defending America's interests in trade abroad. He wistfully hoped that he could move out of that level of politics into something more glamorous in the next administration—say, the Ambassadorship to Moscow, or something equally grand—which would crown his services with historic achievement. But before that he would perform this last great service to his friend, Richard Nixon—he would raise the money to re-elect the President.

Stans ran his own team—the Finance Committee to Re-Elect being only a roof committee, embracing and controlling special finance committees such as the Media Committee to Re-Elect, state finance committees, and scores of fictitious receptacle committees. Like the Colson team, the Chapin-Segretti team and other Nixon teams criss-crossing the backfield because there was no quarterback to direct them, the Stans team was sure it was doing what the coach wanted—and it had extraordinary zest. By hobby, Stans was a big-game hunter; trophies of his African safaris hung in his home. He was now tracking down big game in America—the long-purse money contributors all across the country, at every level. He had raised $34,000,000 for Nixon in 1968—in 1972 he was to raise $52,000,000.

There was a special spur to Stans's efforts. Early in 1972, Congress had passed the new Federal Election Campaign Act, requiring each party to record publicly all its sources of funds over $10 and report to the General Accounting Office those over $100 from April 7th, 1972, on. Up until that date, it would be open season for private hunting; after that, all sources of political funds and the spending of them would be publicly recorded. For Stans and the Finance Committee, the spring of 1972 was the time—get the hay in the barn while the sun shines ($10,000,000 of it, as it turned out later). For a limited period, Stans could promise big-money contributors that news of what they paid into the President's campaign fund would never reach light of day—if delivered before April 7th. Thus the grotesqueries which so intrigued the press later as Stans, straining to the limit his interpretation of the new law, tried to absorb money before the publicity deadline—money float-ing through Mexican banks, money arriving in wads of cash. $25,000 in cash (for example) was secretly deposited by one of Hubert Hum-phrey's principal long-time contributors (Dwayne Andreas of Minne-sota) in a safe-deposit box (#305) in the Seaview Hotel in Miami Beach, which Andreas owned—placed there apparently before midnight of April 7th but not collected, presumably by a slip-up, until Sunday, the 9th, after the legal deadline. In the frantic last weeks of March and the first week of April, the Finance Committee to Re-Elect was harvest-ing money with an almost manic glee—it probably would have accepted Confederate dollars or wampum, too, if those currencies had any value. Checks had to be collected and deposited. But so much cash money was coming in from so many different sources, through so many different channels, it was physically difficult to keep track of it all. One safe in Maurice Stans's office held wads of cash which at one time, according to reports, ran up to $250,000. Through another safe down the corridor, in the office of Hugh Sloan, the Committee's treasurer, passed another $1,000,000. From both these safes a total of $199,000 in cash was to go to Gordon Liddy. Trying to trace the flow of this cash is like trying to trace the flow of underground streams. Cash, theoretically, went out only on the signature of Mitchell or Magruder ordering Stans or Sloan to deliver. But cash went out also to a coffer under H. R. Haldeman's jurisdiction ($350,000) and to another under the jurisdiction of Herbert Kalmbach ($250,000). Such movement of cash, it should be stressed, is not necessarily illegal; politicians in both parties have used cash wher-ever necessary—to pay for services, to pay the bills of wary political printers, to tide volunteers over the weekend, to hustle up votes by en-couraging minor leaders in critical wards. "Money is the mother's milk of politics," said Jesse Unruh of California in a dictum that has become famous.

What must be stressed, in the matter of political finance, particu-larly since two former Cabinet members are under indictment at this moment of writing, is the distinction between the traditional squalor of political money-raising and outright crime.

Money-raising is one of the more disgraceful forms of American practice in politics. Rarely does any senior politician, particularly a Presidential candidate, know exactly where all his money comes from—his campaign treasurer is supposed to insulate him from the more sor-did transactions. Benjamin Harrison attributed his close election in 1888 to Providence. "He ought to know that Providence didn't have a damn thing to do with it," retorted Matt Quay, the Republican boss of Pennsylvania, who had been shaking down the big business of the coal-and-steel state for campaign funds. Over the years, money-raising has become more subtle, less coarse, less than ever the outright bribe-andboodle of the days of the Grant or Harding administrations or of Tammany operations in New York. Money now flows into national politics chiefly to buy influence and comes from recognizable seekers of influence. There are the great old patrician families of America—the Pews, the Whitneys, the Rockefellers, the Mellons—who contribute hugely out of high disinterested tradition, but want a say in the evolution of tradition. There are the Texas oil millionaires, whose heyday of involvement came in the late 1950's and early 1960's. There are the Southern California millionaires. There is what is called the "big Jewish money," which has been involved in politics since the days of Theodore Roosevelt's first campaign but which, between 1948 and 1972, went chiefly to Democrats. There is "cause" money—rich old ladies and idealistic young scions of great fortunes who will contribute hundreds of thousands of dollars to be able to talk to "their Senator" or the President about mental care, better hospitals, cleaner environment. There is corporate money, labor-union money, fund-raising-dinner money. Recently, beginning with Barry Goldwater's campaign, a more altruistic kind of money has been coming into politics—grass-roots money, raised by direct-mail or television appeals to ordinary people. At this level of conscience money, the McGovern campaign of 1972, under the direction of Henry Kimelman and Morris Dees, probably did better than any previous campaign in American history—and by its success may have begun a hopeful revolution for the future. Only at a local level, of state and municipal politics, is hard money delivered for purchased favors. The money that comes from contractors, sewer-pipe manufacturers, racetrack operators, distinguished architectural firms requires a very specific *quid pro quo* before delivery.

What almost all types of contributors desire in return for their money is quite simple: access. Some want merely access and invitations to the inaugural ball. Others want more. The archives of the Kennedy Presidency, which I once examined, contain some of the more plaintive passages of human eloquence, in letters from $5,000 contributors whose wives complained that they had never once been invited to dinner at the White House. Other contributors are teased with hopes of Ambassadorships or appointments to Presidential commissions. Most large contributors, however, want much more substantial access: they want to be able to talk to a government official, whether at the Internal Revenue Service, or the Pentagon, or the Department of Justice, or the Departments of Agriculture, Interior or Commerce, about some problem that concerns them greatly. Most contributors pay not for an expected fix, but for the right to skip the slowness of bureaucratic channels and plead their case, quickly, sharply to the policy-making officials who will make the critical decisions. This pressure for access to officialdom has always been there—but it has been growing year by year in the postwar world as government regulatory agencies have extended their authority further and further into American daily life. From oil quotas to sugar prices, from drug inspection to smokestacks, from school textbooks to television franchises, from approval of giant conglomerate mergers to merchant-marine subsidies, the reach of government touches, directly or remotely, everyone who does business in America today. These organs of business are willing to pay for quick access, for quick decision one way or another; and since wage-and-price responsibility was assumed by government in the first Nixon administration, the pressure for access to sensitive decision-making in that area may be expected to increase exponentially. The wonder is that the American Federal civil service has so consistently—indeed, almost totally—maintained its integrity and honor under such pressure although occasional breakthroughs take place.

This stimulus of large contributions—the need for access—works as much for Democrats as for Republicans. The usual response of a finance chairman in a Presidential campaign ("You won't be forgotten") is to imply that access will be open; usually, the response is covered with an admonition that there will be no intervention, no appointment, no pressure, no fix in return for the contribution. It is in this area of access that, as I write, former Attorney General John Mitchell and former Commerce Secretary Maurice Stans find themselves indicted for aid and assistance to one Robert L. Vesco, a shady financier who looted a huge mutual-fund investment trust. Several things are clearly charged in the indictments: that on April 10th (a Monday, three days after the legal Friday, April 7th, deadline) an emissary of Vesco delivered $200,000 in $100 bills to Maurice Stans in Washington; this money was unreported; but within hours, that very day, John Mitchell had arranged for the emissary to meet with the top personalities of the Securities and Exchange Commission, which was pursuing Vesco for fraud. It should be noted that Vesco's plea and $200,000 contribution did no good—eight months later the Securities and Exchange Commission was issuing fraud charges against Vesco and he was a fugitive from justice. The courts will decide whether his contribution was the traditional delivery of cash in expectation of access, or the delivery of a bribe in expectation of a criminal fix.

More important is the connection of Republican money-raising to the calculated crime of Watergate.

"Naïve" is probably the last adjective Maurice Stans's friends would apply to him. But Stans *was* naïve—as are most businessmen when they involve themselves in politics. Stans's duty was to raise money. In a well-ordered corporation, the treasurer-controller is obliged to check on whether the money appropriated for a given purpose is in fact spent for that purpose. But on the second floor of the First National Bank Building, Stans limited himself to raising the money—and left to others the spending of the money, without checking. He had recognized early that the new Federal Election Campaign laws imposed complicated new rules for money-raising. He needed legal counsel, yet without seeking his own counsel he let Magruder shift Gordon Liddy from the Magruder staff to his own. When particularly delicate collection or contribution problems came up, Liddy would offer to take charge himself. "He was a good lawyer," said Stans later, "he was hard-working, he attended staff meetings, he worked full-time—whatever he did, he did in his off hours. He only took two days off for personal business."

Stans had a sound businessman's irritation with what appeared to be the vapors of the Committee to Re-Elect the President. The top men of the Finance Committee and the Re-Elect Committee met occasionally for summit discussions. The tone of such meetings seemed familiar to Stans—he had once been Eisenhower's Director of the Budget and, as he recalled later, the strategy conferences at 1701 Pennsylvania Avenue raised echoes of the past. "When I was Director of the Budget," said Stans, "the Army, the Navy, the Air Force would all come in with their requests for weapons. All of them wanted enough money to destroy Russia single-handedly, all by themselves." Now the Committee wanted enough money for every one of its divisions—direct mail, media, ethnics, volunteer organization—as if each division were going to wipe out the Democrats all by itself. Like a good budget maker, Stans might grumble that money did not grow on trees. But what the political committee wanted, he must finance. One day, furious, he walked out of a meeting with Committee personnel because he could not find out what the money was being spent on. But the budget line for intelligence and security operations was a very small one—$350,000 out of a total budget originally set at $42,000,000, later to rise to $52,000,000. A detail.

"I never asked when I came aboard," said Stans later, "what this intelligence operation was all about. I heard it was about the possibility of a demonstration at San Diego—where we planned to hold the convention—and about bodyguards and protection for the surrogates who would be traveling to campaign. When I read the Watergate story on June 18th, I didn't even know the Democrats had a headquarters in Watergate. I didn't even know the names of Hunt and Barker. . . ."

But Stans had performed too well. The Committee was afloat and awash with money, enough to over-fertilize the imagination and ambitions of the most balanced minds. Among these was a team known as the Plumbers Group.

The Plumbers Group expressed in new and precise form the war between the administration and the press.

On June 30th, 1971, as the fiscal year in government came to its end, as the President's ratings in the polls still lagged behind those of

Edmund Muskie, the Supreme Court of the United States decided that
The New York Times could not be prevented from publishing the famous
Pentagon Papers, containing secret documents stolen from government
files and copied. The decision brought the administration to a turning
point in its thinking. Nixon had already been embittered by the publication in *The New York Times* of technical details of American prepara-
tion for the SALT talks with Russia, details which dealt with innermost
matters of American nuclear strategy. So, too, with *The New York
Times*'s revelation in May of 1969 that B-52's were bombing in Cambodia. The Australian government had already protested to the American government, diplomatically, that their most private exchanges were
being leaked; the Australians stopped just a rhetorical step short of describing the security of the American government as a sieve. Still later
the President was to be driven to an extremity of anger at the publication of National Security Council minutes on the war in Bangladesh by
columnist Jack Anderson, an unguided journalistic missile with multiple
warheads likely to strike anywhere. Quoting dialogue from critical meetings, the Anderson columns stripped bare the essential privacy of national-security planners as never before. But by then, and since the end
of June, 1971, the Nixon administration had been moving, undercover,
through a number of branches, to convert its feud with the adversary
press into full-scale guerrilla warfare, espionage and harassment.

Obsessed with foreign policy, as Nixon had always been, prevented
by the Supreme Court from enjoining the press to secrecy, the administration now saw the leaks as a matter of highest national concern. All
Presidents have been plagued by leaks; leakage of inside information is
part of the play and leverage within government politics. But the Nixon
administration was more sensitive than most. Nixon had first come to national prominence pursuing Alger Hiss for his part in the leakage of
national-security information to the Russians. Now he himself was being
leaked—not just casually, but persistently. Somewhere in the bureaucracy
were culprits who must be caught—and the bureaucracy was made up,
essentially, of Democrats, installed for decades. In his second administration Nixon proposed to shake up that bureaucracy from top to bottom, to
bring it under Presidential control. But for now, in the words of one of
the hard men of his staff, "we were a film of dust on top of the table;
underneath was the bureaucracy. Ike did nothing to replace the bureaucracy. Democratic appointees are all through the woodwork of this government." In the minds of many at the White House, with the publication of the Pentagon Papers it seemed that something akin to political
treason was going on in the administration. The staff men at the White
House, in their late thirties or mid-forties, had all come to maturity in
the postwar period of atom spies, Pumpkin Papers, charges of conspiracy in and out of government. What was going on now appeared to
fit the shape of the world they had grown up in.

One can only invent an imaginary scene to explain it all—a scene akin to that in the court of Henry II when that intemperate king burst out in the hearing of all, "Oh, who will rid me of this troublesome priest!" and a band of knights set out that day at dusk to murder Thomas à Becket at the high altar of Canterbury's cathedral. Historians, playwrights and novelists have mused ever since whether it was the king's intent to incite murder in the cathedral; they have generally blamed the act, for which Henry II did such grievous penance, on swordsmen who misinterpreted his wishes. The same kind of debate will follow the Nixon administration through history; but this moment is much too early for any outsider to pass judgment.

However it was, the President wanted the leaks plugged. He could not play at the table of international diplomacy with an open hand while his adversaries abroad held hands sealed and closed by the rules their countries gave their leadership. No other great world leader with whom Nixon dealt suffered from the inspection and exposure of a press as vigorous and searching as America's.

Yet it was more than hostility to the press, or the use of the press to embarrass him, that incubated what was to follow. Nixon had authorized, as early as 1969, a series of leak-plugging wire-taps on some twenty telephones. These taps, all of them legally permissible at the time in the name of national security, had proven only marginally successful in giving him the privacy of decision he sought. But in 1969, and even more intensely in 1970, he had come to see national security as involving not only America's enemies abroad, but the state's enemies at home, too.

One must recapture the mood of 1970. In all reality, terrorists had surfaced in America. On March 6th of that year, a quiet brownstone house on sedate West 11th Street in New York had exploded—and the city learned that a crude but effective bomb-making factory had been operating in one of its most fashionable neighborhoods. Three dead bodies were found in the ruins; two unidentified young women had fled. A week later, on March 13th, bomb threats caused the evacuation of 15,000 people from their work places in Manhattan. Two weeks later, two more people were blown up at a bomb-making factory in lower Manhattan. (By December of that year, the nationwide count of the FBI read: 3,000 bombings, and 50,000 threats of bombings sufficient to cause search or evacuation of buildings.) On August 7th, black militants seized a courtroom in San Rafael, California, and in the ensuing fracas the judge as well as three others were killed. A few weeks later, the mathematics research center at the University of Wisconsin was bombed, and an innocent research associate killed.

Such a wave of random political violence had never before been known in American history. Such episodes swept through the year as common weekly news, but the crest had come in spring—with Nixon's invasion of Cambodia, the following eruption of America's college campuses, the killings at Kent State University. The ferocity of press criticism and the violence of campus protest had touched the President more directly than any other event in his administration up to then. One of the three men closest to him said to me that fall, "They'd driven one President from office, they'd broken Johnson's will. Were they going to break another President? They had him on the edge of nervous breakdown." From outside, it appeared as if Richard Nixon had lost control. "Whirl is King," wrote Richard Rovere in *The New Yorker,* "and Richard Nixon is First Minister."

Richard Nixon had, however, not lost control. He was in that phase of his administration when he was still trying "to get a grip on things" and, with a quality characteristic of him, was passing on to overkill. He had on June 5th, 1970, met with the four chiefs of the main branches of the "American Intelligence Community"—the chiefs of the FBI, the CIA, the NSA (National Security Agency), the DIA (Defense Intelligence Agency), and sought an answer from them to what he suspected might be a nationwide conspiracy of terror and violence with possible international connections and support. What emerged from their discussions a few weeks later was a series of recommendations that, apparently, envisioned an American domestic espionage apparatus of a nature and scope unprecedented in the American process of democracy. Burglary, breaking and entering, wire-tapping—all such practices, legal and illegal, would, by this plan, be used against American private citizens to protect the state and the larger public interest against the unknown terrorists of the left who, likewise, recognized no legality and had already killed innocents. The full nature of this plan is unknown as yet except that its frightening scope was sufficient to cause John Dean, the prime figure at the crossroads of the Watergate affair, to sequester the papers as his best leverage for buying his way out of penalty.

The plan, as it was approved by the President, came to naught. J. Edgar Hoover, hate-figure of liberals for so many decades, opposed it; his opposition was on record, and decisive. The CIA, too, objected—it could find no foreign conspiracy inciting the new American terrorism. The plan never became operative. But the President's thinking was now established. "Out There," where Richard Nixon operated, were enemies as well as friends. If the President's critics were, later, never to understand his support Out There, the President's loyalists were never to understand the nature of his enemies Out There. And, in their pursuit of the enemy Out There, they were finally to outrage the tradition, of friends and enemies alike.

The President had thus, by the end of 1970, created a private climate of intemperance at the White House, yet taken or authorized no acts of illegality. And then, as we have noted, the Supreme Court had

made of national security a new kind of game—any newspaper was free
to publish whatever it could learn of national-security matters; yet the
government was still free to pursue those individuals in its administration
who had breached the law in making such information available. The
opposition of J. Edgar Hoover had frustrated the President in creating
a new governmental agency to police internal security by illegal means.
Now, with the leakage of the Pentagon papers, clearly stolen from national-security files, Nixon would set up his own White House "Special
Investigations Unit." The assignment was given to John Ehrlichman;
from Ehrlichman it was handed on to a deputy, Egil Krogh, Jr., a
straight-arrow man, utterly devoted to his immediate superior, Ehrlichman, and his supreme chief, Nixon. Said the President later, "I did impress upon Mr. Krogh the vital importance to the national security of
his assignment. . . . Because of the emphasis I put on the crucial importance of protecting the national security, I can understand how
highly motivated individuals could have felt justified in engaging in specific activities that I would have disapproved had they been brought to
my attention." Thus it became possible for some of his staff to indulge
themselves in an impossible casuistry: that there could be moral absolution for those who attempted to save the nation by whatever means,
legal or illegal; that they could use at home against American citizens
the same means used by the CIA against enemies abroad.

The leaks must be plugged, plumbers must be found—and so the
next question was how to staff the Plumbers Group. On the recommendation of Charles Colson, one E. Howard Hunt was recruited. On the
recommendation of Egil Krogh, G. Gordon Liddy was recruited. To this
group was added David Young, of Kissinger's national-security staff—
Kissinger being told simply that Young was going to work in Ehrlichman's office on "classification" of government documents. By July 6th,
Hunt was officially a $100-a-day "consultant" to the White House. By
July 19th, G. Gordon Liddy was aboard. And all three were soon installed in Room 16 in the basement of the Executive Office Building. The
dove-gray Executive Office Building, one of the largest in the capital,
once housed, in the days of American innocence, the entire State Department, War Department and Navy Department of the American government. It now houses the President's special staff in some of the more
beautiful offices of the capital, spacious high-ceilinged rooms with wood-
burning fireplaces. Few visitors venture down to its basement—which
holds the paymaster's office, Secret Service offices, the baggage room,
a cafeteria, a gymnasium and various dreary janitorial and administrative functionaries. It is a good place of concealment; the soldiers mobilized by the Army for the riots expected in 1970 during the Cambodian
invasion were concealed there; what else may be concealed is not of

record. But in Room 16 the Plumbers Group had an enclave of its own, with a private telephone line that bypassed the White House switchboard, and a roving commission inviting wild flights of the imagination. And these men had imagination.

The most interesting of the Plumbers Group was E. Howard Hunt, then fifty-two years old—a former CIA agent, a man who considered himself a patriot, a man with energy and imagination enough to have written more than forty-five spy-thrillers during his service in and out of government. Life had not been kind to Howard Hunt—he had never gone far in the CIA; he had been connected with the CIA Bay of Pigs fiasco, and at an early age he had retired from service. In his novels one can trace the disillusion, the growing bitterness of spirit of a man who felt his country was headed on a disaster course. Phrases in the mouths of his imaginary characters express a strange view of the world. Contempt: "So you hooked a job with the government, the last refuge of the inept and incompetent. Don't try to impress me with what you can push around" (From *Angel Eyes,* by Robert Dietrich, pseudonym for E. Howard Hunt). Ends and Means: Jake Webb, a hero in Hunt's novel *The Judas Hour,* is disturbed by the need to poison a mysterious industrialist called Palmer who advocates trade with Russia; Webb studies the contents of Palmer's briefcase, and then muses—"He had not liked the idea of poison, but now that he had read Palmer's notes and convinced himself that Palmer had been a smirking traitor, the thought of poison no longer bothered him." On Politics in Washington: "Behind the glittering diplomatic façade and the simpering sanctimoniousness it's a dirty gutter, as tough as anything north of 98th Street in New York." On National Purpose: One of Hunt's mythical heroes encounters a retired colonel in Lafayette Park and talks of war; the old colonel muses about the Korean War, ". . . the war we lost. Of it a famous officer said that it happened in the wrong place at the wrong time. I happen to disagree. If our concept of defense is to fight only wars of our own choosing then we have no defense at all. None at all. There was, however, one important thing lacking in your war, sir. . . . The will to win. Always an essential ingredient." And thus, on and on through the novels that Hunt ground out in his spare time, his heroes standing firm against homosexuality, graft, corruption, hypocrisy. But in the half-real, half-imaginary world where Hunt had once seen himself as a large actor, he had been reduced to a functionary in a Washington public-relations firm until resurrected and brought back to the White House with a national-affairs responsibility by his fellow Brown University alumnus Chuck Colson.

Hunt was now teamed with a character of another sort: G. Gordon Liddy, forty years old—pugnacious, violent, erratic or, if you will, a nut. Liddy had been sucked up almost automatically by the political-intake process. A hard-core right-winger, he had been a field agent and then a bureau supervisor for the FBI in Washington before moving into a position as deputy prosecutor in the district attorney's office in Dutchess County, New York, where he won the nickname "Cowboy." Liddy was a flamboyant—once he fired off a pistol with blanks to impress a jury before which he was pleading. A ferocious prosecutor, a difficult neighbor for those who lived close to him, he enjoyed himself once by leaping from a garage roof "like Batman" to frighten small children. Liddy won the Conservative Party's nomination for Congress in New York's then 28th Congressional District in 1968, but bowed out to endorse his incumbent rival, Congressman Hamilton Fish, Republican, in the general election. It was then arranged that he get a Washington job in the Nixon administration—as deputy to Assistant Treasury Secretary Eugene Rossides. Rossides was a determined advocate of gun control; but Liddy loved guns; and after Liddy had made an impassioned speech against gun control before the National Rifle Association, he was quietly let out of the Treasury Department. By this time Liddy had made friends in the administration—and was there, waiting for reassignment, when Krogh tapped him as just the man to help plumb the leaks that the administration wanted plugged. A thoroughly dangerous man.

Thus, then, a romantic and a hothead were matched and paired in partnership in the basement of the Executive Office Building, to find out who was leaking the secrets of the United States government to the press—with all the authority of the White House behind them, the magic switchboard ("the White House calling") opening access to all files and secrets and commanding all assistance from the State Department, CIA, FBI or Department of Justice. These two men had no sense of legality to restrain them. For them a higher "morality" of their own imagination gave sanction to their acts. And, however lowly their rank or responsibility in the many tiers between them and the top, it is with their morality that the later sense of national horror at Watergate begins. If these were instruments of the American government, if these could not be controlled, then no American anywhere was safe in home or privacy once someone at the top had invoked the cause of national security or "reasons of state." And they and their direct superiors interpreted the President's character and spirit as authority for their work.

Very few at the White House knew about the existence of the Plumbers Group. But for those who did, it became a roving service organization. Its first assignment, of course, was to investigate the leakage of the Pentagon Papers. Hunt and Liddy were equal to that. Flying out to Los Angeles, they "cased" the layout of offices of the psychiatrist who had treated Daniel Ellsberg, the thief of the Pentagon Papers. And then, conscripting CIA help, they mounted the entry and burglary of those offices. Other assignments followed. Colson wanted to find out more

about Senator Edward Kennedy's behavior on the night of Chappaquiddick—Hunt allegedly was available for a journey to New England
to gather information. Kennedy was a potential threat, as Democratic
candidate, to the President's 1972 race. Since State Department documents were available to him, Hunt pasted up with Scotch tape and Xerox
machines a totally fabricated cable purporting to make President John F.
Kennedy, Senator Kennedy's brother, a knowing party to and instigator
of the assassination of Ngo Dinh Diem, the unfortunate leader of South
Vietnam, in 1963. As in all Hunt's identifiable operations, a quality of
Walter Mittyish unreality colors the effort—how such a false cable could
have been floated while the then Secretary of State (Dean Rusk), the
then Ambassador to Vietnam (Henry Cabot Lodge) and the then National Security Adviser (McGeorge Bundy) were all still alive to denounce it as spurious passes understanding.

It was some time toward the end of 1971, the date still unclear,
that a moral line was crossed at the White House, and at the highest
level—by one of the apparently gentle group around the President, John
Ehrlichman. One should linger over the personality of John Ehrlichman.
Most men at the Nixon White House gave loyalty to the President only—
not to substance, not to cause, but to the person. Ehrlichman not only
gave loyalty to the President, but was concerned with the cause of good
government. He was one of those indispensable individuals, moreover,
who could translate policy, once set, into program and action. Over the
years, I had watched him transformed from the brisk and bustling
campaign administrator of 1968 to a grave public servant, slowly growing portly, with ever widening horizons. His shop was one of the few at
the White House where ideas were seriously entertained—good ideas,
too, on energy, on land-use policy, on urbanization, on preservation of
the American environment. Always courteous, mild, affable, an Eagle
Scout, he had an almost limitless capacity for work and a sense of history. It is this last, this sense of history he entertained, that makes the
tragedy of the man so poignant, his actions so incomprehensible until
courts or public hearings pass final judgment.

Ehrlichman was that man in authority at the White House who
might have been expected to recognize and then to stop in time the
rupture of morality that later poisoned the electoral campaign of the
President. In late fall of 1971, Ehrlichman discovered that the Plumbers
Group, over whom his office exercised jurisdiction, had gone far beyond
its technical mandate of leak plugging—it had burglarized the offices of
the psychiatrist of Daniel Ellsberg, an outrage. Had Ehrlichman then
summoned Hunt and Liddy to his office, leaned across the desk and done
the most difficult thing an administrator must sometimes do—which is
to say, "You're fired, and you may have to go to jail"—no Watergate
scandal would have occurred. According to the testimony of the FBI,

however, Ehrlichman simply said that he "did not agree with this method of investigation" and instructed the Plumbers "not to do this again." The two criminals were thus safe—gently chided but not punished, and free to go on. Ehrlichman had condoned a crime in the name of what seemed to him a higher principle; and his career, like that of so many others, was to be wrecked.

The work of the Plumbers at the White House, the Special Investigations Unit, tapered off, according to the President, "at the end of 1971." Though Hunt still maintained offices at the White House, both he and Gordon Liddy were, from 1972 on, devoting their energy and frenzied imaginations to the President's Committee to Re-Elect. It was the first time either had been involved in a Presidential campaign, and for two men with no scruples, large, if indefinite, ambitions, and no firm executive control from above, the opportunities were irresistibly tempting. Soon they were planting spies in the camp of Edmund Muskie; and later were attempting to plant spies in, or bug the offices of, George McGovern's headquarters. The catalogue of their caprices remains to be explored fully—as it will be by Congress. But they had brought with them, from their work at the White House, a moral absolution to breach the law, which now engendered a larger fancy, accepted by the leaders of the Committee to Re-Elect: They would wire-tap the very center of the opposition, the Democratic Party. The Plumbers Group could do it.

One must pause to absorb the political stupidity of the concept.

The Democratic Party today scarcely exists as a national organization—it is a national idea.[2] Its strength comes from its ideas, as did its disaster in 1972. Its national mechanisms and national secrets are almost non-existent, except when a Democratic President occupies the White House. In 1972, its Washington headquarters was a particularly forlorn place. It had moved in 1967, during the lush days of Lyndon Johnson's Presidency, from its old headquarters on K Street to splendid new offices of 17,000 square feet on the sixth floor of the Watergate Office Building at 2600 Virginia Avenue, where its annual rent was $97,750. The Watergate development was the capital city's exemplar of those shopping malls and centers we have examined previously. A real-estate developer's dream, financed substantially from abroad, a tax-shelter investment for the very rich, it provided in one self-contained package, behind its curving frontage, restaurants, apartments, bookstores, drugstores, meeting centers, halls, office space and a magnificent view of the Potomac. It was a fashionable place to be; fashionable people bought or rented apartments there, liked to be seen in its restaurants, and its floating population was always very large.

For political people, its chief attraction was the sixth-floor offices of the Democratic National Committee. There, all through 1971 and

2 See *The Making of the President—1968*, pp. 62-70.

1972, the Democratic National Committee's chief problem was simply how to stay alive. Its most intense internal conversations concerned the deficit of $9,000,000 that hung over the party from the 1968 campaign. For all its forlorn mood, the Democratic National Committee's headquarters was a pleasant place to visit—it was warm with that air of casual friendship which has vanished from most bureaucracies. One entered through plate-glass doors, and whether the receptionist recognized you or not, your smile of entry was your best credential. You passed in, wandered around, sat on people's desks, talked. Rarely did you need an appointment with anyone except Chairman Larry O'Brien or Treasurer Robert Strauss. And if you did talk with O'Brien, he had few secrets. His problems were public—he would pick up the latest Gallup Poll or Harris Poll and discuss it with you. His problem was to hold the party together—the labor people, the city people, the young people, the organization people, the black people, the wild liberals. He told his problems to everyone: Democratic newspapermen, Republican newspapermen, independent writers, college editors, all could get the same story from O'Brien—and one could always read about it in the papers. O'Brien in 1972 was a man presiding over an on-going disaster which was as public as the Watergate scandal was to become in 1973; he would speak about it mournfully but openly. A good clipping service would have provided the Committee to Re-Elect with more information than any number of wire-taps.

Nonetheless, in the enlarged imaginations of Hunt, Liddy and their amateur superiors, the bugging of the Democratic National Committee seemed a glistening target. Hunt had, by March, 1972, gone underground, as it were, and his private line in the White House had been disconnected. Liddy had moved in December of 1971, apparently on John Dean's recommendation, from the White House to the Committee to Re-Elect. There he had been assigned to the office of Jeb Magruder, as counsel to the acting chairman. Liddy and Magruder, according to Magruder, did not get along—Liddy was too hard, too ambitious, too difficult a character for anyone to get along with. When Magruder finally rid himself of Liddy, Liddy was reassigned in April as legal counsel to Maurice Stans, chairman of the Finance Committee.

At this point, the narrative becomes obscure. Stans would turn over no money to anybody without the authorization of John Mitchell or Jeb Magruder. According to the cover story told at the first Watergate trial, the money turned over to men like Hunt, Liddy and company was paid for general security purposes—and they then went off on their own, wildly, to violate Democratic national headquarters. According to later statements by Magruder, he had been present when the violation of the Democratic Party had been discussed first on January 24th, 1972, at the Department of Justice, in the presence of John Mitchell, then Attorney General, and of John Dean, then legal counsel to the President. The project had been repeatedly discussed in February and March, until the word to go and breach the law had been given.

On Memorial Day weekend, the first bugging devices were planted in Democratic national headquarters—one on a telephone line to the desk of Lawrence O'Brien, the National Chairman; the other on the line of R. Spencer Oliver, executive director of the Democratic Committee's State Chairmen's Association—and the first photographs of Democratic Party documents had been taken. The bug on Spencer Oliver's phone worked, but the bug on O'Brien's did not. According to hearsay testimony, the "takes," or transcripts of this first effort, pleased John Mitchell, the former Attorney General, but he wanted more. All in all, perhaps 200 telephone conversations had been recorded up to this point, over a period of little more than two weeks. According to the testimony of James McCord, the electronics expert who supervised the bugging, appetite was growing: Could an efficient bug be installed on the O'Brien phone and perhaps something more effective—not only a phone tap, but a bug to pick up conversations in O'Brien's room? On the night of June 16th–17th this act was to be performed.

The absurdity of the idea still appalls in retrospect—the idea that there *were* secrets of value to anyone in the brawling, boisterous, open Democratic Party, whose appeal to the American people for so many generations had come from its air of humanity, its common vulgarity. The National Democratic Party is not a conspiracy; it is a continuing commotion, baffling to all logical, managerial-minded men. But the buggers and their superiors were insisting on penetrating what they thought must be a conspiracy, and they had to do better than bug the phone of Spencer Oliver. Somewhere on the sixth floor of the Watergate there must be secrets, and certainly on the wire of Lawrence O'Brien, if anywhere. Thus, on June 17th they moved to find the secrets on O'Brien's phone, like primitives trying to puzzle out an enemy tribe's baffling and superior magic. The conspiratorial theory of history was about to destroy its true believers.

What was going on reached the public for the first time in the morning papers of June 18th, 1972; and what people learned as they opened their papers, if their papers carried the story at all, read like farce.

At 2:30 on the morning of June 17th, 1972, a night watchman at one of the Watergate office buildings noticed that someone had taped back the latch on the door to the stairwell leading up from the basement garage. The watchman removed the tape. Twenty minutes later, returning, he noticed that the latch had been retaped. He called the police, and three roving plainclothesmen of Washington's beefed-up crime patrol responded and found that the latch on every door leading off the stairwell on every floor of the building up to the sixth was taped; so was the latch at the eighth floor. But on the sixth floor, the door to the offices of the Democratic National Committee had been jimmied. The police burst in with guns drawn, the first stories reported. From behind a partition near Chairman Lawrence O'Brien's office came the plea, "Don't shoot," and out came five men, hands up, wearing surgical gloves and possessing at that moment either in person or in their hotel rooms a kitful of burglary tools, two 35 mm. cameras, forty rolls of unexposed film, three tear-gas pens, a radio transmitter-receiver, two bugging devices, a wig and $5,300 in crisp, consecutively numbered $100 bills.

The scene as first described was burlesque. Five cowering criminals caught red-handed, three of them Cubans, the fourth a Miami businessman with a taste for adventure and intrigue, the fifth a former CIA security specialist. All were marched off in handcuffs to police headquarters, where investigation began—an investigation that was to go on, and on, and on for over a full year, setting off the most dramatic shake-up of American government in its history.

For the moment, however, the story seemed modest. On Sunday, June 18th, 1972, the Washington *Post* printed as its second lead on the front page: "5 HELD IN PLOT TO BUG DEMOCRAT PARTY OFFICE." The next day's headline read: "GOP SECURITY AIDE AMONG 5 ARRESTED IN BUGGING AFFAIR," bylined by Bob Woodward and Carl Bernstein, a joint signature that was to become famous. On the 20th, Eugene Bachinski, another Washington *Post* reporter, turned up from police sources the information that two little notebooks carried by the culprits contained notations bearing the name of E. Howard Hunt. Beside the name in one notebook were the initials "W.H."; in the other was written "W. House." From these notebooks all trails would lead, finally, to the White House itself.

It was clear to Howard Hunt and Gordon Liddy, from the moment their walkie-talkie communication with the burglars in Watergate ended in disaster, that they were in trouble. Hunt, reportedly, went to the Howard Johnson Motel across the street to telephone a lawyer, then to his White House office to pick up $8,500 in cash, then to visit his lawyer at 3:30 in the morning, and shortly thereafter fled to California to think things over before returning to Washington. Liddy was more practical. By midday, Saturday, he was in the offices of the Committee to Re-Elect shredding as many documents as he could as fast as he could. And by this time word of the episode had reached California, where John Mitchell, Jeb Magruder, and two other Committee functionaries, Frederick LaRue and Robert C. Mardian, were all weekending with their wives. Magruder immediately telephoned to his personal assistant, Robert Reisner, back in Washington, to remove the folder marked "Gemstone," which made Magruder's complicity in the Watergate affair quite clear. The visitors in California knew they were in trouble. But at the White House it was worse.

At the White House, a minor panic had set in. The President was weekending in Key Biscayne—his trip to Moscow had taken a good deal of energy and emotion, and he was still unwinding. From the police, staff members at the White House had learned almost immediately, even before the Washington *Post,* that the seized notebooks contained the name of Howard Hunt and a connection to the White House. Some time between 5:00 and 6:00 P.M. on Saturday, Ehrlichman, who had been well aware of the Plumbers Group's general operations, called Colson to find out where Howard Hunt was. Colson could not locate him. By Sunday, Hunt's office in the Executive Office Building had been cleared out. The President's legal counsel, John Dean, had the safe in Hunt's office opened and emptied; eight cartons of documents were swiftly carried away to safekeeping. There remained now the problem of cover-up: how to restrain, contain, manipulate a story which, in essence, was that of conspiracy, crime and contempt for the democratic process.

At this point, this writer must suspend the story as narrative, for he can bring no original testimony to bear which will not, some time in 1973, become available in public-hearing or court-tested facts as to exactly who authorized the Watergate conspiracy. And—even more importantly—how and when the full facts became known to the President, and how large a role the members of his staff had in preventing the arrest, indictment and conviction of the true criminals. Obstruction of justice is at least as great a crime as burglary itself, and, in this case, politically far more significant. A liberal administration is always made vulnerable by its many promises—it promises so much to so many that always it is forced to betray one or another of the groups to which it has made conflicting promises. A conservative administration makes only one overriding promise—it promises the citizens that they will have law-and-order. When it betrays this promise, it betrays all; when it breaches law, it invites savagery; and those who betrayed the promise of this conservative cause in 1972 were traitors not only to the law and country, but to their own cause as well. Nixon had made the conservative promise his own in the campaign of 1968. "We're going to have a new Attorney General," he promised repeatedly, scoring Johnson's Attorney General Ramsay Clark as soft on crime. And as supreme keeper of his law-and-order promise Nixon named John Mitchell.

There remain, then, certain observations which justice and fairness require to be made to explain the actions of the guilty—but in no sense to exonerate their defiling of the political process of a free people.

§ The case of the guilty, as I have heard it, runs as follows:
From 1968 on, the American political process had been increas-

ingly subject to violence, to riot, to mob pressure. The Democratic convention in Chicago was made a carnival of violence by the planning, plot-
ting and conspiracy of a band of men who, in the name of peace, attempted to take over the streets and bludgeon a Democratic convention
to compliance with their will. This violence, so runs the story, was
brought home to Richard Nixon personally on the night of October 29th,
1970, when he saw its raw and ugly face while he was campaigning in
San Jose, California—demonstrators throwing eggs and rocks at his car,
trying to smash the windows, pounding on its sides. "You had to see
their faces," said someone who was in the car with Richard Nixon that
night, "the hate in those faces—it got to him."

Thus, according to their story, it was their job to see to it that the
Republican convention of 1972, originally called to meet in San Diego,
would not be subject to violence, or the television portrait of violence.
This, they claim, was why they set up a security and intelligence operation at the Committee to Re-Elect: to find out how much violence might
spurt in San Diego, in volatile Southern California—what demonstrations the Democrats or their outriders might be planning in order to
make the Republican convention as vivid a scar on memory as the
demonstrations in Chicago, 1968.

This explanation does not, in any sense, even begin to explain the
operations of the Plumbers and the other groups at the White House;
they had begun to breach the law as early as 1971; others, perhaps earlier. It explains only how higher authorities deluded themselves into con-
doning what was going on.

§ There is the memory of self-delusion, at which most of us—including this writer, who considered himself so experienced—must wince.
It was impossible to believe what was going on, while it was happening.

I remember receiving a telephone call from the office of Jeb Magruder in early October, 1972, saying that he would like to see me next
time I was in Washington. Invitation on the Committee's part to come
and call was rare, so I went.

Magruder was confiding in me, in his most earnest and warming
manner. Watergate? "This operation was peanuts," he said, "they were
using junk stuff." He sneered at the equipment used—if the Committee
had really been involved, it would have been done competently, he implied. It was inconceivable, as he told his story so straightforwardly,
that this boyish man could be lying.

"Liddy and Hunt and the Cubans," said Magruder, "were zealots.
Liddy and I never got along, so he went down to work for Maury Stans.
We had thirty-five different divisions here. Three out of every four dollars were spent at my direction—if there was a secret fund, I didn't
know about it. We agreed on what levels of expenditure for each period
of time. Once I authorized them, the finance division paid them out of

the general funds. Once I sign off on these funds, I don't know where they're going. . . ."

At this point, Magruder thrust a paper across the desk to me. It was an authorization for $1,625,000 to be sent to the television-radio November Group of Peter Dailey, the budget for the last two weeks of advertising. "Do you think Clark [MacGregor] and I will ever know what stations he's going to be running programs on? Or what every one of these messages or programs will say? We authorize funds for activities. We authorized funds for Gordon Liddy for our convention at San Diego, to get as much information on the rioters and brawlers who might be there as we could. We changed the site from San Diego to Miami because we were told that there might be 250,000 demonstrators who would tear the city down. Liddy did a good job on that. . . . I can't guarantee you that someone else didn't ask him to slip over to the Democratic National Committee. . . ." Magruder presented himself as innocent. And I trusted him. So did almost everyone else. "How could that All-American boy with that sweet wife and those wonderful children turn out to be such a viper?" asked John Mitchell of a friend later, shortly after Magruder had implicated both Mitchell and John Dean in foreknowledge of the Watergate bugging.

Magruder made a final observation in our conversation about Watergate. I asked him about the flow of cash through the headquarters, which by now was incomprehensible. The use of cash, said Magruder, was something that had developed from the experience of the 1968 campaign. In the 1968 campaign, the Republicans had operated on credit cards. Credit cards always enlarge the imaginations and appetites of operatives sent out on the road—lobster and steak, wine and spirits, fine suites and first-class flights can be put on a credit-card tab and when the bills come in months later all is forgotten in the euphoria of victory. The Republican campaign of 1968 had wound up with something like $3,000,000 worth of unexpected credit-card tabs. Mitchell would have none of that this time. Participants in the much larger enterprise of 1972 would be required to turn in vouchers for funds—they would pay cash for their tickets, their hotel bills and the necessary purchases of local advertising, local radio time, local advance work. Local purveyors of services, who deal with politicians, usually demand cash payment in advance. The campaign would operate, where it could, on cash advances to people sent on specific assignment.

Unhappily, Maurice Stans was too successful—there was too much cash around.

§ The exposure of the Watergate scandal was a triumph of the press and of the fortitude of a Federal judge, John J. Sirica. In this exposure, the Washington *Post* led the way, CBS followed, *The New York Times* ran third—exactly as they placed on the imaginary White House hate-list. The rest of the American press came in nowhere. When, finally, in 1973, the rest of the press joined in the hunt, it reminded one of Eugene McCarthy's famous description in 1968—"the press is a little like the blackbirds in the fall—one flies off the telephone line, the others all fly away; and the other one comes back and sits down and they all circle and they all come down and sit . . . in a row again." By the spring of 1973, long after the campaign was over, the press was swooping and wheeling over the bodies of the Nixon administration, without mercy or compassion, in full-pack cry; and as the administration seemed to be coming apart, every man who had had a part in it was made a target for whatever charge, whatever allegation, could be milked from whatever source. The outcry, the tumult, the juiciness of personalities and details was to make of Watergate a story outrunning in its continuous daily headlines and excitement even the outbreak of World War II.

But there was in this outcry the danger that the voice of the American people themselves, their expression of opinion on the known facts, on the clear issues of 1972, might be forgotten. So there remained then, in any reporter's mind, the question: How much did the Watergate affair influence the plebiscite of 1972?

Considerably, but not critically, is the judgment of this reporter. It was customary, during and after the campaign, to say that the American people did not care. Wise men agreed, and the polls supported them, that it meant little—that Americans had become callous, too cynical to worry about morality in government. Yes, they had heard about Watergate and Republican money shenanigans by early October, reported the Gallup Poll—52 percent of all those queried had read or heard of the scandal; but four out of five felt it was not really a strong reason for voting for George McGovern. Two weeks later, by October 19th, the Harris Poll reported that 76 percent of all those polled had heard about or were following the story—and 62 percent of all those polled dismissed the matter as "just politics." Thus stood the majority opinion at the time.

This writer, who followed the campaign from beginning to end, enters here a dissenting opinion. Without any statistical or hard evidence except that which his ear brought him from conversations with anonymous Americans at doorsteps, rallies, the wire enclosures at airports where they gathered to watch candidates arrive, this reporter found that Americans were talking about Watergate—and they were bothered by it.

Watergate did not, demonstrably, change the minds of those who went to the polls and voted for Richard Nixon by 61 to 38 percent. But those who went to the polls in 1972 were disconcertingly few. The number of actual voters fell to the lowest percentage of eligible voters in a quarter of a century. A remarkable pattern was perceived in this voting, reported first by Pat Caddell, McGovern's vote analyst, in a post-election

study. Always previously in a national election, in those states where a
Governor or a Senator runs in the same year as a President, the voting
on the Presidential line has exceeded the number of those who voted in
the Gubernatorial or Senatorial races. It has always been as if the voters
come to the polls to choose a President and thousands of them simply
do not bother to cast a vote for the lesser men who govern locally. Not
so in 1972. Of the forty-two states that offered their voters such multiple
choices in November, 1972, the votes for Governor or Senator in nineteen states of the Union exceeded the votes cast for the Presidential
candidates—millions of Americans rejected both national candidates.
And in twenty-three states of the Union, despite the enormous number
of potential new voters from eighteen to twenty-one years of age added
by the youth amendment, the total vote for President was actually *less*
than it had been in 1968. McGovern had lost the nation by August; yet
Nixon somehow, for some reason, failed to maximize his potential support.

In this writer's opinion, it is possible that at least three or four
million Americans were so disillusioned by both candidates that they
chose not to vote at all. Had it not been for Watergate, it is quite possible that Richard Nixon's margin would have been increased by another three or four million votes—that, indeed, his stunning 61–38
victory might have gone as high as 65–35, for a record that might
never again be approached in American two-party history. The Watergate affair blew that opportunity.

Contrariwise—had the full story of the Watergate scandal and its
companion fund-raising scandals been thoroughly exposed during the
campaign, Nixon's margin would probably have been diminished to that
of most ordinary candidates who run in the 55–45 area of choice. But
it is doubtful that in 1972, given the moods, emotions and public issues
of that year, George McGovern or any other Democrat could have been
elected.

The facts remain—and the after-myth of a contrived or rigged
election cannot change them. Americans were given an open choice of
ideas, a free choice of directions, and they chose Richard Nixon. The
mandate he received was of historic dimensions; whether or not Watergate was to erase the meaning of that mandate as the Vietnam War erased
Lyndon Johnson's mandate of 1964, and as court-packing eroded Franklin D. Roosevelt's of 1936, remains to be seen. But the shaping of the
Nixon mandate in the public mind in the fall of 1972 remains one of the
watershed markers of the end of the postwar world. And with the shaping of that mandate, in the fall campaign, this story proceeds.

CHAPTER TWELVE

THE SHAPING OF THE MANDATE: MEN AND MACHINERY

The clearest over-all view of the campaign was at all times the President's own.

I called on him in mid-September. I had seen him last in China—this was the first time since the campaign had begun. McGovern was in full swing across the country and the President was thought to be eluding battle.

He was tired at the end of the day, and came out from behind his desk to sit on the small chair beside the fireplace, offering a choice of drinks—milk, coffee or Coca-Cola. I said that the Oval Office was beautiful these days, that Mrs. Nixon's taste for bright yellow seemed to light the room up. "We call it gold," he corrected crisply. Then, as we began to talk, Ted Kennedy's name came up, and the President volunteered that after the shooting of George Wallace he had provided Secret Service protection for Kennedy, although Kennedy was not a candidate. "His mother called me up," explained the President, then added that he felt he should provide the guards—next to himself, Teddy Kennedy received more threatening mail than anyone in the country. "I felt I should," he repeated several times. Then he turned directly to the campaign.

"The new majority," he said, was what this election was all about. His speechwriters at the convention had wanted him to call it "the new coalition." Others had argued for "the new Republican majority." He insisted on "the new majority," however, because he felt he wasn't putting groups together in a coaliton the way Roosevelt had—he was trying to cut across groups, binding people in every group who had the same ideas. The Republicans, he said, had been the natural majority party from 1864 to 1928—Wilson had been a minority President in 1912, would have gone down in 1916 "except for the war." Since 1932, however, it had been the other way around, the Democrats had been the natural majority party.

What, I asked, was he doing in September, 1972, to achieve another such reversal?

He fielded the question technically, with precision. "My role from the standpoint of operations is limited until the last two or three weeks, both by necessity and politics. There'll be one event a week until the last three weeks, and then only the big states—New York, Pennsylvania, Illinois, Michigan, Ohio, California, Texas." And, "I'm not going into the states for the purpose of supporting Senate or House candidates, the way FDR did, or the way I did in 1970."

Then, on his own, in the way in which he likes to wheel a conversation by his own logic, "Now let me give you the reasons back of that," he said.

In his opinion, Congressional candidates went up or down in a Presidential year by the national sweep, and this business of a President going in, putting his arm around a local candidate was "at best a mixed bag." He wanted the Republican candidates to do it on their own—to tie themselves to the President on foreign policy, particularly, and "on domestic policy as much as they can." It was up to them to tie their local opponents to McGovern. Agnew was going to circulate, supporting Congressional candidates—"That's his job, that's a Vice-President's job, I did it in 1956"—and the President's family was campaigning for local candidates also.

Then, I asked, would there be no Truman-style "Give 'em Hell" campaign against the Democratic Congress?

"No, sir," he said vehemently.

The public polls, he explained, were giving him a 34-point lead, the greatest indicated margin in American history, but "I have no illusions about polls, and neither have you, Teddy. No President except Washington ever won by two to one. The best was 63/37 for Roosevelt. The optimum for a Republican, from a smaller base, was the Eisenhower landslide of 1956—that was 57½ to 42½. And unemployment in '56 was less than 5 percent, plus the 3-point bulge on Hungary and Suez that Ike picked up at the end. That campaign—the spread between Ike and Stevenson was never more than 10 points from September 1st on."

He, Nixon, was working for this new majority, not a Republican majority, because, "Well," he said, "I'm not stupid." He was working to get the people he called Truman Democrats. Not only people like John Connally, but people like Eugene Klein and Eugene Wyman. They were calling him up. I appeared surprised that Wyman, Humphrey's chief fund-raiser, was now helping Nixon. He chuckled. A lot more Democrats were coming over to him than met the eye, he said, but they couldn't come out publicly for fear of hurting the Congressmen and Senators they supported.

At this point he was becoming very animated, his hands weaving, leaning forward, persuading. Democratic Presidential candidates usually ran *behind* their local Congressmen, he said, as Truman had in 1948. But Republicans like himself usually ran *ahead* of their local Congressmen. Everywhere this year, in his polls, there was at least a 10-point spread between what Richard Nixon was drawing and what the local Republican Congressmen were drawing. The moment he tied himself to the theme of a "new Republican majority," well, "the moment I do that, I pull myself down to their level, and . . . part of our problem is that we have a lot of lousy candidates; the good ones will go up with me, the bad ones will go down.

"My view," he said, "is to continue to go out and campaign for a 'new majority.' Suppose after the election we win by 55 over 45—the Ike majority over Stevenson. Then, after that, you still have the problem of governing the country. If I don't succeed [in pulling a Republican Congressional majority in with him], I then have that problem." He spoke about the need of being able to use his mandate, the effect of a landslide that didn't pull along a Republican Congress, the need of holding Southern Democrats who would be willing to go along with him. And, summing it up, "I have to not have drawn the sword on the Congress I'll be working with."

It was a Presidential view of the campaign, and then he passed from his onetime favorite subject, the politics of politics, to his new view, the politics of state.

He needed this coming mandate for foreign affairs. His administration had been able to do more in foreign affairs than he had ever dreamed of when he came in—except for the hope of finding a more rational North Vietnam. China. Russia. Western Europe. Progress everywhere. The Middle East was still difficult, "but it's a hell of a lot better for them not to be killing each other every day." We were going to keep our commitments to Israel, but the job had to be finished there. Africa he regarded more as a European problem than as an American one; but Latin America was an American problem, we needed new initiatives there. "For twenty-five years we were frozen in ice, and now it's thawing. But we can slip into the water and drown. When ice thaws, it's the period of greatest danger as well as greatest hope."

Thus, back to the politics of 1972, why he needed this mandate. "We come in with 43 percent of the vote, with the establishment giving us nothing but a kick in the butt, the press kicking the bejeezus out of us, the intellectuals against us." He admitted they had given him a little credit for the opening with China and Russia. But he had operated from a position of weakness because foreign powers thought he had no support at all; they read *Time* Magazine and the Washington *Post* and *The New York Times,* and thought he had no support; so it all had to be done by personal diplomacy. And the May 8th decision—that was the biggest gamble of all.

Now, if he got this mandate, the expressed support of the people— "If we can win and win well, we can talk to China with great authority, to the Soviet Union, to Japan." We, America, had to take the lead in reducing tensions, in reducing the burden of arms everywhere. SALT Talks I had been difficult, SALT Talks II would be even more difficult. He needed that personal mandate. He'd been reflecting—except for Chou En-lai, he now was the senior statesman in the world. The others were all gone, Adenauer, Churchill, Macmillan, De Gaulle. There were new faces in Russia, in Japan. A solid majority would give him the authority to speak and act.

He was not very worried about his ability to lead in foreign policy if he got the mandate he hoped for. In the foreign field, the President leads and Congress follows. Take the Truman 80th Congress (Republican-dominated), he said. They passed the Marshall Plan and the Greece-Turkey aid plan. "Truman led, and we followed. I voted for them." It was George McGovern's departure from bipartisan foreign policy that was "his major mistake—that was the real cruncher, that's what got to men like George Meany; what makes a man leave his party is foreign policy and national defense.

"But in domestic policy," said the President, "you can't count on Congress following." In the 80th Congress, he himself had split with Truman on the Taft-Hartley Act, civil rights, price controls. The most a President could expect even with a landslide, if the mandate was big enough, was that they'd follow him for the first year. He was going to say, in this instance, the country has spoken, and put out his own views on welfare, on a program of fiscal responsibility, on other matters.

I said that by the time he ended his second term it would be 1976, two hundred years since Independence, and suggested that perhaps now was the moment for the entire Constitution to be overhauled—how could you govern the cities under the old Constitution?

He shook his head decisively. He rejected the idea of a Constitutional revision. "When you talk of something as radical, as far-reaching as a Constitutional Convention or reorganizing the cities—the American people, they're fed up with being used as an experiment. What you're seeing now is a very pragmatic administration."

Then he rose from his chair, went to his desk, pulled out a three-page paper and said, "Look at this—this is history in the making."

The paper was a ribbon copy, with hand-scrawled corrections, of a memorandum that Nelson Rockefeller had just sent him. It had impressed the President, and as I tried to scan the memorandum while he talked, his conversation and the words of the memorandum blurred. The memorandum, as my eye tried to grab it, was a summation of what Nelson Rockefeller had learned in fourteen years of state and national politics. Rockefeller was writing about the different levels of government in America, how they denied people a "sense of control," how all these levels of Federal, state, city, county government had to be separated out in the public mind, each with its own responsibilities, each with its own tax resources. All the while the President was continuing to talk, saying, "What Nelson feels is that we've got to get at what will work and what won't work."

The President rejected my approach to the Constitution and the cities as "revolutionary." He was saying, "We know how things work here—Ehrlichman's crowd, Kissinger's crowd, they know how things work. Lou Harris used the phrase 'change that works.' We don't want too violent a change. We know all the plays, we're going to be in a position to present to the country changes in the system that will work."

He went on to reflect on the first four years in domestic policy. "Let me say this—those first four years weren't an easy period. When I came in, LBJ couldn't even leave the White House—he was right, he shouldn't have subjected himself to violence. But I can travel in all fifty states now. We started with the country in a hell of a shape. You've forgotten the days when 200,000 people marched on the White House. We've been fighting uphill on foreign policy. But domestic policy! It's been uphill all the way; we didn't have the mandate, we didn't have the Congress. Now we've got an opportunity we couldn't even dream of four years ago, but I don't see it in terms of a revolutionary hundred days. We've got to look over our institutions and return them to old values. . . ."

It was now well past my allotted hour with the President, but he seemed more cheerful and animated than when he had begun. He invited me to stroll with him from the White House over the street to the Executive Office Building, where people were waiting for him. The guards came to attention with a click as he passed; an umbrella mysteriously appeared in the hand of a guard to shelter him from the rain, and he was now making casual conversation. I was asking him about China and he was saying that it was too sensitive to talk about because both the Russians and the Chinese were so security-conscious. But as we walked he rambled about Chou En-lai—the charm of that man, how gay, how humorous Chou was. They said Chou was getting old, recalled the President, but he was tough. Chou En-lai could sit through a negotiating session of six or seven hours at a stretch; but he, Nixon, so much younger, couldn't take more than four such hours. And how both Chou and Mao still liked to talk about their Long March. Then we were in his hideaway at the Executive Office Building, where he wanted to show me his Asian mementoes—vases, jars, lacquers. He was particularly fond of a Gandhara head someone had sent him—"That's a Greek Buddha head from Afghanistan," he said. It was a perfect piece.

It was time to go, and I noted that waiting for him were Senator Bill Brock of Tennessee and Ken Rietz, the youth coordinator of the Committee for the Re-Election of the President, obviously there to talk the youth politics of the election campaign. The President gave them a brief session, then returned to the White House to dine alone. He had been up early that day—and, in campaign terms, had scored in the news by addressing the State Department's international conference on narcotics control. Most of his day had been spent privately on foreign affairs and Vietnam, and three days later Bloody Thursday's figures would come up with a historic marker. Bloody Thursday this week, on September 21st, 1972, would show zero Americans killed. In between, 46,000 had died in combat. The U.S. role in the war was winding down, and the President was thrusting his main campaign at the people as the politics of state. He would begin his personal campaign on Friday, when he would fly to Texas to stop overnight at the ranch of John Connally and apply himself, without much relish, to a re-election that was in the bag.

For George McGovern, the campaign was sadly different.

The drain on McGovern himself, up to early September, had already been exhaustive. There had been not only the spring march across the country and the excitement of Miami Beach; there had been a full year of campaigning before that, in 1971. This claim on his energy had been met by all the physical resources that years of clean living and a country-boy upbringing had stored up. He had begun to drain his last nervous and emotional energy during the six-week challenge on the California delegation; then, after the convention, when his schedulers had finally granted him a two-week respite for thought and rest in South Dakota, the Eagleton affair had piled up on him. August had been a month of disaster—not only the Eagleton affair, but the Salinger affair, and the futile courtship of the AFL/CIO, the wooing of Daley of Chicago and Lyndon Johnson in Texas. And on top of that, his headquarters in Washington dripped gossip and steamed with dissent, like a boiler leaking at every joint.

Thus, for months, when the real campaign began, he had been engaged in crisis. Yet the campaign required, above all, concept, theme and organization. The first of his final themes came almost by chance. He had been invited in late August, with several key members of his staff, to dinner at the Governor's mansion in Minnesota, and the old champion of liberal democracy, Hubert Humphrey, had come bustling in late. Humphrey had been crisp and eloquent. The first job, he said, was to reunite the party; and the best way to reunite the party, old and new elements, was to remind all of them that it was still the party of "little guys against the big guys" and raise the question of who owned this government anyhow. Humphrey reflected that in 1968 he had wanted to talk about bread-and-butter issues, but had been harried to desperation by people who wanted him to talk about the war. Now the roles were reversed—George wanted to talk about the war, but people in 1972 wanted to hear about bread-and-butter.

George had agreed. George McGovern was a man of the Senate who liked to please his colleagues, and was eager to agree with any good-willed proposition brought to him by a friend. The inner compass of the man had been set on course long before, in his youth, and the grand strategy of the campaign had been set in his heart years ago. His theme, always, undeviatingly, was Good against Evil, Light against Darkness. But for now, the pragmatic campaign themes would be little guys against big guys, and bread-and-butter.

It was late to be selecting themes and concepts, but McGovern flew back to Washington and, on August 30th, summoned the squabbling chieftains of his staff to an evening at his home. There, in his mild way, he tried to crack heads together, assign responsibilities, insist on coordination of themes, statements, travel, research and schedules, and prepared to take off on Labor Day, with eight weeks left to go.

I joined the McGovern campaign Labor Day week seeking some coherence, mindful of how much all of us reporters had underrated George McGovern only eight months before in January. The planning as it had been explained to me now seemed clear—and I wanted to see it work. This week would be "tax week," devoted to the inequities of the national tax structure; next week would be "inflation week," on the "cost to you" of this unending war; then would come "corruption week," on the scandals of the Republican Party; and other weeks would follow, each week geared to a single theme, a single message to be pounded home to Americans. As the candidate moved, so ran the plan, the television campaign would begin—on September 10th. On September 25th they would review the planning after having measured, via Pat Caddell's polling, where the best chance for the 270 electoral votes bearing victory lay. By October 10th they would have chosen the targets of concentration for the last three-week drive; and thus, in a garrison finish, over the line to victory on November 7th, as McGovern finally made the people realize what Richard Nixon was doing to them.

The red-white-and-blue *Dakota Queen II* howled out of Washington Sunday night before Labor Day; and suddenly one was transported back to 1960, when Richard Nixon, too, thought he could swallow the continent in a gulp, coast to coast in a single day. McGovern was off: to Hilton Head, South Carolina, to meet with Southern Governors; to

Barberton and Chippewa Lake, Ohio, to address union rallies; to Oakland, California, and then by helicopter to a labor rally at the Alameda County fairgrounds; and on to Seattle, for a late-night street rally. On the next day, beating down the West Coast—to a surplus-food distribution center for the unemployed in Seattle, to illustrate before the cameras his concern about people; to a senior citizens' retirement center in Portland; and on to Los Angeles that night. The next day, starting in Los Angeles, even more strenuous: an address to the Board of Rabbis of Southern California, to shore up the shaky Jewish vote ("You've got to admit George McGovern's got courage," said one of his advisers, "he says the same thing all across the country, the same thing to the rabbis in Los Angeles as he says to the rabbis in New York"); a noon address to the quadrennial convention of the International Association of Machinists and Aerospace Workers in Los Angeles; a visit to a San Diego aerospace plant; and then, that afternoon, back across the Southwest to Dallas, Texas.

The Dallas rally was a first-class rally. In Dallas, liberal Democrats are still an underground, suppressed by the dominant ethic of the money men and the tyranny of the proprietary press, as hostile to McGovern as the liberal press was to Nixon. (The Dallas *Morning News,* for example, had announced McGovern's arrival and rally on its eighth page, the front page being dominated by a local hotdog-eating contest.) Despite all, the McGovern loyalists turned out a night crowd of 3,000 enthusiasts, waving their blue banners, signs held high: "MAKE AMERICA HAPPEN AGAIN, MC GOVERN." "MC GOVERN—WE LOVE YOU." "COME HOME AMERICA—MC GOVERN." "FOUR MORE YEARS—NO THANKS." Tired as he was, McGovern was buoyed by the crowd. No longer the Gentle George of his television commercials but George the Wrathful, he struck out on the week's pre-planned theme, the inequity of the tax structure: "A businessman can deduct the price of his $20 martini lunch and you help pay for it, but a workingman can't even deduct the price of his bologna sandwich."

The crowd loved every word, cheering and rocking with excitement, at one with McGovern. But, watching the faces of the crowd, standing among them, slowly at that point I perceived a pattern in the threads of the week's campaign. But not at all the pattern described to me a few days before in Washington. The problem in Texas, I had been told by the locals, was to "de-radicalize" George McGovern's image. But the crowd gathered here was the same kind of crowd George McGovern's volunteers had assembled for the primaries—young people, blond, handsome, loose-limbed in loose clothing, with the look, many of them, of students. They wanted the radical, crusading George McGovern—he was giving the audience what it wanted. But there were no blacks in this group, and there were few Latin-Americans. Moreover, on the terrace from which he spoke, another element was missing. The most prominent Democrat in Dallas, for example, Robert S. Strauss, was not there. Strauss, the Democratic Committee's former National Treasurer, soon to be its new National Chairman, had found it necessary to be out of town the day his party's candidate for President was scheduled to arrive. So, too, had Dolph Briscoe, the Democratic nominee for Governor. Two state commissioners, Democrats, were indeed on the platform. But no Congressmen, nor the Democratic County Chairman.

The next day reinforced the pattern, and the long day, typical, ran like this:

§ McGovern up early to wander through a Safeway supermarket, where he paused by the meat counter to look at ground beef and comment to the housewives ("The Nixon inflation is ground into every pound of hamburger that you buy"), then to examine prices of cornflakes, pears, bananas for the benefit of the cameras to score home the story of inflation for the evening news shows; off to Houston, where NASA's Manned Spacecraft Center had been scheduled as a "visual" stop for the television cameras; and after examining with the intelligent curiosity of a serious man the modules, space chambers and experiments in the garish-painted barn-like halls, he left in the rain. And as he left, he was told that back in Washington two other disputes had exploded in his headquarters, the resignation of his voter-registration chief, Congressman Frank Thompson, and the reported, but untrue, resignation of Gordon Weil. Momentarily depressed, he turned to his press secretary, Dick Dougherty, and said, "I feel like one of those guys up there in space, walking out of the space ship, and the guy down there below who should be pumping the oxygen, he's walking out on you."

§ From Houston up the valley of the Mississippi. Late-afternoon stop in Peoria, Illinois—the home of good whiskey and the giant Caterpillar Tractor plant. At the Caterpillar plant, skilled workers make $6 an hour, and with the plant working on overtime, wages in 1972 were running $180–$200 a week in central Illinois; the land around was green and the fall hunting was good. Here the United Automobile Workers had learned to live with management; the plant produced great earth-movers, exported them around the world; and the union squeezed the last dollar it could from the corporation. The United Automobile Workers was the main labor force going for McGovern in the industrial Midwest, and the union leaders had scheduled a visit to the Peoria plant because they controlled it right down to the sweepers. Supposedly, they controlled the 17,000 workers for McGovern, but there was no crowd at the airport, no reception. The Democratic Mayor of Peoria was absent; so, too, was the chief of the city council, Democrat.

One sits down with McGovern at a bench in the cafeteria where the night shift is beginning to eat before going to work. But, obviously, this is a television happening, set for the cameras and microphones to identify McGovern visually with traditional blue-collar men on the line. It is, of course, too late in the afternoon for this "visual" stop to reach any major national network, and probably it is useless in terms of Presidential campaigning. So I move down the row of benches, to escape the crowd cluster of reporters about the candidate, and fall in with three workers about to go on line. They are wearing their local union's button, and are proud of it. But apparently, this year, they are not taking their politics from the union. All three are veterans, combat veterans, as are so many blue-collar workers. The youngest of them, a Democrat, declares that he was in the invasion of Cambodia in the 1970 strike at Parrot's Peak. "Best thing Nixon ever did," he says. "We cleaned them out. It was a good job." The oldest says he was in the Marines when Ike sent them into Lebanon in 1958. He had landed on the beaches there, recalls it proudly—good job, too. All three are against amnesty—or what they're told McGovern says about amnesty. Most of all, they don't like this welfare thing, giving everyone $1,000 free. They work for a living. But no race prejudice among them. When I try to talk about busing, they say, "We've got twelve school districts and twelve high schools." The blacks have their school district, they have theirs, and they get along.

§ From Peoria up to Rockford, Illinois ("the hardware capital of the world"), where, late at night, the local Democrats suddenly come together in a throb, recalling the party as it used to be. The old regular politicians, under Daley's influence, have turned out their people to cheer; the United Auto Workers have turned out their blue-collars in Rockford; and the McGovern organizers, under Gene Pokorny's first drive from Chicago, have turned out a young crowd. The rousing rally is the day's high point and McGovern wallops the "special interests" with old eloquence; the dismal day ends on a bright note.

§ Next day: McGovern meets with the labor leaders in Rockford. Then visits an old folks' high-rise apartment house to show concern for the aged. Then gears up for one of the major stories of the campaign—the grain scandal. He has learned, and his staff has researched the story, of how inside information was leaked to four big grain exporters, allowing them to mulct the United States government of $131,600,000 in export subsidies for wheat just sold to Russia. It is one of those transactions at the second level of the Nixon administration where the blurring of morality, though not illegal, is outrageous. This is the kind of story perfectly tailored for McGovern's moral indignation, and he is about to make the most of it. All the way up the Mississippi Valley he flies, to Superior, Wisconsin, and there he stands before the cameras and thirty-five people in the hot sun. The visual shot is beautiful—McGovern in a yellow hard hat, his backdrop the towering gray cylinders of grain elevators rising against the sky like the columns of Karnak. And he scores—aesthetically, politically, morally, technically. It is well timed, shortly after the noon hour—every national network will have to use it.

Since the scorethrough is clean, the day should be over; were this the only visual McGovern story of the day, its impact would be sweeping. But the day goes on. From Duluth, Minnesota, down to Des Moines, Iowa, for another visual, a visit to farmer Philip E. Broderick's 260 acres, twenty minutes' drive from the airport.

Mr. Broderick's home is a white frame house with a bricked-in, glass-paneled sun porch. Against this backdrop, forefront on the green lawn, is spread a little table on which are a pitcher of pink lemonade and a plate of brownies and chocolate-chip cookies. With microphones poking over the table, McGovern discusses the grain scandal with Farmer Broderick and his friends. At this point, McGovern seems relaxed—he really likes cookies and pink lemonade and is at home with dirt farmers.

But by now it is late afternoon; the national reporters, both of the press and of broadcasting, know that the day is over for them—their papers and networks can take no more for the day. This visual is for the benefit of the seven Iowa television stations that have sent crews to cover the event and may or may not show a snatch of it on their eleven-o'clock news. Thus, the entourage observes like drama critics how the local road performance is going. We look at the scenery, the petunias and the asters blooming now in late fall in the neat garden, the locust tree that arches over the fine lawn, a weathered pear tree, and move on from there to the performance. There is a large pigpen, full of sullen pink-and-brown hogs; the pigs charge forward, then rush away, reluctant to perform. McGovern stands there leaning over the staves of the fence, as flies and reporters buzz around him while beaters try to drive the pigs into camera view, but the pigs squeal and dart uncontrollably—they will not cooperate for the picture. So we move to the cattle lot, and the city correspondents of the national press debate: What do we call these cows? Since they are not black cows, they can't be Black Angus. They can't be Brahma cattle, they have no hump. As the cows are finally forced into the same camera span as the candidate, we all agree to call them Hereford cattle. But it is now late—back to Des Moines, an airport rally, and through the night to Albuquerque.

The mood of the press now, at the end of the first week of the revived McGovern campaign, is more clinical than ever. "Fuselage journalism" is what the newsmen call their assignment—what you observe or learn from inside the candidate's plane. And the candidate's campaign as seen from the plane is quite different from the one described in Washington headquarters. The traveling campaign is based on media markets—and the candidate's imperative is to expose himself to television networks for three shots every day, plus a few more exposures aimed at local or regional evening news shows at eleven o'clock. All issues are blurred in this approach for the Presidency; it is concern for national defense in Seattle, concern for Israel in Los Angeles, concern for aerospace workers in San Diego, concern for the tax problem in Dallas, outrage against the war all through Illinois, indignation against the grain steal in Minnesota and Iowa—all of it illustrated by a jet that streaks from city to city, coast to coast, television market to television market, hopefully tracing across the evening news shows what George McGovern is all about with a camera pencil.

Richard Nixon has had no need to trace his politics across the country. With the power, facility and authority of the Presidency he has casually pin-pricked only three messages on the public mind all this week. From his San Clemente hideaway in California he has on Labor Day delivered a radio address to labor on the work ethic. En route back to Washington for work, Air Force One has stopped to let him off in San Francisco for a brief appearance before the Citizens Advisory Committee on Environmental Quality. The next weekend he will spend in Camp David, and lift off by helicopter for a quick afternoon view of the ravages of the 1972 Pennsylvania flood. He has thus, almost effortlessly, praised labor; shown concern for the environment; and will have expressed alarm for the desolated citizens in Pennsylvania's coal valley.

The White House press grumbles about Nixon's inaccessibility, but on the plane out of Des Moines to Albuquerque, at the close of McGovern's first week of full-time campaigning, the traveling press is also in revolt. They have been reporting a series of dramatic presentations for television, but what they want to do is to give the McGovern story some coherence, some meaning, some shape in this early phase. Albuquerque, New Mexico, has been scheduled by the McGovern planners as a weekend of semi-rest, one more attempt to let the candidate catch his breath and think a bit. But the rising pressure from the press is too great, and he must rise early on Saturday morning to prepare for a press breakfast and press conference to appease the writing reporters. Thus, he must review once more, in complex detail, his version of the Salinger affair; must be available for several exclusive television interviews, including one with a Dutch television crew that has been following him for days because of someone's promise that it would get a visual exclusive alone with him; must receive a deputation of twelve Pueblo Indian chiefs, who want to talk land and education policy with him, and who are received only because the New Mexico McGovern leaders insist the Indian vote is critical there.

So he was very, very tired, on this day that had been reserved for rest and thought, when he arrived at the poolside of the hotel, carrying blue folders of speech material with him, to be assailed once more by this writer. McGovern ordered a cheeseburger and coffee, for he had not eaten lunch yet, though it was 2:30, and rubbed himself with sun-tan oil.

He had changed in the long months I had been following the campaign. His chest hair was now frosty with white; his face had become seamed, craggy with weariness. And he had hardened in some way. The last time I had been able to spend a relaxed outdoor moment by a pool-side with him had been at a hotel in Miami, on Florida primary day in March. That day he had known he was to be crushed in the Florida free-for-all, but his strategic objective then was to put Lindsay out of the race by splitting the liberal vote with his rival on the left. He was almost a detached observer that day in Florida and I remember him saying as he lay in the sun, "Sometimes I wonder—does it make any difference at all who gets elected President of the United States? The country goes on anyway." He was still, in September, in Albuquerque, reflective and philosophic—but the philosophy had changed. He was bitter at Richard Nixon, with a bitterness of conviction. He believed in America as Isaiah had believed in Israel . . . and Israel had followed false gods.

I asked him flatly where he thought he stood now in the campaign.

He reflected wearily before speaking, and said that the others in his campaign had a scenario—"Frank and Gary have a scenario, but I don't see it as a scenario. I have this feeling I'm working with a historical trend, history is going for me. This country is going to pieces, if you can make the people see what Richard Nixon is doing to them . . ." and he, McGovern, could make the people see, he would.

He was planning now on that assumption—and there unrolled yet another McGovern plan, to be filed with all the other campaign plans one had heard in the previous three weeks—only this one was the candidate's own. Yes, next week was the Ted Kennedy week—Teddy was going to campaign with him from Minneapolis across the Great Lakes states eastward to New York. They would not be saying anything special, but the crowds, he was sure, would be great. Then they would come into Boston and he would begin, finally, on the grand themes of the campaign. The first would come on Thursday night next week, out of Faneuil Hall in Boston, the Cradle of Liberty. There, where the Sons of Liberty had planned the Boston Tea Party, McGovern would speak on the great Constitutional issues of our times—on the Nixon assault on freedom in America. He would ask what is a radical? What is a conservative? He would demonstrate that Nixon, with his assault on American freedoms, was the radical, and he, McGovern, defending them, was the conservative. It was the history professor in McGovern speaking, and speaking beautifully. He would go on to discuss this theme of what is radical, what is conservative, what is American, what is un-American, in other places. There would be a speech in Chicago on preserving American traditions—on how vital it was to preserve our country places, our villages, our small towns, our city neighborhoods. He, McGovern, wanted to preserve these values; what were Richard Nixon's values? Somewhere in there, in this sequence of grand themes, would also be a major speech on the problem of the cities and their plight. And then there would be a climactic speech on Vietnam and peace—not about the bombing of North Vietnam, but about the ravage of our bombing in South Vietnam. "We're ruining South Vietnam, we're killing people, killing, we're bringing that society to barbarism."

And all of these things would be said by the end of September. Then the campaign would take off.

There was still in the weary talk an echo of the romance which had stirred the primary voters to see McGovern as a folk hero of the plains. He had grown up on the plains, and felt the wind blow down from Canada on the farm people of the North, and listened to church-singing on Sundays, and it was all in him; what he wanted to do, he said, was to reach the moral, the idealistic strains in American life.

We moved on again and I pressed on him that idea which has become obsessive with me after twenty years of American politics—of how the cities as they are cannot be saved, any more than the Vietnam war could be won. The cities need to be reorganized, depopulated—how would he get at that, I asked, could he get at that? And he said bluntly, almost as bluntly as Richard Nixon, "But how do you talk about that without talking about the race problem?" Without saying it, he gave the impression he could not talk about the race problem in the city. There had to be some way of reversing the trend, he said, of people moving from farms and small towns to the cities, but—"How do we reverse it?" He had no answers.

As for specific planning: He felt he was going to carry both California and New York. Then, the main fight would come in five states: Illinois, New Jersey, Ohio, Michigan, Pennsylvania. He felt he would do well in Protestant suburbia, and he felt he might do especially well in Ohio, where there was a strong strain of country Protestant evangelism in the small towns. "Our main problem," he said, "is the blue-collar Catholic worker." His record in the primaries, he said, had been "erratic" in those factory towns—"You just didn't know what would reach them." His primary campaign had done well in South Milwaukee, Wisconsin, and in some factory towns in Ohio, but they had broken through cleanly only in Massachusetts. Michigan was going to be very tough. So was New Jersey. Again and again he reverted to New Jersey. He had written off states like Indiana—one talk at the University of Notre Dame, and that was all the time he could give to Indiana.

It would be a close election, he summarized—like 1960, but in the end he would win. He knew he was way behind, acknowledged it, but he had been way behind in the primaries; somehow, history would start working for him again. "We're trying to identify our themes," he said, and if only he could get the message through about how Nixon was perverting the entire American tradition, "the corruption, the thievery, the combines behind this Nixon administration," if the American people saw it—he would come out ahead.

He was fingering his blue folders of speech material at this point, so I left, recognizing that George McGovern, in mid-September, though troubled, was not a man in despair. He had not given up, as Barry Goldwater had given up by September of 1964. He could still see his way dimly forward to the Presidency, for this was his plan—to make the campaign, as the primaries had been, a struggle between the forces of light and darkness.

It was only later that I realized that his plan and the plans of his campaigners had almost nothing in common. There was to be no Faneuil Hall speech in Boston on Constitutional liberties next week; no following speech in Chicago on the preservation of the small towns and neighborhoods; the Vietnam speech would not come until October 10th. So it was back to Washington, to look at McGovern's headquarters again, to define, if possible, what the McGovern campaign organizers were trying to do—how they proposed to mesh plans to persuade the American people that the national power should be passed to them.

Disorganization is characteristic of all Presidential campaign headquarters, because Presidential campaigns are always run by amateurs. But the McGovern campaign added a new variety of disorganization. There is no West Point for the doctrine of political war, and the officers of each Presidential army must win their commissions on the battlefield. Even for veterans of state and local politics the mechanics of a national campaign are bewildering. There are the claims for manpower, money and candidate's time from across the continent, each community demanding its own unreasonable share. There are the instant and startling resentments that sprout from the bruised self-importance of famous men who consider themselves more useful than they really are. There are the sudden fights between old friends when the pressure grows; there are demands by equally persuasive advocates on the limited money—for television time, for travel funds, for mailings, for vote-buying, for literature. And, above all, there is that mysterious, complex American mood which must be reached by those clear, simple themes that only the candidate himself can define.

In the process of learning Presidential politics one lesson needs to be learned early—the candidate must have one manager whom he trusts entirely, who will make all the administrative decisions and free the candidate's personality for the one thing he alone can do: communicate with the voters. The candidate cannot be both horse and jockey—he is the horse, he must choose his jockey. For John F. Kennedy it had been his brother Robert. For Richard Nixon, after the learning experience of 1960, it had become H. R. Haldeman. George S. McGovern had no one.

There was no place that fall to get an overview of the McGovern campaign—not from the desk of Frank Mankiewicz, or of Gary Hart, or of Larry O'Brien, each of whom had a title suggesting he might be the boss. One could get the picture of a creative new financial approach to politics from the desk of Henry Kimelman or Morris Dees. One could get a philosopher's view of television in politics from producer Charles Guggenheim. One could hear the scheduling plans of the candidate from scheduling chieftain Steve Robbins, and the rationale for that scheduling, which was convincing. Or one could listen to Pat Caddell analyzing the ladders of preference and personality characteristics, the plateaus of cognition and resistance, and they were indelibly impressive. But each office had its own plan, its own approach. There were five, six, seven or more major plans for winning the election, which is natural in any national headquarters. Only no two of them fitted together.

The flaw fissured from the top down. "George McGovern," said Gary Hart, "just doesn't understand organization. He has an inordinate inclination to take every phone call. It flows from South Dakota politics." In South Dakota, everyone can reach the candidate for a hearing. For Hart, preservation of the integrity of the organization, McGovern's army, was the essential thing. Hart felt that old-timers like Larry O'Brien didn't understand how the primaries had been won. The old-timers felt the campaign needed a manager with a blacksnake whip; Hart disagreed —that was old-fashioned hierarchical organization; Hart believed in a theory he called "the concentric matrix." The "concentric matrix" theory of organization and decision required the confirmation of the initiative, responsibility, ability, equality of the enormously skilled, highly talented volunteers who had won the guerrilla war of the primaries. Hart insisted he was the campaign manager; George McGovern had said so. Hart liked O'Brien, whom McGovern had also told he was campaign director. O'Brien, in Hart's eyes, was the spokesman dealing with the old regulars. But as one went on reporting, it all became confused. The regulars were a state of mind, not a managerial group. And no one was in charge of reaching the state of mind of confused Democrats around the country. Hart did, indeed, manage his volunteer storefront organizations; but no one coordinated the ideas of the campaign, the themes of the campaign, the television of the campaign, the travels of the campaign. The campaign had begun with a control group which met every morning for a fifteen-minute session—a stand-up huddle of quick-fire questions, quick-fire answers. When the stand-up sessions aroused irritation, top-level coordination was changed to a pattern of one-hour sit-down sessions, once a week on Wednesdays—but soon twenty people were participating and their influence quickly decayed.

Time spent exploring McGovern's headquarters for ideas in late August, even into the first week of September, had been exhilarating. Time spent there in late September or October colored the day with melancholy.

In August, when one entered the headquarters, one immediately recognized that here were comrades who had slept on hard floors and in walk-ups across the country, and carried off the primary victory eating hamburgers and potato chips. No matter that it had taken them three weeks to get headquarters telephones working; the heart was still there. The sunflower motif in the posters carried the gaiety of springtime; the maps of the U.S.A., printed in psychedelic colors, jabbered. "LET THE SUN SHINE IN," read one poster. "WAR IS NOT HEALTHY FOR CHILDREN AND OTHER LIVING THINGS." "NIXON HAS A SECRET PLAN TO END THE WAR—HE'S VOTING FOR GEORGE MC GOVERN." And the bronze-and-copper campaign portrait of George McGovern glowed.

By October, however, starting from the entrance hall and rising to the eighth floor, the scene, except for Lawrence O'Brien's office, could only be described as filthy. Wastebaskets spilled over; cigarette butts littered the floor; paper cluttered offices; the corridors smelled; plates of stew and beans carried up in elevators fumed. Xerox machines, clogged with paper clips, might or might not work; mail might or might not get out that day, except for the always efficient finance mailing operation which sucked into its maw any incoming check, whether addressed to it or not. Children roamed the floors; volunteer mothers worked mimeograph machines, their toddlers by their sides; pre-adolescents earnestly lugged cartons and licked stamps. Volunteers as young as twelve or thirteen years old rode up and down on elevators, on some afternoons making headquarters seem like a playground as they pushed the buttons for fun, resentfully obeying when told to stop holding elevator doors open by force, or saying, "I hope you get stuck." The language one overheard was the language of old Tammany or the new college campuses—but if one overheard a young man in jeans saying "F--- you" over the phone, he might be saying it either to an old friend of the spring army or to a county chairman in Illinois, whose affront one would hear about later as one traveled.

The headquarters reflected the family struggle within the Democratic Party. There was no real reception room, no place where visiting dignitaries, or self-supposed dignitaries, could be given a pleasant seat and a perfunctory but courteous hearing so they might go back home, inflate the visit and say, "I was in headquarters the other day and saw . . ." One day one could see John F. Kennedy's Postmaster General, J. Edward Day, wandering around as if in a daze, simply looking for campaign buttons—totally unrecognized except by one of the "old people," a lady of forty. Tom Turner, the black president of the Wayne County AFL/CIO Council, the powerhouse of Detroit politics, visited the headquarters and later said, "I didn't mind a bit that they didn't know who I was. What bothered me is that even after they found out, they didn't give a damn." The men who controlled this headquarters had won the primaries; they had pulled off the largest coup in American party politics since the Goldwater people had seized the Republican nomination of 1964—and done it with lieutenants barely out of college. Among these lieutenants history ran shallow. Sargent Shriver, the Vice-Presidential candidate, was scheduled to visit Louisville, Kentucky, during mid-campaign. One old-timer inquired of a young scheduler whether anybody had bothered to call Barry Bingham, not only one of the great monuments of civilization in the Democratic Party but, as publisher of the Louisville *Courier-Journal* and *Times,* also a political powerhouse. "Who's he?" came the reply. When Bingham was described as not only the most important Democrat in Kentucky but also a Kennedy friend, the response was, "Oh, one of those 1960 freaks."

The new people had in their minds their own structure of politics—their own activist cadres plus a national reserve of volunteers who would eventually carry the cause. Old-timers called it the politics of exclusion. It was not that at all; it was rather the politics of the faithful few. Said Lester Hyman, onetime Massachusetts State Democratic Chairman, after his post-convention offer of help had been ignored, "They felt that they owned George McGovern; they had him long before anybody else, and, by God, they weren't going to share him." And those who felt left out were not only the old politicians. Sargent Shriver was upset throughout the campaign by the absence of black faces at headquarters; headquarters was almost all white, except for the faithful few blacks who had been there early. Women were left out. The trio of women who could reach George McGovern were those who had given their personal loyalty to him in the spring campaign—Liz Stevens, Shirley MacLaine and Jean Westwood. Out there in such housecoat belts as Ohio, West Virginia and Kentucky, where women's Democratic organizations had achieved over the years a singularly effective political weight, women were ignored. Many Midwestern lady Democrats enjoyed being women and the power they could swing as women. They could not speak in the idiom of Manhattan's women's-rights movement, but they could mobilize a different kind of woman power based on mothers and housewives who packed the man's lunch box, got the kids off to school in the morning, kept a clean house and were proud of it. Such women were lineal descendants of Carry Nation and the prohibitionists. They knew their worth, were interested in politics, and could be ignored only at great risk. McGovern headquarters, in effect, ignored them.

As one prowled through headquarters, one was impressed not only by what was happening—the finance mailing operation, the storefronts sprouting like mushrooms in the spring, the Caddell polling analyses—but also by what was *not* happening. In every campaign, a campaign newspaper is required. A campaign newspaper is a boring, unglamorous, unromantic, bread-and-butter item which is designed to nourish local politicians with the current week's clichés and table-thumping points for the precinct workers. Not until mid-October did McGovern headquarters produce its first issue of the McGovern-Shriver newsletter; and this first issue was the last. Headquarters should have a speakers' bureau to deliver famous names or, at least, competent experts to satisfy the insatiable appetite of local groups for "events" that let them call people together for a meeting. The Republican Committee to Re-Elect had elevated its speakers' bureau to a magnificence entitled "The Surrogate Operation," to which $2,000,000 and much time of Robert Finch, Chuck Colson and Jeb Magruder were devoted. In both the 1964 and 1968 Democratic campaigns, Democratic headquarters had had twelve teams of two people each manning desks all around the clock to meet the demand. In 1972 the Democrats' Big Four—George and Eleanor McGovern, Sargent and Eunice Shriver—had their own scheduling team. But as for the rest—one young lady and one assistant tried to handle all requests for speakers, their efficiency diminished by the fact that they scarcely recognized the names of the famous Democrats willing, available, but untapped to go out and spread the message.

One sought the standard center of ethnic operations. One found, finally, on the fourth floor of headquarters, in a shabby backroom, two young men, Kenneth Schlossberg and Gerald Cassidy—indignant. They had been pleading since early spring that "attention must be paid" to other minority groups besides blacks, Chicanos and youth. But the staff command had talked itself into believing, they said, that McGovern *had* the ethnics, that the primaries had shown his triumph with the blue-collars. "They never tried to understand the Wallace vote," said Schlossberg. "Our people deluded themselves. They were angry when we pointed out that what the workingman resented was us." Schlossberg and Cassidy had asked for a budget of $250,000 to reach the blue-collar ethnics; they felt they had won McGovern's commitment to the program in August; were then cut to a budget of $50,000—and were finally given the sum of $12,000 to spend in reaching the multi-million ethnics. Their first literature was not printed until October 10th. Even then it was a mailing of only 1,000 sample copies to each of the large industrial states in the hope that local McGovern campaigners might reproduce the appeals. (Down the street, in addition to the massive mailings and special-interest committees [see pp. 320 ff.], the Committee to Re-Elect was budgeting and spending $2,000,000 to reach these same core groups of traditional Democratic loyalists.) "McGovern," said Schlossberg, "doesn't understand the East. He finally got to be able to deal with blacks in a meaningful way, though he never turned them on. He didn't resent them the way he came to resent the ethnics. The ethnics were the opposition, and his people shared his resentment—it became a campaign which couldn't understand its own vote."

One could run on and on through the ingredients of classical campaigning and turn up blanks. Not until October 16th did a limited number of "issues" books arrive at headquarters, to make available a fundamental compendium of basic statements. Until then, one had to descend to the second floor, where friendly press personnel might or might not be able to produce a text of what George McGovern had or had not said on key issues. The most convenient source was the White House, which kept McGovern's vulnerable statements in one easy-to-hand big black looseleaf binder. And if the Republicans did not have the record, then the Republican National Committee's research arm had on computer tapes everything McGovern had ever said.

There were at least six plans for waging the uphill fight against Richard Nixon. There was the early thought, in August, that McGovern should base his campaign on "listening"—responding to a supposed feeling among Americans that their government was inattentive, that "nobody's listening to us." That idea was discarded when the candidate accepted Humphrey's more activist notion of polarizing the little guys (Democrats) against the big guys (Republicans). The candidate was open to suggestion at all times. When Stewart Udall suggested he needed "authority" performances, not stump performances, serious statements before sit-down audiences on major issues of the day, the campaign plan tilted that way for a while. But nothing came of this plan.

By mid-September the opportunity issue was clearly corruption. No retrospective sadness about the McGovern campaign is more poignant than the failure of this issue to cut. In Washington, McGovern accused the Nixon administration of being "the most corrupt" in two centuries of American government, charging that the President "has no constant principle except opportunism and manipulation. . . . At no time have we witnessed official corruption as wide or as deep as the mess in Washington right now." In Detroit, talking of Republicans' espionage against the Democrats, he placed the "whole ugly mess of corruption, of sabotage, of wire-tapping right squarely in the lap of Richard Nixon," whose administration had created "a moral and Constitutional crisis of unprecedented dimensions." On this issue, McGovern was closer to the jugular of national concern than on any other, except peace, and did his best. Whatever he said, however, was discounted as hysterical moralizing. No fault could be ascribed either to him or to his staff in their attempt to maximize the issue. McGovern was simply ahead of his time—the charges, on his lips, seemed fashioned not by facts but by the hyperbole of his conscience. As a historian himself, McGovern could take consolation only from Lord Acton, who declared that it was the historian's duty "to suffer no man and no cause to escape the undying penalty which history has the power to inflict on wrong."

There followed then the fireside-chat period of the campaign on television, starting with the McGovern speech on the Vietnam War, delivered on October 10th. Then Howard Metzenbaum of Ohio, who had narrowly lost a Senate race in 1970 to Robert Taft, persuaded McGovern that telethons could rescue the faltering campaign and there was a question-and-answer telethon phase of the campaign. But there was to be only one speech on the cities and the urban crisis. His major speech dealing with the race confrontation in the big cities was delivered in Detroit—McGovern assailed Nixon for using the "busing" issue for "cheap political purposes in the most cynical and demagogic way possible to divert attention from that record of indifference," but advanced no philosophy of his own beyond supporting the courts. There was to be one major speech on the environment, and, finally, in the last two weeks, he reverted to being George McGovern, his prose becoming both lyrical and biblical, reaching for the scriptural allusions which would mobilize the angelic hosts against the legions of darkness.

McGovern's shifting patterns tried the ingenuity of his scheduling team to its utmost. "We sit here," said Steve Robbins, chief of McGovern scheduling operations, "and we get a phone call from the road, McGovern wants to do a moral, uplift, issues speech on the 15th. So we send a team up to Maine to shop around and we find a beautiful church to do it in; then four days later we hear he wants it to be an inflation speech, and we have to shift overnight to a hotel in Portland." "It was bewildering," said Frank Mankiewicz, "I'd go to sleep at three in the morning, knowing that we were going to Detroit to talk about the tax problem. And at six Tony Podesta would wake me up to tell me we weren't, we were staying in Washington because McGovern wanted to work on a statement on Vietnam." "It all reminds me of Groucho Marx's story," said one of the electronic chieftains whom George McGovern trusted. "Groucho said once that any club that would accept him as a member, he wouldn't want to join. Any man who trusted my judgment so completely—I wouldn't want him to be President." Or another: "I'd vote for George McGovern for God, any time. He'd be great. But I don't know whether I'd vote for him for President again."

By mid-October the McGovern campaign was over; it had lost its own loyalties. Its base would remain solid—those Democrats who had been taught over a quarter-century to either distrust or despise Richard Nixon. But it would be unable in the age of ticket-splitters to reach out beyond that base to people whose votes were no longer swayed by party affiliation or loyalty. Pat Caddell would bring his polling results to headquarters and, as he said of himself, "I felt like the recreation director on the *Titanic*." But one day he had good news, from a telephone survey in Ohio. He rushed into headquarters to report the good news—here it is: we're behind in the last survey in Ohio by only six percentage points! Pierre Salinger, who had just come back from stumping in Ohio, responded: "Yeah? Where did you take that poll—in McGovern's headquarters?" In Delaware, a Democratic county committeewoman told her friends, "The only way to save this party is for us to lose big."

"It's like watching Mandrake the Magician trying to trap Donald Duck," said Meg Greenfield, the Sappho of the Washington *Post,* as she watched McGovern's reeling irregulars fall back before the hussars and fusiliers of Richard Nixon's campaign organization. By midsummer the Committee for the Re-Election of the President had been dubbed with the acronym CREEP, first by the disgruntled old-line organization men of the Republican National Committee, then by the press and the Democrats. But whether it was called "The Committee," as the White House preferred, or CREEP, as it usually was, it was important—it was the managerial revolution brought to politics.

When Democrats spoke of the New Politics, they meant the romantic insurgency of 1968 or the hope-filled ideologies of 1970–1972. But when Republicans spoke about the New Politics, they meant the specific technology which, at the Committee, was being perfected and mastered. At McGovern's headquarters on 19th Street, as a matter of principle there were no charts or tables or organization. "We don't fit people into boxes here," they said. At the Committee, two blocks away, everyone fitted into a box on a table of organization which defined his function—or he left.

"Executive Row" of the Committee lay on the fourth floor of the First National Bank Building; the Committee also occupied the entire third floor, suites on the eighth, ninth and eleventh floors, several floors of a building across the street. The First National Bank Building also held the offices of John Mitchell and, on the second floor, the offices of Maurice Stans's Finance Committee. But all authority lay on the fourth and second floors.

If you could suppress the nausea that still lingered and rose in your throat from the Watergate scandal; if you could wipe from memory the knowledge that someone on this fourth floor *must* have authorized the break-in at the Watergate; if you could do this, then you had to recognize that by late August the Committee had mounted one of the most spectacularly efficient exercises in political technology of the entire postwar era. At the level of their operations, they were pioneers. Now, in September, as the campaign moved into high, they were writing a new chapter of political history.

The Committee had begun as an idea in the minds of Nixon, Haldeman and Mitchell in the spring of 1971 [1] with what was apparently a classically orthodox perception of the American political system—the

[1] See Chapter Eleven.

Committee would be designed to go outside the Republican Party and deal with the Americans as discrete voter blocs. All American politicians have done this since the turn of the century; but the Committee, with the gush of funds that Maurice Stans was to tap, was to perform the classic turn better than anyone else had ever done before. There were to be separate operations for the aged, for the farmers, for the ethnics, for the Jews, for the women, and on down the line. And there would be an entirely separate Youth Committee. ("Nixon was uptight on the youth vote," said one of the planners who met him in 1971, "that was his main concern then.") [2]

The Committee had barely turned its wheels all through the spring of 1972, apart from the spectacular fund-raising of Maurice Stans. Its nominal acting chief, Jeb Magruder, was responsible to both Mitchell and Haldeman. Caught under the weight of two such personalities, he contented himself with design, planning and, as it turned out later, espionage. The designs, by the time of Watergate, were all there; and so were the shells of paper committees in every state in the union as well as a polling operation, a media operation on standby, and voter-bloc groups described and analyzed. But authority, decision-making, action were areas where Magruder had to tiptoe, for Mitchell neither delegated nor assumed control of policy. Mitchell had been trapped in controversy from the beginning of the year chiefly concerning his role in the ITT affair—an episode in which that rogue corporation had contributed $400,000 to help finance the Republican convention, and been accused of soliciting and receiving special favor from Mitchell's Justice Department in return. "The ITT affair was a bastard," said one of Mitchell's friends. "John had very little time or emotional energy to spend on the Committee. John grew pale, he was wan, his hands were beginning to shake. And he had Martha on his back, because Martha was really stressed by the ITT thing and seeing John paraded back and forth on the front pages." By the time the ITT affair had subsided in the prints and Mitchell had gone off on a Florida vacation, men at the White House were already debating whether Mitchell should or should not be brought back as head of the Committee. Then, with the Watergate affair, it was clear that Mitchell could not be brought back to direct publicly the President's reelection campaign.

It was, thus, only on July 1st that the Committee began its real and extraordinary effort, for on that day the White House moved in a new chairman, Clark MacGregor, and a second deputy chairman, Fred-

[2] I know of no complete list of all the voter blocs separately managed out of the Committee to Re-Elect. But they included: the Hairdressers Committee for the Re-Election of the President, the Funeral Directors Committee, the Motorcyclists Committee, the Aviators Committee, the Veterinarians Committee, the Optometrists Committee, the Indians-Aleuts-and-Eskimos Committee, the Volunteer Firemen's Committee, the Travel Agents Committee and on and on and on, as well as the traditional committees for lawyers, insurance agents, architects, bankers, savings-and-loan officials, doctors, etc.

eric V. Malek—Mr. Smiles and Mr. Ice, as they came to be called.

Clark MacGregor was a large, burly, jovial man, a former Congressman from Minnesota, a defeated rival of Hubert Humphrey's for the Senate in 1970, next a White House liaison with Congress, a man of the same family of civic Republicans that had bred such greater figures as Paul Hoffman, Nelson Rockefeller, George Romney. MacGregor's capacity for enthusiasm was igniting; one could imagine him in knee pants as Scoutmaster on weekends. But his honesty was self-evident; he winced over the Watergate affair as few other White House confidants except Robert Finch did; and his good mind and large energies were offended by what he found at the Committee when he took over.

"There was no sense of urgency," said MacGregor later, recalling his arrival. "Everyone was a planner. Down to the third level—they were all planning, sitting around holding meetings. It was absurd—they were engaged in strategy planning. I canceled all those meetings." In the key states, states like New York, Pennsylvania, Michigan, no allocation had yet been made from the swollen central budget to the local budgets of operation.

MacGregor's principle of operation was clear. "Our candidate is the President," he said. "He decides the issues. Finances belong to Maurice Stans—he handles that. The job of this Committee is to get bodies to the polls. That's page one of the Abraham Lincoln handbook of politics." In the mythical Abraham Lincoln handbook which MacGregor was fond of citing, the job of politics was simple: Go out and find your friends. Identify your voters. Get them into the polls. Only now in 1972, with 210,000,000 Americans to court, this job had become administratively immense. MacGregor had been impressed, then astounded, by the spring march of the McGovern army climaxing in California. On his wall hung a large blow-up of a statement made by Gary Hart to the Washington *Post* early in June. In oversize print it read, "I hope the Nixon people do to George McGovern what the Democrats did—underestimate him. If they do, we'll kill them." MacGregor proposed not to underestimate what Gary Hart and the volunteer army could do; if the strength of the McGovern campaign had rested on the person-to-person, voice-to-voice contact with voters, the Republicans must match it. Budget planning was putting too much money into TV, unrealistically; he would move the money into "the people operation." An initial transfer of $3,400,000 would begin the creation of a contact organization. (Later the sum would grow to $12,000,000, the largest single expenditure of the Committee's $42,000,000 budget.)

Contact operation was the province of Fred Malek. Blue-eyed, tow-haired, muscular, Malek could by no means be described as jovial. His mind was tough and decisive. A West Point graduate, later a Green Beret in Vietnam, later yet a Harvard Business School graduate,

Malek had distinguished himself in a management-consultant firm in Los Angeles; then, with two partners, bought into a business of his own and had already become a millionaire at the age of thirty-three when he had been invited to work with Finch at HEW in 1969. Malek was one of those Southern Californians who were admired by both Finch and Haldeman, and from HEW Malek had moved to the White House as a specialist in personnel management. From there he was sent by Haldeman to help MacGregor clean up the mess at the Committee.

Few at the Committee liked Malek, but all respected him. "This guy," said one of the younger Committee men, "operates like a corporate raider taking over." "There were a lot of people on that staff who had to be fired—so we needed a Fred Malek," said another.

If, then, in MacGregor's opinion, the person-to-person operation had to be energized by a nationwide storefront operation, the energizer was to be Malek. Malek confessed that he knew little or nothing about politics, or about what motivates political volunteers, but the process intrigued him. "Best job I ever had," he later said, with the enthusiasm of an amateur discovering how simple politics apparently is. Storefronts cost approximately $1,000 to $1,200 a month, he estimated. (At McGovern headquarters the estimate was $600 to $800.) Storefronts were not there to show presence—they were there to canvass, to make the calls, to identify. On August 1st there had been fewer than 100 Republican volunteer storefronts; by September 1st, 800. By October 1st Malek's planning target had been hit—2,000 Republican storefronts across the nation. Motivation or destiny concerned Malek little. Nixon and Haldeman decided what the country would do; they made policy as a general sets strategy; his job was to occupy and organize the emotions by grassroots reinforcement. "We don't have any legitimate role in issues," said Malek. "Our thrust is to identify our people and get them to the polls. We can't let apathy keep them home. We've got 170 storefronts in California, 40 telephone centers, 30,000 precinct-walking volunteers. Every storefront calls in here on a WATS line every Monday, and we post the results at the end of the next day; every headquarters has to make 150 local calls a day; we measure production; it's just like a profit-and-loss statement in business. We have more volunteers in the field today than McGovern has."

The mind of Malek impressed a visitor—for it was, quintessentially, something as different from the mind of an old-breed Republican politician as it was from the mind of Gary Hart or Eli Segal or Gene Pokorny, with whom one might enjoy a drink after the day's work was over. Malek's mind was managerial, not political. The structure, not the purpose, held him in thrall. How things worked—whether in storefronts or in government—was the measure of achievement. Men lived in boxes; they performed or they disappeared. The men in the boxes might be warm, easy-going, enthusiastic or thoughtful. But the neat charts, the criss-crossed boxes pegged them all to their tasks.

Old people? The box led to robust young Webster B. (Dan) Todd, Jr., thirty-three years old, operating across the street from main head-quarters on Pennsylvania Avenue. Todd's huge slice of the vote-getting operation was the 29,700,000 Americans over the age of sixty. Until 1971 Todd's specialty in the Nixon administration had been aviation policy. Assigned to old folks, he had now generated not only an enthusi-asm for his aging-voter target but a warmth that made him excep-tional in any Committee office but MacGregor's. "Any other society keeps its older people involved and active until they die; we don't. They're lonesome. The whole problem is to involve them, to make them feel wanted and useful." Eighty-six percent of the aged were registered voters—and Todd by mid-October had 30,000 of the aged involving other aged, from suburbs to walk-up apartments, from nursing homes to hospitals. Todd did not like the cost-efficiency operators at main head-quarters; he had been a liberal New Jersey state legislator; he was sensi-tive, ebullient, worried about what the Republican Party might become; but, dollar for dollar, his budget probably delivered more voters than any other division.

Young people? That box occupied a separate chart of its own. Ken-neth Rietz, thirty, ran the youth operation. He had come up through Wisconsin and Tennessee politics. At main headquarters some of his more suspicious superiors thought it was unwise to let Rietz run this semi-autonomous operation—Rietz might be creating a skeleton youth corps of his own which could develop at some future date as Clif White's young Republicans had once developed into the takeover group that staged the Goldwater coup of 1964. But Rietz had insisted on com-plete autonomy, on his own volunteer army. When challenged by Mac-Gregor to show what he could do with all the money he had been spending, Rietz's youth corps was able to field 25,000 volunteers on an August Saturday to deliver almost 300,000 new registrations by super-market and precinct walking; he then went largely his own way.

In between age and youth were a dozen other boxes. For demo-graphic theoretical analysis, there was young Arthur Finkelstein, who coined the mothering phrase of the campaign's strategic target, the "peripheral urban ethnic." For the farmers, Clayton Yeutter. For labor, another name; for each of six specific geographical regions, a specific responsible deputy; and each Monday all regional chieftains assembled in Malek's office to report and be held to account.

Direct contact took the largest share of the funds Maurice Stans had raised—in all, finally, some $12,000,000. But following the line items of the Committee's budget down the list, one could see the relative values that the managerial mind assigned to political priorities.

Direct-mail and telephone batteries, at costs of $5,000,000 and $3-000,000 respectively, washed each other's hands, marrying their results with the storefront results, feeding names into computers. Magruder supervised these operations, and did it well. However much his private inner thought must have been haunted by the Watergate affair, he functioned with efficiency at the office. Computers sliced up the nation's census tracts into patterns; the storefront operators in the counties that Malek had "prioritized" had identified independents, wavering Democrats and "don't knows"; the 250 telephone batteries in ten key states had poured other names into the computer. And by the end of October the computer was taking over—there would be in the last week eight million "mailgrams" to the nine largest states, cut and coded by county, by age, by income, by Spanish-speaking, by black, by ethnic origin, plus 9,000,000 letters to Republicans. A computer software firm in Texas cut the tapes; mail-list houses around the country sorted names; the Donnelley plant in Chicago printed and mailed—17,000,000 pieces in all, in the largest single roundhouse swing by mail in American politics. As one leafed through the master samples on Magruder's desk, the profile of the operation became very hard. "NEW JERSEY," read one batch of coded letters, each master envelope with its prototype text labeled:

N.J.—Democrats for Nixon, Italian
N.J.—Democrats for Nixon, Veteran
N.J.—Democrats for Nixon, Middle Income
N.J.—Older Republican
N.J.—Democrats for Nixon, Older Peripheral Ethnic
N.J.—Democrats for Nixon, Peripheral Urban Ethnic
N.J.—Concerned Citizens

Then:

Pennsylvania—Democrats for Nixon, Irish
        Democrats for Nixon, Polish
Pennsylvania—Democrats for Nixon, Italian

and on down the rest of the list, through California, Illinois, Ohio and others.

As one examined the operational clockwork of the Nixon organization, it grew more impressive; and, indeed, more impressive because of what it had learned from the past.

All advertising, for example, was concentrated not in Washington but in New York, at an inconspicuous office at 909 Third Avenue where the "November Group" met. There were to be no more books written, like *The Selling of the President: 1968,* from the unguarded conversations of advertising buccaneers to titillate readers with what went on in the backrooms of the studios. The November Group, which Haldeman, a former advertising executive himself, had conceived, was recruited from true-blue, sworn-true-to-Nixon advertising executives who volunteered to serve full-time for Nixon for one year—on leave of absence from their own firms, distracted by no other accounts but the campaign. The November Group wrote, printed, controlled all pamphlet material and literature—material stored in four regional warehouses, each warehouse with incoming WATS line to serve state and local campaigners; orders computerized, checked out, triple-manifolded. Unlike a commercial agency which spurs more and more advertising because each new slice of advertising earns the agency a 15-percent commission, the *ad hoc* November Group could caution restraint on television spending.

"We're the nay-sayers," said Peter Dailey, the forty-one-year-old friend of Haldeman who directed the November Group. "We don't need a silver bullet to win this election." There had been no television expenditure by the November Group in the primary campaigns. There was to be none in August. The Democrats started television nationally on September 10th; the Republicans—not until September 25th. "Never has so much talent been put together for so little output," said Dailey in mid-September as he resisted pressure to go on air. Dailey had a quite clear idea of what his instructions were all about, for he was one of the few who could talk to Haldeman directly. He had taken over as head of the advertising group in January of 1972, when all Republican minds had been haunted by the nemesis figure of 43 percent. Good times, bad times, success or failure, Nixon rode at 43 percent in all the polls. The turn had come in the spring, and now Nixon, in the fall, was riding at 60 percent plus. McGovern had kicked away his core Democratic voters, thought Dailey. "Anything we do," he continued, "that makes their crossover decision to Nixon difficult is wrong—like trying to get a Republican Congress. This is not a campaign of Republicans against Democrats, it's Richard Nixon against George McGovern. If we harden them on party lines—that could go wrong. There's one President and one candidate, and we're going to do nothing to bring our man down from the level of the President to the level of the candidate. We aren't ever going to get caught in the trap where the evening news shows say, 'And now on the road, let's look at the candidates today.'" Dailey was to end up spending only $4,000,000 on all national air media, only 63 percent of the sum spent on the Nixon campaign in 1968, and substantially less than the $6,200,000 that McGovern's media people spent. The local TV advertising might vary from place to place as the computers and polls defined the varying concerns of the twenty major media markets in whose framework advertising was placed—the aerospace issue was hot in California, the property tax in Wisconsin, the busing issue in Michigan. But the national message, when it was launched September 25th, was sharp-cut: national defense (a hand wiping out half the Navy, a third of the divisions, most of the Air Force); the work ethic (a hard-hat, high on a girder, talking about people who work for a living and McGovern's welfare proposals); and McGovern's face on a weathervane, revolving in the wind.

Another man who could speak directly to Haldeman was Robert M. Teeter, thirty-three, the head of the Committee's polling operation, budgeted at $1,300,000. The White House had come to rely on the public polls (Harris, Gallup, Sindlinger) for its head-to-head gross counts. Teeter conducted only three large national polling operations for the Committee during the year—a sampling of 1,500 on January 1st, another on June 1st, another just after Labor Day. These, however, were buttressed by in-depth surveys of fifteen to nineteen key states each time, and further supplemented by precision questions on issues, suggested either by Teeter or by the White House. As, for example, a testing of feeling on "amnesty," or Watergate. (By September, Teeter reported, 70 percent of those polled were aware of the Watergate scandal, but only 6 percent thought that Richard Nixon had anything to do with it; the rest of those aware of the matter thought it was the work of CREEP.)

Teeter, too, had begun the year haunted by the bedrock Nixon rating of 43 to 44 percent in the American public mind. The Nixon figure had begun to move only after the California debates—"that was when Nixon moved up from 44 percent approval to 52/53," said Teeter. "It was Hubert Humphrey who put McGovern away; no other Democrat could have done it to him like Hubert. Not only did Hubert give it to him, but that was the first time McGovern got adversary treatment." From then on, as the Democratic convention reached the viewers, and then the Eagleton affair, then the Salinger affair, the cutting edge, in Teeter's mind, had become clear—it was not what the voters thought of Richard Nixon, as it had been early in 1972, but what they thought of George McGovern.

By September, Teeter had set up for the Committee, as Pat Caddell had set up for McGovern headquarters, a daily sampling of 500 people by long lines across the country, rotating from state to state each day. By October, Teeter was fully confident. By his analysis, 58 or 59 percent of all American voters were now committed to Nixon against McGovern, and the undecided would bring a few more. "Each week," he said in October, "as the undecided come down for a candidate, we pick up one and McGovern picks up two. McGovern is picking them up from the hard-core low end of the income scale of the working class —or from the eighteen-to-twenty-four-year-old undecideds. We're picking up ours from the high-end income scale of skilled workers." With the ease and largeness that a comfortable seat on the winning side affords, Teeter's pre-election thoughts were graphic. "In the last ten years," said Teeter, "the quality of dynamism seems to have less and less impact on the voters. Five years ago when I was polling in Michigan and Minnesota, the characteristic of 'youth' was about fourth or fifth in importance to a voter. Now, 'youth' ranks about tenth in good qualities. And 'maturity' is usually first or second. What McGovern represents in issues, people are afraid of; his positions bomb out the older working people. Permissiveness isn't what I'm talking about. I'm talking about a mind set. What you have in this election is the movement of an entire social class, the man who works for a living. The old ticket-splitter was suburban—but now the ticket-splitter is the workingman. There are two kinds of ticket-splitters—the man who's just plain independent, and the guy who's on his way, leaving his own past. McGovern's driven the workingman there ten years earlier than he would have got there otherwise."

There were, in effect, two levels to the Nixon campaign. The critically important level was the White House level. Nixon's ideas about how his nation worked and what its groups sought, matched against George McGovern's ideas, would have won, Watergate or no Watergate, organization or no organization, in 1972. Then there was the second, or CREEP, level, of manipulation, organization and mobilization of votes, far less important—but occasionally, at the CREEP level, as intriguing to a reporter as a science-fiction preview of future politics. And the science-fiction view climaxed in the Situation Room of the Committee to Re-Elect.

The Situation Room was on the south side of Pennsylvania Avenue, across the street from the Committee's headquarters. It was always security-tight, so I joined John Ehrlichman, eleven days before the election of 1972, to watch Fred Malek demonstrate visually to the White House man's inspection how the Committee read the political state of the nation.

The room was windowless, and might have been sunk deep in the ground, as is the Pentagon's subterranean triple-depth war room. It glistened in the brilliant overhead lights. Fifty-three glassined panels, seven feet high, bordered in red-white-and-blue, swung on their hinges from high ceiling posts, so that one could turn them with a touch of a finger as one walked down the U-loop circuit. Each state had one panel, except for Texas, which, with 254 counties, had two; there was a panel for the District of Columbia; and a summary panel for the entire nation made the total of 53.

The panel for each individual state listed all the state's counties on their own lines and then was vertically cross-cut with canvassing, telephone and polling results. The Committee could, in sum, report to the White House that some direct personal contact had reached 15,932,000 American households—by phone or visit. States were listed by priority counties—all 3,000-plus counties in the United States, with the precise percentage of the total households in each county already visited. More people, we were told, had been reached in these households than actually voted for the President in 1968. The households were now coded as to (1) those which would surely vote for the President, (2) those inclined but not sure to vote for him and (3) those which needed just a bit more urging, contact or a mailgram to tip them to the President. The practice of voter identification was, to be sure, exactly the same as that of McGovern's army in the spring primaries. But CREEP had far outdistanced the McGoverns in reach. Each of the 2,000 Malek storefronts was calling in on a direct line to change the postings every Monday or Tuesday; and they hoped to rack up between two or three million more calls in the next week. The Election Day effort was already, on this day, Friday, October 27th, moving, as Malek's military D-Day plan took over—the briefings of get-out-the-vote teams were under way; final check-off lists were being prepared; each storefront was ready to check off on Election Day its first list of voters by one o'clock, then again at two, at three, and at 6:30. "You've got to know where your ducks are, in order to bring them in," said someone, and as one sauntered down the aisles, finger-flipping the gleaming charts, the ducks had all been identified in their counties and coveys, from Alabama to Wyoming. These people took their politics seriously, just as seriously as the McGovern people, although with much less music. As I left, I noticed the large panel that hung over the center of the room: "WINNING IN POLITICS ISN'T EVERYTHING," it said, "IT'S THE ONLY THING."

CHAPTER THIRTEEN

APPEAL TO THE PEOPLE: VERDICT IN NOVEMBER

O NE might imagine, reporting the Committee in Washington, that it was all like this, all bloodless, all managerial, all computerized, all planned. Except for those rare moments when one could follow the President in the flesh, see him raw, hear his voice ring free of the speeches written for him or hand-tooled in his own notes on the yellow legal pads.

And then, hearing him, one grasped what George McGovern was running against—a man, and a set of ideas, more formidable than his computers or his unrecognized espionage apparatus.

For example, October 28th, ten days before election, in Ohio.

No one had known, when the Ohio trip was planned, that the duel of war and diplomacy would be leading to a blurred pre-climax of the Vietnam war; that the negotiations in Paris, which had apparently been going so well for the previous three weeks, would be announced first out of Hanoi; and that Henry Kissinger, carried away by a momentary euphoria, would give the nation from the White House, on Thursday, October 26th, those most beautiful of all words, "Peace is at hand." Or that the next day so great a relief would sweep the entire country that when Richard Nixon landed at Hopkins Airport, near Cleveland, it would be a day for the book of memory.

I had followed Richard Nixon through four campaigns, and seen him ill on the road in 1960; indignant in 1962; fatalistic in 1968. He was now, on this day, both totally exhausted and totally happy, and at ease with himself in public as I had never seen him before, the simplest of his emotions, personal and political, bubbling to the surface.

The day began with almost military precision, the President's plane touching down at 12:08, two minutes from plot time. The airport scene was exactly as the Committee's pre-planning would have had it. He was to move this day, in a very old-fashioned motorcade, across northern Ohio, from the suburbs of Cleveland to the steel town of Warren, his target again the ethnic vote. One could make out the wording on the sign held by the "DEUTSCHE MUSIKSCHULE SACHSENHEIM," or the "YOUTH FOR NIXON" signs in English. But then there were the signs in strange languages, lofted by "LITHUANIANS FOR NIXON" or "UKRAINIANS FOR NIXON." And signs in Greek. Signs in Serbian. Signs the local TV cameras had to pick up, if they were to cover Nixon's arrival at all.

Then, quickly, the Nixon motorcade moved out of the airport, through the industrial belt that surrounds Cleveland, past the Ford plant, with its tall plumes of white steam slanting through the air, past the machine shops, and on to Parma, Ohio, the Middletown of the "peripheral urban ethnics" who work in the heavy industry of the area. Nixon's advance men had laid it on. But there could be no doubt that the crowds which lined the road, whether stirred by peace or by Nixon's presence, were authentically jubilant. And hard. "MC GOVERN TALKS BULLSHIT," read one of the signs in the first five minutes; and for the next hour, people almost five deep crowded either side of the procession as the motorcade passed. Nixon has always, from his first campaign, been able to call up the little peppermint-striped flags that children wave, and the flags were out. They were waving at him, each group in its custom—some giving him the Roman salute, hand-high for Caesar; others had turned their young ladies out in Balkan or Slavic peasant costume with gypsy-colored billowing skirts and white puffed sleeves. And the Boy Scouts, cub scouts, senior scouts, American Legionnaires. The signs in the ethnic belt were standard ("ITALIANS FOR NIXON," "WE LOVE YOU MR. PRESIDENT," "NIXON AND YOUTH," "PUT PRAYER BACK IN OUR SCHOOLS," "WE NEED NIXON").

We passed quickly, in less than an hour, through the ethnic belt, and then the clean lawns, the neat houses, the autumn gardens of the ethnics gave way to countryside where the names on the mailboxes changed from the unpronounceable to straight Smith, Jones, Miller, and the faces became the faces of Grant Wood canvases.

Here in the farming country, where the crowds were less thick, one could observe Nixon himself—standing in tan topcoat, leaning out of the open hatch of his limousine, letting the air blow over him. He rested on his elbow as he stood in the open hatch, as if the air and the cool of Halloween season could blow vigor into him; his face, sun-tanned by days in Key Biscayne and San Clemente, was nonetheless so lined with weariness, so heavy from the neck as it swayed and nodded, that one could only imagine how much the week's negotiations with Hanoi and the wind-down of war had punished him. He had, he was sure at that moment, ended a war. Now, leaning out of the car, he was looking at his people, as few Presidents have been able to do, at what he and they believed to be the moment of peace.

The signs and the bands and the colors of the uniforms were making it a grand day for him: "NIXON GAVE PEACE A CHANCE TO WALK," "TRICKY DICK TOOK THE TRICK," "MY DADDY WILL BE HOME FOR CHRISTMAS," "NIXON IS MY HERO," "RIGHT ON MR. PRESIDENT," "DO YOURSELF A FAVOR, VOTE NIXON," "TRY HIM, YOU'LL LIKE HIM," "WELCOME CHIEF, WE'RE WITH YOU," "HELLO MR. PRESIDENT, HANG IN THERE SIR," "NIXON, THE MAN FOR NO MORE NAM," "A KISS FOR KISSINGER," "HAPPINESS IS PEACE," "SEE DICK. SEE DICK RUN. SEE DICK WIN," "NIXON IS OUR PRESIDENT," "THANK YOU FOR BRINGING JOHNNY BACK HOME," "PEACE TIME IS NIXON TIME," "TRICK OR TREAT, NIXON CAN'T BE BEAT." And on and on—as the high-school bands and the veterans' clubs stood at attention; the pretty girls with their tall shakos prancing, pompoms bobbing about their ankles; the blown-cheek boys tonguing the air furiously into their trumpets and trombones; the paunchy veterans lined up. And also the McGovern pockets, wherever they showed, with a gallantry inviting lynching by Nixon's adoring crowds, chasing after him in university towns, headbands around their heads, chanting "On, McGovern," flaunting their signs, too—"TRICKY DICK, STOP CHISELING ON THE WAR AGAIN, SIGN UP BY THE 31ST," "THIEU AND HEROIN EQUALS NIXON." But the McGovern signs were rare. Nixon had carried Ohio by 90,000 votes against Hubert Humphrey in 1968, but lost these working-class towns by over 150,000 votes. He would carry Ohio this time by 882,000 votes and he could sense it, feel it.

I had never seen him more weary, never felt such deep weight of aging in a contemporary. This day, in elation, his hair graying, he was old. He had been negotiating on war and peace all that week. Now, this afternoon, he was released from his own compulsory orderliness, to ramble in his own words, leaning out of his car with a hand-held mike, as the stump speaker, in which role he had begun his career.

He did it first that day in North Royalton, Ohio, about twenty-five miles out of Cleveland. The crowd had clotted at a crossroads, and he halted his cavalcade to walk about, shake hands, then come back, then put forth a thought:

". . . as we drove through Parma, Ohio, I saw that the flags were at half-mast. . . . I asked one of our Secret Service, a man who has . . . risked his life many times, why the flags were at half-mast. He told me that . . . just two days ago a policeman, in the line of duty, trying to apprehend a criminal—who proved to be a criminal, certainly, by his actions in killing the policeman—was murdered. . . . The town . . . was paying its respects to that man of the law. . . . Let me tell you, you can't pay these men what it is really worth. You can't pay a man enough to risk his life to help you keep your life. One thing you can do is this: Respect him, honor him. I have seen on occasion over these years sometimes some scroungy-looking people that are spitting on policemen and calling them pigs and the rest. It makes my blood boil."

On went the President, talking to his people and his voters from his heart. He stopped just before entering Mantua Corners, Ohio, for someone he recognized holding a sign—and it was Al Doyle, a Navy veteran who had served with Nixon on Guadalcanal. Of course, it was old Al Doyle, and the President lingered for a minute. Here's a pen, he said, it's a White House pen. Hey, said the President, remember when old so-and-so (I missed the name) cracked up that new tractor on Guadalcanal? Someday at the White House we ought to have a reunion of our Navy service crowd, got to get together. And thus, on.

In Mantua Corners, on a grass knoll stood a white frame house with a huge sign reading "MR. PRESIDENT MAY I PLEASE SHAKE YOUR HAND. WE LOST OUR SON IN VIETNAM." The President stopped his cavalcade. Mr. Frank Lorence, a tall, lean man with a sharp nose, standing with his wife, was waiting there, surrounded by children and grandchildren. They had lost their son, Sp-4 John Lorence, somewhere near Truang Banh. "I don't want to feel like he went for nothing," said Mrs. Lorence after the President had promised her that he wished he "could bring him back. We're going to do everything we can to see that it doesn't happen to . . . other boys. That's what we're going to do."

The President went on: "They give up their lives, but they do it to serve their country, and the few hundred that deserted this country, the draft-dodgers, are never going to get amnesty when boys like yours died. Never. They are going to have to pay a penalty for what they did. That's the way I feel." [1]

---

[1] A day later, back in Washington, the President told a group of his staff people what the day had meant to him. The episode at Mantua Corners had scored deeply. His remarks, abbreviated here from a transcript, express the essential Nixon and his relation to his people as well as anything I can recall: "Some of you read of the motorcade yesterday and a stop that I made, one that was unplanned, one that came about because we saw a sign on the side of the road. . . .

"After I had gone by the sign, I stopped the car, got out and walked back. I talked to the mother, to the father, to the brother of the man who had been killed. . . . I shook hands with them. Anyone who has been in politics and who shakes hands a lot can tell a lot about people by how they shake hands, and also the feel of their hands. I shook hands with the man. His hands were not soft. I don't mean that most of us who have soft hands because we don't do manual work have anything to be ashamed of, but he obviously was a working man; he was a farmer. It was a callused hand, but strong and firm.

"But what impressed me even more was the mother. I shook hands with her. Her hands also were somewhat rough, and I looked at them and they were red. She obviously cannot have a dishwasher, and she didn't have all those fancy things that you read about in *Vogue* and the rest as to how to make your hands pretty and lovely and the rest. I thought of my own mother and father. My father had hard hands too, because he worked all of his life. My mother's hands were not pretty, but I always thought they were beautiful because I knew how much she did and how hard she worked all day, baking pies at four o'clock in the morning to send four kids to college, hoping they could, or helping other people.

And on and on, the President sniffing the sycamores as he leaned out, the fall turn of the earth, his eye watching the somber change of Ohio seasons, these people loving him, not only because he had brought peace but because he spoke their language. He paused more frequently as he relaxed, stepping from his car, revealing himself to his people as Caliph Harun al-Rashid might have done had he coursed Route 82 in Ohio the week of Halloween. He was behind schedule, which is an odious offense in the Nixon organization, when, as he entered Warren, Ohio, he passed a field on which some pre-adolescents had set a table and sign which said, "STOP AND GET A FREE PUMPKIN MR. PRESIDENT." So he stopped the caravan again, the press buses in the rear, a quarter of a mile beyond, wondering what kind of Presidential campaign this was anyway. How much were these pumpkins? the President asked, before the crowd could run up and cluster around him. The children, overwhelmed, said the pumpkins were free. Oh, no, said the President—he was against that, they had to be paid for their pumpkins, how much would three cost? A dollar? And he peeled off a dollar and paid it out. Carrying his three pumpkins, the President strolled back to his limousine and was accosted by a young man who introduced himself as a Vietnam vet. How was it going to come out? the veteran asked. The President, being President, replied, "I think we've had significant progress. I think it's going to come out all right. But you'll have to read about it in the papers."

Thus, finally, as evening approached, into Warren, near Youngstown, Ohio, fourth-ranking steel center of the country, and a quick, political speech plugging the local Congressman, and noting the money that Warren, Ohio, would soon get from the Federal government, from

---

"I thought as I talked to this woman and to this man that they were really what makes this country great. . . .

"The mother said, very simply, not out of anger toward those who are in Canada or who deserted the country, but simply speaking about her son, she said, 'We put the sign up because,' she said, 'we just don't want our boy to have died for nothing.'

". . . We could have ended this [war] in the beginning of our administration. But ending it by getting out of Vietnam would have left our POW's to the mercy of the enemy. We would have had to beg or crawl in order to get them back. Ending it without some sort of an agreement would have meant that we would have gotten out, but the killing would go on, the North Vietnamese would kill the South Vietnamese and the Cambodians and the Laotians.

". . . If the United States were to withdraw, if the United States were to surrender, in effect, and throw up our hands, it means that 50,000 Americans, including the son of that wonderful man and woman that I saw on that Ohio farm, they would have died for nothing. It would mean that the grandchildren that I saw—one was six; another was eight; another was ten—they may be fighting in another war. I can't guarantee to them or to you that there will not be another war, but I do know this:

"By ending the war in Vietnam in the right way, in a way that discourages aggression, that does not reward it, gives them a better chance for the sons and the younger brothers of those who have died in Vietnam to grow up in a world of peace."

his scheme of revenue-sharing. And into the plane for one more stop at Saginaw, Michigan.

Michigan was a busing state, where the issue cut deep. Nixon emerged from Air Force One at the end of the day, too tired to move farther than the platform of the plane staircase which had been rolled up to him. In the light of television, he looked as young and tough as he ever had. One hand tucked into his coat, he urged these voters to vote for his Republican friend Senator Robert P. Griffin: "The Senate needs Bob Griffin standing against any kind of program that would bus children away from their homes across town. . . . The best education is the education you get in the school that is closest to your home."

Then, into the plane and back to Washington. On the scoreboard of national politics, he had scored his points that day on ethnics, on busing, on "work-fare," on peace, on amnesty, on law-and-order. The mark on the inner scoreboard of the President was probably just as important: The people he had seen today liked him, understood him, were with him. And thousands of them undoubtedly loved him, which was most important of all.

So the campaign came to its end.

The great storyteller Sholom Aleichem might have told it best. Sholom Aleichem has a story about the rich man's funeral and the poor man's funeral. At the rich man's funeral the sun shines, the flowers nod in the grass, the horses prance, the carriage rolls noiselessly. At the poor man's funeral the horses droop, the wheels squeak—and it rains.

Shifting back and forth between candidacies, it was usually my misfortune, after the primaries were over, to follow George McGovern on cloudy days when it rained—or threatened to rain.

The cloud that hung over George McGovern was, however, more real than rain. The mind of the country had set; and the will of his staff had crumbled. Whatever mysterious thing it is that sets national opinion, that evoked a community judgment from November's 210,000,000 Americans, that mysterious thing froze against George McGovern, whether in the national polls, or in the Committee to Re-Elect's polls, or in his own polls.

By the beginning of October, Caddell had identified for the McGovern staff, and for his candidate, who now glanced at the polls ever more infrequently, what the condition of their campaign was. Caddell's polls were realistic. McGovern, in the analyses Caddell was doing, was now seen as more concerned about people than ever. But the problem in the public mind was, simply, his competence. Americans take their vote for the Presidency very seriously—a sense of obligation weighs on that vote. They are concerned, of course, by issues. But beyond that there is another concern—can the man do the job? And in August and September, Caddell, sampling as optimistically as he could, was reporting to his headquarters roughly what Teeter was reporting to the Republicans: Since July there had been a 35-percent shift of McGovern voters away from their candidate—either to the undecided column or to Nixon. Does George McGovern understand how things work? asked Caddell in an agree/disagree question of orthodox polling. Forty-nine percent of those polled by Caddell agreed that McGovern didn't understand; 39 percent thought he did. Caddell tried paneling questions on personality characteristics. In July the favorable qualities people had perceived in McGovern had led the unfavorable by three to one. By the beginning of October the perceptions had shifted to three to one against McGovern, headed by "indecisive," "impractical," "the Eagleton experience." A specific sample in New Jersey, a key state for McGovern, had come out with such results on personality characteristics as: *Strong*—Nixon 64, McGovern 16. *Honest*—Nixon 32, McGovern 30 (!). *Foolish*—Nixon 11, McGovern 44. *Sneaky*—Nixon 32, McGovern 13. *Practical*—Nixon 56, McGovern 16. There was movement, always movement, for, according to Caddell, no one really loved Nixon, nor did any voter believe that the government could do anything about what bothered him most. (When do you think the war will be over? asked Caddell, and 30 percent replied, "Don't know"; 40 percent, "A year or longer"; 12 percent, "In the next six months"—and 12 percent, "Never.") George McGovern, in the voters' eyes, by his own polls, was less competent to get things done than Richard Nixon. "This thing keeps me up all night," said Caddell. "I lie awake at night trying to figure out a way that he can break this competence issue, how do we break that one basic question? And I don't know. In the primaries we had the war issue going for us, and the alienation issue. Now our problem is at the top. We've always been light in the idea sector, we got left without any strategy of ideas, we play one thing, then we play another thing, and it all contributes to his image, to this lack of consistency and competency."

At the beginning of October it had been decided that McGovern would combine his one great positive issue (America's disgust with the war) with his one greatest weakness ("competence") and make a nationwide broadcast on the Vietnam war. Only this time he would be specific. There would be a timetable of specific actions to bring the war to an end and the boys home—a workable, practical proposal. The speech told as much as any other episode about George McGovern's political valor and political weakness.

The best Democratic brains worked over the Vietnam speech. Former Defense Secretary Clark Clifford and former Assistant Secretary of Defense Paul Warnke advised on its first draft. McGovern was dissatisfied, and Ted Van Dyk and the issues theme team worked it over. Then

McGovern handed it over to his personal staff writers; then he worked it over himself for three or four more hours to final edited form. Finally, on October 10th, his nationwide commercial on CBS showed the floodlit Capitol, panned in to George McGovern behind his desk and he was off with a superlative performance. The indignation was McGovern's, the eloquence was McGovern's, the high yearning morality was McGovern's. It was a seven-point solid construction, one more in the countless succession of solutions put before the American people in the long war; but the essence of McGovern was in the last of his practical proposals. He had inserted this last proposal over the advice of most of his staff—to wit, that all those who had fled the war, all those who had sought refuge from the draft overseas, be pardoned, forgiven once the war was over and the prisoners had been brought home. McGovern's conscience insisted that amnesty, one of the chief moral controversies of the year, be thrust forth now, at this moment. But there were voters whose consciences had dictated that they be ready to answer the call to die, if necessary, for their country. They could not, in their conscience, forgive men of other conscience who had refused either to kill or to die for their country.

There was deep conscience going on both sides, two tenacious views of patriotism and moral responsibility. Neither McGovern nor Nixon could recognize conscience on the other side. Two and a half million American veterans had answered the call to arms in Vietnam; only 14,000 had answered a contrary call of conscience which insisted they must escape the service. The numbers and emotions ran for Nixon.

McGovern's leaders had looked forward to the speech of October 10th as a turning point, the 1972 equivalent of Hubert Humphrey's Salt Lake City speech of September 30th in 1968, which had reversed the tide of opinion. In one way the McGovern speech *was* a stunning success —perhaps the most successful in terms of dollar response of any in modern times, drawing in the next four days $800,000 from the committed peace-lovers who had always been McGovern's base. But the effect of the speech on the over-all electorate was that of a pin dropping.

McGovern had now in the last month of the campaign come home to the Vietnam issue; he and Eleanor had decided he would speak to that. Two days after the peace broadcast he was on the University of Minnesota campus, stunning the students with a tape-recording of horror, the voice of a Vietnam veteran recalling the remains of human bodies "fused together" by napalm bombings, "like pieces of metal that had been soldered. Sometimes you couldn't tell whether they were people or animals." One day later he was again before a cheering audience of 25,000 in the San Francisco Cow Palace, lifting his listeners to frenzy as he called on "them" to "give us back our country."

McGovern was no longer happy in Washington. As he said later to

James M. Naughton of *The New York Times,* "I had to stay out of
Washington to keep my morale up and every time I'd go back to Washington and start reading those polls and talking to people back there,
God, I felt [this thing was hopeless]. Then I'd get out among the people,
you know, and you'd see a different thing. You'd see that there were
really masses of people who wanted a fundamental change." On the
road, the faithful, the moralists, the young still cheered; the McGovern
army could still turn out volunteers to make crowds. But McGovern
was wise to stay out of Washington. At his Washington headquarters, by
the second half of October, when the upturn had failed to come, a condition had set in which I had never known before; it was not the condition of bleak despair, or the black-humor surliness of the Goldwater
headquarters in 1964; it was a condition that passed disloyalty. Men and
women I had known for over a year as disciples now despised their own
candidate. They were not disaffected with the cause, but contemptuous
of the man; betrayed not by his beliefs, which they still shared, but by
the absence of that hard quality of leadership which they sought. He had
failed them not in honor or devotion—but in craftsmanship.

A political reporter could carve out of the McGovern schedule in
the last three weeks whatever story or pattern he wanted. His plan, to
appease some, included one college-campus appearance a day, a "visual" for the cameras. To appease others, the plan called for hitting big
cities in big states, to show the ethnic flag. With all goodwill, obedient
to schedule, decisions and compromises in Washington, McGovern went
through his travels. But the only image worth carving out of the last
weeks of the campaign was the image of the man himself, as it broke
through the frames and time blocks set for him: He was the preacher,
calling for repentance.

Dressed in white robe and bearing rod or staff, he might have been
a minor prophet; dressed in starched black, he might have been a
circuit-riding Wesleyan. Alighting in Texas, he could recall his Sunday-
school days when the children in Avon, South Dakota, chanted, "Red
and yellow, black and white, all are precious in His sight." In Wheaton,
Illinois, he told the Evangelical School of Wheaton College that the
Scripture clearly assigns to mankind "the ministry and the mission of
change." Not only would he change the course in Vietnam, but he would
"also change those things in our national heritage which turned us astray,
away from the truth that the people of Vietnam are, like us, the children
of God. . . . So, Christians have a responsibility to speak the questions of
the spirit which ultimately determine the state of the material world."
That day McGovern had chosen as his text a passage from the Book of
Micah: "What doth the Lord require of thee, but to do justly, and to love
mercy, and to walk humbly with thy God?"

Yet McGovern, though he quoted Micah, was a proud man ("a

humble, self-effacing egomaniac" is the way one of his disillusioned saw him). And so, two weeks after his quoting of Micah came one of those moments which so endeared him to correspondents, who now winced at his humiliation. He had come into Battle Creek, Michigan, that evening five days before the election, shaking hands at the fence as candidates do, and encountered a stout young man wearing Nixon buttons, who heckled him with coarseness. McGovern beckoned to the young man, saying, "I've got a secret for you." Then, quite audibly to all around him, the farm boy from South Dakota said what he had to say. "Kiss my ass," said the Presidential candidate. He really no longer cared about rounding up votes—he was speaking from his heart.

By the last week of the campaign, his text had become what it was in the very beginning: Repentance. And: Beware. His voice was cracking, his throat was sore as he traveled from Chicago to Waco and Corpus Christi, Texas; to Little Rock, Arkansas; to Granite City and Moline, Illinois; to St. Louis, Missouri. But the war and its killings lay heavy on him, and his spirit was burdened.

He took to the air, on a nationwide telecast Friday night, to warn the American people about Richard Nixon and the war in Vietnam. By the text of McGovern, the American government was deceiving the American people with this talk of peace, this "cruel political deception" that Nixon and Kissinger were perpetrating. President Nixon was only "pretending"; he had actually "closed the door to peace once again." The entire exercise of Kissinger diplomacy in October, prematurely exposed, was a fraudulent bit of election trickery. Hammering his message home, he told a news conference in Chicago that he was making his charges "as a patriot and not as a candidate. He has no plan for ending this war," McGovern said of Nixon. ". . . He's not going to let that corrupt Thieu regime in Saigon collapse. . . . He's going to stay there. He's going to keep our troops there. He's going to keep the bombers flying. He's going to confine our prisoners to their cells in Hanoi for whatever time it takes for him to keep his friend General Thieu in office." It was, in short, as George McGovern presented it in its final weeks, a contest between an alliance of monsters, Nixon and Thieu, versus a saint named McGovern.

He made a final television appearance—again on Vietnam—on Sunday night after having been scheduled into a dismal tour of the ethnic boroughs of inner New York by downcast local regulars. He took off Monday, after a walk on New York's Fifth Avenue in the morning, and his schedulers moved him that day (while Richard Nixon rested in San Clemente, doing nothing but plan the reorganization of government) to Philadelphia, to Wichita, Kansas, and late at night to a mismanaged rally at Long Beach, California—from which he flew back through the night to Sioux Falls, South Dakota, which was home.

All others in the McGovern camp had given up hope weeks before. As he himself recalled it, he thought there might be an upset until the Monday before the election. And then it was clear even to him that it would not work. Thus, Tuesday, Election Day, was tranquil for the candidate. He left Sioux Falls rather late in the morning to vote for the straight Democratic ticket in the education building of the Congregational Church in Mitchell, South Dakota, his home town. After voting, the candidate went to the Campus Center building of Dakota Wesleyan, where he had once taught, and gave a lecture on civics to high-school students from all over the state. A reporter in the hall reflected that it was very difficult to think of this happening in any other country. All America was voting that day on its Presidency and here was one of the two candidates eating cookies and drinking coffee with old faculty friends, then talking to high-school students—but you had to grasp the fact that George McGovern had always, really, been the Senator from South Dakota, and a teacher. He was doing his own thing as he spoke to the students, instructing them; he fitted more appropriately into this hall than any other on the long campaign trail.

The drive back from Mitchell to Sioux Falls takes about an hour and a half; and before McGovern had left, Frank Mankiewicz had telephoned him from Washington. Mankiewicz had already received two foreboding calls that morning. One reported that, by the early turnout of voters, it seemed that Detroit would be voting 100,000 less than expected that day—which was bad for McGovern. And, even worse, the second call had come from Suffolk County in New York, which was voting exceptionally heavy that day—which was good for Mr. Nixon. But Mankiewicz was flying out from Washington that evening anyway to join his chief in Sioux Falls for the vespers of the campaign.

So it was over.

And yet not.

It was impossible to dismiss George McGovern as one of the traceless losers of American Presidential politics, like the Coxes or Landons who passed into the record books leaving no more than sterile voting totals behind to mark their defeats.

There would be a permanent residue of the McGovern campaign. Never again would the Pentagon's budget be accepted by the American people and their Congress as sacred. Never again would a President's right to make war abroad without consent of Congress go unquestioned. And someday, shortly, certainly, his attack on the ramshackle and jerry-built tax structure of America, with all its inequities, would result in law.

More than that. Like Stevenson and Goldwater, McGovern had introduced a new generation of young people to politics. Most would pass on, discouraged, to other things, the campaign of 1972 fading to a memory of their lives at springtime. But others, a handful, would remain to live and act within their party, wiser perhaps than before; and, like the Stevenson and Goldwater men, they would change their party, in structure and nature, from what it had been before.

It was what these young people had learned from the McGovern campaign that would, finally, give ultimate meaning to the McGovern phenomenon of 1972. The McGovern phenomenon had been something more than a movement, something more than a party coup. It had been a rhythm, a sound in the hearts of millions of Americans, a rhythm that came to crest that night in Miami when George McGovern looked down from the rostrum and the hall was singing, black and white chanting together.

And then, after that, the magic left. The music which moved the McGovern phenomenon was the oldest music in American life—the music of the religious ones, of the American crusaders, the abolitionists, the good-cause people, the cold-war people, a music that inspires some and frightens others. On the long march of the American people to the uplands, most have usually been willing to go along so long as they feel that they or their children will not be discarded, or crushed, or sacrificed in the journey; they will follow so long as they feel those at the head of the march have a competence, a skill, a practical understanding of affairs which touch their lives. At Miami the music began to frighten people.

From Miami on, the rhythm was broken. The hard work remained to be done, work for which magic was no substitute; the McGoverns had been frivolous in choosing a Vice-President, showing a contempt for the process which they proclaimed sacred. "It was like a doorbell ringing during love-making," said a young McGovern volunteer of the Eagleton affair and its impact. They then showed themselves incompetent in organizing a campaign, auguring badly for their ability to organize a government. They remained pure at heart—but the system rejected their purity as unsafe. The rhythm beat on, of course, in the inner ear of the faithful; but fewer and fewer Americans cared to join that dance.

Mr. Nixon and Mr. McGovern conducted their campaigns for two different audiences, never joining issues in one central place, but setting up their tents, offering different music, on different terrains of American culture, inviting America to divide. When the Americans did, the majority went to Richard Nixon because they felt most at home there, most safe. Though McGovern himself would never again run for President, the rhythm and music of spirit that had moved him would persist in politics, as it had persisted through American culture from its beginning. And so, too, would Mr. Nixon's.

Thus, finally:

On November 7th, 1972, Richard Milhous Nixon, 37th President of the United States, was re-elected for a second term—only four of the thirteen Presidents of the United States in this century had won two such votes of confidence from the American people.

Of the 77,681,461 Americans who voted—the largest number in history—he carried 47,167,319, as against 29,168,509, to defeat his Democratic rival, George Stanley McGovern, by 17,998,810, the largest numerical margin in American history.[2] The Nixon landslide was overwhelming. In percentage terms, he won 60.7 percent of the entire national vote, and stands second in history by only a tiny margin to Lyndon Johnson's record-breaking 61.1-percent landslide of 1964. At the same time, the American people were electing a Congress of remarkable stability, untouched by the landslide: Of the 378 incumbent Congressmen running for re-election, only 13 were defeated. Over-all, the Republicans gained 12 seats in the House, to send back a Congress in which they were still a minority—192 Republicans against 243 Democrats. In the Senate, remarkably, the Republicans suffered a net loss of two seats, to become a diminished minority of 43 against 57 Democrats.

But the national contest of man against man, idea against idea, campaign against campaign, was enough to give the historian pause: Here, with 18,000,000 votes, was the largest numerical margin of decision ever recorded. Here, with a victory in 49 states, Nixon had carried the largest number of states ever carried by any President. Here were the most electoral votes ever recorded for any Republican (521[3]), only two short of Franklin Roosevelt's 523 in 1936. (McGovern won 17 electoral votes.) Whatever later would be made of this mandate, however much its mechanics would cast shadow on it, it was a major statement by the American people. And they had stated their preference for Richard Nixon.

The simple numbers spurned quick analysis—they were numbers that might have turned the head of a more secure personality than Richard Nixon. Unlike most landslides, Nixon's had been truly national; there had been no Harding, Eisenhower or Johnson landslide in the South. Only the Roosevelt landslide of 1936 compared with Nixon's in the deadly uniformity of the returns in every region. The President's percentages ranged from the merely huge (in the high fifties or the low sixties) for the East, Middle West and Far West to absolutely enormous (over 70 percent) in some Southern states.

The landslide scrambled historic patterns. New York, which in Nixon's previous two races had voted decisively against him, gave him a larger ratio of victory than did Iowa—which had twice before voted

---

[2] All the figures used in this passage are taken from the final tabulations of the Associated Press, as is traditional in this series. A full tabulation of the vote by states and including splinter-party candidates, also made available by the kindness of the Associated Press, is to be found in Appendix A.

[3] Nixon won 521 electoral votes, but the official record reads 520; one of Nixon's electors from Virginia defected to cast a vote for John Hospers, Libertarian.

for him by decisive margins. Connecticut, which had twice rejected him, embraced him this time with a greater percentage than did his thrice-faithful native California.

In this scrambling of patterns, one could detect the hardening of shapes that had begun to jell over previous years.

The Nixon victory in the South was something with which history had been pregnant for almost a generation. Franklin D. Roosevelt had been the last Democratic President to carry all eleven states of a once-traditional "Solid South." In 1948, Harry Truman had lost four of those states to Strom Thurmond. In 1952, Dwight D. Eisenhower had also ripped off four—Virginia, Florida, Texas, Tennessee. John F. Kennedy, in 1960, Catholic though he was, carried seven of the states of the old Confederacy. Johnson, in 1964, could hold only six. Hubert Humphrey, in 1968, could hold only one, Texas. But Richard Nixon, in 1972, carried the entire "Solid South" for the Republican Party. In doing so, he blew apart voting numbers that had prevailed only four years before. Mississippi, his poorest state in 1968 (with 13.5 percent of the vote), was his best state in 1972—with 78 percent. Georgia, Nixon's second-best state in 1972, had been 47th four years before. Of the eight states which gave the President 70 percent of their vote or better in 1972, all but Nebraska and Oklahoma were in Dixie. And Nebraska, Nixon's best state in both his previous elections, trailed five Southern states in 1972.

Another shape, just as significant though fuzzier in profile, had been emerging over the years in American voting—the shape of voting in the big industrial centers of the Northeast. Here, in 1972, Nixon scored another major breakthrough—but that breakthrough, like his final occupation of the "Solid South," could be understood only by what had happened to the Wallace vote.

As one approaches analysis of the Wallace vote, one must confront again the most brutal reality of domestic American politics—which is that white people fear black people all across the country. In the spring, McGovern theorists had argued that the huge Wallace vote in the primaries was an expression of "alienation," of general lack of trust in the process of American government, and that, under their skins, Wallace and McGovern voters shared similar emotions. In the fall, as McGovern's campaign was collapsing, months after Wallace had been gunned out, they argued that Nixon was inheriting the Wallace vote, a racist vote.

The election results proved the theory both true and untrue. In the South, the Wallace vote moved en masse to Richard Nixon. A CBS analysis of some 17,000 American voters on election day,[4] pinioning

---

[4] The CBS News Election Day Survey was conducted in 143 voting precincts throughout the country. It caught an unprecedented sample of 17,405 voters leaving the polls, the largest sample ever taken of the national electorate—large enough

them for questioning as they left the polls, showed that the 1968 Wallace voters in the South had gone for Richard Nixon by three to one. In a remarkable number of Southern states, the 1972 Nixon vote was within a point or two of the combined Nixon-Wallace vote four years earlier: Georgia, South Carolina, Tennessee, Louisiana, Arkansas.

But in the rest of the country—North, East and Midwest—the same CBS survey showed that the Wallace voters of 1968 split between Nixon and McGovern by almost equal numbers, six to five for Nixon over McGovern. What carried the North, East, West and the industrial centers for Nixon was Nixon's new strategy—his courtship of the blue-collar, working-class, ethnic voters on issues clearly voiced to appeal to them.

One of the crucial elements of the Nixon strategy had been his discernment of the emotions of the mass of American Catholics, most of whom had come of late-nineteenth-century immigration, who had fought their way up to the status, the comfort, the neighborhoods in which they now dwelt—and wanted to preserve their neighborhoods and way of life against the tide of change. In Eastern industrial states, Catholics had achieved a rough voting parity with Protestants in the electorate; and now, by the CBS analysis, in the election of 1972 the once heavily Democratic Catholics had gone Republican for the first time in any American Presidential election. Nixon spoke to them. Rhode Island, the most heavily Catholic state in the Union, had gone against Nixon by two to one in 1968; in 1972 Rhode Island voted for him. Even Providence County, which had gone for Hubert Humphrey by 70 percent in 1968, gave Nixon a majority in 1972. All through the East, the same way: Hudson County, New Jersey; Allegheny County (Pittsburgh), Pennsylvania; Albany and Erie counties (Buffalo), New York; Hartford County, Connecticut—all heavily Catholic, and all, utterly out of previous political character, voted for the Republican Protestant from Yorba Linda, California.

New York State was perhaps, outside the South, the chief triumph of the Nixon strategy. Twice—in 1960 and 1968—it had humiliated Richard Nixon as Presidential candidate by cruel margins. This year, the Empire State gave Nixon his largest numerical majority in the nation. The campaign on Nixon's behalf was managed by the elaborate political technocracy of Nelson Rockefeller. But the stars of the campaign team were Liberal Jewish Senator Jacob Javits and Conservative Irish-Catholic Senator James Buckley. Both did valiantly for the President, but Buckley was

---

to produce for the first time sub-samples of groups (such as Jews and voters under twenty-five) which had never been sampled before in numbers large enough to give statistical validity to their results. The survey was designed and conducted by Warren Mitofsky, associate director of the CBS News Election Unit, and supervised by Robert Chandler, then its director and now a CBS News vice-president.

the better spokesman of the Nixon strategy. In the CBS News analysis, Catholic voters in New York supported the President by the unheard-of margin of two to one! By so doing, they almost enabled the President to carry Brooklyn—as inconceivable a thought to American politicians as it would be, in Britain, for a Tory to carry Nye Bevan's old Welsh mining district of Ebbw Vale. Nixon lost New York City by only 82,000 votes, compared to the 700,000 by which he lost it in 1968! And he carried the whole state by almost a million and a quarter votes—1,241,694—as against his larger native California, fourth largest in plurality, in which he led by 1,126,249.

If campaign planning is something more serious than the simple mechanics and manipulation of media and vote registration, its historic rationale has to lie in the governing concepts of the men who seek to lead the nation, how they see the nation. The final votes measure these thoughts and concepts. The home strategy of George McGovern had been one of universal brotherhood; the home strategy of Richard Nixon had been one of self-respecting, interacting yet independent communities. At Key Biscayne, he had decided he would make such communities—previously ignored by Republicans as "ethnics"—his primary target. They had voted Democratic previously because they had had no place else to go. He would take them away.

The votes record the success of this strategy. In the CBS polling, as in every other public poll, the defection of Democrats from their loyalties is one of the high ridges of the election results. Of people who identified themselves as Democrats, 37 percent voted for Richard Nixon. This compared with only 8 percent of Republicans who supported McGovern. The Democratic defection in 1972 is without precedent—in neither of his huge victories did Eisenhower win over more than 23 percent of Americans who claimed to be Democrats; and in Johnson's huge landslide, only 20 percent of the Republicans defected. The response of Democrats in 1972 was, thus, unique.

For a detailed breakdown of how Nixon's strategies worked—what the final markers were in the Polish wards of the big cities; the Italian wards of Cleveland, Boston, Chicago; the Irish wards of St. Paul; the Jewish districts of Los Angeles—one is best referred to the final analysis of the voting results by the Research Division of the Republican Party, always one of the best analyses in statistics, detail and general meaning, and usually ignored by the leaders of the Republican Party.[5] The ethnic, blue-collar strategy of Richard Nixon, according to this analysis of results, ran thus: Among Italian-Americans, Nixon ran his margin up

[5] See *1973 Republican Almanac, State Political Profiles, 1972 Election Summary,* produced by Political/Research Division, Republican National Committee, 310 First Street S.E., Washington, D.C.

to 51 percent of their total, from 22 percent in 1968; among Polish-Americans, he increased his totals in various big cities by 12 to 30 percent of the vote; among Spanish-American voters, he ran his total up from an average 18 percent in 1968 to 31 percent in 1972.

The massive CBS Election Day survey threw up other readings that provoke reflection—on blue-collar workers, union members, Catholics.

Blue-collar workers gave Nixon 55 percent of their major-party vote, up from 41 percent in the Gallup survey of 1968. The families of union members, which gave 34 percent of their major-party vote to Nixon in 1968, awarded him 51 percent in 1972. Catholics, 36 percent for Nixon in the Gallup survey of 1968, were 53 percent for him in the CBS survey of 1972. The rise in Nixon's white-collar vote, by contrast, was much less pronounced. From the 1968 Gallup survey to the 1972 CBS survey, the white-collar vote for Nixon rose only eight points— from 55 to 63 percent.

The Presidential strategy had been to develop and exploit a new majority. Its most striking effect, in the heavily blue-collar, strongly Catholic, larger states of the East which Nixon had lost in both his prior races, was to turn those states around and produce in them landslides as great as, and in some cases greater than, those in the states which he had carried in the past.

An NBC survey indicates that the Jewish vote across the nation rose from 18 percent for Nixon in 1968 to 37 percent in 1972. The CBS survey estimates that the percentage of Jews voting for Nixon came to 32 percent. These figures fall in a rough area of agreement. Nelson Rockefeller's private polls had always given him pride that Jews, who normally voted only 15 percent Republican in the Empire State, would vote for him up to 30 percent in his gubernatorial races. Nixon, then, had pulled enough Jews over to the Republican side, nationwide, to match, or possibly surpass, Rockefeller's record.

Of the Irish-American voting and German-American voting, so important in past history, there are as yet no realistic measures.

There were two elections going on in 1972, as Professor Walter De Vries has written—that for the Presidency and that between the parties. The election for the Presidency was over by August. There remained after that, according to De Vries, another campaign—that of the two old parties in the cities and states. That was a real contest. Here the Americans split, in bewildering fracture patterns. In the twelve states where both a Governor and a Senator were running for office, six split their votes between the Republican and Democratic victors. Eighteen states split their control of state legislatures. More Americans split their votes between the local candidates of the two parties than ever before.

They were searching not in parties but in personalities for answers to problems that baffled them.

So large, diffuse and provocative are the data which the election of 1972 poured out that reporters, like this one, must wait for fine shades of meaning on the slow thought and dissection of results by scholar-psephologists, who sort out the pebbles—on the forthcoming stories of Richard Scammon and Benjamin Wattenberg; of Walter Dean Burnham; of the scholars of the Michigan Research Institute. Buried somewhere under every great historic landslide are the ripples of counter-movement, nodules of resistance to the general sweep. What they represent is not yet quite clear, now in 1973. But a few should be noted.

For example:

Everywhere across the country, the President ran ahead of his party, partly by design and partly by construction—but in the rare cases when Senate Republican candidates ran ahead of the landslide Republican President, generally it was a *liberal* Republican who did so—Case in New Jersey, Percy in Illinois, Hatfield in Oregon, Brooke in Massachusetts. Nixon landslides of 58 percent or better did not prevent liberal Democrats from upsetting Republican Senatorial incumbents in Delaware, Maine, Colorado, Iowa.

One is intrigued, also, by those areas where George McGovern outran the record of Hubert Humphrey, however unfortunate his record was in the rest of the country. McGovern carried Alameda County, California—seat of the University of California at Berkeley. He carried Dane County, Wisconsin, better than Humphrey had—the seat of the University of Wisconsin. He did the same in Washtenaw County of Michigan—seat of the University of Michigan at Ann Arbor. And Johnson County, Iowa, seat of the University of Iowa.

One is intrigued by the pattern of black voting. The blacks were the only group in the country among whom Richard Nixon's appeal failed to fatten preference for him substantially. He had received only 13 percent of the black vote in 1968; in 1972, he could move that up only to 14 percent.

There were other illusory dynamics in the planning of the campaign of 1972 which turned out not to be realities. The youth vote, on which George McGovern's strategists had based so much of their hope, failed to materialize. The women's vote, that potential which McGovern's planners had mobilized in the primaries, developed little force in the general election. The women, insofar as the polls can determine, voted for Richard Nixon over George McGovern in even larger proportions (62 to 38) than they had voted for Richard Nixon over John F. Kennedy, the lanceman of Camelot, in 1960 (51 to 49).

One of the more stubborn realities that showed in the results of the "other" election, where people decided who should govern, or speak for them, in their own states, was the continuing power of the AFL/CIO.

The AFL/CIO powerhouse deserves more space than it gets in this book; its influence and muscle spread over the middle ground of working men and women who lie between the thuggery of the teamsters' leaders (pro-Nixon) and the idealism of the auto workers' leadership (pro-McGovern). The working men and women of the AFL/CIO are independent of their leaders at the national level of issues and candidates, where, like most Americans, they make up their minds by what television and press tell them. But when it comes to local voting to choose who speaks for them in Congress, they will go with the union leadership. Messrs. Meany, Kirkland and Barkan, who control this system of loyalties, opted out of the Presidential contest. But at the Congressional and Senatorial level, they delivered maximum impact. In Maine, they decided Margaret Chase Smith could be eliminated—not out of any malice but because labor needed every Senatorial vote it could get. Their contribution of $10,000 to William D. Hathaway, Democrat, was probably the largest single contribution to his campaign; yet more important was the mobilization of the building-trades, textile workers' and service workers' unions to support him. AFL/CIO's COPE moved in Delaware to support young Joseph Biden against J. Caleb Boggs, an apparently hopeless race which Biden finally won. Labor financed and helped the Iowa campaign of Dick Clark, who ran a spectacular race on his own, against the surprising loser, Republican Senator Jack Miller. In Rhode Island, the AFL/CIO machinery was certainly the largest factor in turning that state's electorate against its former Governor, John Chafee, Republican, to support incumbent Democratic Senator Claiborne Pell in what had appeared, in early fall, an almost sure win for Chafee. The AFL/CIO managed to pump $103,000 into various committees of Pell's campaign, as well as manpower. In the Senate, where Richard Nixon now faces his Constitutional challenge, the AFL/CIO probably provided the critical handful of votes that may swing decision. So, too, in the races for the House. AFL/CIO political effort concentrated on eighty-two marginal House districts. Most incumbents, as we have seen, were re-elected; only thirteen lost; but all five of the Republican losers were replaced by liberal Democrats whom the AFL/CIO had backed to the hilt; and in the new Congressional districts—approximately a dozen, chiefly in the middle-class suburbs, carved out by the reapportionment required by the Census—AFL/CIO-endorsed candidates won four.

The last message of the voting record of 1972 to history was its most bleak: its shriveled size. Americans, numbed by words, headlines and TV shows, cozened, courted, cross-analyzed by canvassers, telephone banks and statisticians of both candidates, simply drew in on themselves. Only 55.7 percent of all Americans old enough to be eligible to vote bothered to cast a vote for President—the lowest percentage since the 51.3 percent who voted in the confusion of the Truman-Dewey-Thurmond-Wallace (Henry) race of 1948. The proportion of eligible Americans who vote has been dropping every four years since the election of John F. Kennedy, whose fight drew 63.8 percent to the polls. Kennedy established a Presidential commission thereafter to find out why so few Americans cared to vote. But the vote continued to drop—to 62.1 percent in 1964, to 61 percent in 1968, to the results of 1972.

Something in this turn of time had made Americans feel that their votes were unconnected with the control they should have over their own lives. "Alienation" was the fashionable word for the vague feeling. What it meant was that in the decade of the 1960's you had lost the right to vote on where your child went to school. You had lost the right to vote on when your son should be drafted, and where he should be sent to fight. Most of the major problems that affected "you"—from taxes to smog, from busing to war—you could not reach by voting for anyone.

Of those who believed that voting could still help *you* control *your* life, the preponderant majority wanted Nixon to set their directions, not George McGovern. They approved of his course, from what they had seen, or heard, or felt in their own lives. That was the mandate for Nixon —to carry on. But fewer Americans than ever in a quarter-century wanted to make a choice.

The phrase that governed traditional contests of the past was "fair choice." In terms of "fair choice," the decision of 1972 was a climax in the thinking of Americans—they voted for the end of the postwar world.

But what if the choice had not been fair? What if the rules had deceived them? What if their President had betrayed the system of fair choice, fair laws, fair chance for which all of them had come here— ethnics, Catholics, Jews, Englishmen, Nordics and Mediterraneans? What if the blacks, who had been dragged here in chains and coffles, now were convinced that "Charlie's" society was phony? Now all of them, black and white, rich and poor, North and South, minorities and majorities, would have to look back on what their choice of power really meant. Here, analysis of election numbers gave no answer.

CHAPTER FOURTEEN

───

TEMPTATION OF POWER

WHEN I came home twenty years ago, after many years abroad, to write of American politics, Richard Nixon was already a major figure of the national scene.

And all he stood for, as nearly as I could make out, I feared. I wrote of him in this style over the years of the fifties and then discovered, to my surprise, that the harsh edge of my reporting was softening. I had the choice, as a reporter, of writing about him from afar—in which case, his rhetoric and public posture made him the most inviting target at which a liberal might wing his eloquence. Or I could pursue him, seek personal contact in order to measure the man I was writing about. This second choice, of course, carried with it an obligation to respect his privacy—and, even more, an obligation to try to understand. I chose the second course, and discovered that the unguarded private man was fascinating.

What was interesting about Richard Nixon was the education life had given him—an education as engrossing as the Education of Henry Adams. Richard Nixon was, to be sure, not a very trusting person. Life had made him that way. There hung over him the wary loneliness of a man always excluded from the company of those he admired; he guarded his hurts. He had been excluded all the way—from the football team at Whittier High School as a boy, from the private upper floor of the White House even after he had become Vice-President. When he came to live in New York, where I sought him out, he was excluded by those who think of themselves as "the best people." Nelson Rockefeller ran New York's Republican party with an iron hand; though the former Vice-President lived in the same apartment block as the Governor, he was excluded from party affairs as completely as if he did not exist. Life was always for him a bare-knuckled fight upward, at every level—and he made friends with difficulty. Most were flatterers in later life; he was a name and a property to be used; yet he hungered for loyalties.

But on the way the mind of the loner had been working, observant of himself as of others. Thus, as I came to know him, to observe his mind changing, my respect began. There was in his private talk a stubborn candor of self-recognition; in his thinking was a muscular quality of grappling with the facts as they were. The recognized pugnacity was there, that toughness of response, even cruelty, with which he could respond to toughness thrust at him. Above all, two qualities: a fatalism of outlook and a personal melancholy which added wisdom to his reflections.

Over the years, thus, I watched Richard Nixon change from the man I had denounced—from the Cold Warrior to the man who sought peace with China; from the red-baiter to the enemy of the John Birch Society; from the unfeeling opponent of every social program in House and Senate to the advocate of a guaranteed annual income, the first modern welfare proposal since Franklin Roosevelt's Social Security Act —and my respect grew.

I was a liberal. He was a conservative. Our mind-sets ran differently. I had come back to the United States in the early 1950's at a moment when poetry passed briefly through American politics—first Adlai Stevenson, then John F. Kennedy gave a music to public affairs. There was no poetry in Richard Nixon. The liberal tradition had heroes running back through Lincoln to Jefferson. The conservative tradition, of which Nixon came, had no ancestor heroes; his mind had to pick its way awkwardly through the facts, the realities, with no governing code, no inherited dream.

The mind, then, was what first intrigued me, both for its toughness and for its range. The range of Richard Nixon's mind was astonishing— it reached from the problems of Singapore to the exports of Japan, to the minutiae of Southern California politics, to the cost factors in political publicity, to the sequence of railway towns in Ohio—just which towns lay north or south of Lima, Ohio, for example, and what people made there. The mind embraced the ethnic pattern of America, personalities at the Pentagon, draft figures and the impact on colleges. Nixon had the courage to face facts even when they did not fit together. In conversation, his mind could go, zip, from what appeared to be a covering banality to the most precise exposition of sustaining and contradictory facts. I remember speaking to him on the telephone in 1969 just fifteen minutes after the astronauts had landed for the first time on the moon, a moment of American drama if there ever was one. He was exhilarated. He had been watching the Cronkite narration on television. First came a football image. Those last twenty seconds before Armstrong and Aldrin landed, he said, were just like the last twenty seconds of a tight football game; and then shifting metaphor, he continued—it was like the explorers of Spain reaching the New World. People miss the whole thing about the Age of Exploration, he said; it wasn't what they brought back at first that counted, it was the lift it gave to man's spirit. Then his mind locked into tight reasoning: we Americans were going to make the adventure in space a free-world enterprise; he wanted to bring other nations in; Kissinger was working on it—the British, the NATO allies, the Japanese to show that Asians were included in space, too. Eventually, the Russians —but that couldn't be done right away, for national security was involved, and Russian pride. But he was sure you could run an integrated multi-national adventure in space. He had problems with the military, of course. But if the allies came into the space adventure, perhaps they could be brought to bear 20 percent of the expense of the space program. His mind had all the facts at hand, had pre-sorted them into patterns—all this within twenty minutes of the time the first men had walked on the moon to plant the American flag.

Talking to Nixon, either before or during his Presidency, left the visitor enlarged in his own re-patterning of facts. The mind of the President was not philosophical. Fatalistic, yes. But questioning, no. He was President, or candidate for President—and the President was the national symbol. Conversations with him, when I first came to know him, had the sound of a male Barbara Frietchie calling "Shoot, if you must, this old gray head, but spare your country's flag." Then it sank in that this *was* the philosophy of Richard Nixon; there was nothing spurious about it. His first duty was to protect the state of America —against all enemies, at home and abroad. This led to the next, the overriding thought in his mind. America needed peace—he would bring peace. When George McGovern spoke of peace all through the campaign of 1972, one understood that the word "peace" meant, for McGovern, brotherhood between all peoples of the world. I have never heard Nixon use the word "brotherhood" privately; if he has used it publicly, it must have been with his fingers crossed behind his back. For Nixon, peace was a need of the American people, to be won by hard, tough negotiations and deals with other hard, tough governments overseas who took the word "brotherhood" as skeptically as did he. Once peace was won, it was his conviction, the American people at home would be able to find their own way into the future, with a minimum of control from the government.

By 1973 I had followed the evolution of his thinking through his Presidency, through his foreign policy, through his liquidation of the burden of the draft on American young men, through his concept of environmental control, through his thrust for revenue-sharing, through his definitions of the communities and constituencies of American life. I had been appalled by the Watergate affair during the campaign, as was everyone; it was, I felt, a clinical indecency in politics which the President should have cauterized immediately, however loyal his lieutenants might have been. I had accepted, finally, the concept of the President as steward of the state's interests abroad, one man expressing the will of the people, but ultimately responsible alone for defining and deciding who were their enemies and friends overseas. But I had not then imagined that in Nixon's mind this power of the state could be stretched to defining enemies and friends at home in America, too.

On balance, however, the record of Richard Nixon had earned from me a high respect which came to crest on Saturday afternoon of March 17th, 1973, the last time I saw the President.

Four days later were to begin those revelations and charges which were to shatter his confidence in himself, the nation's confidence in him, and raise for everyone who writes of American history or politics those unavoidable questions: Would he go down in history as the President of Peace or the President of Watergate? Had the President of the United States broken the law? What were the limits of power for the office and the man?

But I asked none of those questions that Saturday afternoon; they did not, at that moment, seem relevant. We were talking about what he had learned of the Presidency, of the nature of the job—running the country—in his first four years. He was answering pragmatic questions in pragmatic style. Watergate was about to burst; but he was at that moment reflective, almost serene, an American President at the height of his authority. We talked for two and a half hours.

We began to talk on a side matter—the recently announced appointment of David Bruce as Ambassador to China in all but title. Both of us were fond of David Bruce, and I told the President how much the appointment pleased everyone. He replied that what was vital in the appointment was its symbolism. Two years earlier he had wanted to send Bruce, not Kissinger, to make the initial contact with China. But the Chinese had refused to accept Bruce because he was then America's negotiator in Paris with North Vietnam—Bruce represented to the Chinese the symbolism of war. They had taken Kissinger instead. But now they would accept Bruce—and in exchange they were sending their number-one diplomat to Washington. It meant, said the President, they accepted the fact that the war in Vietnam was over. And so did we.

I wanted to turn the conversation to home affairs; and I said that I had once quoted him on the Presidency and the nation in a conversation of 1967, in which he had said, "I've always thought this country could run itself domestically without a President; all you need is a competent Cabinet to run the country at home. . . ." Since that remark had been requoted and misinterpreted so often, what about it?

He was easy this afternoon, and toyed with the question as if trying to find a shape to the answer. "People don't respond in domestic affairs," he said. "Unless it touches them directly—like busing—they don't give a damn. But when it comes to foreign affairs, everyone wants to be Secretary of State, every columnist, every commentator, every writer." Domestic questions, he felt, just weren't that exciting. Take a question like revenue-sharing—only the specialists wanted to probe around that one.

The reason for the importance of the Presidency in foreign affairs was that if a President made a mistake in that area it could mean the destruction of the world; or it could mean you miss the opportunity for an uneasy peace, and "the best we can hope for is an uneasy peace." In domestic affairs, take the economy, for example—the economy was so strong that, despite its ups and downs, "it would take a genius to wreck it." A President and his Cabinet could meddle with it, foul it up, but it got along, it continued to grow. "A mistake in domestic affairs isn't necessarily fatal—but in foreign policy it is fatal." In foreign affairs a President had to call the shots "as clearly as he can to the ultimate."

So the domestic field was where Presidents usually ran into trouble. The nation tended to unite behind a President on foreign policy. But on domestic policy "Presidents are usually losers, because domestic affairs divide." FDR had had an emergency at home, the Depression, which united people behind him—but it was sad that so many of our great Presidents had to have a war to unite people behind them.

What we had now, in the domestic field, was an opportunity to get the nation mobilized to solve domestic issues—but that wasn't going to be easy.

This got him into the nature of his job: running the country. "A President can only concentrate on a few issues," he said. "It gets back to what they said about Cleveland—that he'd rather do something poorly himself than delegate it to someone else to do well." He spoke of Lyndon Johnson, who "insisted on making all the calls—the White House even intervened on target selection in Vietnam. That was Johnson's way. But it's not the best way. A President is basically elected to make those decisions well that no one else can really make."

The President reminisced about what he had learned on the job in the previous four years, on what it is to be a President. Take Kissinger's shop. In those first few months they'd been sending the President notes on practically every proposal and problem—notes on the Ecuadorian fisheries; on Central Africa; on Denmark and the salmon problem. He had had to "turn them around" on that—"we've got people who can and should make the answers on that kind of thing." The President's time should be devoted to matters like nuclear-arms limitation. And "when a President gets involved, he should not just preside—he should participate." But it was up to the President to decide what questions required his time.

The Office of the Presidency was overburdened with councils, committees, Cabinet members who wanted the President to sit and listen and be briefed. You tried to listen to something like the President's Science Advisory Committee, but you learned you couldn't listen to every single one of those committees. What you had to do was to put able people in government, then "trust them and back them up. . . . The most important thing I've learned is to get free time, time when the President just thinks. I'd recommend it to any future President—just call in someone and say, 'Let's talk about this for an hour.' "

"In the domestic field," he said, "I'm going to do the same thing. I'm getting the government reorganized in such a way that the President can spend more time on the most important things—though everything is important, and what's important will change from time to time—and we'll see how successfully we can do that. My disposition is to see that the President's time is not frittered away. I've found a way to do it. I'm a reader, not a buller. Most of the boys at the Law School had long bull sessions about their cases. I studied my cases alone. The space committee, the medical committee, the science committee—if they give me a paper, I'll read it."

He seemed amused as he recalled his on-the-job training, learning to recognize what papers a President should and shouldn't read. By law, of course, he was supposed to read them all. His first week in office, the first paper put at him was a paper from the Civil Aeronautics Board. By law, the CAB requires Presidential approval before granting any airline a franchise on a foreign route; the CAB had thrust a route application by Continental Airlines at him. "I spent hours reading it, just considering it," he said ruefully. "At present I wouldn't *think* of doing that. I don't want anti-trust cases to get in here, or cable television franchises, or licenses. I'm not going to get into that."

He broke off, half chuckling. "The Tariff Commission sent over something the other day on pianos." The President is, by law, supposed to break a tie vote when the Tariff Commission is split. "When I first came to office, I would have spent hours reading about the piano industry." By now his staff had been trained to make papers precise for him. "I took ten minutes to read a split paper and made the decision." Things like that were for people down below to be responsible for—he didn't want his mind "cluttered up" with that sort of thing.

What, then, were the kinds of things for which a President was responsible now in 1973 in domestic policy? There was, obviously, no listed portfolio in his mind, and what came uppermost as he leaned back, his feet on the table, was a cluster of matters for which he felt no one except a President could be responsible. Uppermost in his mind at that moment were energy, civil rights, the economy, the budget.

Energy was the first.

"Right now I'm spending a lot of time on energy. I have to make the calls there. It involves—it involves foreign policy, the Soviet pipe-

line, the Middle East, are we going to have brown-outs?" The President
was listing his major problems in the order in which he saw them, weaving their interconnections back and forth through the long conversation,
and when, as now, I try to assemble his thoughts it is because he kept
returning to the energy problem. We have to make a long-term decision
there, said the President. It involved getting rid of quotas, tariffs, barriers; it involved defense policy, agricultural policy, policies of subsidies,
wages, prices, some twenty different agencies of government. "Energy
won't get the public attention it deserves until people run out of it, and
then they'll blame the government—'What were those guys doing?' Environment didn't affect the country as an issue directly until it became
the water you drank, the air you breathed, the park you wanted to go
to. Well, we've got to do the right thing now, and that involves the
Alaska pipeline, the Middle East oil, possibly something with the Russians, nuclear energy, shale-oil recovery. In energy, it's got to be the
President. These questions cut across the gamut of interests, and the
fighting in the bureaucracy's been vicious, and between good men, too.
They all want to do it—State, Interior, Defense. So it's got to be a decision in the White House—I want to make those decisions."

As for civil rights, he volunteered that as the next most important
domestic problem on his mind. He felt he'd moved things forward in
civil rights, "but that took time." And he was doing it his way. Take
segregation. The "professional civil-rightser" was interested in confrontation, in rhetoric more than in result. If he'd denounced the racist
South, that would have pleased the civil-rights crowd. "But in actually
desegregating the schools in the South, it wouldn't have done it. There
would have been police at every school door, the President would have
given them confrontation—and who knows what might have happened?"
He had done it his own way. He hadn't got much of the black vote anywhere, but he could call in the black leaders and white leaders of the
South, quietly, to the White House and tell them what had to be done,
that it had to be done by law, and done peacefully. Only the President
could have brought those people together—*that* was a Presidential job.
He'd attended only one public session on black and white school problems, in New Orleans. Nonetheless, there was a lot less segregation in
Southern schools now than in Northern big cities.

He moved along to the economy. There the President *had* to act—
all across the board. "There's seven billion dollars' worth of material in
the stockpiles, for example, far more than we need." We'd kept prices
high for a long time, for various reasons; by inference I gathered he felt
the stockpiles had to be used to bring prices down. But take tin, for example—that involved foreign policy as well as prices. Bolivia, Malaysia,
Thailand, our allies, depended on tin, which we stockpiled, for exports—
"I have to balance the loss to Malaysia and Thailand against the present

price crisis." So, too, he had to balance labor's demands for protection against the world abroad. "That's not only foreign policy—that's jobs. I talk to George Meany and his crowd and I point out, 'You say fifty billion worth of imports means [could cost us] fifty billion worth of jobs. I'm worried about that, too. But we export fifty billion worth, too—and I don't want to lose *those* jobs.' Sure, we could be tough with Japan and we could be tough with Europe, so tough they'd change to anti-American." To adopt a tough policy on imports just wouldn't serve American political interests abroad. So when it came to a point where jobs at home and America's interests abroad had to be balanced—that was a Presidential duty.

This problem focused in the budget—that was Presidential. "The budget determines the health of the economy, it determines inflation, it determines the role of government in social areas." The budget decided functions. Here he gave an example. He was dismantling the Office of Economic Opportunity. He'd taken the Head Start program and put it in HEW and actually *increased* the money for it. He'd taken Manpower Training and put it where it belonged. But when it came to such a thing as the Community Action Program, that was different. During its existence CAP had spent, over the years, $2.3 billion—of which 85 percent had gone to the bureaucrats who ran it and only 15 percent actually got to poor people. So, "out with it"—here, a slash of his hand.

The budget was a Presidential function, it was one of the larger controls a President had over the whole scene (here, I am paraphrasing the President's thought). But, said he, "I've been rather amused, this attack on the administration for impounding funds." LBJ impounded an average of 6 percent of the money appropriated; Nixon was impounding substantially less than LBJ—less than the Presidential average over the past fifty years. " 'This President is grasping for power,' they say. What I'm trying to do is to get power out of here."

From this point he went on to what is, in the public mind, one of the dreariest and dustiest of his major achievements: revenue-sharing. There, said the President, "we come to a difference of philosophy. Those who oppose us don't want to say so. Virtually every politician pays lip service to the idea of the decentralization of the Federal government. But there's this considerable body of opinion, especially among scholars, that local government isn't as competent as Federal government. If you accept that premise, then our whole approach is wrong, it falls on its face. If you accept that approach, then all our governors, all our mayors are necessarily clerks, lobbyists, messenger boys spending the dough as people here in Washington determine. . . . Whether it's a government abroad, a city, a county, a state, if you help them too much they remain weak, incompetent and, frequently, corrupt." The President's opinion was that you simply had to take the great revenues the Internal Revenue Service collected and share them out with cities and states, and let the mayor or governor decide what that city or state needed. "When Washington makes a mistake, it's a beaut, it covers the whole country. When California or New York makes a mistake, it covers one tenth of the country. When Wyoming makes a mistake, it covers only one sixtieth of the country. Nelson Rockefeller says it's pretty dangerous to let the Mayor of Utica make the decisions for Utica. But we're freely expressing a faith—the right and responsibility of self-government. The states and cities can do things we might never approach, or even see; we're trying to get more brains and ability on the job."

He felt that domestic revenue-sharing was like the Nixon doctrine abroad: The American government helps, but local governments have got to do it on their own. As in South Vietnam—"We've trained them, armed them, and it's up to them to defend themselves with our assistance. That's the only way they're going to get the strength and experience to run their country." That was the way American cities and states should run themselves—with Federal help, not Federal control. This was his concept of the Presidency, and the direction he had set in domestic affairs. It was quite clear, on that afternoon, that he felt himself at the peak of power. He had taken the old Lincolnian concept of government and moved it, theoretically, a step further. Lincoln had felt that government was necessary to do those things best which the people could not do for themselves. Nixon had extended that concept: The President must decide only those matters which the government cannot decide by itself. "Too many people," he said, "who write about politics get bogged down in trivia. You've got to get up there and be in tune with the forces. If you're out of tune with the forces, like McGovern, you're not going to make it."

Nor had that been easy for him. It was quite clear where his heart and attention still lay as we came back to talk of foreign affairs. We talked of his visit to China; of his May 8th decision to mine Haiphong and bomb Hanoi. Those were Presidential tasks.

The worst of all the tasks came at Christmas, 1972.

So the election had occurred, he said, "a big victory," the people thought the war was over. Then Henry Kissinger went to Paris for the last details of the agreement with Hanoi—and found "a complete turnaround, a prolonged filibuster." The other side had reneged on the DMZ, reneged on our prisoners of war. Now they wouldn't release our prisoners of war unless Thieu released civilian prisoners in South Vietnam. We'd already told Thieu that if we got the right deal, we'd sign and he'd have to go along. Kissinger negotiated for ten days, but the deal had come unstuck; Hanoi had new conditions we couldn't accept. There was Christmas coming up, and the Christmas spirit. And Congress coming back to session in January—"If we didn't have a settlement, they'd blow us up."

"What you needed was they [Hanoi] had to know, so far as I was concerned," said the President, "without regard for any opinion here or around the world, that I was determined to bring this war to an end." And he was going to do it with whatever force was necessary. Weather over Hanoi is bad in December. Fighter planes could not do it. All-weather B-52's might. The Defense Department did not want to use B-52's over Hanoi; they estimated a loss rate of 3 or 4 percent (which proved correct). The President inquired how many B-52's were operational around the world; was told the numbers; then decided himself, alone, that if that was what it took to end the war, that was what it took. On December 18th the bombing started. Then the loss of three planes the first day, four the next, five the next. And everyone demanding he go on air to explain the reason for the bombing. Even the Chicago *Tribune.*

"I didn't go on air," said the President. "That would have been counter-productive." The United States had sent a private message to Hanoi, saying that as soon as they came back to the table to talk in terms of the October agreement, the bombing would stop. But to say that publicly would have been tantamount to an ultimatum (I am paraphrasing the President's remarks here), and to have given a public ultimatum would have made it impossible for Hanoi to come back to the table. "So I just had to take the heat," said the President. The alternative was to let the war drag on into the next year and let the war be voted out, in effect, by Congress; the prisoners would have been held forever—"they would never have given them to us."

Every editorialist in the country was demanding that the President either stop the bombing or explain. Because of the international date line, the one-day Christmas bombing pause became a thirty-six-hour bombing pause. He talked to no one about the matter, not even to his wife and family. "That was the toughest day—we had no word." The day after Christmas he telephoned Admiral Moorer, Chairman of the Joint Chiefs of Staff, and said, "Admiral, everything that can fly is going to go over next day." And thirty-six hours later, after the bombing was resumed, messages came from Hanoi saying that, after all, things could be worked out at the conference table. The main thing was the goal, said the President; the goal does not guarantee South Vietnamese freedom, it gives them a chance to defend their own freedom, and that "presumably was what the war was all about."

It was not quite over yet, though. A few days later the Senate Democratic caucus voted, as the President put it, "for a bug-out on the prisoners." Would it affect Hanoi? Kissinger was already in Paris. But by January 9th Kissinger had telephoned to say that the major breakthrough had come, there would be peace. And January 9th was the President's sixtieth birthday.

The President was now, in our conversation, almost through with his tour of Presidential responsibilities, playing with his watch. I thought I must have tired him. But he continued, "What caused me the pain was not what Trudeau, nor the Australians, nor Pompidou, nor what the American press said. No. The thing that concerned me were those crews, five a day. I knew they had to go. It wasn't an easy Christmas."

When it was clear, after the bombing halt, that things were brightening, he called Lyndon Johnson, the day after New Year's. LBJ's voice was hoarse, the President recalled; he'd been to the Cotton Bowl game and yelled too much. LBJ told the President, "I've got some terrible heart pains." Nixon told Johnson that negotiations were on the track again; LBJ said he was praying for Richard Nixon. Nixon's recollection was that he himself replied, "I'm just doing the right thing. You did, too. If it does come out all right, your position in history is assured." Then, just three days before LBJ died on January 22nd, 1973, Henry Kissinger was told by the President to telephone the ex-President and say the deal was made; furthermore, the President directed that the texts of the documents be sent to Johnson.

LBJ, the President thought, might have done it differently. "He was obsessed by the media, he'd look at those television sets every night. I followed what was going on. But I made my decisions in the cold light of day. I had to build a shield around myself."

My judgment, suspended at that date, would have cast Richard Nixon as one of the major Presidents of the twentieth century, in a rank just after Franklin Roosevelt, on a level with Truman, Wilson, Eisenhower, Kennedy.

Thus the view from Olympus, on March 17th, 1973, as Nixon described his use of a President's power. And then, within a few days, the view was to be shattered. I was to be brought down from Olympus to consider, with the President and millions of other Americans, the housekeeping of power—and its abuse. By early April the nation and the President were both to learn that the deputy director of his political mobilization, Jeb Magruder, had alleged that both his Attorney General, John Mitchell, and his legal counsel, John Dean, had knowingly participated in the planning of the Watergate conspiracy. A few weeks later the nation was to hear the President on television declare that he was accepting the resignations of H. R. Haldeman and John Ehrlichman, two men of his great trust and affection. Less than two weeks later his former Attorney General and his former Secretary of Commerce were indicted for helping a swindler. The leaders of his own Republican Party were removing themselves from him as they would from a leper. And the privacy of his inner life and actions, a privacy so essential to the personality of Richard Nixon, was being made a daily television show, a variation of the ancient parable: How Have The Mighty Fallen! Having so implacably pursued the press, he was in turn pursued by a press which was now equally implacable. Chivvied and harassed as no President before him had ever been, he was either an object of national sympathy and a victim, or else the first President about to be found guilty of breach of law. In 1968, Richard Nixon had begun his final push for the Presidency in a speech in riot-torn Chicago. "My friends," he had thundered, "let me make one thing clear. This is a nation of laws and, as Abraham Lincoln said, no one is above the law, no one is below the law. And we're going to enforce the law." Now, in 1973, it was up to him to keep that pledge, however far down the path of tragedy it took him; for the use of power at home was as important as the use of power abroad.

For those who loathed Nixon, it was easy to explain Watergate: All of it, bugging, burglary, fund-raising, wire-tapping, dirty tricks, pay-offs for silence, tampering with witnesses, the miasma of fear—all flowed from the character and personality of Richard Nixon.

Those who drew up the indictment in public opinion, or clamored for his official impeachment, reached back to Nixon's past, and as they dredged it, they uncovered much that seemed to cling to the President. Here was the man Nixon who had begun in politics by savaging one of the champions of the liberal cause, Congressman Jerry Voorhis. He had gone on to rip another liberal champion, Helen Gahagan Douglas, in a campaign which, even in California terms, was one of the most ferocious of the postwar years. He had been exposed as accepting a private gift fund from rich Californians in the campaign of 1952—and wriggled off by playing the emotions of Americans like a guitar. He had been an ally, they said, of Joe McCarthy in the red hunts of the late forties and early fifties. His campaigns had been marked by the use of every phony-front dirty trick in the book. Thus, in the view of those who called for his impeachment, the White House had been seized by a group of men who reflected the essential character of their chief; these men would stop at nothing, observe no law, preserve no decencies in their ambitions, and sell government favors at random to dairy men, grain men, conglomerates, investors all alike for cash contributions. All of this, they alleged, flowed from the character and career of Richard Nixon.

Yet reality was more complicated than that. Most of the allegations against Richard Nixon rested on hard fact. He had led a hard, tough political career on his way up, pressing the accepted rules of American politics to their limit. But there were other facts, too. And when one assembled them all, there was an enigma in Richard Nixon which lay at the heart of the Watergate affair—his view of the state, its limits and responsibilities.

There were these facts, for example: He had campaigned in 1960 against John F. Kennedy embittered by Kennedy's charge that a "missile gap" was giving the Soviet Union a lead of terror over American defense; at the time, the missile gap in reality was overwhelmingly in America's favor; but Nixon would not use the information in the campaign, for to do so would breach security of the state. He had been beaten by Kennedy by two tenths of one percent of the national vote in an election marked by vote stealing and irregularities in three or four states, so brazen that any court would have entertained a challenge for recount. For a few days, Nixon considered demanding such a recount, then rejected the thought—the need of state required that America not wait two or three months to find out the name of its next President. He had instructed his campaigners in 1968 to put as much distance between his campaign and the racist Wallace campaign as they could, no matter what the cost—if elected, he could not govern a state which race issues had split. As President, he found himself again and again forced to act as authoritarian chief of state—he had no support in Congress except on defense policy; he could enact only one major piece of structural legislation: revenue-sharing. What he did—whether it was abolition of the draft, or the reorganization of environmental controls, or negotiations with foreign chiefs of state—he did alone, as President; as Richard Nixon, not Mr. Republican.

There was much in the life-journey of Richard Nixon through politics that explained the facts, both hurtful and helpful to his public image. That life-journey had begun in California just after the war, when the old party system was breaking down. That party system in a state of newcomers, two thirds of its people born out of state, had no cohesion, no organizations, no party principles when Richard Nixon entered politics. It was, for example, a state where, until the late 1950's, Republicans might run in Democratic primaries and Democrats in Republican primaries under the state's peculiar tradition of "cross-filing." Republicans like Earl Warren or Bill Knowland might win both primaries and run as both Republican and Democratic candidates for state office. So, too, might Democrats—and did. Democrats formed front committees under Republican names; Republicans did the same under Democratic names. Dirty tricks flourished. Both parties were open to wild, extremist groups of right or left which might seize and control parts of a party's nominal machinery. Public-relations men perfected those arts of image manipulation and image destruction which became common in Eastern politics only much later when party structures began to erode there, too. Miraculously, the California system provided excellent state government, a system which could administer and make attractively livable a state whose population was doubling in a generation; it could provide great roads and a superb system of education; it developed a responsible and competent body of state legislators; and it could train a statesman of the quality of Earl Warren. But its very newness, the strangeness of its newcomers to each other, made the state increasingly, as it is today, subject to gusts of political passion, swept by violent opinions.

Out of this system came Richard Nixon, trained in the hit-and-cut style of California media politics, learning to slash messages on people's minds to get attention without benefit of party help or party loyalties. He arrived in Washington at the moment of the breakdown of America's wartime alliance with Stalinist Russia, to be intrigued by the spy hunts and witch hunts of the Cold War. He made his first mark on fame by tracing the leakage of what he considered to be critical State Department information, national-security information, at a time when, actually as well as mythically, Russian espionage had penetrated the American government. Many liberals and good thinkers had been ensnared by the mood of the war and the times to rhapsodize over an alliance with Russia made necessary by survival; and thus, later, by false allegation, to be charged with implied treason. The slanders of those days still linger in the minds of liberals and color all their thinking of Richard Nixon—the hit-and-slash man, the spy-hunter, the conspiratorial thinker. From the days of Joe McCarthy on (though Joe McCarthy might and did growl that "Richard Nixon is no friend of mine"), Nixon has appeared in liberal prose always as if the brand of Cain were on him. And Nixon distrusted such domestic enemies—the liberals, not the Democrats—as much as they distrusted him. If, in his mind, reasons of state required precautionary action against them, he would not be squeamish.

Thus, then he became President, regarding politics as mechanics; bred in the old California school of dirty tricks and cut-and-slash; wary of conspiracies; obsessed with the President's role as chief of state in speaking for America in foreign affairs—and a man without executive experience.

This executive job of the Presidency is without parallel. Shortly after talking to the President for the last time, I tried to find out just what the minimum legal burden of the executive was, in hard law. I learned the following: He is by statute responsible for choosing men and making the policy decisions for over fifty executive departments and agencies. He must appoint the policy makers who serve in 197 departments, agencies, commissions and committees. He must direct the basic policy of all the statutory departments, some of which (such as HEW) have no less than 254 separate programs, on each of which he is supposed to give policy guidance. Plus Congress. In the year 1972, for example, 483 bills arrived at the White House from the Hill to be read and signed, which he did. Seventeen more arrived which he considered at length and then vetoed. In addition, he issued 55 Executive Orders to the government, and 77 Proclamations; moreover, he transmitted to Congress 110 reports from Presidential commissions and task forces, all of which, by law, were supposed to reflect his thinking. This was the statutory burden. Beyond that were the trips to China and to Russia, the receptions for and conferences with foreign chiefs of state, the unrecorded demands on his time from a thousand sources. And, finally, a campaign for re-election to manage.

The mechanics of the campaign were the easiest matter to export from the White House—across the street to the Committee to Re-Elect, and to the Finance Committee. Nixon had mastered that craft long ago; its details still amused him and occasionally he would talk about such details as a senior general might reminisce on his experience as a battalion commander. He could appreciate or criticize good or bad advance work in the field; was aware of the performance of such people as Maurice Stans in totals of money coming in, separated from details of its collection. His preoccupation now was the grand strategy of state, the concepts of the campaign.

To his operational teams, thus, was delivered only one imperative—performance. What they took from Nixon, and their reading of his past politics, was a reading of politics as a game in which one had to run up the score, no matter how. What was lacking was more important: a vision, a binding cause, a sense of purpose beyond just winning, beyond just making a record to serve personal ambition within palace politics. Nixon gave that inspiration only to a handful of people, all of them at the White House, none of them in politics. He gave it to Moynihan, who dropped out after two years; to Kissinger, who stayed; to Weinberger and Finch, who wanted to make the system work, as did the President; to his three personal speechwriters, Buchanan, Price and Safire. But the nation beyond absorbed little of that inspiration of purpose, that "lift of a driving dream," which he had promised in 1968. People voted in 1972 for the man most competent to do the job; they were uneasy about the spirit and dreams of George McGovern. The conservative cause in 1972 might have been, and someday may be, transformed into a genuine movement of spirit. But Nixon in 1972 failed to seize the moment to give his cause, or his campaign team, that horizon of spirit and dream which urges men to deny themselves evil.

I doubt that new laws, though they may be useful, will prevent repetition of such an episode as the Watergate affair; the laws of the United States already forbade the family of crimes included in that term. New laws will not help because the Watergate affair gets to the use and temptation of power in a world that grows more and more complicated. And the temptation of power is no less corrosive in a democracy than in a dictatorship.

In America, I think, temptation of power starts with the traditional impatience of a nation that demands quick solutions; and this impatience builds to a pressure that has increased through the administrations of all the Presidents I have known except Eisenhower. A military executive most of his life, Eisenhower had learned to recognize those moments that call for the quick stroke of action, and to distinguish them from the slow responsibilities of garrison duty. Eisenhower conducted his Presidency as a benign garrison command. All other Presidents of the postwar world, from Truman on, have suffered from this national impatience for results; and they have all pressed the laws of the United States to the limit to get results.

There is a membrane of morality which, indefinably, gives the White House its sacerdotal quality. It is a delicate and flexible membrane, but vital: it must contain policy and national action within the law. When that membrane hemorrhages—danger.

This membrane had been strained well before Nixon. John F. Kennedy, whom I cherished, read the FBI wire-taps on Martin Luther King with relish—but took no action based on them. Lyndon Johnson pressed further on the membrane, enjoying the power of prying and gossip that access to secret tax files and FBI reports gave him; he pressed it as far as the launching of an unauthorized war. Neither man, however, pressed the membrane to rupture. In the Nixon administration, the membrane did rupture—and peritonitis, a seepage of lawlessness, began to work its way through the system, from employees of the White House down. It had been characteristic of the late sixties and early seventies, as the postwar world was ending, that others, too, were pressing on the general membrane of morality which, in a civilized society, keeps action within the law—rioters in the street, bombers, direct-action causists, students subject to conscription and death in an illegal war, good-willed citizens using conscience as an excuse for violence. So, too, was the press pushing to its limits another membrane of law, that which protects the privacy of courts and government decision. But the White House is the place of law itself, where the law must be executed in all its precise purity; and in the White House, in 1972, pressure tempted power to the final, poisonous rupture of the membrane.

Temptation of power usually stirs when those who wield it grow impatient at its limitations—and impatience infects everyone who works at the White House. The President requires a statement today—and a dozen bureaucrats must drop all other work to provide the data that may or may not be used tomorrow. A decision must move now—and all through the bureaucracy, from the Pentagon to Interior, men at the remotest fringe of responsibility tingle to the need—moreover, feel privileged to be included in it. Credit goes to those who respond fastest, the credit rising level by level to the final person who enters personally to the President, or whose paper reaches his desk fastest, with the most coherent summary. The sound of the cracking whip—"Get it up to the boss"—sets the rhythm of the White House. A President may muse, "I wonder whether we're going to have trouble with demonstrators at San Diego, it might look bad on TV"—and down the line his musing becomes a command, credit going to those fastest off the mark. Or the President may explode at the printing and publishing of a national-security paper, and say, "Who the hell did that? Find out!"

So—Fast! Speed is required.

In the Nixon White House, perhaps more than in any other except the Johnson White House, this impatience prevailed. In the great foreign-policy decisions where the President himself governed, the weaving of strands was masterful and slow. But in the mechanics of politics and its details—there the unspoken imperative was always: "Move it, get it done, don't bother him with detail." The pressure on anyone who works or lives in the White House is continuously enormous; it became even more enormous under Nixon, when men had to rise at 6:00 in the morning to get to staff conferences at 7:30 so the President could be briefed at 9:00 A.M. Privileges, too, are enormous. There is the switchboard that links your calls anywhere around the globe, whether the call is to a child traveling abroad or to a traveling mission of state. There is the White House car, to pick you up in the rain at 7:00 A.M. or take you home after midnight—should the President's staff stand in the street and frantically hail taxicabs? There is the deference from famous men who visit, from the bureaucracy below. Life at the White House exhausts—but intoxicates. Beyond the daily pressure shimmer many dreams. The dreamers hope to move from the White House to sub-Cabinet or Cabinet posts, and thus be recorded in history forever; they may change the shape of the country; and, at the very least, no matter what happens, if they perform well, there are all those jobs that come attendant on the exposure or experience they acquire at the White House—jobs in industry, or jobs in foundations, or jobs in grandly titled lobbies, which pay $75,000 or $100,000 or $200,000 a year. But all depends on performance, on moving by performance step by step through the tiers of the White House to public responsibility and note. This pressure to perform, this intoxication with the power and privileges available to achieve performance overcame the men who worked for Richard Nixon—and surfaced in what will remain in American history as the nightmare of the Watergate affair. Whether they acted in his spirit or with his knowledge is the matter before American judgment as this book closes.

At best, Richard Nixon, however magnificent his management of American power abroad, is guilty of gross negligence in management of the power of the White House at home.

And at the worst?

At the worst, which his enemies and friends alike debate at the moment, he would be found guilty of a specific crime, "misprision of justice." The crime alleged is both specific and peculiar, for the word "misprision" comes from the old French word *"mesprendre,"* to make a mistake. The word came into English from the Norman kings, who required that all officials of the strange Anglo-Saxon country they conquered report crimes against the state to them. One commits misprision of justice when one fails to recognize felony or treason, or aids and abets in concealing or covering up such felony or treason from the courts of law. The running question that pursues the President of the United States is whether or not he knew felony was being committed, and whether he made a mistake in not acting on such knowledge. Such a mistake in the President of the United States is unforgivable—and he would have to leave. But to indict a President only on hearsay evidence or gossip is equally unforgivable.

The Watergate affair is inexplicable in terms of older forms of corruption in American history, where men broke laws for private gain or privilege. The dynamics of its irrationality are compounded further by stupidity. The men involved were involved at a moment, in 1972, when history was moving their way. They were trying to speed it by any means, fair or foul. By so doing perhaps they wrecked their own victory. And that, as history may record, compounds their personal felonies with national tragedy.

For it would be no less than national tragedy if men came to regard the election of 1972 as fraud; or attempted to reverse the verdict of the people at the polls on the technicalities of a burglary, in a spasm of morality approaching the hysterical.

The view of the 1972 election as fraud is comforting to many who, intellectually, have been unable to accept the proportions of the 1972 vote. Watergate has, curiously, restored their faith in the American people. The people had, according to this theory of fraud, simply been hoodwinked, bamboozled, tricked into a giant mistake. According to this theory, the people could be rehabilitated and forgiven for what they had done—had they known the truth, they would have turned Richard Nixon out.

Of all the ironies of 1972, this could become, if accepted, the greatest.

There have been four American campaigns in living memory in which the issues were clearly stated—the Roosevelt campaigns of 1932 and 1936, the Goldwater-Johnson contest of 1964, the McGovern-Nixon contest of 1972. All others have been contests of personalities or of party organization. If anything, the election of 1972 was an invitation to the American people, eloquently expressed by both candidates, to consider the use of power in their country. Americans had lived through a postwar world where impatience of power had led either to questionable result or to disaster. Vietnam had been explained to them first as a war in a high cause where, with the investment of several battalions of American troops, a quick mop-up could be effected in a few months against ragged guerrillas—and with a few more troops, the war would be over by Christmas . . . 1965, 1966, 1967. The great cause of civil rights had also been simply explained, its rallying cry "Freedom Now!" "All deliberate speed" had been the judicial formulation, but the accent had been on speed; and the rush had brought results as much of sorrow and agony as of brotherhood and hope. The Russians had been ahead of us in the race to the moon, we were told, which was true; and so, with all the speed and impatience of American power, the rush to the moon was on, with what large benefits no one can yet perceive.

The Republican campaign of 1972 was explained to me by many of its own participants and leaders, but several of the explanations that echo longest in memory come from the defeated of the headquarters of George McGovern. "The Republican Party is the place where people vote when they want to go slow, and I think they want to go slow now," said veteran Ted Van Dyk, McGovern's chief speechwriter, in late October. Much later young Pat Caddell added, "America is not a place in geography, it's an idea. Watergate fouled up the idea."

Between them, they spanned the giant irony. The idea that prevailed in the election of 1972 was that the power should go slow. Go slow abroad, go slow in the cities, go slow with power wherever it interfered with how a child grew up, where she went to school, or where he was sent to die. The election itself was a dull election in the reporting, a refutation of drama, as if the American people were spitting in the wind of history, demanding of time that it stand still. Richard Nixon promised them that—a curb on power. And then, once he was elected, the Americans learned that his administration had been guilty of the grossest abuse of power.

Yet the people had spoken their will. All the dirty tricks, all the dirty money, all the devices known and still to be revealed were as nothing compared to the massive exposure that television and the press—"the system"—gave to what the candidates thought, said, actually did. Reform of national election laws has been overdue for twenty-five years, to make them conform to the new shape of the new America. But no reform yet suggested could have affected the outcome in 1972.

The Americans were for slowing the pace of power, and they chose Richard Nixon.

They would not be ready to march again, or vote again in counter-landslide, until the ideas to make them march or vote had matured wherever they might mysteriously be making themselves ready. For the moment, all the old ideas of the postwar world were dead—and America, which was born of ideas, was an intellectual wasteland. Its most eloquent accepted political thinkers were largely advocates of dead partisan causes; its *avant-garde* thinkers had lacquered over outworn dogmas with new phraseology; the primitive thinkers who opposed them had forgotten, or could not express, the values that had given strength to their tradition. It is characteristic of an age of passage, as a country moves from one set of crumbling ideas to another yet undefined, that palace politics reaches maximum power; goals cease to be national goals and become administrative.

Thus, a man like Richard Nixon must envy a man like Harry Truman.

Truman came to power at a time of crisis, with a country unified behind him, its purpose clear—to destroy Fascism. So, too, were its purposes at home clear to Harry Truman—to eliminate the pestilence of unemployment; to give the black people equal access with whites to American opportunity; to endow and reward education; to make it possible for ordinary people to build and own their own homes. Truman was an amateur in foreign affairs, and his first two years of learning resulted in the needless tragedy of American enmity with China, the awkward intervention of America in a third world it did not understand. But, at least at the beginning, Truman was in no doubt either of his purpose or of his moral authority as President, and I remember best of all the stories I have heard from or about Presidents one that Dr. Robert Oppenheimer told me.

Oppenheimer was the prime creator of the atom bomb. This knowledge haunted him. He, Dean Acheson, David Lilienthal and others had wanted to share the secrets of nuclear power with other nations. The White House resisted. Oppenheimer asked to be received by President Harry Truman, who had dropped the bomb which killed so many. Oppenheimer had never met a President before.

As I heard the story from Oppenheimer, a few weeks before he died—the great scientist already gaunt, his throat seared with the red glaze of radiation where the cancer was being treated, knowing the end was coming—we talked of the relation of thinkers to power, of intellectuals to national decision. He recalled that when he saw Truman he had pleaded as persuasively as he could for Presidential approval of the Oppenheimer-Acheson-Lilienthal plan. Truman asked why Oppenheimer seemed so agitated by the problem, why he seemed so upset. Oppenheimer recalled that he held out his two hands and said, "Mr. President, I have blood on my hands." Truman paused, reached in his pocket and pulled out a handkerchief. Then he said, "I'm the President. I dropped the bomb. Take my handkerchief and wipe the blood off your hands."

A President can absolve, pardon or wipe guilt from any citizen's hands when national goals are clear enough—as Truman did, offering absolution to Oppenheimer. A President can even deny liberty—as

Abraham Lincoln did during the Civil War when he suspended *habeas corpus;* or Franklin Roosevelt when he interned the Japanese of California in 1942. But when there are no overriding national goals, when purposes and directions for the next era are still shaping, then the democratic process itself becomes vital. There can then be no absolution for anyone who has tampered with the supreme need of a passing time—that the process be kept fair and open, that the process proceed without fear, so that new men can think through what the problems of the new era are and what choice of solutions may be offered.

The Americans stand, thus, in the presence of not one, but two mandates.

There is, as I write, the current mandate of Watergate—that the process be kept clean. It reads that no one—not the President, nor his staff, nor anyone using their names—may abuse the law. That mandate spreads far beyond palace politics. It requires that Americans recognize that impatience in any form of power, whether expressed in street riot, demonstration or government espionage, be recognized as the begetter of crime against the democratic process. It requires that the press, too, recognize the limitations on its power—a recognition that the privacy essential to government is equivalent to the privacy essential to newsmen's sources. But the beginning of the current mandate is pointed at the President: that he purge, at whatever cost in affection or personal loyalties, those who defiled the process of law which he promised to uphold. "The abuse of greatness," said Shakespeare, "is when it disjoins remorse from power."

But then there is the governing mandate—of the election.

Americans have a propensity for re-inventing a past in order to serve the needs of the present, for rewriting history to prove a contemporary point. Yet if there is a purpose to history, it is to make men conscious of what in the past can be useful for the present—for, after all, the past shaped the present, and an amnesiac nation is as helpless as a wanderer in the streets.

This second mandate, that of the people speaking at the polls in 1972, closed a generation.

Rudely but compellingly, every thirty or forty years, the ideas of one generation become the prison of the generation that follows. The more powerful the idea, the more confining the imprisonment. The idea of compromise with slavery had been accepted in American politics in 1820 as imperative for saving the Union. By 1860 such compromise had frozen politics so completely that it could be released only by the Civil War. The creative domestic ideas of Abraham Lincoln during that war opened new horizons. The war Congresses of the 1860's sought to open the plains by giving a free hand to the railroads, free soil to the settlers, all the while encouraging industry in the cities and new thinking leadership by vast land grants to universities. Thirty years later all these ideas had succeeded—and the horizons had shrunk. Their success had left the settlers of the plains victims of the railroads, the unorganized workers the prey of industrial brutality, the beauty of the country despoiled. So thirty years later came the political upheaval of the 1890's—inspirited by the intellectual and political leadership of the land-grant colleges the same ideas had so casually endowed.

We live, similarly, at the end of a generation, when the ideas of hope and grandeur that moved the decades of the 1930's and 1940's, having achieved their triumphs, imprisoned new thinking. Those ideas increased the power of the state beyond the experience of any previous generation —the power of the state to make war or make peace abroad, to create suburbs with Federal credit, or destroy cities with Federal roads and tax burdens, to broaden education and opportunity, to command the deployment of children in schools, to heal and to build. The extrapolation of those ideas by George McGovern frightened too many Americans; too many had been hurt along that road. The majority wished to pursue those ideas no further now; the Democratic Party, which called itself the party of the future, had become, in their eyes, the party of the past. They turned instead to Richard Nixon, affirming the change of direction he declared he was giving to government—a restraint on the power and reach of the Federal state into daily life. However his use of the power of state may be defined in the months or years to come, this restraint on power and its excess was what the majority voted for. For this time, they preferred to live their own lives privately—unplagued by moralities, or war, or riots, or violence. In the alternation of the sequences of American history, in the cycle between poetry and pragmatism, in those generational shifts of mood characteristic of the adventure in democracy, certainly the ideas of the minority who voted for McGovern would come into their time again. Those ideas still stirred in the spirit of the nation. But until those ideas had new form, new shape, new perspective, the majority of Americans would not be called out to march in their cause. Such was their mandate in 1972.

APPENDIX A

THE VOTING OF 1972

The following table of voting results by state and nation is based on the compilation of the Associated Press and is used here by permission. There is still no such thing as an official national vote count in the United States; but the Associated Press table, based on official returns state by state, is the closest to accurate that I have found.

State	Electoral Vote	Nixon Vote	Pct.	McGovern Vote	Pct.	Schmitz Vote	Pct.
ALABAMA	9	728,701	73	256,923	26	11,918	1
ALASKA	3	55,349	58	32,967	35	6,903	7
ARIZONA	6	402,812	62	198,540	30	21,208	3
ARKANSAS	6	445,751	69	198,899	31	3,016	—
CALIFORNIA	45	4,602,096	55	3,475,847	42	232,554	3
COLORADO	7	597,189	63	329,980	35	17,268	2
CONNECTICUT	8	810,763	59	555,498	40	17,239	1
DELAWARE	3	140,357	60	92,283	39	2,638	1
DISTRICT OF COLUMBIA	3	35,226	22	127,627	78	—	—
FLORIDA	17	1,857,759	72	718,117	28	—	—
GEORGIA	12	881,496	75	289,529	25	815	—
HAWAII	4	168,865	62	101,409	38	—	—
IDAHO	4	199,384	65	80,826	26	28,869	9
ILLINOIS	26	2,788,179	59	1,913,472	41	2,471	—
INDIANA	13	1,405,154	68	708,568	32	—	—
IOWA	8	706,207	58	496,206	41	22,056	1
KANSAS	7	619,812	68	270,287	30	21,808	2
KENTUCKY	9	676,446	64	371,159	35	17,627	1
LOUISIANA	10	686,852	66	298,142	29	52,099	5
MAINE	4	256,458	61	160,584	39	—	—
MARYLAND	10	829,305	61	505,781	37	18,726	1
MASSACHUSETTS	14	1,112,078	45	1,332,540	54	2,877	—
MICHIGAN	21	1,961,721	56	1,459,435	42	63,321	2
MINNESOTA	10	898,269	52	802,346	46	31,407	2
MISSISSIPPI	7	505,125	78	126,782	20	11,598	2
MISSOURI	12	1,154,050	62	698,531	38	3,110	—
MONTANA	4	183,976	58	120,197	38	13,430	4
NEBRASKA	5	406,298	71	169,991	29	—	—
NEVADA	3	115,750	64	66,016	36	—	—
NEW HAMPSHIRE	4	213,724	64	116,435	35	3,386	1
NEW JERSEY	17	1,845,502	62	1,102,211	37	34,378	1
NEW MEXICO	4	235,606	61	141,084	37	8,767	2
NEW YORK	41	4,192,778	59	2,951,084	41	—	—
NORTH CAROLINA	13	1,054,889	70	438,705	30	9,039	—
NORTH DAKOTA	3	174,109	62	100,384	36	5,646	2
OHIO	25	2,441,827	60	1,558,889	38	80,067	2
OKLAHOMA	8	759,025	72	247,147	24	23,728	2
OREGON	6	486,686	53	392,760	42	46,211	5
PENNSYLVANIA	27	2,714,521	59	1,796,951	39	70,593	2
RHODE ISLAND	4	220,383	53	194,645	47	—	—
SOUTH CAROLINA	8	477,044	71	184,525	27	10,075	1
SOUTH DAKOTA	4	166,476	54	139,945	46	—	—
TENNESSEE	10	813,147	68	357,293	30	30,373	2
TEXAS	26	2,298,896	67	1,154,289	33	—	—
UTAH	4	323,643	68	126,284	26	28,549	6
VERMONT	3	117,149	63	68,174	37	—	—

State	Electoral Vote	Nixon Vote	Pct.	McGovern Vote	Pct.	Schmitz Vote	Pct.
VIRGINIA	12	988,493	68	438,887	30	19,721	1
WASHINGTON	9	837,135	57	568,334	39	58,906	4
WEST VIRGINIA	6	484,964	64	277,435	36	—	—
WISCONSIN	11	989,430	54	810,174	44	47,525	2
WYOMING	3	100,464	69	44,358	30	748	1

Popular Vote Totals

	Votes	Pct.
Nixon	47,167,319	60.7
McGovern	29,168,509	37.5
Schmitz	1,080,670	1.3
Others	264,963	0.5
Total Vote	77,681,461	

McGovern's vote total in Alabama includes 219,108 votes on the regular Democratic ticket and 37,815 votes under the listing of the National Democratic Party of Alabama.

MINOR PARTY CANDIDATES:

Dr. Benjamin Spock, People's Party: California 55,167, Colorado 2,403, Idaho 903, Indiana 4,544, Kentucky 1,118, Massachusetts 101, Minnesota 2,855, New Jersey 5,355, Vermont 1,010, Washington 2,644, Wisconsin 2,701. Total: 78,801.

Linda Jenness or Evelyn Reed, Socialist Workers Party: Colorado 666, District of Columbia 316, Indiana 5,575, Iowa 488, Kentucky 635, Louisiana 14,398, Massachusetts 10,600, Michigan 1,603, Minnesota 940, Mississippi 2,458, New Hampshire 368, New Jersey 2,233, New Mexico 474, New York 7,797, North Dakota 288, Pennsylvania 4,639, Rhode Island 729, South Dakota 944, Texas 8,664, Vermont 296, Washington 623, Wisconsin 506. Total: 65,290.

Louis Fisher, Socialist Labor Party: Colorado 4,361, Illinois 12,344, Indiana 1,688, Iowa 195, Massachusetts 129, Michigan 2,437, Minnesota 4,261, New Jersey 4,544, New York 4,530, Ohio 7,107, Virginia 9,918, Washington 1,102, Wisconsin 998. Total: 53,614.

Gus Hall, Communist Party: Colorado 432, District of Columbia 252, Illinois 4,541, Iowa 272, Kentucky 464, Massachusetts 46, Michigan 1,210, Minnesota 662, New Jersey 1,263, New York 5,641, North Dakota 87, Ohio 6,437, Pennsylvania 2,686, Washington 566, Wisconsin 663. Total: 25,222.

Earle H. Munn, Prohibition Party: Alabama 8,551, Colorado 467, Delaware 238, Kansas 4,188. Total: 13,444.

John Hospers, Libertarian Party: Colorado 1,111, Washington 1,537, Massachusetts 43. Total: 2,691.

John Mahalchik, America First Party: New Jersey 1,743.

Gabriel Green, Universal Party: Iowa 199.

Others: 23,959.

APPENDIX B

The report of the Credentials Committee, adopted by the Democratic Convention on August 27th, 1968, without debate, read:

This Committee recommends that the Chairman of the Democratic National Committee establish a Special Committee to:

A. Study the delegation selection processes in effect in the various states, in the context of the peculiar circumstances, needs and traditions in which each state's laws and practices find their roots.

B. Recommend to the Democratic National Committee such improvements as can assure even broader citizen participation in the delegate selection process.

C. Aid the state Democratic parties in working toward relevant changes in state law and party rules.

D. Report its findings and recommendations to the Democratic National Committee and make them available to the 1972 Convention and the committees thereof. . . .

Be it resolved, that this Convention instruct the Democratic National Committee that it shall include in the Call for the 1972 Convention the following addition to Section 1:

"It is the further understanding that a state Democratic party, in selecting and certifying delegates and alternates to the Democratic National Convention, thereby undertakes to assure that all Democrats of the state will have meaningful and timely opportunities to participate fully in the election or selection of such delegates and alternates."

Be it further resolved, that the Chairman of the Democratic National Committee shall establish a Special Committee to aid the state Democratic parties in fully meeting the responsibilities and assurances required for inclusion in the Call for the 1972 Democratic National Convention, said Committee to report to the Democratic National Committee concerning its efforts and findings and said report to be available to the 1972 Convention and the committees thereof. . . .

The minority report of the Rules Committee, adopted by the Democratic Convention on August 27th, 1968, read:

Be it resolved, that the Call to the 1972 Democratic National Convention shall contain the following language:

It is understood that a state Democratic party, in selecting and certifying delegates to the National Convention, thereby undertakes to assure that such delegates have been selected through a process in which all Democratic voters have had full and timely opportunity to participate. In determining whether a state party has complied with this mandate, the convention shall require that:

(1) The unit rule not be used in any stage of the delegate selection process; and

(2) All feasible efforts have been made to assure that delegates are selected through party primary, convention, or committee procedures open to public participation within the calendar year of the National Convention.

INDEX